T0214185

Lecture Notes in Business Information Processing 372

More information about this series at http://www.springer.com/series/7911

María José Escalona · Francisco Domínguez Mayo ·
Tim A. Majchrzak · Valérie Monfort (Eds.)

Web Information
Systems and Technologies

14th International Conference, WEBIST 2018
Seville, Spain, September 18–20, 2018
Revised Selected Papers

 Springer

Editors
María José Escalona
University of Seville
Seville, Spain

Francisco Domínguez Mayo
University of Seville
Seville, Spain

Tim A. Majchrzak ⓘ
University of Agder
Kristiansand, Norway

Valérie Monfort
University of Paris 1
Paris, France

ISSN 1865-1348 ISSN 1865-1356 (electronic)
Lecture Notes in Business Information Processing
ISBN 978-3-030-35329-2 ISBN 978-3-030-35330-8 (eBook)
https://doi.org/10.1007/978-3-030-35330-8

This Springer imprint is published by the registered company Springer Nature Switzerland AG
The registered company address is: Gewerbestrasse 11, 6330 Cham, Switzerland

Preface

The present book includes extended and revised versions of a set of selected papers from the 14th International Conference on Web Information Systems and Technologies (WEBIST 2018), held in Seville, Spain, during September 18–20, 2018.

WEBIST 2018 received 68 paper submissions from 24 countries, of which 18% are included in this book. The papers were selected by the event chairs and their selection was based on several criteria that included the classifications and comments provided by the Program Committee members, the session chairs' assessment, and the program chairs' global view of all papers included in the technical program. The authors of selected papers were then invited to submit a revised and extended version of their papers having at least 30% new material.

The purpose of WEBIST 2018 was to bring together researchers, engineers, and practitioners interested in the technological advances and business applications of Web-based information systems. The conference had five main tracks, covering different aspects of Web Information Systems, namely Internet Technology; Mobile and NLP Information Systems; Service Based Information Systems, Platforms and Eco-Systems; Web Intelligence; and Web Interfaces.

The papers selected to be included in this book contribute to the understanding of relevant trends of current research on Web Information Systems and Technologies, including:

- Data Protection and Authentication
- Personalization, Recommendations, and Evaluation
- User Interfaces
- Semantic Modeling
- Voice Services
- Reliability
- Web Services and Microservices

We would like to thank all the authors for their contributions and also the reviewers who helped to ensure the quality of this publication.

September 2018

María José Escalona
Francisco Domínguez Mayo
Tim A. Majchrzak
Valérie Monfort

Organization

Conference Chair

Valérie Monfort   LAMIH, UMR CNRS 8201, Université de
Valenciennes, France

Program Co-chairs

Maria Jose Escalona	Universidad de Sevilla, Spain
Francisco Domínguez Mayo	Universidad de Sevilla, Spain
Tim A. Majchrzak	University of Agder, Norway

Program Committee

Mohd Helmy Abd Wahab	Universiti Tun Hussein Onn Malaysia, Malaysia
Diana Andone	Universitatea Politehnica Timişoara, Romania
Jesús Arias Fisteus	Universidad Carlos III de Madrid, Spain
Noushin Ashrafi	University of Massachusetts Boston, USA
Elarbi Badidi	United Arab Emirates University, UAE
Vítor Basto-Fernandes	Instituto Universitário de Lisboa (Iscte-Iul) and University Institute of Lisbon (Istar-Iul), Portugal
Werner Beuschel	Technische Hochschule Brandenburg, Germany
Adelaide Bianchini	Universidad Simón Bolívar, Venezuela
Boyan Bontchev	Sofia University, "St. Kliment Ohridski," Bulgaria
Philipp Brune	Neu-Ulm University of Applied Sciences, Germany
Christoph Bussler	Google, Inc., USA
Maria Claudia Buzzi	Consiglio Nazionale delle Ricerche, Italy
Pasquina Campanella	University of Bari Aldo Moro, Italy
Shiping Chen	CSIRO, Australia
Martine De Cock	Ghent University, Belgium
Isabelle Comyn-Wattiau	Cnam and ESSEC, France
Christophe Cruz	Le2i - Laboratoire Electrique, Informatique et Image, France
Guglielmo De Angelis	CNR-IASI, Italy
Valeria De Antonellis	University of Brescia, Italy
Toon De Pessemier	iMinds, Ghent University, Belgium
Steven Demurjian	University of Connecticut, USA
Enrico Denti	Alma Mater Studiorum, Università di Bologna, Italy
Luigi Di Caro	Università di Torino, Italy
Francesco Di Cerbo	SAP Labs, France
Francisco Domínguez Mayo	Universidad de Sevilla, Spain
Georg Dr. Schneider	Trier University of Applied Sciences, Germany

Martin Drlik	Constantine the Philosopher University in Nitra, Slovinia
Karim El Guemhioui	Université du Québec en Outaouais, Canada
Atilla Elci	Aksaray University, Turkey
Larbi Esmahi	Athabasca University, Canada
Joao Ferreira	ISEL, Portugal
Luis Ferreira Pires	University of Twente, The Netherlands
Josep-Lluis Ferrer-Gomila	Balearic Islands University, Spain
Karla Fook	Aeronautics Institute of Technology (ITA), Brazil
Pasi Fränti	University of Eastern Finland, Finland
Xiang Fu	Hofstra University, USA
Ombretta Gaggi	Università di Padova, Italy
Carolina Gallardo Pérez	Universidad Politécnica de Madrid, Spain
John Garofalakis	University of Patras, Greece
Panagiotis Germanakos	University of Cyprus, Cyprus
Henrique Gil	Escola Superior de Educação do Instituto Politécnico de Castelo Branco, Portugal
Nuno Gonçalves	Superior School of Technology, Polithecnic Institute of Setúbal, Portugal
José González Enríquez	Universidad de Sevilla, Spain
Annamaria Goy	Università di Torino, Italy
Carlos Granell	Universitat Jaume I, Spain
Ratvinder Grewal	Laurentian University, Canada
Daniela Grigori	Université Paris-Dauphine, France
Foteini Grivokostopoulou	University of Patras, Greece
Angela Guercio	Kent State University, USA
Francesco Guerra	University of Modena and Reggio Emilia, Italy
Fayçal Hamdi	Conservatoire National des Arts et Métiers, France
Azza Harbaoui	Laboratoire RIADI, ENSI, Tunisia
Shanmugasundaram Hariharan	Saveetha Engineering College, India
Ioannis Hatzilygeroudis	University of Patras, Greece
A. Henten	Aalborg University, Denmark
Jose Herrero Agustin	Universidad de Extremadura, Spain
Hanno Hildmann	TNO, The Netherlands
Yuh-Jong Hu	National Chengchi University (NCCU), Taiwan
Sergio Ilarri	Universidad de Zaragoza, Spain
Kai Jakobs	RWTH Aachen University, Germany
Monique Janneck	Luebeck University of Applied Sciences, Germany
Zhuoren Jiang	Sun Yat-sen University, China
Maria Jose Escalona	Universidad de Sevilla, Spain
Kennedy Kambona	Vrije Universiteit Brussel, Belgium
Andreas Kanavos	University of Patras, Greece
Georgia Kapitsaki	University of Cyprus, Cyprus
Vaggelis Kapoulas	The Computer Technology Institute and Press "Diophantus," Greece

Sokratis Katsikas	Norwegian University of Science and Technology (NTNU), Norway
Takahiro Kawamura	Japan Science and Technology Agency, Japan
Matthias Klusch	German Research Center for Artificial Intelligence (DFKI GmbH), Germany
In-Young Ko	Korea Advanced Institute of Science and Technology, South Korea
Hiroshi Koide	Kyushu University, Japan
Tsvi Kuflik	University of Haifa, Israel
Dongxi Liu	CSIRO, Australia
Michael Mackay	Liverpool John Moores University, UK
Tim A. Majchrzak	University of Agder, Norway
Andrea Marrella	Università degli Studi di Roma La Sapienza, Italy
Kazutaka Maruyama	Meisei University, Japan
Wojciech Mazurczyk	Warsaw University of Technology, Poland
Luca Mazzola	Lucerne University of Applied Sciences, Switzerland
Hakima Mellah	Research Center in Scientific and Technical Information, Algeria
Ingo Melzer	Daimler AG, Germany
Marzal Miguel Ángel	Universidad Carlos III De Madrid, Spain
Alex Norta	Tallinn University of Technology, Estonia
Declan O'Sullivan	University of Dublin Trinity College, Ireland
Eric Pardede	La Trobe University, Australia
Kalpdrum Passi	Laurentian University, Canada
David Paul	The University of New England, Australia
José Pereira	Instituto Poliécnico de Setúbal, Escola Superior de Tecnologia de Setúbal, Portugal
Isidoros Perikos	University of Patras, Greece
Simona Popa	Universidad Católica San Antonio de Murcia, Spain
Jim Prentzas	Democritus University of Thrace, Greece
Birgit Pröll	Johannes Kepler Universität Linz, Austria
Claudia Raibulet	University of Milano-Bicocca, Italy
Thomas Risse	University Library Johann Christian Senckenberg, Germany
Davide Rossi	Università di Bologna, Italy
Gustavo Rossi	Lifia, Argentina
Yacine Sam	Université de Tours, France
Comai Sara	Politecnico di Milano, Italy
Claudio Schifanella	Università di Torino, Italy
Wieland Schwinger	Johannes Kepler Universität Linz, Austria
Rami Sellami	CETIC, Belgium
Tacha Serif	Yeditepe University, Turkey
Pavel Shapkin	National Research Nuclear University MEPhI (Moscow Engineering Physics Institute), Russia
Weiming Shen	National Research Council Canada, Canada
John Shepherd	University of New South Wales, Australia

Invited Speakers

Contents

Client-Side Cornucopia: Comparing the Built-In Application Architecture Models in the Web Browser

Antero Taivalsaari[1], Tommi Mikkonen[2], Cesare Pautasso[3], and Kari Systä[4(✉)]

[1] Nokia Bell Labs, Tampere, Finland
antero.taivalsaari@nokia.com
[2] University of Helsinki, Helsinki, Finland
tommi.mikkonen@helsinki.fi
[3] University of Lugano, Lugano, Switzerland
cesare.pautasso@usi.ch
[4] Tampere University, Tampere, Finland
kari.systa@tuni.fi

Abstract. The programming capabilities of the Web can be viewed as an afterthought, designed originally by non-programmers for relatively simple scripting tasks. This has resulted in cornucopia of partially overlapping options for building applications. Depending on one's viewpoint, a generic standards-compatible web browser supports three, four or five built-in application rendering and programming models. In this paper, we give an overview and comparison of these built-in client-side web application architectures in light of the established software engineering principles. We also reflect on our earlier work in this area, and provide an expanded discussion of the current situation. In conclusion, while the dominance of the base HTML/CSS/JS technologies cannot be ignored, we expect Web Components and WebGL to gain more popularity as the world moves towards increasingly complex web applications, including systems supporting virtual and augmented reality.

Keywords: Web programming · Single page web applications · Web Components · Web application architectures · Rendering engines · Web rendering · Web browser

1 Introduction

The World Wide Web has become such an integral part of our lives that it is often forgotten that the Web has existed only about thirty years. The original design sketches related to the World Wide Web date back to the late 1980s. The first web browser prototype for the NeXT computer was completed by Tim Berners-Lee in December 1990. The first version of the Mosaic web browser was made available publicly in February 1993, and the first commercially successful browser – Netscape Navigator – was released in late 1994. Widespread commercial use of the Web took off in the late 1990s.

© Springer Nature Switzerland AG 2019
M. J. Escalona et al. (Eds.): WEBIST 2018, LNBIP 372, pp. 1–24, 2019.
https://doi.org/10.1007/978-3-030-35330-8_1

In the end of the 1990s and in the early 2000s, the web browser became the most commonly used computer program, sparking a revolution that has transformed not only commerce but communication, social life and politics as well. In desktop computers, nearly all the important tasks are now performed using the web browser. Even mobile applications today can be viewed merely as "mirrors into the cloud". While native mobile apps may still offer UI frameworks and widgets that are (at least for now) better suited to the limited screen size and input modalities of the devices, valuable content has moved gradually away from mobile devices to cloud-based services, thus reducing the original role of the mobile apps considerably.

Interestingly, the programming capabilities of the Web have largely been an afterthought – designed originally by non-programmers for relatively simple scripting tasks. Due to different needs and motivations, there are many ways to make things on the Web – many more than people generally realize. Furthermore, over the years these features have evolved in a rather haphazard fashion. Consequently, there are various ways to build applications on the Web – even without considering any extensions or thousands of add-on libraries. Depending on one's viewpoint, the web browser natively supports three, four or five different built-in application rendering and development models. Thousands of libraries and frameworks have then been implemented on top of these built-in models. Furthermore, in addition to application architectures that partition applications more coarsely into server and client side components, it is increasingly possible to fine-tune the application logic by moving code flexibly between the client and the server, as originally noted in [15].

Even though a lot of the application logic in web applications may run on the server, the rendering capabilities of the web browser are crucial in creating the presentation layer of the applications. In this paper, we provide a comparison of the *built-in client-side web application architectures*, i.e., the programming capabilities that the web browsers provide out-of-the-box before any additional libraries are loaded. This is a topic that has received surprisingly little attention in the literature. While there are countless articles on specific web development technologies, and thousands of libraries have been developed *on top of the browser*, there are few if any papers comparing the built-in user interface development models offered by the browser itself. The choice between these alternative development models has a significant impact on the overall architecture and structure of the resulting web applications. The choices are made more difficult by the fact that the web browser offers a number of overlapping features to accomplish even basic tasks, reflecting the historical, organic evolution of the web browser as an application platform.

This paper is motivated by the *recent trend toward simpler, more basic approaches in web development*. According to a study carried out a few years ago, the vast majority (up to 86%) of web developers felt that the Web and JavaScript ecosystems have become far too complex (http://stateofjs.com/2016). There is a movement to go back to the roots of web application development by building directly upon what the web browser can provide without the added layers introduced by various libraries and frameworks. The *"zero framework manifesto"* crystallizes this desire for simplicity [3]. However, as will be shown in this paper, even the "vanilla" browser offers a cornucopia of choices when it comes to application development. The paper is based on our earlier articles [27,29], and it has been extended from those to provide a more comprehensive view to web development in general as well as deeper technical discussion on the implications.

The structure of this paper is as follows. In Sect. 2, we provide an overview on the evolution of the web browser as an application platform. In Sect. 3, we dive into the built-in user interface development and rendering models offered by modern web browsers: (1) DOM, (2) Canvas, (3) WebGL, (4) SVG, and (5) Web Components. In Sect. 4, we provide a comparison and presumed use cases of the presented technologies, and in Sect. 5, we list some broader considerations and observations. In Sect. 6, we revisit our earlier predictions made in [27,29], followed by avenues for future work in Sect. 7. Finally, Sect. 8 concludes the paper with some final remarks.

2 Evolution of the Web Browser as an Application Platform

The history of computing and the software industry is characterized by disruptive periods and paradigm shifts that have typically occurred every 10–15 years. Back in the 1960s and 1970s, mainframe computers gave way to minicomputers. In the early 1980s personal computers sparked a revolution, making computers affordable to ordinary people, and ultimately killing a number of very successful minicomputer manufacturers such as Digital Equipment Corporation as a side effect. In the 1990s, the emergence of the World Wide Web transformed personal computers from standalone computing "islands" to network-connected web terminals. In the early 2000s, mobile phones were opened up for third party application development as well. Today, the dominant computing environment clearly is the Web, with native apps complementing it in various ways especially in the mobile domain [17,18].

Over time, the World Wide Web has evolved from its humble origins as a *document sharing system* to a massively popular hypermedia application and content distribution environment – in short, the most powerful information dissemination environment in the history of humankind. This evolution has not taken place in a fortnight; it has not followed a carefully designed master plan either. Although the World Wide Web Consortium (W3C) has seemingly been in charge of the evolution of the Web, in practice the evolution has been driven largely by dominant web browser vendors: Mozilla, Microsoft, Apple, Google and (to a lesser degree) Opera. Over the years, these companies have had divergent, often misaligned business interests. While browser compatibility has improved dramatically in recent years, the browser landscape is still truly a mosaic or cornucopia of features, reflecting organic evolution – or a tug of war if you will – between different commercial vendors over time.

Before delving into more technical topics, let us briefly revisit the evolution of the web browser as a software platform [1, 24, 26].

Classic Web. In the early life of the Web, web pages were truly *pages*, i.e., page-structured documents that contained primarily text with interspersed images, without animation or any interactive content. Navigation between pages was based on simple *hyperlinks*, and a new web page was loaded from the web server each time the user clicked on a link. There was no need for asynchronous network communication between the browser and the web server. For reading used input some pages were presented as *forms*, with simple textual fields and the possibility to use basic widgets such as buttons and combo (selection) boxes. These types of "classic web" pages were characteristic of the early life of the Web in the early 1990s.

Hybrid Web. In the second phase, web pages became increasingly interactive. Web pages started containing animated graphics and plug-in components that allowed richer, more interactive content to be displayed. This phase coincided with the commercial takeoff of the Web during the dot-com boom of the late 1990s when companies realized that they could create commercially valuable web sites by displaying advertisements or by selling merchandise and services over the Web. Plug-in components such as Flash, RealPlayer, Quicktime and Shockwave were introduced to make it possible to construct web pages with visually enticing, interactive multimedia, allowing advanced animations, movie clips and audio tracks to be inserted in web pages.

With the introduction of *DHTML* – the combination of HTML, Cascading Style Sheets (CSS), the JavaScript language [6], and the Document Object Model (DOM) – it became possible to create interactive web pages with built-in support for more advanced graphics and animation. The JavaScript language, introduced in Netscape Navigator version 2.0 B almost as an afterthought in December 1995, made it possible to build animated interactive content by scripting directly the web browser.

In this phase, the Web started moving in directions that were unforeseen by its original designer, with web sites behaving more like multimedia presentations rather than static pages. Content mashups and web site cross-linking became popular and communication protocols between the browser and the server became increasingly advanced. Navigation was no longer based solely on hyperlinks. For instance, Flash apps supported drag-and-drop and direct clicking/events on various types of objects, whereas originally no support for such features existed in browsers.

The Web as an Application Platform. In the early 2000s, the concept of Software as a Service (SaaS) emerged. Salesforce.com pioneered the use of the Web as a CRM application platform in the early 2000s, demonstrating and validating the use of the Web and the web browser as a viable target platform for business applications. At that point, people realized that the ability to offer software applications seamlessly over the Web and then perform instant worldwide software updates could offer unsurpassed business benefits.

As a result of these observed benefits, people started to build web sites that behave much like desktop applications, for example, by allowing web pages to be updated partially, rather than requiring the entire page to be refreshed. Such systems often eschewed link-based navigation and utilized direct manipulation techniques (e.g., drag and drop features) borrowed from desktop-style applications instead. Interest in the use of the browser as an application platform was reinforced by the introduction of Ajax (Asynchronous JavaScript and XML) [8]. The key idea in Ajax was to use *asynchronous network communication* between the client and the server to decouple user interface updates from network requests. This made it possible to build web sites that do not necessarily block when interacting with the server and thus behave much like desktop applications, for example, by allowing web pages to be updated asynchronously one user interface element at a time, rather than requiring the entire page to be updated each and every time something changed. Although Ajax was primarily a specific technique rather than a complete development model or platform, it fueled further interest in building "Web 2.0" applications that could run in a standard web browser. This also increased the demand for a full-fledged programming language that could be used directly from inside the web browser instead of relying on any external plug-in components.

After the introduction of Ajax and the concept of *Single Page Applications* (SPAs) [12], the number of web development frameworks on top of the web browser has exploded. Today, there are over 1,400 officially listed JavaScript libraries (see http://www.javascripting.com/).

Server-Side JavaScript. The use of client-side web development technologies has spread also to other domains. For instance, after the introduction of the V8 high-performance JavaScript engine (https://developers.google.com/v8/), the use of the JavaScript language has quickly spread into server-side development as well. As a result, Node.js (https://nodejs.org/) has become a vast ecosystem of its own; according to a popular saying, there is an "NPM module for nearly everything". In fact, the NPM (Node Package Manager) ecosystem has been growing even faster in recent years than the client-side JavaScript ecosystem. According to npmjs.com, there are more than 800,000 NPM packages at the time of this writing.

As already mentioned earlier, in this paper we shall focus only on client-side technologies and only on those technologies that have been included natively in standards-compatible web browsers. We feel that this is an area that is surprisingly poorly covered by existing research.

Non-standard Development Models and Architectures. For the sake of completeness, it should be mentioned that over the years web browsers have supported various additional client-side rendering and development models. For instance, Java applets were an early attempt to include Java language and Java virtual machine (JVM) support directly in a web browser. However, because of the immaturity of the technology (e.g., inadequate performance of early JVMs) and Microsoft's vigilant resistance, applets never became an officially supported browser feature. For years, Microsoft had their alternative technologies, such as

ActiveX, available (only) in Microsoft Internet Explorer. For a while, the use of various browser plug-in components offering application execution capabilities – such as Adobe Flash or Shockwave – was extremely popular.

In the late 2000s, so called *Rich Internet Application* (RIA) platforms such as Adobe AIR or Microsoft Silverlight were very much in vogue. RIA systems were an attempt to reintroduce alternative programming languages and libraries in the context of the Web in the form of browser plug-in components that each provided a complete platform runtime. For a comprehensive overview of RIA systems, refer to Castelyn's survey [4]. However, just as it was predicted in [24], the RIA phenomenon turned out to be rather short-lived. The same seems to be true also of various attempts to support native code execution directly from within the web browser. For instance, Google's Native Client offers a sandbox for running compiled C and C++ code in the browser, but it has not become very popular. Mozilla's classic NPAPI (Netscape Plugin Application Programming Interface) – introduced originally by Netscape in 1995 – has effectively been removed from all the major browsers; for instance, Google Chrome stopped supporting it already in 2015. Although there are some interesting ongoing efforts in this area – such as the W3C WebAssembly effort (http://webassembly.org/), it is now increasingly difficult to extend the programming capabilities of the web browser without modifying the source code of the browser itself (and thus creating non-standard, custom browsers).

3   Client-Side Web Rendering Architectures – An Underview

As summarized above, the history of the Web has undergone a number of evolutionary phases, reflecting the *document-oriented* – as opposed to *application-oriented* – origins of the Web. Nearly all the application development capabilities of the Web have been an afterthought, and have emerged as a result of divergent technical needs and business interests instead of careful planning and coordination.

As a result of the browser evolution that has occurred in the past two decades, today's web browsers support a mishmash of complementary, partially overlapping rendering and development models. These include the dominant "holy trinity" of HTML, CSS and JavaScript, and its underlying Document Object Model (DOM) rendering architecture. They also include the *Canvas 2D Context API* as well as *WebGL*. Additionally, there are important technologies such as *Scalable Vector Graphics* (SVG) and *Web Components* that complement the basic DOM architecture.

The choice between the rendering architectures can have significant implications on the structure of client-side web applications. Effectively, all of the technologies mentioned above introduce their own distinct programming models and approaches that the developers are expected to use. Furthermore, all of them have varying levels of framework, library and tool support available to simplify the actual application development work on top of the underlying development model. The DOM-based approach is by far the most popular and most deeply ingrained, but the other technologies deserve a fair glimpse as well.

Below we will dive more deeply into each technology. We will start with the DOM, Canvas and WebGL models, because these three technologies can be regarded more distinctly as three separate technologies. We will then dive into SVG and Web Components, which introduce their own programming models but which are closely coupled with the underlying DOM architecture at the implementation level.

3.1 DOM/DHTML

In web parlance, the *Document Object Model* (DOM) is a platform-neutral API that allows programs and scripts to dynamically access and update the content, structure and style of web documents. Document Object Model in the foundation for *Dynamic HTML* – the combination of HTML, Cascading Style Sheets (CSS) and JavaScript – that allows web documents to be created and manipulated using a combination of declarative and imperative development styles. Logically, the DOM can be viewed as an *attribute tree* that represents the contents of the web page that is currently displayed by the web browser. Programmatic interfaces are provided for manipulating the contents of the DOM tree from HTML, CSS and JavaScript.

In the web browser, the DOM serves as the foundation for a *retained (automatically managed) graphics architecture*. In such a system, the application developer has no direct, immediate control over rendering. Rather, all the drawing is performed indirectly by manipulating the DOM tree by adding, removing and modifying its nodes; the browser will then decide how to optimally lay out and render the display after each change.

Over the years, the capabilities of the DOM have evolved significantly. The evolution of the DOM has been described in a number of sources, including Flanagan's JavaScript "bible" [6]. In this paper we will not go into details, but it is useful to provide a summary since this evolution partially explains why the browser offers such a cornucopia of overlapping functionality.

- *DOM Level 1* specification – published in 1998 – defines the core HTML (and XML) document models. It specifies the basic functionality for document navigation.
- *DOM Level 2* specification – published in 2000 – defines the stylesheet object model, and provides methods for manipulating the style information attached to a document. It also enables traversals on the document and provides support for XML namespaces. Furthermore, it defines the *event model* for web documents, including the event listener and event flow, capturing, bubbling, and cancellation functionality.
- *DOM Level 3* specification – released as a number of separate documents in 2001–2004 – defines document loading and saving capabilities, as well as provides document validation support. In addition, it also addresses document views and formatting, and specifies the keyboard events and event groups, and how to handle them.

– *DOM Level 4* specification refers to a "living document" that is kept up to date with the latest decisions of the WHATWG/DOM working group[1].

DOM attributes can be manipulated from HTML, CSS, JavaScript, and to some extent also XML code. As a result, a number of entirely different development styles are possible, ranging from purely imperative usage to a combination of declarative styles using HTML and CSS. For instance, it is possible to create impressive 2D/3D animations using the CSS animation capabilities without writing a single line of imperative JavaScript code.

Below is a "classic" DHTML example that defines a text paragraph and an input button in HTML. The input button definition includes an `onclick` event handler function that – when clicked – hides the text paragraph by changing its visibility style attribute to '`hidden`'.

```
<!DOCTYPE html>
<html><body>
<p id="text">This is a piece of text.</p>

<input type="button" value="Hide text"
onclick="document.getElementById('text').style.visibility='
    hidden'">

</body></html>
```

In practice, very few developers use the raw, low-level DOM interfaces directly nowadays. The DOM and DHTML serve as the foundation for an extremely rich library and tool ecosystem that has emerged on top of the base technologies. The manipulation of DOM attributes is usually performed using higher-level convenience functions provided by popular JavaScript/CSS libraries and frameworks.

3.2 Canvas

The Canvas (officially known as the *Canvas 2D Context API*) is an HTML5 feature that enables dynamic, scriptable rendering of two-dimensional (2D) shapes and bitmap images (https://www.w3.org/TR/2dcontext/). It is a low level, imperative API that does not provide any built-in scene graph or advanced event handling capabilities. It that regard, Canvas offers much lower level graphics support than the DOM or SVG APIs that will automatically manage and (re)render complex graphics elements.

Canvas objects are drawn in *immediate mode*. This means that once a shape such as a rectangle is drawn using Canvas API calls, the rectangle is immediately forgotten by the system. If the position of the rectangle needs to be changed, the entire scene needs to be repainted, including any objects that might have been invalidated (covered) by the rectangle. In the equivalent DOM or SVG case, one could simply change the position attributes of the rectangle, and the browser

---

[1] https://dom.spec.whatwg.org/.

would then automatically determine how to optimally re-render all the affected objects.

The code snippet below provides a minimal example of Canvas API usage. In this example, we first instantiate a 2D canvas graphics context of size 100×100 after declaring the corresponding HTML element. We then imperatively draw a full circle with a 40 pixel radius in the middle of the canvas using the Canvas 2D Context JavaScript API.

```
1  <!DOCTYPE html>
2  <html><body>
3
4  <canvas id="myCanvas" width="100" height="100">
5  <script>
6  var c = document.getElementById("myCanvas");
7  var ctx = c.getContext("2d");
8  ctx.beginPath();
9  ctx.arc(50,50,40,0,2*Math.PI);
10 ctx.stroke();
11 </script>
12
13 </body></html>
```

Note that in these simple examples we are mixing HTML and JavaScript code. In real-world examples, it would be a good practice to keep declarative HTML code and imperative JavaScript code in separate files. We will discuss programming style implications later in Sect. 4.

The event handling capabilities of the Canvas API are minimal. A limited form of event handling is supported by the Canvas API with *hit regions* (https://developer.mozilla.org/en-US/docs/Web/API/Canvas_API/ Tutorial/Hit_regions_and_accessibility).

Conceptually, Canvas is a low level API upon which a higher-level rendering engine might be built. Although canvas elements are created in the browser as subelements in the DOM, it is entirely possible to create just one large canvas element, and then perform all the application rendering and event handling inside that element. There are JavaScript libraries that add event handling and scene graph capabilities to the canvas element. For instance, with *Paper.js* (http:// paperjs.org/) or *Fabric.js* (http://fabricjs.com/) libraries, it is possible to paint a canvas in layers, and then recreate specific layers, instead of having to repaint the entire scene manually each time. Thus, the Canvas API can be used as a full-fledged application rendering model of its own.

The Canvas element was initially introduced by Apple in 2004 for use inside their own Mac OS X WebKit component in order to support applications such as Dashboard widgets in the Safari browser. In 2005, the Canvas element was adopted in version 1.8 of Gecko browsers and Opera in 2006. The Canvas API was later standardized by the Web Hypertext Application Technology Working Group (WHATWG).

The adoption of the Canvas API was originally hindered by Apple's intellectual property claims over this API. From technical viewpoint, adoption was also slowed down by the fact that the Canvas API expressiveness is significantly more limited than the well-established, mature immediate-mode graphics APIs that were available in mainstream operating systems already a decade or two earlier. Microsoft's DirectX API – originally introduced in Windows 95 – is a good example of a substantially more comprehensive API. Nowadays the Canvas API is supported by all the main web browsers; in spite of its technical limitations, the Canvas API has a thriving library ecosystem as well.

3.3   WebGL

WebGL (http://www.khronos.org/webgl/) is a cross-platform web standard for hardware accelerated 3D graphics API developed by Khronos Group, Mozilla, and a consortium of other companies including Apple, Google and Opera. The main feature that WebGL brings to the Web is the ability to display 3D graphics natively in the web browser without any plug-in components. WebGL is based on OpenGL ES 2.0 (http://www.khronos.org/opengles), and it leverages the OpenGL shading language GLSL. A comprehensive JavaScript API is provided to open up OpenGL programming capabilities to JavaScript programmers.

In a nutshell, WebGL provides a JavaScript API for rendering interactive, immediate-mode 3D (and 2D) graphics within any compatible web browser without the use of plug-in components. WebGL is integrated into major web browsers, enabling Graphics Processing Unit (GPU) accelerated usage of physics and image processing and effects in web applications. WebGL applications consist of control code written in JavaScript and shader code that is typically executed on a GPU.

WebGL is widely supported in modern desktop browsers. Today, even all the major mobile browsers (excluding Opera Mini) support WebGL by default. However, actual usability of WebGL functions is dependent on various factors such as the GPU supporting it. Even in many desktop computers WebGL applications may run poorly unless the computer has a graphics card that provides sufficient capabilities to process OpenGL functions efficiently.

Just like the Canvas API discussed above, the WebGL API is a rather low-level API that does not automatically manage rendering or support high-level events. From the application developer's viewpoint, the WebGL API is in fact too cumbersome to use directly without utility libraries. For instance, setting up typical view transformation shaders (e.g., for view frustum), loading scene graphs and 3D objects in the popular industry formats can be very tedious and requires writing a lot of source code.

Given the verbosity of shader definitions, we do not provide any code samples here. However, there are excellent WebGL examples on the Web. For instance, the following link contains a great example of an animated, rotating, textured cube with lighting effects: http://www.sw-engineering-candies.com/snippets/webgl/hello-world/.

Because of the complexity and the low level nature of the raw WebGL APIs, many JavaScript convenience libraries have been built or ported onto WebGL in order to facilitate development. Examples of such libraries include *A-Frame, BabylonJS, three.js, O3D, OSG.JS, CopperLicht* and *GLGE*.

3.4   SVG

Scalable Vector Graphics (SVG) is an XML-based vector image format for two-dimensional graphics with support for interactivity, affine transformations and animation. The *SVG Specification* [30] is an open standard published by the World Wide Web Consortium (W3C) originally in 2001. Although bitmap images were supported since the early days of the Web (the `<IMG>` tag was introduced in the Mosaic browser in 1992), vector graphics support came much later via SVG.

The code snippet below provides a simple example of an SVG object definition that renders an automatically scaling W3C logo to the screen[2].

```
<div id="w3clogo">
<svg xmlns='http://www.w3.org/2000/svg' viewBox="0 0 131 76
    ">
   <path d="M36,5l12,41l12-41h33v41-13,21c30,10,2,69-21,28l7
      -2c15,27,33,-22,3,-19v-4l12-20h-15l-17,59h-11-13-42l
      -12,42h-11-20-67h9l12,41l8-28l-4-13h9" fill='#005A9C'/>
   <path d="M94,53c15,32,30,14,35,71-1-7c-16,26-32,3-34,0
      M122,16c-10-21-34,0-21,30c-5-30 16,-38 23,-21l5-10l-2-9
      "/>
</svg>
</div>
```

While SVG was originally just a vector image format, SVG support has been integrated closely with the web browser to provide comprehensive means for creating interactive, resolution-independent content for the Web. Just like with the HTML DOM, SVG images can be manipulated using DOM APIs via HTML, CSS and JavaScript code. This makes it possible to create shapes such as lines, Bezier/elliptical curves, polygons, paths and text and images that be resized, rescaled and rotated programmatically using a set of built-in affine transformation and matrix functions.

The code sample below serves as an example of interactive SVG that defines a circle object that is capable of changing its size in response to mouse input.

```
<!DOCTYPE svg PUBLIC "-//W3C//DTD SVG 1.1//EN"
  "http://www.w3.org/Graphics/SVG/1.1/DTD/svg11.dtd">

<svg width="6cm" height="5cm" viewBox="0 0 600 500" xmlns="
    http://www.w3.org/2000/svg" version="1.1">

  <!-- Change the radius with each click -->
```

---

[2] https://dev.w3.org/SVG/tools/svgweb/samples/svg-files/w3c.svg.

```
7   <script type="application/ecmascript">
8     function circle_click(evt) {
9       var circle = evt.target;
10      var currentRadius = circle.getAttribute("r");
11      if (currentRadius == 100) {
12        circle.setAttribute("r", currentRadius*2);
13      } else {
14        circle.setAttribute("r", currentRadius*0.5);
15      }
16    }
17  </script>
18
19  <!-- Define circle with onclick event handler -->
20  <circle onclick="circle_click(evt)" cx="300" cy="225" r="
        100" fill="blue"/>
21 </svg>
```

As illustrated in the example, the SVG scene graph enables event handlers to be associated with objects, so a circle object may respond to an `onClick` event or other events. To get the same functionality with Canvas, one would have to implement the code to manually match the coordinates of the mouse click with the coordinates of the drawn circle in order to determine whether it was clicked.

Just like with the HTML DOM, SVG support in the web browser is based on a *retained (managed) graphics architecture*. Inside the browser, each SVG shape is represented as an object in a *scene graph* that is rendered to the display automatically by the web browser. When the attributes of an SVG object are changed, the browser will calculate the most optimal way to re-render the scene, including the other objects that may have been impacted by the change.

In the earlier days of the Web, SVG was the only mechanism to implement a scalable, "morphic" graphics system, which is why the SVG DOM API was used as the foundation for graphics implementation, e.g., in the original Lively Kernel web programming system that provided a self-supporting development environment inside the browser [11,26]. The following link provides a reference to a more comprehensive, "Lively-like" example of an SVG-based application that includes interactive capabilities (image rescaling and rotation based on mouse events) as well: https://dev.w3.org/SVG/tools/svgweb/samples/svg-files/photos.svg/.

In general, it is important to summarize that in the context of the Web, SVG is *much more than just an image format*. Together with event handling capabilities, affine transformations, gradient support, clipping, masking and composition features, SVG can be used as the basis for a full-fledged, standalone graphical application architecture or windowing system.

3.5   Web Components

Web Components (https://www.w3.org/TR/#tr_Web_Components) are a set of features added to the HTML and DOM specifications to enable the creation of reusable widgets or components in web documents and applications. The intention behind web components is to bring component-based software engineering principles to the World Wide Web, including the interoperability of higher-level HTML elements, encapsulation, information hiding and the general ability to create reusable, higher-level UI components that can be added flexibly to web applications.

An important motivation for web components is the *fundamentally brittle nature of the Document Object Model*. The brittleness comes from the global nature of elements in the DOM created by HTML, CSS and JavaScript code. For example, when you use a new HTML `id` or `class` in your web application or page, there is no easy way to find out if it will conflict with an existing name used by the page already earlier. Subtle bugs creep up, style selectors can suddenly go out of control, and performance can suffer, especially when attempting to combine code written by multiple authors [16]. Over the years various tools and libraries have been invented circumvent the issues, but the fundamental brittleness issues remain. The other important motivation is the *fixed nature of the standard set of HTML elements*. Web components make it possible to extend the basic set of components and support dynamically downloadable components across different web pages or applications.

Web components are built on top of a concept known as the *Shadow DOM*. In technical terms, the Shadow DOM introduces the concept of parallel "shadow" subtrees in the Document Object Model. These subtrees can be viewed conceptually as "icebergs" that expose only their tip while the implementation details remain invisible (and inaccessible) under the surface. Unlike regular branches in the DOM tree, shadow trees provide support for *scoped styles* and *DOM encapsulation*, thus obeying the well-known separation of concerns and modularity principles that encourage strong decoupling between public interfaces and implementation details [19]. Utilizing the Shadow DOM, the programmer can bundle CSS with HTML markup, hide implementation details, and create self-contained reusable components in vanilla JavaScript without exposing the implementation details or having to follow awkward naming conventions to ensure unique naming.

At the technical level, a shadow DOM tree is just normal DOM tree with two differences: (1) how it is created and used, and (2) how it behaves in relation to the rest of the web page. Normally, the programmer creates DOM nodes and appends those nodes as children of another element. With shadow DOM, the programmer creates a *scoped DOM tree* that is attached to the element but that is separate from its actual children. The element it is attached to is its *shadow host*. Anything that the programmer adds to the shadow tree becomes local to the hosting element, including `<style>`. This is how shadow DOM achieves CSS style scoping.

The following listing presents a minimal web component example that creates a text editor that automatically resizes itself as text is entered in the text area:

```
<!DOCTYPE html>
<html><head>
<link rel="import" href="basic-autosize-textarea.html" >
</head><body>
<p>Automatically resizing text input component:</p>
<basic-autosize-textarea>Edit me!
</basic-autosize-textarea>
</body></html>
```

Note that up until recently, many browsers did not support web components yet. Therefore, they had to be emulated in the form of *polyfill libraries* that implement the missing functionality (http://webcomponents.org/polyfills/). As of this writing, native support for the Shadow DOM is available all major web browsers except Microsoft Explorer and Microsoft Edge. For latest status, refer to http://caniuse.com/#feat=shadowdom/.

4   Comparison and Primary Use Cases

The technologies described in the previous section are rather different, with divergent design goals and varying and partially overlapping functionality. As a result, it is not easy to perform an objective comparison, or provide measurements on, e.g., development efficiency or ease of use. In general, ease of development or use in the context of the Web is highly subjective and dependent on one's background, e.g., whether the developer is a classically trained software engineer or a web developer who has never written software for target platforms other than the Web.

In this section we first provide a comparison that begins with an overview table that gives a summary of the basic differences between the presented technologies. Second, we discuss the primary use cases for the different technologies. Broader technical and architectural implications will be discussed separately in Sect. 5.

4.1   Technology Comparison: An Overview

An overview and a summary of the different approaches is presented in Table 1. The table covers topics such as the overall development paradigm (imperative vs. declarative), rendering architecture (retained/managed vs. immediate), information hiding support, primary intended usage domain and current popularity. We also provide impressions on more subjective factors such as technology maturity, abstraction level and ease of code reuse. Finally, the table summarizes whether each technology provides support for defining animations in a declarative fashion (as opposed to having to write lengthy JavaScript timer scripts to drive animations), as well as whether the technology is supported by mobile browsers.

4.2   Primary Use Cases

While the presented five technologies are all fully functional and Turing complete in the sense that they can be used for writing any imaginable application within the context of the sandbox offered by the web browser, these technologies are originally intended for different purposes and use cases. To begin with,

Table 1. Comparison of built-in client-side rendering technologies [29].

	DOM/DHTML	Canvas	WebGL	SVG	Web components
Development paradigm	Declarative and imperative	Imperative	Imperative	Declarative and imperative	Declarative and imperative
Rendering architecture	Retained	Immediate (explicit repainting required)	Immediate (explicit repainting required)	Retained	Retained
Information hiding	No	Not applicable (no namespace support)	Not applicable	No (except when creating multiple SVG images)	Yes (Shadow DOM encapsulation and scoped styles)
Primary usage domain	Documents and forms	2D graphics (e.g., in games)	3D/2D graphics especially in games and VR/AR	2D image rendering	Web applications and graphical user interfaces
Popularity	Ubiquitous	Popular in specific use cases	Limited	Popular in specific use cases	Growing
Technology maturity	Mature	Mature	Mature	Mature	Emerging (standardization underway)
Abstraction level	Medium	Very low	Low	Medium	High
Ease of code reuse	Low to medium	Low	Medium (shaders)	Low to high (high as an image format)	High
Declarative animation support	Yes	No	No	Yes	Yes
Mobile browser support	Yes	Yes	Yes	Yes	Not in Microsoft browsers

each of the technologies introduces their own distinct programming style(s). This is especially true of the Canvas and WebGL technologies that are much lower level, imperative APIs that require significantly more manual labor, e.g., in the placement of graphics and in driving the rendering process. In contrast, DOM/DHTML, SVG and Web Component programming is performed at a higher level and require much less imperative control and attention over rendering. That said, DOM/DHTML and SVG programming can be performed in a number of very different ways depending on whether the developer prefers a declarative development style (relying only on HTML and CSS) or imperative development style (developing primarily in JavaScript).

The following bullets provide a basic characterization on the primary baseline use cases for each technology.

– *DOM/DHTML*. HTML was originally developed as a declarative markup language for creating static documents and forms. Over the years, the use of DOM/DHTML has expanded to almost every imaginable use case. Today, DOM-based development approach dominates the web development landscape. This approach is declarative in nature, so the browser largely decides about rendering; this simplifies the development of web sites that look like documents, but can complicate the creation of sites that should behave like desktop applications or require control of the display at pixel level.
– *Canvas*. The Canvas API was introduced at a time when there was no other way to render lines, circles, rectangles or other low-level graphics imperatively inside the browser. For a number of reasons that were highlighted earlier, the Canvas API is significantly less capable that it ideally should be. Currently, the Canvas API is utilized primarily by game developers. It is also used occasionally inside regular web pages to include custom graphical content, although the majority of such use cases can often be completed more conveniently in SVG.
– *WebGL*. From technical viewpoint, WebGL is basically a thin JavaScript wrapper over native OpenGL interfaces for providing a programmatic API inside the web browser to achieve hardware-accelerated (GPU) rendering. As a result, the use cases of WebGL are a direct derivative of the OpenGL use cases, including (especially) game development, computer-aided design (CAD), scientific visualization, flight simulation, virtual reality, or any other case in which advanced 3D (or 2D) graphics rendering capabilities are needed. WebGL is an imperative, low-level API that places a lot of requirements on developer skills. Until recent years, the use of WebGL was still marginal, but it has steadily gained importance as the need to render VR/AR content in the web browser increases.
– *SVG*. In the context of the web browser, SVG has a dual role. First and foremost, SVG is a vector image format for rendering scalable graphics content on web pages. However, SVG can also be used as a rich, generic graphics context to drive scene graph based applications with support for complex event handling, affine transformations (rotation, zooming, scaling, shearing), gradients, clipping, masking and object composition. Given that the basic

DOM has evolved over the years to support these capabilities, in practice SVG is used mainly as an image format. Thus, the importance of the broader application development use cases for SVG is nowadays small.

- *Web Components.* Web components are the "dark horse" in web development – they are still little known to most developers, and it is difficult to place betting odds on their eventual success. Web components reintroduce well-known (but hitherto missing) software engineering principles and practices into the web browser, including modularity and the ability to create higher-level, general-purpose UI components that can be flexibly added to web applications. Web components cater to nearly any imaginable use case but they are especially well-suited to the development of full-fledged web applications that require an extensible set of GUI widgets.

5   Broader Considerations

According to MacLennan's classic software engineering principles [13], some of the most fundamental principles in software development are *simplicity* and *consistency*: There should be a minimum number of concepts with simple rules for their combination; things that are similar should also look similar, and different things should look different. Unfortunately, the web browser violates these and several other key principles in a number of ways, as evidenced by the above observations.

Overlapping Capabilities. Ideally, in a software development environment there should be only one, clearly the best and most obvious way to accomplish each task. However, in web development – even in a generic web browser without add-on components or libraries – there are several overlapping ways to accomplish even the most basic rendering tasks. It is not easy to provide recommendations on specific technologies to use, except for those tasks in which immediate-mode graphics is required (in which case either the Canvas or WebGL API will have to be utilized). In most cases, developers will end up using the basic DOM/DHTML approach, complemented with various libraries.

Mismatching Development Styles. When composing web applications even using the basic DOM/DHTML approach, the developers commonly face a mixture of declarative and imperative programming styles. They may also have to use a combination of retained and immediate-mode graphics especially when aiming at applications that are usable across different screen sizes – following responsive web design [14]. In general, imperative versus declarative and unmanaged versus managed graphics rendering provide different facilities and require different considerations, and the implementation mechanisms can be completely different. In fact, such adaptation could have been yet another dimension to compare.

Incompatible and Incoherent Abstractions. The abstractions and programming patterns supported by Canvas and WebGL APIs are very different from DOM/DHTML and SVG programming. Web components introduce yet another abstraction layer that has been patched on top of the DOM/DHTML. In general, the features supported by the browser reflect organic evolution of features over the years rather than any carefully master-planned architectural design. For instance, patterns and styles required for Canvas and WebGL programming are very different from DOM or SVG; Web Component (Shadow DOM) programming requires yet another programming style. When these programming patterns are combined – as often happens when using code from other parties – confusing situations may emerge.

Given the organic evolution of the web ecosystem, it is nevertheless fairly safe to predict that we will not go back to a less diverse web ecosystem or have a chance to radically simplify the feature set of the web browser. It is impossible to put the genie back to the bottle. For example, recent versions of the JavaScript language – from ECMAScript6 to ECMAScript9 – have introduced a lot of new language functionality (promises, generators and decorators, to list a few), thus ensuring that library rewriting and evolution will be swift in the coming years, creating further diversity and potential confusion for application developers.

Fashion-Driven Development. Over the past years there has been a notable trend in the library area towards fashion-driven development. By this we refer to the developers' tendency to surf on the wave of newest and most dominant "alpha" development frameworks. For instance, the once hugely popular *Prototype.js* and *JQuery.js* libraries were largely replaced by *Knockout.js* and *Backbone.js* in 2012. Back in 2014, *Angular.js* was by far the most dominant alpha framework, while in 2016–2017 it was the *React.js + Redux.js* ecosystem that seemed to be capturing the majority of developer attention, with *Vue.js* then foreseen as the most likely next dominant framework. As witnessed by the somewhat unfortunate evolution of the Angular ecosystem over the years, the alpha frameworks have a tendency to evolve very quickly once they get developers' attention, leading into compatibility issues. To make the matters worse, once the next fashionable alpha framework emerges and hordes of developers start jumping ship onto the new one, it becomes questionable to what extent one can build long-lasting business-critical applications and services, e.g., for the medical industry in which products must commonly have a minimum lifetime of twenty years. With the present pace of upgrades, the browser and the web server as the runtime environment would be almost completely replaced by patches, upgrades, and updates; similarly, most of the libraries would be replaced several times by newer, more fashionable ones.

Opportunistic Design and "cargo cult" Programming. In web development there has historically been a strong tradition of *mashup-based development*: searching, selecting, pickling, mashing up and glueing together disparate libraries and pieces of software [9]. Often such development has the characteristics of *cargo cult programming*: ritually including code and program structures that serve no real purpose or that the programmer has chosen to include because hundreds of other developers have done so – without really understanding why. The popularity of opportunistic design has exploded because of the success of *Node.js* (https://nodejs.org/) and its *Node Package Manager (NPM)* ecosystem (https://www.npmjs.com/) – nowadays, there are over 800,000 reusable NPM modules available for nearly all imaginable tasks. While this approach can save a lot of work and open up interesting opportunities for large-scale code reuse [21], this approach does not foster development of reliable, long-lasting applications, because even the smallest changes in the constituent components – each of which evolves separately and independently – can break applications [22].

Violation of Established Software Engineering Principles. Although many web developers may not realize this, the web browser violates many established software engineering principles, including the lack of *information hiding*, lack of *manifest interfaces*, lack of *orthogonality*, and lack of (aforementioned) simplicity and consistency [13]. These observations were reported already over ten years ago [16], but little has happened to fix the issues, apart from libraries that aim at introducing their own way of engineering web applications. The absence of solid engineering principles is easy to understand given that the web browser was originally designed to be a document distribution environment rather than a "real" application execution environment. However, the current popularity of the Web as the software platform makes it very unfortunate that these important principles have been ignored. Currently the web components are the best – and perhaps also the only – chance to reintroduce some of these important principles to the heart of the Web.

In the broader picture, the deficiencies of the web browser as a software platform are being tackled with an abundance of libraries. As of this writing, there are more than 1,400 officially listed JavaScript libraries in javascripting.com, with new ones being introduced on a weekly if not daily basis. Although many of the libraries are domain-specific, a lot of them are aimed squarely at solving the architectural limitations of the web browser, e.g., to provide a consistent set of manifest interfaces to perform various programming tasks. Over the years, JavaScript libraries have evolved from mere convenience function libraries to full-fledged Model-View-Controller (MVC) frameworks providing extensive UI component sets, application state management, network communication and database interfaces, and so on. In general, these will not necessarily help in tackling the above characteristics but may rather add a new layer of complexity on top of them.

6   Revisiting Our Earlier Predictions and Considerations

As mentioned in the beginning, this paper is an expanded, revisited version of papers that were published earlier [27,29]. In this section, we will revisit our earlier predictions and considerations in the light of more recent technologies and approaches to web applications.

The Emergence of Virtual DOM Technologies. Out of the technologies discussed in [27,29], DOM/DHTML has maintained its dominant role as the baseline technology as we predicted. The majority of libraries and applications that have been developed over the years are built on top of the standard

DOM/DHTML approach. What we did not foresee, however, was the introduction of techniques that effectively replicate and virtualize the behavior of the Document Object Model in order to gain additional programmatic control over rendering. These new approaches can be viewed as a derivative of the Shadow DOM model introduced by Web Components, except that in these approaches the DOM is externalized and replicated outside the built-in Document Object Model, thus allowing libraries and applications to work around some of the limitations and built-in assumptions that the web browser imposes on application development. Simply put, Virtual DOM trees (see https://bitsofco.de/understanding-the-virtual-dom/) are copies of the original DOM; these copies can be manipulated and updated independently of the browser-level DOM APIs, thus bypassing any immediate impact on the browser's rendering process. Once all the updates have been made in the virtual DOM, the changes need to pushed back (copied) to the original DOM in an optimized way. The Virtual DOM approach can considerably improve rendering performance as well as enhance the overall smoothness of web user interfaces in comparison to traditional DOM manipulation in which applications have very limited control over rendering.

Emerging Support for Virtual and Augmented Reality. In our previous work, we foresaw increased popularity of WebGL that enables browser-based, installation-free, high-performance applications for viewing VR/AR content. These features will inevitably gain more popularity, as the world moves towards richer media experiences, and the standard DOM/DHTML model is unable to support the necessary features. To this end, further rendering and visualization techniques that build on WebGL have been proposed. These include *WebVR* (https://webvr.info/) and *WebXR Device API* (https://immersive-web.github.io/webxr/), which take the Web towards virtual and augmented reality rendering with new APIs. In addition, we predicted that WebGL would also be increasingly important for game developers; however, the elimination of the "last safe bastion" of traditional binary applications (as indicated in our earlier paper) – allowing the creation of portable high-performance applications in the context of the web browser – has not yet taken place. Similarly, we pointed out that the Web would benefit from a high-performance, low-level 2D graphics API that would provide a more comprehensive feature set and direct drawing capabilities without any historical development baggage of the Canvas API. However, at the time of this writing, there is no such standardization effort in sight.

Web Components. Regarding web components, it is still too early to declare victory or failure. Since web components offer a more disciplined approach to DOM/DHTML programming, reintroduce established software engineering principles, and generally alleviate the "spaghetti code" issues that have resurfaced with the Web [25], we would certainly like to see them succeed. In reality, the main obstacle to the wider adoption of web components are the predominant JavaScript libraries that also provide additional abstraction layers on top of the underlying DOM and basic browser features. Hence, the future of web components is fundamentally affected by the evolution of JavaScript library landscape and associated features.

JavaScript Library Landscape. Earlier in this paper, we noted that JavaScript library evolution has followed a fashion-driven approach in which a few frameworks have dominated the landscape for a few years, only to be superseded by new dominant frameworks some years later. Interestingly, this trend seems to have waned in the past two years. While the flood of new, lesser known front-end and backend frameworks has continued as strongly as ever (as witnessed in http://www.javascripting.com/ or in the constantly increasing number of NPM packages), the popularity of top three dominant front-end libraries has not changed much in the past two years.

When writing the first manuscripts of our earlier papers in late 2016/early 2017 [27,29], the top five frontend frameworks were Vue.js, React, Angular, Angular 1, and Inferno (https://risingstars.js.org/2016/en/). As of this writing (January 2019), Vue.js, React, and Angular are still the top three, followed by Hyperapp and Omi (https://risingstars.js.org/2018/en/#section-framework). At the same time, jQuery is still used rather extensively (https://w3techs.com/technologies/details/js-jquery/all/all), implying that some web frameworks can also have an extended lifespan. However, the introduction and enamoration with new, fashionable frameworks is by no means over. For instance, *Weex* (https://weex.incubator.apache.org/) has recently gained popularity rapidly in the mobile domain.

7   Future Work

In this paper we have scratched only the surface of architectural issues related to web applications, as we intentionally narrowed down our analysis into one specific area: the built-in application rendering technologies in a modern web browser. The web ecosystem provides a cornucopia of choices in many other areas. Consequently, there are several avenues for future research and directions to expand this work towards different dimensions of the Web as an application platform.

We are currently encouraging ourselves and our students to perform similar studies, e.g., on the cornucopia of communication mechanisms and methods used in web applications, including Ajax [8], Comet [5], Server-Sent Events [10], Web-Sockets [20], WebRTC [2]), and to some extent also Web/Shared Workers [31]. In addition, persistent storage in the context of the web browser is an interesting topic, although the design space in that context is far more limited.

Cornucopia associated with front-end Web frameworks is an even more diverse area to study than the technologies inside the browser itself. So far, we have briefly studied only the most popular mainstream frameworks, but a more in-depth look would definitely be an interesting direction for future work, in particular since the many libraries provide facilities that are similar to those of the technologies inside the browser.

Finally, server-side web development is yet another rich area for future work. As already mentioned, over the past few years, an extremely prolific ecosystem has emerged around Node.js, and there are a lot of additional open source technologies for nearly every imaginable aspect of server-side development. For instance, data acquisition and analytics solutions such as Apache Kafka, Storm and Spark have become very popular. From architectural standpoint, the recent trend towards *isomorphic JavaScript* is also extremely relevant. In web development, an isomorphic application is one whose code can run unmodified both in the server and the client [23]. Such capabilities are relevant, e.g., in realizing *liquid software* that allows applications to seamlessly migrate across multiple devices [7,28].

8 Conclusions

Over the past twenty-five years or so, the World Wide Web has evolved from a document sharing system to a full-fledged programming environment. This evolution has taken place organically, and new technologies have been constantly introduced to help developers create compelling web systems.

As a consequence, web development today presents a cornucopia of choices on all fronts. Both on the client side and the server side, there exist a large number of competing, overlapping technologies, and new libraries and tools become available almost on a daily basis. The rapid pace of innovation has put the developers in a complex position in which there are numerous ways to build applications on the Web – many more than most people realize, and also arguably more than are really needed.

In this paper, we have investigated one of the perhaps most overlooked areas in web development: the client-side web rendering architectures that have been built into the generic web browser. We compared five built-in rendering and application development models, followed by some predictions, discussion and avenues for future research.

As Alan Kay once aptly put it, "simple things should be simple, and complex things should be possible". In web development today, pretty much everything is possible, but really not at all in the simplest possible way. While the World Wide Web is one of the most important innovations for humankind, for web application developers things are still likely to get even more complicated until they get any simpler.

References

1. Anttonen, M., Salminen, A., Mikkonen, T., Taivalsaari, A.: Transforming the web into a real application platform: new technologies, emerging trends and missing pieces. In: Proceedings of the 2011 ACM Symposium on Applied Computing, pp. 800–807. ACM (2011)
2. Bergkvist, A., et al.: WebRTC 1.0: real-time communication between browsers. W3C Candidate Recommendation, 27 September 2018. https://www.w3.org/TR/webrtc/
3. Bitworking.org: Zero Framework Manifesto: No More JS Frameworks (2014). https://bitworking.org/news/2014/05/zero_framework_manifesto

4. Casteleyn, S., Garrigós, I., Mazón, J.N.: Ten years of Rich Internet Applications: a systematic mapping study, and beyond. ACM Trans. Web **8**(3), 18:1–18:46 (2014). https://doi.org/10.1145/2626369. http://doi.acm.org/10.1145/2626369
5. Crane, D., McCarthy, P.: What Are Comet and Reverse Ajax?. Springer, Heidelberg (2009)
6. Flanagan, D.: JavaScript: The Definitive Guide, 6th edn. O'Reilly Media, Sebastopol (2011)
7. Gallidabino, A., et al.: On the architecture of liquid software: technology alternatives and design space. In: Proceedings of WICSA (2016)
8. Garrett, J.J.: Ajax: a new approach to web applications, 18 February 2005. http://adaptivepath.org/ideas/ajax-new-approach-web-applications/
9. Hartmann, B., Doorley, S., Klemmer, S.R.: Hacking, mashing, gluing: understanding opportunistic design. IEEE Pervasive Comput. **7**(3), 46–54 (2008)
10. Hickson, I.: Server-sent events. W3C Recommendation, 3 February 2015. http://www.w3.org/TR/eventsource/
11. Ingalls, D., Palacz, K., Uhler, S., Taivalsaari, A., Mikkonen, T.: The lively kernel a self-supporting system on a web page. In: Hirschfeld, R., Rose, K. (eds.) S3 2008. LNCS, vol. 5146, pp. 31–50. Springer, Heidelberg (2008). https://doi.org/10.1007/978-3-540-89275-5_2
12. Jadhav, M.A., Sawant, B.R., Deshmukh, A.: Single page application using AngularJS. Int. J. Comput. Sci. Inf. Technol. **6**(3), 2876–2879 (2015)
13. MacLennan, B.J.: Principles of Programming Languages: Design, Evaluation, and Implementation, 3rd edn. Oxford University Press, Oxford (1999)
14. Marcotte, E.: Responsive Web Design. Editions Eyrolles (2011)
15. Meijer, E.: Democratizing the cloud. In: Companion Proceedings of OOPSLA 2007, pp. 858–859 (2007). https://doi.org/10.1145/1297846.1297925. http://doi.acm.org/10.1145/1297846.1297925
16. Mikkonen, T., Taivalsaari, A.: Web applications – spaghetti code for the 21st century. In: Proceedings of the International Conference on Software Engineering Research, Management and Applications, SERA 2008, Prague, Czech Republic, 20–22 August 2008, pp. 319–328. IEEE Computer Society (2008)
17. Mikkonen, T., Taivalsaari, A.: Apps vs. open web: the battle of the decade. In: Proceedings of the 2nd Workshop on Software Engineering for Mobile Application Development, MSE, Santa Monica, CA, pp. 22–26 (2011)
18. Mikkonen, T., Taivalsaari, A.: Cloud computing and its impact on mobile software development: two roads diverged. J. Syst. Softw. **86**(9), 2318–2320 (2013)
19. Parnas, D.L.: On the criteria to be used in decomposing systems into modules. Commun. ACM **15**(12), 1053–1058 (1972)
20. Pimentel, V., Nickerson, B.G.: Communicating and displaying real-time data with WebSocket. IEEE Internet Comput. **16**(4), 45–53 (2012)
21. Salminen, A., Mikkonen, T.: Mashups: software ecosystems for the web era. In: IWSECO@ ICSOB, pp. 18–32 (2012)
22. Salminen, A., Mikkonen, T., Nyrhinen, F., Taivalsaari, A.: Developing client-side mashups: experiences, guidelines and the road ahead. In: Proceedings of the 14th International Academic MindTrek Conference: Envisioning Future Media Environments, pp. 161–168. ACM (2010)
23. Strimpel, J., Najim, M.: Building Isomorphic JavaScript Apps: From Concept to Implementation to Real-World Solutions. O'Reilly Media Inc., Sebastopol (2016)
24. Taivalsaari, A., Mikkonen, T.: The web as an application platform: the saga continues. In: 37th EUROMICRO Conference on Software Engineering and Advanced Applications, pp. 170–174. IEEE (2011)

25. Taivalsaari, A., Mikkonen, T.: Return of the great spaghetti monster: learnings from a twelve-year adventure in web software development. In: Majchrzak, T.A., Traverso, P., Krempels, K.-H., Monfort, V. (eds.) WEBIST 2017. LNBIP, vol. 322, pp. 21–44. Springer, Cham (2018). https://doi.org/10.1007/978-3-319-93527-0_2

26. Taivalsaari, A., Mikkonen, T., Ingalls, D., Palacz, K.: Web browser as an application platform: the lively kernel experience. Sun Labs Technical report TR-2008-175, January 2008

27. Taivalsaari, A., Mikkonen, T., Pautasso, C., Systä, K.: Comparing the built-in application architecture models in the web browser. In: 2017 IEEE International Conference on Software Architecture (ICSA), pp. 51–54. IEEE (2017)

28. Taivalsaari, A., Mikkonen, T., Systä, K.: Liquid software manifesto: the era of multiple device ownership and its implications for software architecture. In: 38th IEEE Computer Software and Applications Conference (COMPSAC), pp. 338–343 (2014)

29. Taivalsaari, A., Mikkonen, T., Systä, K., Pautasso, C.: Web user interface implementation technologies: an underview. In: Proceedings of the 14th International Conference on Web Information Systems and Technologies, WEBIST 2018, Seville, Spain, 18–20 September 2018, pp. 127–136 (2018). https://doi.org/10.5220/0006885401270136

30. W3C: Scalable Vector Graphics (SVG) Specification 1.1, 2nd edn. (2011). https://www.w3.org/TR/SVG/

31. W3Schools: HTML5 Web Workers. http://www.w3schools.com/html/html5_webworkers.asp

Hybrid Is Better: Why and How Test Coverage and Software Reliability Can Benefit Each Other

Antonia Bertolino[1](✉), Breno Miranda[2], Roberto Pietrantuono[3],
and Stefano Russo[3]

[1] ISTI - CNR, Pisa, Italy
antonia.bertolino@isti.cnr.it
[2] Federal University of Pernambuco, Recife, Brazil
bafm@cin.ufpe.br
[3] Università degli Studi di Napoli Federico II, Napoli, Italy
{roberto.pietrantuono,stefano.russo}@unina.it

Abstract. Functional, structural and operational testing are three broad categories of software testing methods driven by the product functionalities, the way it is implemented, and the way it is expected to be used, respectively. A large body of the software testing literature is devoted to evaluate and compare test techniques in these categories. Although it appears reasonable to devise hybrid methods to merge their different strengths - because different techniques may complement each other by targeting different types of faults and/or using different artifacts - we still miss clear guidelines on how to best combine them.

We discuss differences and limitations of two popular testing approaches, namely coverage-driven and operational-profile testing, belonging to structural and operational testing, respectively. We show *why* and *how* test coverage and operational profile can cross-fertilize each other, improving the effectiveness of structural testing or, conversely, the product reliability achievable by operational testing.

Keywords: Software testing · Reliability · Structural testing · Operational testing

1 Introduction

Testing is an essential part of the software development and maintenance processes. It consists of the dynamic assessment of software behavior on a finite sample of executions. To make testing systematic and to measure progress while tests are executed, some strategy is necessary. It will help testers to keep costs within reasonable bounds and to identify those test cases deemed the most effective.

Broadly speaking, systematic testing strategies are driven by three major aspects of the software under test (SUT): *(i)* what it is expected to do, *(ii)* how

© Springer Nature Switzerland AG 2019
M. J. Escalona et al. (Eds.): WEBIST 2018, LNBIP 372, pp. 25–38, 2019.
https://doi.org/10.1007/978-3-030-35330-8_2

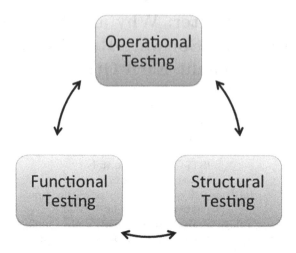

Fig. 1. Test strategies and their potential relations.

it is implemented, and *(iii)* how it will be used. Such three aspects correspond to three major categories of software testing techniques, namely functional, structural and operational testing (Fig. 1).

Each category relies on different assumptions and artifacts, and a broad variety of techniques and tools for each one has been proposed.

Since the early years of software testing discipline, researchers have conducted analytical and empirical studies to evaluate and compare the effectiveness of the different test techniques, in search for the most cost-effective approach.

From such studies we have learned that testing techniques may suffer from saturation effects and from various other limitations, and that there exist no one technique which best suits all circumstances. Different test techniques target different types of faults and thus may complement each other. For this reason, it is reasonable to invest resources by properly combining different techniques, rather than employing all the testing budget in only one selected strategy.

However, there are not many proposals for hybrid techniques merging the respective strengths of functional, structural and operational testing (examples are [7,8,10]), and no widely accepted guidelines on how different methods could be combined into one effective strategy are available. Further research is needed to understand how such strategies could be combined, depending on the testing purpose and the available artifacts.

As a step forward in this direction, we discuss the differences and respective limitations of two popular testing approaches: techniques driven by code coverage information, and techniques driven by the operational profile. Traditionally these two test approaches are adopted to address different purposes: coverage-driven testing aims at finding as many faults as possible, whereas operational-profile driven testing aims at improving software reliability. So, apparently, they seem to belong to two worlds apart, and in fact there is little overlap between research progresses. However, we have found that on the one side coverage criteria can be made more effective if not all entities are considered equal, but software usage in operation is referred to assign them different weights. On the other side, software reliability testing can be made more effective as well if coverage information is considered alongside the operational profile in selecting the test cases.

Our reported results provide only an incomplete vision of several other potential "hybridizations". For instance, we have not considered yet the usage of functional strategies where software specifications or models are available. In presenting how coverage criteria and reliability improvement can benefit each other our contribution is one step towards unleashing the potential of many more useful combination of techniques.

The chapter is structured as follows. Section 2 describes the main concepts of test coverage and related measures in *debug testing*. Section 3 presents the rationale behind software *reliability testing* techniques. Section 4 discusses the relationship between coverage and reliability, and how these can benefit each other. Section 5 describes related work on combining white-box and operational testing. Section 6 concludes the chapter.

2   On Test Coverage Measures

Software testing can pursue different goals. Along the development process, testing may aim at detecting as many faults as possible so that these can be removed before the software goes in production. For this reason, this type of testing is referred to in the literature as *debug testing* [15].

Measures of effectiveness of debug testing techniques are related with its faults finding capability. For example, a test technique would be evaluated more effective than another if it detects the first fault by executing a lower number of test cases, or otherwise if by executing an equal number of test cases the former finds a higher number of faults than the latter.

Along such line of reasoning, measuring the coverage of which and how many program elements are exercised during test execution is seen by many as an appealing proxy for assessing fault finding effectiveness. The intuition is that if a fault resides in a part of code that is never tested, such fault would never be activated and hence would survive testing, probably remaining undetected until the final user will eventually trigger it. In his seminal and highly-referenced book on "Software Testing Techniques" [3], Beizer defined leaving parts of code untested as "*stupid, shortsighted and irresponsible*".

Depending on which elements of code are targeted, in the years a broad variety of test coverage criteria have been proposed [16,47]. All of them basically share the following scheme: an element of the program source code is identified as the type of entity to be covered. This element can be as basic as every statement or every branch of the program control flow, or become more sophisticated, such as for example every association between the definition of a variable and all its potential usages, for every variable in the program (all definition-use associations [16]). Then the source code of the SUT is parsed and instrumented, so that the coverage of the targeted elements can be monitored during testing. While test proceeds, a quantitative assessment of the thoroughness of testing is provided by the ratio between the number of entities that have been already covered and the cardinality of the whole set of entities, expressed by the percentage:

$$\text{Test coverage} = \frac{\#\ of\ covered\ entities}{\#\ of\ available\ entities} \cdot 100(\%). \tag{1}$$

The underlying idea of coverage criteria is that until there remain entities that have not been exercised, the testing cannot be deemed complete, and more test cases have to be executed that can increase the above ratio. Therefore, coverage measures provide both a practical stopping rule (when a satisfying coverage is achieved), and a guide for the selection of additional test cases (*i.e.*, those covering yet uncovered entities).

There exist no proven direct relation, for any of the existing criteria, that when complete test coverage is achieved, then the SUT can be guaranteed to be defect-free. Since testing is essentially a sampling from a practically infinite set of executions [4], it is obvious to everyone that no finite test campaign can ensure correctness. Indeed, the most famous quotation about software testing is probably Dijkstra's aphorism that *software testing can only show the presence of bugs, but never their absence* [13]. In search for more effective testing strategies, the realistic goal is not to remove all faults, but rather to maximize the likelihood of revealing potential failures.

Coverage criteria can be considered as belonging to *partition testing* strategies that divide the input domain into equivalence classes (even though they generally create overlapping subdomains and not true partitions), and ensure to pick representative test cases (at least one) from each class. Theoretical analyses of partition testing strategies [44] have early shown that their effectiveness depends on how and where the failure-causing inputs are located, which is of course beyond testers' control and knowledge. The root of the problem is what Roper called the *"missing link"*: we still cannot (will we *ever* be able to?) establish a logical or practical *"link between the adequacy criteria and attributes of the program under test such as its reliability or number of faults"* [37]. Thus, the only way to establish whether a relation exists between coverage of some entity type and fault finding effectiveness is through empirical studies, and in fact a series of such studies has been and continues to be undertaken by several researchers, *e.g.*, [23,43], but no definitive answers are available yet.

More properly, we must understand that what coverage measures provide us is an assessment of a *test suite thoroughness*. At the same time, some researchers have raised concerns against misusing coverage as the main goal of testing [18,27]. In such light, additional test cases that do not contribute to increase coverage would be considered "redundant" and not useful, however such test cases could indeed be able to catch still undetected faults. We should also never forget the cost in terms of time consumed in monitoring coverage, which makes white-box testing impractical on large scales [21].

In conclusion, coverage criteria provide a very useful and practical means towards systematic thorough testing. However, "*100% coverage should always be the result of good testing but it makes few sense as a goal in itself*" [36].

3   On Software Reliability

Testing to find as many faults as possible may seem a good strategy. However, in real-world production we have to face stringent time and budget constraints, which make Herzig note that "*There's never enough time to do all the testing you want*" [20]. Henceforth, this strategy could not be the best choice.

The point is that debug testing targets all faults indiscriminately, without considering the important difference between a *fault* (the cause) and a *failure* (its manifestation), nor the likelihood and potential impacts of the failure originating from a given fault. Indeed, *not all faults are created equal*. An early seminal study by Adams [1] showed, for example, that the 30% of the faults found in the systems he studied (at the time in IBM production) would each show itself less then once every 5,000 years of operational use. Clearly any testing effort spent to find these "tiny" faults would not be well employed.

This brings us to the fundamental concept of *software reliability*, which is "the probability of failure-free operation for a specified period of time in a specified environment" [24]. When the SUT is not safety-critical, testing to improve software reliability may be a more convenient aim than debug testing: in other words, we acknowledge that we would never be able to find all faults, and aim at focusing our efforts towards those ones whose removal mostly contributes to increase reliability.

Pioneered in the 70's by Musa [30], software reliability testing is based on the notion of the *operational profile* [31,40], which provides a quantitative characterization of how a system will be used in the field. In operational profile-based testing (OP testing in the following), the SUT is thus tested by trying to reproduce how its final users will exercise it, so that the failures are detected with the same likelihood they would be experimented by those users in operation.

The operational profile is normally built by associating the points in the input domain D with values representing the probability to be invoked in operation. Making such association is a difficult task; the best case is when historical data are available, otherwise this can be done by domain experts. Usually, D is divided into M subdomains $D_1, \ldots, D_m$, so that the inputs within a partition are estimated as having the same probability of occurrence in operation. The operational profile is then defined by a probability distribution over the partitions D_i: a value p_i denotes the probability that in operation an input is selected from D_i, with $\sum_{i=1}^{M} p_i = 1$. The software reliability, R, can then be defined [15] as:

$$R = 1 - \sum_{t \in F} p_t \qquad (2)$$

where F is the (unknown) set of failure-causing inputs and p_t is the expected probability of occurrence in operation of input t.

OP testing has been shown to be an effective strategy, both in theory [15] and in practice, *e.g.*, [14,42]. With this strategy, when the test is stopped (for instance because of imperative schedule constraints) and the software released, testers are ensured that the most-frequently invoked operations have received the greatest attention, so that the delivered reliability is at the maximum level achievable under the given test resources [26].

However, OP testing faces difficult challenges that may hinder its broad take-up: first, an operational profile may not be readily available and its derivation can be costly and complex [22]; second, as more frequent failures are detected and removed, the application of OP testing may progressively lose efficacy.

The latter problem is known as the *saturation effect* [22]. Actually, it is not a prerogative of OP testing, but could affect any test technique. To counteract saturation, research has shown that it is convenient to always consider a *combination* of different testing strategies, which target different types of faults and can together achieve higher effectiveness than the individual application of the most effective technique [25]. Considering specifically reliability improvement, the authors of [11] suggest that the combination of techniques should aim at exposing failures with high occurrence probability, but also as many *failure regions* as possible.[1]

4   How Are Coverage and Reliability Related?

4.1   Ways of Combining Coverage Measures and Operational Profile

In the previous sections we have overviewed two widely used testing strategies, which employ different techniques and pursue different goals. Indeed, coverage testing and OP testing have formed two separate threads of the software testing literature, with little overlaps (see Sect. 5).

In recent work, we have addressed the question whether and how coverage and OP testing techniques could mutually benefit each other towards the goal of increasing software testing effectiveness for reliability improvement. Indeed, we have achieved encouraging results in either directions.

On the one hand, we have found that coverage testing can be made more cost-effective if not all entities are indiscriminately targeted, but a subset of entities is selected based on their relevance for the final user. In other terms, we have somehow embedded a notion of operational profile within the definition of coverage measures. This research has been presented in [29], and is summarized in Sect. 4.2.

On the other hand, we have found that using coverage information can help prevent the saturation effect of OP testing and achieve higher effectiveness in reliability improvement. In other terms, to further improve reliability beyond a certain point, within a selected input subdomain the testing should target those entities that are the most rarely covered. This research has been presented in [5], and is summarized in Sect. 4.3.

---

[1] A failure region is the set of failure points eliminated by a program change [15].

4.2 Mimicking Operational Profile by Means of Coverage Count Spectrum

The leading idea of OP testing is exercising the SUT in similar way to how their final users would do. OP testing is inherently a black-box technique, since it disregards the SUT internal structure. Conversely, in coverage testing, a tester tries to exercise the SUT thoroughly without leaving parts untested, no matter of whether and how final users will exercise them. One attractive feature of coverage testing is the availability of a simple and intuitive stopping rule, which is provided, as said, by the coverage measure. On its side, OP testing lacks such a straightforward adequacy criterion.

In traditional coverage testing, while testing proceeds each entity is marked as covered or not covered, *i.e.*, from monitoring code coverage testers derive the so-called *hit spectrum*. In general, a program spectrum [19] characterizes a program's behavior by recording the set of entities that are exercised as it executes. The hit spectrum, in particular, records if an entity is covered ("hit") or not. When used in operation, the different program entities will be covered with different frequencies. Some entities will never be exercised, others will be accessed only few times, and others will be covered very frequently. The hit spectrum does not give any information about this varied usage of program entities, beyond revealing that some entities have never been exercised and hence are probably "out-of-scope". Conversely, the *count spectrum* records how many times an entity is exercised: by referring during coverage testing to the count spectrum rather than to the normally used hit spectrum, we keep track of the frequency with which each entity is covered.

As an example, Table 1 displays the *branch-hit* and *branch-count* spectra of two test cases TC_1 and TC_2 exercised during a test campaign. Both TC_1 and TC_2 cover the same set of branches, thus their hit spectra are identical. If we look at their count spectra, we can notice that TC_1 and TC_2 exercise the SUT quite differently.

Table 1. An example of branch-hit and branch-count spectra.

Branch ID	*Branch-hit* spectrum		*Branch-count* spectrum	
	TC_1	TC_2	TC_1	TC_2
b_1	1	1	5	23
b_2	0	0	0	0
b_3	1	1	1	1
b_4	0	0	0	0
b_5	1	1	85	394
b_6	1	1	9	42
b_7	0	0	0	0
b_8	1	1	28	129
b_9	0	0	0	0

Hence, the count spectrum could be used to obtain an approximate representation of how the final users behaviour impacts on the SUT code. Such intuition inspired us the idea of *"operational coverage"*: using the count spectrum, it measures code coverage taking into account whether and how the entities are relevant with respect to a user's operational profile.

In principle, the notion can be applied to any existing coverage criterion. In previous work [28,29], we studied operational coverage for three types of entities, namely statements, branches and functions.

To measure operational coverage, we developed the following method. First, program entities are classified into different importance groups based on the count spectrum. Consider, for instance, three importance groups, denominated *high*, *medium*, and *low*. To cluster entities into these three groups, the list of entities is ordered according to their usage frequency; the first 1/3 entities are assigned to the *high* frequency group; the second 1/3 entities to the *medium* frequency group; and the last 1/3 entities to the *low* frequency group. Of course, different grouping schemes could be adopted.

Then, different weights are assigned to the importance groups to reflect the operational profile. We gave the highest weight to entities in the *high* group, and the lowest weight to the *low* group. Entities that are never covered are assign a zero weight (they are out-of-scope).

Finally, the operational coverage is computed as the weighted arithmetic mean of the rate of covered entities according to the Equation:

$$\text{Operational coverage} = \frac{\sum_{i=1}^{3} w_i \cdot x_i}{\sum_{i=1}^{3} w_i} \cdot 100(\%) \tag{3}$$

where: x_i is the rate of covered entities from group i; w_i is the weight assigned to group i. Note that reducing the above formula to only one group we re-obtain the formula of traditional coverage as per Eq. 1.

Operational coverage can be used both as an adequacy criterion and as a selection criterion. In the former case, we use operational coverage for deciding when to stop testing: intuitively, the coverage measure that we achieve during testing gives a weighted estimation of how many of the entities that are more relevant for the final users have been covered. The weights allow testers to take into account if the not yet covered entities may have a large impact on the delivered reliability. For the same reason, using operational coverage in test selection provides a criterion to prioritize the next test cases to be executed.

In [29], we performed some empirical studies to assess operational coverage and the results confirmed the above intuition. Precisely, operational coverage is better correlated than traditional coverage with the probability that the next test case will not fail while performing OP testing. Regarding test case selection, operational coverage on average outperforms traditional coverage in terms of test suite size and fault detection capability.

4.3   Boosting Reliability Improvement by Targeting the Lowest Covered Entities

As described in Sect. 3, in OP testing the test cases are selected from the operational profile, aiming at finding the failure-causing inputs that have the highest likelihood of being invoked in operation. However, as we already observed, due to the saturation effect [22], after some testing campaign in which the most frequent faults have been revealed and removed, continuing to perform OP testing will progressively lose its efficacy.

Saturation is a well-known problem, and advanced approaches have been proposed to counteract it. For example, Cotroneo and coauthors [11] have recently developed the RELAI technique that uses an adaptive scheme for redefining the operational profile, dynamically learning from the test outcomes. Indeed, to continue improving reliability, at a certain point it becomes necessary to find a proper strategy to move farther from the most frequently exercised operations and start "digging" in less frequent zones of the input domain.

In line with [25] that suggests to combine different testing approaches, we explored whether considering code coverage as an additional information to the operational profile helps achieving higher reliability. The intuition is that coverage-driven selection can point to parts of the program that have not been exercised by the operational profile driven test cases and that may contain faults. However, even so, we would like to take into account the user's profile, because the aim remains to improve reliability.

Along such line of reasoning, we have recently developed a hybrid approach that relies on both operational profile and coverage information, the latter specifically considering the above introduced count spectrum [5]. The approach, called *covrel*, works in iterations: each iteration dynamically uses the test outcomes from previous iteration to re-arrange the operational profile. This adaptation is based on an inference method called *Importance Sampling* (IS) method [6], which was previously used in the already cited work [11].

Each iteration consists of two steps. First, a partition of the input domain into subdomains D_i is dynamically redefined. In line with traditional OP testing (see Sect. 3), this step allows to assign probability values to inputs. More precisely, at each iteration the output of the first step is the number of test cases to execute from within each partition (for more details we refer the reader to [5]). In the second step, among all the inputs within a partition (*i.e.*, having a same occurrence probability), *covrel* selects those that exercise the least covered entities according to the count spectrum. This is the novel aspect of *covrel*, in comparison with the more usual approach of selecting such test cases in random way. Of course, to do so *covrel* assumes that the SUT is instrumented and test traces are tracked, as in any white-box testing strategy.

Note that similarly to operational coverage (Sect. 4.2), the *covrel* strategy derives the count spectrum and classifies the entities into three different importance groups: *high, medium,* and *low*. However, differently from operational coverage, in *covrel* we are interested in covering the most "hidden" entities. Therefore, we assign the weights for the importance groups prioritizing the low group.

Then, for each partition, we select the test cases with the highest ranks. The two steps are repeated until the available budget of test cases exhausts.

In [5] we have evaluated *covrel* against traditional OP testing with controlled experiments. The results showed that *covrel* can outperform OP testing and achieve faster a given reliability value. The performance of *covrel* is better considering high values of reliability, confirming the intuition that the extra costs it requires for coverage measurement do pay when a high value of reliability is required.

5 Related Work

While a huge literature exists about the topics of coverage testing and OP testing considered individually, here we are concerned with the interplay between the two worlds. As anticipated in Sect. 4.1, there have been only few overlaps between the two research communities. These overlaps have interested mostly the investigation of the effectiveness of coverage testing in terms of reliability improvement instead of fault finding, as, *e.g.*, in [12,17] and the usage of coverage information for refining software reliability growth models, as surveyed in [2].

Related approaches of interest are those exploring some direct or indirect knowledge derived from the program code (i.e., white-box information) or from the development process in order to either improve or assess reliability.

Smidts *et al.* consider operational testing as a means to *corroborate* (rather than to assess) an already assessed reliability, by complementing evidences gained in previous phases of the development process (e.g., by white-box testing) [39]. This is a problem particularly felt in ultra-reliable systems, where no failures are observed during testing, making operational testing not able, by itself, to give confidence about reliability.

Neil *et al.* propose to use Bayesian networks (BN) as a means to combine evidences: in their example, many pieces of information coming from development-time activities, including code coverage and operational profile, are used together with test results as evidence to assess reliability [32]. A Bayesian approach is also proposed by Singh *et al.*, who use reliability prediction obtained from UML models as the prior belief for reliability assessment in system operational testing [38].

In a PhD proposal by Omri [33], white-box information is used in combination with the operational profile, again with the aim of estimating reliability; the author applies symbolic execution combined with stratified sampling to derive the most favorable partitions for minimizing the variance of the estimate. We too have conjectured the usage of white-box information such as coverage as a means to modify the belief about the partitions' failure proneness, with the aim of driving the profile-based test generation process [34,35].

All these approaches try to augment the profile-based testing with other pieces of information so as to expose more reliability-impacting failing inputs. None, however, directly embeds code coverage information into the test selection or generation process like *covrel* [5].

Our operational coverage and *covrel* approaches rely on the coverage count spectrum. The idea of using program spectra to help software validation tasks is not new: program spectra have been used, among others, for fault localization [45] and regression testing [46]. To the best of our knowledge, however, we are the first to compute coverage measures based on program count spectra, for the purpose of reflecting the importance of program entities.

One more feature of our approaches is adaptivity. Many authors have exploited adaptivity for improving testing. A noticeable example is the well-known family of *Adaptive Random Testing* (ART) techniques by Chen et al. [8], in which the intuition is to improve random testing by using test results online in order to evenly distribute test cases across the input domain. ART is aimed at debug testing; as such, it does not explicitly target reliability improvement and/or assessment like OP testing. *Adaptive testing*, proposed by Cai et al., uses the operational profile for reliability assessment and foresees adaptation (via controlled Markov chains) in the assignment of test cases to partitions [7]. Both these approaches use neither coverage nor any other development-time information to boost reliability.

To implement adaptivity, we used *Importance Sampling*, a statistical sampling method to approximate the true distribution of a variable of interest [6]. We used it to approximate the unknown distribution of the number of test cases for each partition to maximize delivered reliability. While Importance Sampling is successfully used in many fields, its usage for testing is limited to few papers: Sridharan and Namin used it to prioritize mutation operators in mutation testing [41]; we ourselves used it for test techniques selection [9].

6 Conclusions

A large part of software testing literature evaluates the effectiveness of testing techniques based on the faults found, irrespectively of the potential likelihood and impact of such faults. In this way, among several test techniques the one that finds the highest number of faults would be considered the most effective, but this might not correspond to reality. If the faults found are never experienced in practice, the test technique would not be very effective.

In this work, considering that test effectiveness should be evaluated based on the delivered reliability [15], we have discussed some results from combining two usually separated test strategies: white-box coverage criteria and black-box operational testing. The former exploits knowledge of program internals, the latter of program usage.

We have overviewed two approaches that mix the two strategies following two different intuitions. In operational coverage, we have augmented coverage testing criteria with a notion of user's relevance. The intuition is that if an entity is rarely or never used in operation, coverage of this entity should contribute to coverage measure with lower weight. On the contrary, entities that, based on operational profile, are frequently covered, should be given higher weights. In covrel, we have augmented OP testing with coverage information, targeting the selection of test cases within a domain partition towards those entities that remain hidden, i.e. yielding a lower coverage count. The intuition here is that monitoring coverage along OP testing may help increasing faster the reliability.

The approaches we have developed are just a first attempt to implement what seems a very attractive perspective: by combining information from coverage and operational profile we can achieve a stronger testing technique that yields both a practical stopping rule and mitigates the inherent saturation problem.

Having opened a novel research thread, we are also aware that a myriad of other potential techniques could be devised, only limited by creativity. For example, we have considered coverage of only three more common entities, statement, branch and function. Other entities could have been considered. Moreover, as we hinted in the introduction, we could consider a model of software behaviour and different combinations also involving functional testing strategies.

Acknowledgements. This work has been partially supported by the PRIN 2015 project "GAUSS" funded by MIUR. B. Miranda wishes to thank the postdoctoral fellowship jointly sponsored by CAPES and FACEPE (APQ-0826-1.03/16; BCT-0204-1.03/17).

References

1. Adams, E.N.: Optimizing preventive service of software products. IBM J. Res. Dev. **28**(1), 2–14 (1984)
2. Alrmuny, D.: A comparative study of test coverage-based software reliability growth models. In: Proceedings of the 11th International Conference on Information Technology: New Generations, pp. 255–259. ITNG, IEEE (2014)
3. Beizer, B.: Software Testing Techniques, 2nd edn. Van Nostrand Reinhold Co., New York (1990)
4. Bertolino, A.: Software testing. In: Bourque, P., Dupuis, R. (eds.) Software Engineering Body of Knowledge (SWEBOK), Chap. 5. IEEE Computer Society (2001)
5. Bertolino, A., Miranda, B., Pietrantuono, R., Russo, S.: Adaptive coverage and operational profile-based testing for reliability improvement. In: Proceedings of the 39th International Conference on Software Engineering, pp. 541–551. ICSE, IEEE (2017)
6. Bishop, C.: Pattern Recognition and Machine Learning. Information Science and Statistics. Springer-Verlag, New York (2006)
7. Cai, K.Y., Li, Y.C., Liu, K.: Optimal and adaptive testing for software reliability assessment. Inf. Softw. Technol. **46**(15), 989–1000 (2004)
8. Chen, T.Y., Leung, H., Mak, I.K.: Adaptive random testing. In: Maher, M.J. (ed.) ASIAN 2004. LNCS, vol. 3321, pp. 320–329. Springer, Heidelberg (2004). https://doi.org/10.1007/978-3-540-30502-6_23
9. Cotroneo, D., Pietrantuono, R., Russo, S.: A learning-based method for combining testing techniques. In: Proceedings of the 35th International Conference on Software Engineering (ICSE), pp. 142–151. IEEE (2013)
10. Cotroneo, D., Pietrantuono, R., Russo, S.: Combining operational and debug testing for improving reliability. IEEE Trans. Reliab. **62**(2), 408–423 (2013)
11. Cotroneo, D., Pietrantuono, R., Russo, S.: RELAI testing: a technique to assess and improve software reliability. IEEE Trans. Software Eng. **42**(5), 452–475 (2016)

12. Del Frate, F., Garg, P., Mathur, A., Pasquini, A.: On the correlation between code coverage and software reliability. In: Proceedings of the 6th International Symposium on Software Reliability Engineering, pp. 124–132. ISSRE, IEEE, October 1995

13. Dijkstra, E.W.: Structured programming. In: N.Buxton, J., Randell, B. (eds.) Software Engineering Techniques. NATO Science Committee (1970)

14. Donnelly, M., Everett, B., Musa, J., Wilson, G., Nikora, A.: Best current practice of SRE. In: Handbook of software Reliability Engineering, Chap. 6, pp. 219–254. IEEE Computer Society Press and McGraw-Hill (1996)

15. Frankl, P.G., Hamlet, R.G., Littlewood, B., Strigini, L.: Evaluating testing methods by delivered reliability. IEEE Trans. Software Eng. **24**(8), 586–601 (1998)

16. Frankl, P.G., Weyuker, E.J.: An applicable family of data flow testing criteria. IEEE Trans. Software Eng. **14**(10), 1483–1498 (1988)

17. Frankl, P.G., Deng, Y.: Comparison of delivered reliability of branch, data flow and operational testing: a case study. ACM SIGSOFT Software Eng. Notes **25**(5), 124–134 (2000)

18. Gay, G., Staats, M., Whalen, M., Heimdahl, M.P.: The risks of coverage-directed test case generation. IEEE Trans. Software Eng. **41**(8), 803–819 (2015)

19. Harrold, M.J., Rothermel, G., Wu, R., Yi, L.: An Empirical Investigation of Program Spectra. In: Proceedings of the 1998 ACM SIGPLAN-SIGSOFT Workshop on Program Analysis for Software Tools and Engineering, pp. 83–90. PASTE, ACM (1998)

20. Herzig, K.: There's never enough time to do all the testing you want. In: Perspectives on Data Science for Software Engineering, pp. 91–95. Elsevier (2016)

21. Herzig, K.: Let's assume we had to pay for testing. In: Keynote at the 11th IEEE/ACM International Workshop on Automation of Software Test (2016). https://www.kim-herzig.de/2016/06/28/keynote-ast-2016/

22. Horgan, J., Mathur, A.: Software testing and reliability. The Handbook of Software Reliability Engineering, pp. 531–565 (1996)

23. Inozemtseva, L., Holmes, R.: Coverage is not strongly correlated with test suite effectiveness. In: Proceedings of the 36th International Conference on Software Engineering, pp. 435–445. ICSE, ACM (2014)

24. Institute of Electrical and Electronic Engineers: IEEE standard glossary of software engineering terminology. IEEE Standard **610** 12, 09 1990

25. Littlewood, B., Popov, P., Strigini, L., Shryane, N.: Modelling the effects of combining diverse software fault detection techniques. In: Hierons, R.M., Bowen, J.P., Harman, M. (eds.) Formal Methods and Testing. LNCS, vol. 4949, pp. 345–366. Springer, Heidelberg (2008). https://doi.org/10.1007/978-3-540-78917-8_12

26. Lyu, M.R.: Software reliability engineering: a roadmap. In: Future of Software Engineering, pp. 153–170. FOSE, IEEE (2007)

27. Marick, B.: How to misuse code coverage. In: Proceedings of the 16th International Conference on Testing Computer Software, pp. 16–18 (1999)

28. Miranda, B., Bertolino, A.: Does code coverage provide a good stopping rule for operational profile based testing? In: Proceedings of the 11th International Workshop on Automation of Software Test, pp. 22–28. AST, ACM (2016)

29. Miranda, B., Bertolino, A.: An assessment of operational coverage as both an adequacy and a selection criterion for operational profile based testing. Software Qual. J. **26**(4), 1571–1594 (2018)

30. Musa, J.D.: A theory of software reliability and its application. IEEE Trans. Software Eng. **SE–1**(3), 312–327 (1975)

31. Musa, J.D.: Operational profiles in software-reliability engineering. IEEE Softw. **10**(2), 14–32 (1993)
32. Neil, M., Fenton, N., Nielson, L.: Building large-scale Bayesian networks. Knowl. Eng. Rev. **15**(3), 257–284 (2000)
33. Omri, F.: Weighted statistical white-box testing with proportional-optimal stratification. In: WCOP 2014 Proceedings of the 19th International Doctoral Symposium on Components and Architecture, pp. 19–24. ACM (2014)
34. Pietrantuono, R., Russo, S.: On adaptive sampling-based testing for software reliability assessment. In: Proceedings of the 27th International Symposium on Software Reliability Engineering, pp. 1–11. ISSRE, IEEE, October 2016
35. Pietrantuono, R., Russo, S.: Probabilistic sampling-based testing for accelerated reliability assessment. In: Proceedings of the IEEE 18th International Conference on Software Quality, Reliability and Security (QRS), pp. 35–46. IEEE, July 2018
36. Prause, C.R., Werner, J., Hornig, K., Bosecker, S., Kuhrmann, M.: Is 100% test coverage a reasonable requirement? Lessons learned from a space software project. In: Felderer, M., Méndez Fernández, D., Turhan, B., Kalinowski, M., Sarro, F., Winkler, D. (eds.) PROFES 2017. LNCS, vol. 10611, pp. 351–367. Springer, Cham (2017). https://doi.org/10.1007/978-3-319-69926-4_25
37. Roper, M.: Software testing–searching for the missing link. Inf. Softw. Technol. **41**(14), 991–994 (1999)
38. Singh, H., Cortellessa, V., Cukic, B., Gunel, E., Bharadwaj, V.: A Bayesian approach to reliability prediction and assessment of component based systems. In: Proceedings of the 12th International Symposium on Software Reliability Engineering, pp. 12–21. ISSRE, November 2001
39. Smidts, C., Cukic, B., Gunel, E., Li, M., Singh, H.: Software reliability corroboration. In: Proceedings of the 27th Annual NASA Goddard/IEEE Software Engineering Workshop, pp. 82–87. IEEE, December 2002
40. Smidts, C., Mutha, C., Rodríguez, M., Gerber, M.J.: Software testing with an operational profile: OP definition. ACM Comput. Surv. **46**(3), 39:1–39:39 (2014)
41. Sridharan, M., Namin, A.: Prioritizing mutation operators based on importance sampling. In: 21st International Symposium on Software Reliability Engineering, pp. 378–387. ISSRE, IEEE, November 2010
42. Tian, J., Lu, P., Palma, J.: Test-execution-based reliability measurement and modeling for large commercial software. IEEE Trans. Software Eng. **21**(5), 405–414 (1995)
43. Wei, Y., Meyer, B., Oriol, M.: Is branch coverage a good measure of testing effectiveness? In: Meyer, B., Nordio, M. (eds.) LASER 2008-2010. LNCS, vol. 7007, pp. 194–212. Springer, Heidelberg (2012). https://doi.org/10.1007/978-3-642-25231-0_5
44. Weyuker, E.J., Jeng, B.: Analyzing partition testing strategies. IEEE Trans. Software Eng. **17**(7), 703–711 (1991)
45. Wong, W., Gao, R., Li, Y., Abreu, R., Wotawa, F.: A survey on software fault localization. IEEE Trans. Software Eng. **42**(8), 707–740 (2016)
46. Xie, T., Notkin, D.: Checking inside the black box: regression testing by comparing value spectra. IEEE Trans. Software Eng. **31**(10), 869–883 (2005)
47. Zhu, H., Hall, P.A.V., May, J.H.R.: Software unit test coverage and adequacy. ACM Comput. Surv. **29**(4), 366–427 (1997)

Consistency and Availability in Microservice Architectures

Davide Rossi[✉]

Department of Computer Science and Engineering,
University of Bologna, Bologna, Italy
rossi@cs.unibo.it

Abstract. For the most part, the first instances of microservice architectures have been deployed for the benefit of the so-called Internet-scale companies in contexts where availability is a critical concern. Their success in this context, along with their promise to be more agile than competing solutions in adapting to changing needs, soon attracted the interest of very diverse classes of business domains characterized by different priorities with respect to non-functional requirements. Microservices embraced this challenge, showing a unique ability to allow for a plethora of solutions, enabling developers to reach the trade-off between consistency and availability that better suits their needs. From a design point of view this translates into a vast solution space. While this can be perceived as an opportunity to enjoy greater freedom with respect to other architectural styles it also means that finding the best solution for the problem at hand can be complex and it is easier to incur in errors that can put a whole project at risk. In this paper we review some possible solutions to address common problems that arise when adopting microservices and we present strategies to address consistency and availability; we also discuss the impact these strategies have on the design space.

Keywords: Microservices architecture · Service-Oriented · Architecture · Software architecture

1 Introduction

All architecture is design but not all design is architecture. Architecture represents the significant design decisions that shape a system, where significant is measured by cost of change (Grady Booch as cited in [1]).

This citation ties together software architecture and design decisions. Implicitly it also ties together software architectures and non-functional requirements since it is obvious to anyone who has been involved in software development that the decisions for which the cost of change is higher are the ones made to address this class of requirements (think about improving the scalability of a system that has not been designed from the start to allow for that). In this respect we can say that non-functional requirements are the main drivers behind the design choices that shape a software architecture [2]. How design decisions and non-functional requirements play together in microservice architectures is the main topic of this paper.

© Springer Nature Switzerland AG 2019
M. J. Escalona et al. (Eds.): WEBIST 2018, LNBIP 372, pp. 39–55, 2019.
https://doi.org/10.1007/978-3-030-35330-8_3

Microservices architecture (or, simply, microservices) represent an architectural style.

Architectural styles are about constraints [3], which means that when an architectural style is adopted the design decision space is constrained.

Service-Oriented Architecture (SOA) represent an architectural style as well, a more generic one with respect to microservices in which the latter impose more stringent constraints on loose coupling, remarking that each service can be developed, deployed, and scaled independently, which is somehow related to the "products not projects" characteristic from the often cited list composed by Lewis and Fowler [4].

Other kinds of SOA exist, of course, one that is often compared to microservices is what in this paper is referred to as Enterprise SOA (E-SOA). The word enterprise here suggests we are addressing architectures designed to support non trivial non-functional qualities, since most enterprise software has to cope with consistency, availability, data integrity, robustness, security and so forth (notice that in this paper availability will often be used as an umbrella term encompassing related qualities such as performance and scalability, the same applies to consistency that encompasses also the likes of integrity and durability).

Most E-SOA solutions adopt some kind of support to ease many of the recurring problems that arise when building critical distributed systems so it is no wonder that many of these solutions are built on top of large platforms like JEE and .NET and adopt infrastructure software systems and middleware services, an example being the ubiquitous Enterprise Service Bus (ESB). Some of these solutions go as far as loading the ESB with too many concerns, even moving part of the business logic in it, a practice that created a bad reputation for a software component that, in some shape, is still needed in modern microservice architectures (this will be discussed more in depth later in this paper).

Using these combinations of platforms and infrastructure services implies that a set of architectural choices are already embodied in the environment hosting the application logic.

This approach is unusual for microservices-based solutions that leverage the large diffusion of enterprise-grade open source software proposing frameworks for various programming languages, data management systems (relational databases, graph databases, document databases, message brokers, ...) and infrastructure services and integrates them in various ways. As a result this opens up an array of choices when composing a microservices solution.

The CAP theorem [5] states that in a partitionable system it is not possible to achieve full consistency and maximum availability. Consistency and availability are in fact the most exemplary contrasting non-functional requirements that large, multi-user, distributed applications struggle with. In practical terms there is a price to pay in consistency to achieve better availability (for example by embracing relaxed consistency models like eventual consistency) and there is a price to pay in availability to achieve better consistency (just think about the contention caused by locking).

We can think about the trade-off between consistency and availability as a slider that moves between best consistency, no availability and best availability, no consistency. A peculiar characteristic of microservice is the ability to allow the slider to be moved in one direction or the other on a service-by-service or even request-by-request basis. This is something that is also possible with different approaches but at the expense of basic internal qualities such as simplicity, understandability and maintainability.

This paper presents a brief list of recipes that can be used in a microservices architecture to find the best balance between these two forces but also analyzes these recipes with respect to the impact they have on the design space. The dimensions of this space we are more interested in, in the context of this paper, are: governance, development, language (polyglot programming), data management (polyglot persistence) and platform/infrastructure. A detailed discussion of these dimensions is presented in Sect. 5.

We could argue that the array of choices allowed by microservices should not be intended as freedom that is here for the developers to take because of their personal preferences (a narration often supported in IT social media), rather as an opportunity to compose the right mix able to face the non-functional requirements needed by the application under development.

Which brings us back to the citation opening this section: architectural errors are the most costly ones, a project building on wrong architectural assumptions is hardly going to become a success story. Developers embracing microservices should be well aware of how their choices impact the non-functional qualities of their application and not be fascinated by IT social media articles.

This paper is structured as follows: in Sect. 2 a simple, yet paradigmatic and ubiquitous problem of microservices-based systems is introduced and a list of possible solutions to address the problem is presented. Section 3 contains an analysis of these solutions with respect to availability and consistency and a set of recipes to improve their ability to better address these concerns. Section 4 discusses relevant dimensions of the design space for microservices and how the aforementioned solutions impact them. Section 5 concludes the paper.

2 The Chain of Calls

Many aspects of a microservices architecture are impacted by non-functional requirements, however this paper focuses on a very simple issue that has the merit of being easy to understand, frequent to encounter and still triggering several of the pain points associated with many relevant design decisions. For each of these points, the best practices facing them will be presented along with a discussion on how these practices impact software qualities and design space.

This issue is here called the *chain of calls*. That name does not imply an actual cascade of invocations but refers to dealing with a request coming from a client that cannot be fully served by a single (micro)service in the system. From a conceptual point of view that means that service A needs a capability exposed by service B which, at its turn needs a capability exposed C and so on.

While this could very well happen with other architectural styles, the frequency of chains of calls is greatly magnified with microservices for the simple fact that they are *micro*, i.e. more focused on specific aspects of the domain so it is more likely that a single request needs the cooperation of multiple services to be served.

This is summarized by the following image, popularly known as the Microservices Death Star, a microservice dependency graph for Netflix's microservices as of 2012 (Fig. 1).

Fig. 1. The Microservices Death Star.

In E-SOA solutions most of the requests coming from clients are fully served by a single service and, for the rare cases in which a cooperation between multiple services is needed, most best practices suggest alternative ways of dealing with them (based on asynchronous messaging) instead of using a chain of calls (and we will see that these solutions work just as well for Microservices).

The section that follows presents some possible design alternatives that can be adopted. In the subsequent sections, following the rationale exposed in the introduction, these solutions are analyzed with respect to two different viewpoints: availability and consistency. A set of recipes to improve these solution's ability to better address these concerns is presented as well.

Running Example: When possible, a reference to the following elementary example will be used in this paper: an e-commerce application receives a request to retrieve information about a product including its description, price and whether it is available in stock (we can assume that a webpage for that product has to be presented to a user). Among the various microservices presented in the system are the `products` microservice (dealing with the domain of products: their description, their price, ...) and `the inventory` microservice (dealing with stock management).

2.1   Chain of Calls: Design Alternatives

As previously discussed, the chain of calls describes a set of cascading logical dependencies between microservices. This does not necessarily turn into an actual sequence of direct invocations. In fact, several strategies can be adopted to implement a chain of calls.

Here we distinguish between two main approaches: one in which actual invocations are performed and one in which the interactions between dependent services are decoupled (usually by using an asynchronous messaging infrastructure).

When actual invocations are performed we can further distinguish between choreography-based solutions and orchestration-based solutions.

Consider the example introduced in the previous section. In a choreography-based scenario, the external request is routed (usually by an API Gateway) to a microservice, possibly `products` since it has access to most of the information that has to be returned, then `products` invokes `inventory` to retrieve stock availability information, packs all the data in a response and returns it to the external client (via the gateway).

This simple scenario can be expanded at will: service A calls service B that calls service C that, depending on some logic decides to either call service D or service E and so forth. This is a choreography: it defines a coordination process between peers in the form of (observable) message exchanges. Each peer is responsible for generating the correct messages depending on the current state of the process.

Orchestration-based solutions, instead, make use of an additional component: an orchestrator that acts as a communication hub managing the interactions between services.

Digression 1, in the Appendix contains a discussion on configurable orchestrators.

In our example the external request is routed to the orchestrator that calls `products` to retrieve the product-related information, then calls `inventory` to retrieve the stock-related information for that product, packs all the data in a response and returns it to the external client.

Let us now see what options are available when using messaging-based solutions.

A very naive approach is to use asynchronous messages, possibly via a message brokering infrastructure, to decouple requests and responses from both a spatial (and possibly also a temporal) perspective: direct invocations are transformed in the emission of command messages from the caller and the emission of corresponding response messages from the callee. Service providers consume command messages while consumers consume response messages.

A peer-to-peer or an orchestrator-based approach can be adopted in this case as well, with the obvious additional indirection caused by the messaging infrastructure.

These solutions, however, are just removing the physical coupling while fully maintaining the logical one: the use of command messages in our example turns out to be not much different with respect to the naive approach previously discussed: when `products` receives a request it creates a command message asking for stock availability, `inventory` listen di this message are creates a reply message that is then consumed by `products`.

Digression 2, in the Appendix contains a discussion on messaging and coupling.

More articulated solutions based on asynchronous messaging exist, while they have been around for many years now it is with the advent of domain-driven design (DDD) [8] that they found a conceptual framing. In DDD bounded contexts are used to separate the conceptual areas of an application domain; bounded contexts are then usually refined into the main components of the resulting application architecture, since DDD suggests that systems should be organized in a way that reflects the conceptual structure of the domain.

One of the possible ways to enable integration between these components is that of using asynchronous messaging in the form of events and commands, specifically domain events signal relevant occurrence in a domain whereas command messages are requests targeted to a domain.

Bounded contexts are not refined into microservices (although it is easy to read someone affirming the opposite, which is obviously wrong because of a granularity mismatch) but this integration mechanism naturally fits microservice architectures.

Let us consider our example again: each time a stock availability value changes in the `inventory` database, a domain event is published; `products` can, by listening to these events, keep a local copy of the availability information that is synchronized with that of `inventory`. With this approach the external request can be fully served by `products` and the chain of calls is actually avoided. This is not always possible, for example when service A needs a specific business function from service B, careful design of microservices and related bounded contexts should however limit this eventuality. This is a well-known approach in the E-SOA community and is gaining adoption in the microservices community as well.

To summarize, here are the available options to implement a chain of calls:

- CC1. Perform direct invocation

  - CC1.1. Use a choreography-based approach
  - CC1.2. Use an orchestration-based approach

- CC2. Use messaging

  - CC2.1. Use a choreography-based or an orchestration-based approach
  - CC2.2. Use a DDD-inspired solution and actually avoid chaining microservices

3 Chain of Calls: Analysis with Respect to Availability and Consistency

We now analyze the impact of the solutions presented in the previous section with respect to availability and consistency.

From an intuitive point of view the aim of this section is to show how the quality slider moves when adopting a specific solution.

We also present known strategies that are usually adopted to improve the limited quality that naive implementations can express with respect to consistency and availability.

Our analysis starts with CC1 (we collapse CC1.1 and CC1.2 here since we discuss overlapping concerns).

In CC1 direct invocations (synchronous calls) between microservices are performed. From an availability point of view the impact of this solution is easily recognizable: the external request can be served only if all the services involved in the chain are available (for simplicity here we assume that no fallback policies are available): if the average chain size is N and the average availability of each service is A, the overall availability of the system cannot be more than N^A, being N minor than 1 this obviously means that the system is less available than its services. For example: if the average availability for the services is 99.999% (also known as five-nines, a measure usually perceived as very good for a real-world system) and the average chain length is 5, the resulting availability will be 99.995%. That means an increase in downtime from 5 min 15 s per year to 26 min 17 s per year (which, for some classes of applications, could be unacceptable).

This very preliminary aspect, however, is largely overshadowed by a considerably more serious one: what happens in the presence of failures/delays.

It is well known that in an IP-based network a crashed process is indistinguishable from a slow one [6], in this context this means that when a response is not received after sending a request to a service that is part of a chain, there is no way to know if a response will eventually arrive or if the called service has crashed. To avoid for requests to be pending indefinitely, the usual approach is to assume a failure after a timeout. The duration of a timeout is usually determined with an heuristic taking into account the trade-off between the risk of considering crashed a service that is actually running (and maybe just experiencing a transient issue) or that of delaying for a long time a request that has no hope to be fulfilled (with obvious negative consequences on availability). The presence of a chain of calls exacerbates the problem of setting a reasonable time out since the slowness of a service impacts all the services that precede it in the chain, so perfectly healthy services can be assumed as crashed only because they are stuck waiting for their dependencies to produce a reply. The current best practice for microservice architectures (which usually employ some kind of virtualized infrastructure), stemming from the empirical observation that most invocation issues are due to transient problems (topology reconfigurations, virtual machine migrations, containers' virtual network modifications, garbage collection, etc.), is to set relatively short timeouts and perform retries.

Notice that retries are acceptable only when a system is designed to handle them, that usually means that services that are subject to retries should be idempotent: multiple invocations of the same request must lead to the same result; this can be achieved by designing requests to respect this semantic (do not allow requests like "decrement bank account by 10" but only requests like "set bank account to 1234", but then the service is exposed to unordered delivery issues) or by using some de-duplication mechanisms for incoming requests. The practice of setting relatively short timeouts and perform retries usually goes hand in hand with another practice that says that a service should be terminated as soon as it starts showing signs of erratic/slow behavior and replaced by existing replicas or newly created instances, an option that has been made possible by modern virtualized infrastructures and containers-based solutions in which the cost (and the time) of creating new service instances is minimized. To implement this approach, a health monitoring infrastructure has to be put in place, the infrastructure should gather health information from the services and interact with the network and the virtualization infrastructure to deal with the rerouting of messages to other services and failed services re-instantiation.

Since most invocation errors are due to transient issues, a simple retry usually solves the problem. There is, however, a minor but not insignificant number of cases in which the timeout is due to a service that is slowing down but still has not been identified by the health monitoring infrastructure and thus terminated. It is very well possible that the service is in a recoverable state and that the slowdown is due to transient overloading, swapping, garbage collection or similar issues. In those cases, however, retries are equivalent to punching a boxer trying to get back to his feet: the amount of requests arises, the service tries to fulfill them and slows further down, because of that the clients enter a timeout-retry loop until the service eventually fails under the overwhelming load. This could easily start a cascading failure effect that propagates to most (otherwise perfectly healthy) services in the system.

Basic mitigations include the use an exponential backoff algorithm to continually increase the delay between retries until the maximum limit is reached and back-pressure measures: when a service is on the verge of being overloaded it starts rejecting requests and sends failure responses signaling that the failure is not due to an error but to overload (however this requires cooperation from the calling services that have to delay their request even further or direct them to other replicas).

Circuit breaker [7] is a pattern vastly employed to improve stability and resiliency in microservice architectures in the presence of direct service-to-service invocation.

A circuit breaker acts as a proxy for operations that might fail. The proxy should monitor the number of recent failures that have occurred, and use this information to decide whether to allow the operation to proceed, or return a failure immediately.

The behavior of the proxy can be easily described as a state machine that can be closed, open or half-open. Details can be found in the aforementioned reference.

Another problem that can arise when dealing with multiple microservices calling each other is related to resources management. Shared resources (such as connection pool, memory, and CPU) when allocated to troubling connections (that suffers from long response times or are engaged in a retry loop) risk to starve other concurrent workloads. Bulkhead [7] is a pattern that suggests to partition service instances into different groups, based on consumer load and availability requirements (so, for example, a specific connection pool is used when communicating with a specific service, instead of using a single shared connection pool).

All these mitigations are usually mixed and require that all services in the system adopt the same policies with respect to them (imagine what could result if some services perform retries while others do not, only some adopt circuit breakers and so forth) so this has a huge impact in terms of governance.

Since it is not reasonable that all microservices deal independently with these recurring issues (otherwise most of the code will be filled with timeouts and retries instead of focusing on business logic) the usual solution is to move all the mentioned mitigations outside of the main code. This can happen with an in-process or with an out-of-process approach.

With the in-process approach a library is used to deal with service-to-service communications. A notable example is Netflix's Hystrix[1] that mixes the circuit breaker and the bulkhead pattern (and, indirectly, retries) but there are many others (e.g. Twitter's Finagle[2]). Of course a project could decide to implement its own library.

With the out-of-process approach an external, but colocated, proxy is used. The sidecar pattern [8] uses this approach, the sidecar usually also takes care of logging, monitoring and configuration issues which is pretty natural when we realize that all the requests are routed through this component.

The disciplined, consistent use of the sidecar pattern is at the roots of what is called a *service mesh* which is defined as a dedicated infrastructure layer for handling service-to-service communication [9]. A service mesh usually needs a lightweight virtualization infrastructure (i.e. containers) and a virtualization orchestrator (like Kubernetes[3]) to be deployed. This obviously results in stringent constraints associated to infrastructural choices.

Whether a system really needs all of these mitigation strategies mostly depends on the quality of service requirements that are imposed. It is important, however, to stress that software engineers should always have full command on the trade-offs between availability, constraints relaxation, and complexity of the systems. This means they should be aware of which solutions can be adopted and understand their impact on the overall architecture (which includes several limitations to the design space).

We now analyze how consistency is addressed when the chain of calls turns into a sequence of direct invocations. In this case, in general, when the involved services modify data, we are dealing with a distributed transaction. The usual solution to address consistency in distributed transactions is the adoption of mechanism based on the two-phase commit protocol. However, as the data management needs of Web 2.0 companies shifted the focus from SQL and ACID to NoSQL and BASE [13], the microservices community is more interested in trade-offs in which a price is paid in terms of consistency in order to achieve better availability. Two-phase commit is thus reserved to a very limited number of critical requests (if any) whereas most of the requests are served with relaxed consistency. Notice that two-phase commit is also very rarely adopted in E-SOA too, where messaging-based solution are usually preferred.

In order to guarantee some degree of consistency, microservices-based solutions, for the most part, adopted ad hoc solutions. These are colloquially known as feral concurrency control [15], that is application-level mechanisms for maintaining data integrity. At least this has been the case since recently, before finally realize that what has been done for twenty years now with E-SOA, WS-BEL and BPMN was often a viable option: explicitly identify choreographies/orchestrations and adopt long running compensating transactions (LTRs, which have now being re-popularized under the Distributed SAGA name in the microservices community, which is slightly inappropriate since in the original proposal [16] a SAGA has specific characteristics associated to interleaving). The basic idea is to define a mechanism to reach a relaxed form of atomicity by compensating the already executed steps of a transaction when the transaction itself fails.

---

[1] https://github.com/Netflix/Hystrix.

[2] https://twitter.github.io/finagle/.

[3] https://kubernetes.io/.

A long running transaction can make use of a coordinator (orchestration approach, which would be a natural mapping for CC1.1) or use a choreography approach (like in CC1.2). This second option, however, can result in some very complex issues that have to be dealt with: the state of the transaction is now a distributed state, in case of failures we must ensure its consistency (something that can be achieved using a robust distributed logging infrastructure). That also means we have problems with visibility and monitoring. This complexity usually leads to the adoption of orchestration-based solutions when consistency is a concern. In order not to compromise the reliability and availability of the system, the orchestrator, usually called the coordinator in this context, should not be a single point of failure and should be highly available (which adds to the overall complexity of the system).

See Digression 3 in the appendix for a discussion on configurable orchestrators and compensating transactions.

To summarize: the CC1 solutions needs quite a lot of effort to address high availability, mainly in the form of mitigation strategies associated to the issues related to the fail fast/retry policies. When this is done, microservice architectures have shown to be able to achieve very high levels of availability when adopting this kind of solutions (this is, for example, the case of Netflix).

On the consistency side, things are more blurred: strong consistency is expensive and is reserved for a limited number of critical requests; a relaxed form of atomicity is achievable by using long-running transactions (but with costs that are usually too high to justify when adopting CC1.1).

We now put CC2 under our microscope: these are solution based on asynchronous messages. The analysis of CC2.1 is quite straightforward: this is a solution of limited applicability since it does not improve significantly over its synchronous choreography or orchestration-based counterparts but it does add significant complexity, more so in the choreography case, which really makes the orchestration-based approach the only viable solution. In this setup the orchestrator becomes an asynchronous message coordinator and, besides the obvious considerations related to this fact, the analysis presented for CC1.2, from both a consistency and an availability perspectives, holds here too.

Much more interesting is the case of CC2.2. To better focus the problems raised by this solution let us get back to the e-commerce example: the adoption of CC2.2 in this case corresponds to implementing the `inventory` microservice in such a way that, when an availability update is persisted in its local database, a domain event is contextually produced. The `products` microservice listens for these events and updates its own copy of the stock availability accordingly.

With no further measures, this results in a system with no consistency guarantees of any kind: if the `inventory` microservice crashes after updating the database but before producing the domain event, the copy in `products` will not be reconciled.

Notice that this may very well be fully acceptable. A one-in-a-million error related to stock availability for a B2C e-commerce site can be just fine. But the same could not apply to a B2B site used by hospitals to acquire life-saving medicines.

Strong consistency, in this scenario, requires that whenever a domain event related to the modification of some information is generated, the persisting of this modification in the originating microservice has to be part of a distributed transaction in which the persisting of the local copies in all interested microservices participate. In general that turns into a distributed transaction (the domain of two-phase commit), which would impact availability (specifically performances and scalability) so severely to restrict strong consistency to a very limited subset of selected operations. The highest level of consistency for general operations in this scenario, in fact, is usually *eventual consistency* which means that is assumed that, if no new updates are made to a given data item, eventually all accesses to that item will return the last updated value [14].

While opting for a relaxed form of consistency can be perceived as just adding a little more complexity, things can be more convoluted than that: to guarantee eventual consistency the database update and the generation of the domain event in the `inventory` microservice have to be atomic. There are a few solutions to achieve this, the easier one is to let the local database and the message queue participate in a multi-party atomic transaction (which is not necessarily a distributed one because they can both be local to the node hosting the `inventory` microservice). This, however, requires that the message broker supports atomic transactions, and the same applies to the database.

Enterprise-proof solutions to manage asynchronous messaging with transactional support have been around for a long time, they usually take the form of products presenting themselves as message queues or message brokers. But a new class of messaging management solutions is on the rise, an evolution that is similar TO the affirming of NoSQL and BASE in the persistence management domain. An example of the new class of messaging platforms is Apache Kafka [10], while other similar solutions are available we will mainly refer to Kafka as a paradigmatic instance of this new class. Kafka is presented as a distributed streaming solution, what makes this different from usual message queuing systems is persistence: events that are produced before a consumer is registered can still be retrieved. The main design goal in Kafka is clearly scalability but its wide adoption and its ease of use (along with its low cost, being an Open Source software solution) is extending its application domain to areas characterized by a large amount of events to process but also by stringent consistency requirements (like financial applications). Stringent consistency, however, usually implies integrity and atomicity and, while Kafka does support transactions, these transactions can be used to guarantee an exactly once delivery semantic but neither integrity nor atomicity (recovery logs are written asynchronously and particular failure patterns can lead to data loss).

Similar considerations can be extended to most NoSQL databases: ACID transaction are usually not supported which means that most combinations of messaging/persistence solutions adopted in microservices does not allow multi-party atomic transactions.

Ad hoc solutions to guarantee atomicity without multi-party atomic transactions do exist but are complex, brittle, need message deduplication support from listeners and, of course, still need some kind of transactional support from the database and/or the message broker. They are essentially an instance of feral concurrency control: for example the database can be used to record the produced domain events in the same transaction in which the update is performed (allowing the implementation of a form of checkpointing) or, conversely, the message queue can be used to store updates and let the service itself update the local database by consuming the same change events it produced (notice however that these are no more domain events, since domain events refer to something that has already taken place in the domain, which breaks some of the basic semantic assumptions in DDD).

From an availability point of view CC2.2 can be seen as an improvement over CC1 solutions under most real-world circumstances: to refer to our example if read requests are more frequent that write requests (i.e. users access product pages more often than they finalize purchases) most request can be served by only interesting the product microservice at the expenses of an event being generated by inventory (and processed by product) at purchase time. Asynchronous messages also promote decoupling between microservices easing the implementation of tailor-made scalability policies.

To summarize: CC2.2 is possibly the best option to meet stringent availability constraints (at the expense of an added complexity due to the managing of an asynchronous messaging infrastructure) but addressing consistency can be a problem: strong consistency can be an option only when serving a minority of the received requests and even eventual consistency adds relevant complexity and poses a relevant number of constraints with respect to the choice of messaging and persistence management infrastructure.

An interesting point that deserves to be emphasized is that an application built on microservices does not need to choose one of the CC solutions we presented but can mix them together and decide to adopt different consistency models depending on the specific task at hand, for example an e-commerce application can use a best effort approach for stock availability (e.g. CC2.2 with no consistency guarantee) until the user decides to finalize a transaction in which case strong consistency is used (e.g. CC1.1 with transactional guarantees) to verify the actual availability of the products.

It is also interesting to note that, as previously discussed, not all requests can be served with relaxed consistency, even in contexts with a large amount of potential clients (and thus with strong availability concerns). This is the case for domains like stock trading, gambling, micropayments and so forth. A very active stream of research focuses on this challenge, for example improving the availability of databases combining the ACID and the BASE models with modular concurrency control, like the SALT proposal [11].

4 Design Space Dimensions and Solutions Impact

In this section we detail some of the axis related to the design decision space that characterize the adoption of a microservices architecture and analyze which is the impact they have on the solutions presented in the previous sections. Of course there are other dimensions that could be discussed but are not presented in this paper, the collection we propose is mainly based on characteristics that are usually depicted as characterizing for microservices.

Governance is about policies. Policies are pervasive and can touch almost every aspect of software development and operations. E-SOA projects are usually characterized by a strong governance in which several aspects of the services (from both a design-time and a run-time point of view) are asserted and enforced. A bad management of governance, focusing only on collecting the larger possible set of policies, can actively inhibit change. Unfortunately far too many large E-SOA projects suffered from this problem. Microservices bring the promise of decentralized governance: centralized governance is perceived as an overhead that should be avoided by supporting service-specific governance and intra-service contracts (which can be promoted by using patterns like *tolerant reader* and *consumer-driven contracts*).

Development: microservices and agile programming have always been tightly coupled. The main reason behind that traces to the fact that to minimize the coupling between microservices they are usually developed as separate products. That translates to separate development projects and it is not unusual to have tenths if not hundreds of microservices in a single system. That calls for development methods with minimal overhead and agile programming is undeniably the best option.

In this respect, when we discuss development freedom we do not intend the freedom to choose between agile or structured approaches but the freedom to adopt different practices within an agile context. Most notably these practices could change between the projects of different microservices within the same application.

In this respect, then, the development category here is just a subset of governance. But since it receives significant interests from the microservices community it is presented separately.

Language: polyglot programming [6] has always been a strong selling point for microservice architectures. Since each microservice is a separate product, it can be developed with the language perceived as the most fitting to solve the specific problems that microservice has to address. This could easily result in an application developed with an array of different languages.

Data Management: just like polyglot programming, polyglot persistence [7] too has always been linked with microservices. A basic characteristics in SOA is that services should be autonomous and thus should take care of their own data. This is reflected in microservices at the conceptual level, where each microservice defines its own data model, but also at the implementation level, where it has the opportunity to select the most appropriate data storage solution.

Platform/Infrastructure: JEE and .NET provide well-defined ecosystems composed by libraries, frameworks and infrastructure services. Microservices can choose à la carte. An array of options is available, which is also possible thanks to the wide diffusion of enterprise-grade open source software.

It is easy to realize that most of the solutions (and mitigations) proposed in the previous sections have a large impact on these design dimensions. What follow is a brief analysis on what this impact is on a dimension by dimension basis.

Decentralized governance is affected by the adoption of policies to be applied to all (or most of the) microservices. This is for example the case of the fail fast/retry practice presented when analyzing CC1.1. We already discussed that it is not reasonable to think that different microservices use different strategies in this respect. When adopting the in-process solution this also immediately affects language: when libraries are used the languages to develop the microservices can only be the ones the libraries support. Human factors affect the choice of languages too: it is not unusual for a microservices-based application to be composed by tens of different microservices. Each microservice has its own development project with its development team. With disjoint teams this could imply a number of developers that only the likes of Amazon and Google can afford. In most circumstances development teams are not disjoint: it is usual for a developer to be part of the teams allocated to four or five microservices. Having microservices written in different languages limit the ability to allocate available developers since it is not realistic to ask developers to wear the Java hat in the morning when they work on microservice A and wear the Python hat in the afternoon when allocated to service B. The same applies to different software development practices like pair programming, code reviews, coding styles and so forth. In this sense the human factor is what, in practice, dooms most dreams of decentralized governance.

Data management can be impacted when consistency requirements need some kind of transactional support, de facto excluding most NoSQL databases. However, as previously discussed, a single microservices application can adopt different consistency levels, thus different data management solutions can indeed be mixed but great care has to be taken to correctly identify whether a microservice is involved or not in requests with stringent consistency requirements.

As for platform/infrastructure, considerations similar to the ones expressed in respect to language can be proposed: it is not reasonable to think that each microservice reinvents the wheel and that infrastructure services are always written from scratch. The decision to embrace a specific event-based framework rather than a specific message broker, however, is not usually made (or at least it should not, to avoid the risk of having to re-think that decision later) simply because of a preference in the programming model or languages supported but first and foremost because of the guarantees that this solution provides in terms of non-functional dimensions.

The adoption of a messaging middleware to support asynchronous message-based solutions also impacts language: while database access drivers are usually available for a plethora of languages, messaging solutions are often restricted to a few languages (or even one).

Another impact of infrastructural decisions is due to the out-of-process mitigation strategies exposed in Sect. 3, from the large impact due to the adoption of a service mesh to the minor, but diffused impact of monitoring and logging solutions.

To summarize our analysis we could say that the design space for microservice architectures is indeed a large one. However, as soon as we start introducing strategies to improve availability and/or consistency, this space shrinks. This outcome is not unexpected since we know that non-functional requirements are the main driver behind software architectures.

The last part of this section deals with another aspect related to design space dimensions: the social one. In the social network era it should be no surprise that software developers tend to form an opinion on technological matters by reading IT social media.

But today's IT social media is flooded with narrations of microservices being the one solution that can bring freedom in software development when developing critical distributed applications, shadowing many of the complex issues that these systems unavoidably embody.

The scientific community is severely lagging behind in this evolution, while it is true that most of the basic mechanisms in what are proposed as modern solutions to these issues have been well known for dozens of years, it is also true that mixing the same ingredients in different doses and with different seasonings can result in a completely different experience. This results in insufficient support to practitioners who are left with no authoritative references when gathering information meant to inform architectural decisions.

Many of the solutions presented in this paper are complex. All this complexity should be no surprise to anyone with a strong background on distributed systems. The real issue is the number of developers with no, or very limited, distributed systems background who joined the microservices bandwagon, fascinated by a narration of freedom and complexity-free solutions. They design their systems without really understanding all the intricacies of a distributed system and they do not realize about the problems until they are in production. Finally, they understand why the very definition of an architectural error is an error that is costly to fix.

5 Conclusions

Microservice architectures can be built on top of very diverse foundations: different languages, different data management solutions, different interaction patterns and so forth. From a software developer point of view this results in a large decision space, allowing the design of applications able to meet a large spectrum of non-functional requirements (summarized in this paper with consistency and availability). A peculiar characteristic of microservices is the ability to adjust the availability/consistency slider on a service-by-service or even request-by-request basis, something that is possible also with different approaches but paying a price in terms of internal software qualities. Unexpectedly, as soon as we start to improve availability and/or consistency our design space dimensions are more and more constrained. Moreover, complexity creeps in, from both a software design and a system maintenance point of view.

All modern software development methods underline the importance of a risk-driven approach [12]: critical decisions should be taken as soon as possible during the development process in order to avoid the need to reconsider them later, which is not just costly but is something that can lead the whole project to a failure.

Developers adopting microservices should be very aware of that: the idea of starting with "something that works" and later "add on top availability and/or consistency" is always wrong. With microservices it is even worse. In practical terms this means that the first thing to do in a microservices-based software project is to clarify the needs in terms of non-functional requirements, decide the strategies to adopt to meet the requirements, understand how the design space changes on the basis of this adoption and pick a solution that is compatible with this design space.

At the end of the day non-functional requirements shape a software architecture. It has been like that for the whole history of software engineering, it is not going to change with microservices.

Acknowledgements. The work presented in this paper was partially supported by the MIUR PRIN 2015 GAUSS Project.

Appendix

Digression 1: The orchestrator is a microservice, which translates in yet another development project to maintain. Even with the minimal overhead imposed by agile methods the explosion of the number of projects can be troublesome. For this reason (and to improve time-to-market) several approaches based on configurable microservices orchestrators are starting to appear, in some sense we are witnessing the (dreaded) orchestration middleware from E-SOA making its appearance in disguise in the microservices world. Examples include Netflix's Conductor[4] (which uses a proprietary DSL) and Zeebe[5] (which uses BPMN).

Digression 2: the indirection caused by a messaging infrastructure in often mistaken by logical decoupling. It is true that with these solutions you could, for example, run each component in isolation and that changes in a component providing a function through messaging to another does not imply a change to the latter (which is an usual definition of dependency) but still a malfunction is going to happen so a form of coupling is present. This is because messaging based solution imply a form of hidden interfaces in which a logical dependency still holds between components but interfaces cannot be used as contracts to certify them. This could be summarized in the observation that message-based solutions are more flexible but the price to pay for that is maintenance.

Digression 3: enhancing existing configurable orchestrators with long-running transaction support seems like a reasonable option. This would essentially result in BPEL for microservices. To the best of the author's knowledge no product able to do that is currently available (albeit Zeebe seems a good candidate), it will be interesting to see what the future holds in this respect.

References

1. Buschmann, F., Henney, K., Schimdt, D.: Pattern-Oriented Software Architecture. On patterns and Pattern Languages, vol. 5. Wiley, New York (2007)
2. Rossi, D., Poggi, F., Ciancarini, P.: Dynamic high-level requirements in self-adaptive systems. In: Proceedings of the 33rd Annual ACM Symposium on Applied Computing, pp. 128–137. ACM, New York, NY, USA (2018)
3. Perry, D.E., Wolf, A.L.: Foundations for the study of software architecture. SIGSOFT Softw. Eng. Notes **17**, 40–52 (1992)
4. Lewis, F., Fowler, M.: Microservices. https://martinfowler.com/articles/microservices.html
5. Gilbert, S., Lynch, N.: Brewer's conjecture and the feasibility of consistent, available partition-tolerant web services. SIGACT News. **33**, 51–59 (2002)
6. Coulouris, G., Dollimore, J., Kindberg, T., Blair, G.: Distributed Systems: Concepts and Design. Pearson, Boston (2011)
7. Nygard, M.T.: Release It! Design and Deploy Production-Ready Software. Pragmatic Bookshelf, Raleigh (2018)

---

[4] https://github.com/Netflix/conductor.

[5] https://zeebe.io.

8. Burns, B., Oppenheimer, D.: Design patterns for container-based distributed systems. Presented at the 8th USENIX Workshop on Hot Topics in Cloud Computing (HotCloud 16) (2016)
9. Morgan, W.: What's a Service Mesh? And Why Do I Need One?. https://dzone.com/articles/whats-a-service-mesh-and-why-do-i-need-one
10. Kreps, J., Narkhede, N., Rao, J., et al.: Kafka: a distributed messaging system for log processing. In: Proceedings of the NetDB, pp. 1–7 (2011)
11. Xie, C., et al.: Salt: combining ACID and BASE in a distributed database. In: OSDI, pp. 495–509 (2014)
12. Boehm, B.W.: Software risk management: principles and practices. IEEE Softw. **8**, 32–41 (1991)
13. Pritchett, D.: BASE: an acid alternative. Queue. **6**, 48–55 (2008). https://doi.org/10.1145/1394127.1394128
14. Vogels, W.: Eventually consistent. Commun. ACM. **52**, 40–44 (2009). https://doi.org/10.1145/1435417.1435432
15. Bailis, P., Fekete, A., Franklin, M.J., Ghodsi, A., Hellerstein, J.M., Stoica, I.: Feral concurrency control: an empirical investigation of modern application integrity. Presented at the Proceedings of the 2015 ACM SIGMOD International Conference on Management of Data, 27 May 2015. https://doi.org/10.1145/2723372.2737784
16. Garcia-Molina, H., Salem, K.: Sagas. In: Proceedings of the 1987 ACM SIGMOD International Conference on Management of Data, pp. 249–259. ACM, New York, NY, USA (1987). https://doi.org/10.1145/38713.38742

Personalization and the Conversational Web

Konstantinos N. Vavliakis[1,2(✉)], Maria Th. Kotouza[1], Andreas L. Symeonidis[1], and Pericles A. Mitkas[1]

[1] Department of Electrical and Computer Engineering,
Aristotle University of Thessaloniki, GR54124 Thessaloniki, Greece
{kvavliak,maria.kotouza,asymeon}@issel.ee.auth.gr, mitkas@auth.gr
[2] Pharm24.gr, GR23057 Dafni, Lakonias, Greece
https://issel.ee.auth.gr/
http://www.pharm24.gr

Abstract. Hyper-personalization intends to maximize the opportunities a marketer has to tailor content that fits each and every customer's wants and needs. Naturally, gathering and analyzing more data is the key to those opportunities. This is were the *"Conversation Web"* comes in, which in the near future is expected to transform to so much more than just conversational interfaces (chat-bots). In a truly Conversation Web, websites and users implicitly *"discuss"* in the form of clicks, mouse scrolls and movements, as well as page views and product purchases. Websites use this information for decoding user interests and profile and provide customized one-to-one services. In this work we proposed an integrated architecture for the conversational Web; consequently we propose a novel hybrid approach for recommendations using offline and online analysis, as well as we propose a novel personalized search strategy that takes into account the strict time performance limitations applied in e-commerce. We evaluate the proposed methods on three different datasets and we show that our personalized search approach provides considerably improvements in search results while being suitable for near real-time search in commercial environments. Regarding personalized recommendations, the proposed approach outperforms current state-of-art methods in small-medium datasets and improves performance in large datasets when combined with other methods.

Keywords: Personalization · Recommendation · Search ·
Elasticsearch · Conversational web · e-Commerce · RFM · Recurrent neural networks

1 Introduction

Over the last twenty years, e-Commerce has grown at an unprecedented rate all over the world and e-commerce applications have become a constantly increasing segment of the retail industry. The future of e-commerce belongs to brands who

© Springer Nature Switzerland AG 2019
M. J. Escalona et al. (Eds.): WEBIST 2018, LNBIP 372, pp. 56–77, 2019.
https://doi.org/10.1007/978-3-030-35330-8_4

create unique experiences that capture attention and keep customers coming back. To achieve this, companies use personalization for providing uniquely customized experiences, as talking to customers in a customized way is much more efficient than using general, uniform mass messages. Personalization techniques became increasingly popular in recent years and are considered key elements in a variety of areas, not only in e-commerce, but in movies, music, news, research articles, search queries and social tags as well. Personalization is broadly used for improving customer satisfaction, sales conversion and marketing results. A website that is not personalized usually shows exactly the same content to each visitor, irrespective of the visitors' profile, interests, preferences or behavior. As a result, only a small percentage of visitors receive an optimal user experience with this type of site. On the other hand, with personalized websites, visitors get different messages as there is no webpage duplication, and each visitor segment experiences different content that exactly fits their interest and needs. Personalization targeted to segments of users requires specific steps in order to launch an effective strategy, such as to identify audience, understand visitors, plan and create different experience for each audience.

Computing power and the use of big data has increased exponentially over the last few years, and improvements in AI-powered systems have made real-time personalized services possible. Towards this end, *"hyper-personalization"* takes personalized marketing a step further by leveraging artificial intelligence (AI) and real-time data to deliver more relevant content, product, and service information to each user on a one-to-one basis. Hyper-personalization is more involved, more complex, and more effective than personalization. It goes beyond customer data to rethinking customer interaction on a one-to-one basis, where we treat each and every customer uniquely and design a customized experience for each one. The key element for hyper-personalization is interacting one-to-one with individuals, not the customer segments they fall in. To anticipate an individual's desires at any point in time, however, requires having deep customer insight, which comes from analyzing granular and big data. Hyper-personalization identifies subtle nuances and details that profiling doesn't catch, in order to provide highly targeted and personalized products, services, promotions and content. To make this happen, it requires the ability to merge customer interactions with demographic and historical data to paint a clear, contextual picture. This leads to the next era of digital marketing; emails that change content based on where a customer is and when the email is opened. Context-aware messages and segments that are build for more relevant communications with customers, pushing only those messages they should like to receive. Except of added value, there are numerous reasons why hyper-personalization has not yet been adopted by the majority of websites, as it requires significant processing power, technical and academic expertise, as well as propose use of actionable data.

The *"Conversational web"* or conversational interfaces, also known as chatbots, is a hybrid user interface (UI) that interacts with users combining chat, voice or any other natural language interface with graphical UI elements like buttons, images, menus, videos, etc. It has recently started to be used in the context chat-bots or virtual assistants, as well as in the context of web services. On the other hand, conversational web services (CWS) refer to web services that communicate multiple times with a client to complete a single task. Conversational interfaces have emerged as a tool for businesses to efficiently provide consumers with relevant information, in a cost effective manner, as they provide ease of access to relevant, contextual information.

Next, we redefine the term Conversational Web in the context of hyper-personalization [38]. Conversational Web refers to dynamic, multiple and asynchronous interactions (implicit conversations) between users and websites. These conversations allow both sides to understand each other and communicate efficiently. We argue that only in a truly conversational system hyper-personalization is possible, as interacting one-to-one with individuals, requires listening the needs and wills of each and every individual. This is only possible within a conversational web where websites and users continuously "discuss" (interact). The discussion takes place in the form of clicks, mouse movement, scrolling, purchases, back or forward movements and time of each page on behalf of customers. On the other hand, websites "hear" customers "talking" and respond in the form of relevant messaging and offers that best address customer needs. Users in turn react to these responses and a new cycle of communication begins.

Hyper-personalization requires processing an over abundant of data for each individual, thus big data analysis is necessary. On the one hand, real time (online) analysis is required for dynamic adapting to each customer's needs, on the other hand offline analysis is necessary as most algorithms are both time and resource consuming tasks, thus hybrid approaches, combining both online and offline analysis are most appropriate in the new era of hyper-personalized web. In any case, although personalization is becoming more than necessary for several web companies, it is rather challenging to effectively apply it, especially in small and medium sized organizations. That is why, while it's always been a focus of e-commerce strategizing, the promise of a personalized online shopping experience, including personalized recommendations and search, remains largely unfulfilled at a commercial level, as even today it is still unclear whether personalization is consistently used in e-commerce sites, especially when looking beyond e-commerce giants such as Amazon, Ebay and Alibaba, as more than half of online marketers are not sure how to implement online personalization [22].

User experience (UX) is another crucial factor for the success of every e-commerce store. UX is connected with usability which refers to how usable and easy to use a website is. Friendly UX cannot be successfully achieved without effectively practising personalization on the search results through actionable data collected from a Conversational Web. Personalized search has been the focus of research communities for many years and many approaches have been proposed in academic studies. Numerous machine learning techniques have been suggested, such as deep neural networks, SVMs and decision trees, as well as a variety of statistical methods, from descriptive statistics to tf-idf, and other linguistic tools like ontologies. Nevertheless, the common ground of all these studies is that despite some of them achieve improved search results, they do not take into account time limitations that require near real-time execution or scalability issues that are a prerequisite for applications in commercially running web systems.

In this paper, we extend our previous work in providing recommendations at a conversational web [38], by extending the application of the conversational web from recommendations to personalization in general, proposing another field of application, namely personalized search. We present an integrated architecture for conversational websites and we claim that hyper-personalization is only possible in a conversational web that adapts to various user profiles feeding them with varying context. Conversational technologies can be applied to all kinds of websites, from the smallest to the biggest ones, thus there cannot be a unique fit-to-all solution, but numerous complementary personalization algorithms and techniques. We exhibit our modular architecture through two different hyper-personalized applications. In the context of the first application we present $PRCW$ (Product Recommendations for Conversation Web), a novel hybrid approach combing both offline and online recommendations using $RFMG$ (Recency-Frequency-Monetary-Gender), an extension of the popular RFM method [10]. Through $PRCW$ partial matching recommendations are combined with deep neural networks that provide improved results. In the context of the second application we present a personalization strategy that takes into account past user actions, product data, as well as the relations among queries, products and customers. We aim in improving search in real e-commerce environments, while at the same time ensuring that queries are executed in a timely fashion, as delays are considered a conversion killer in e-commerce environments. In both cases we evaluate the proposed methods on publicly available datasets, as well as in a working e-commerce site.

The remainder of this paper is organized as follows: Sect. 2 introduces related work on personalization as well as recommender and search systems. Section 3 presents in detail our framework for the Conversational Web. Section 4 introduces two novel and modular approaches for personalization, the first is discussed in Sect. 4.1 where a new approach for personalized recommendations is presented and the second one in Sect. 4.2 where our methodology for personalized search results in e-commerce is discussed. Both our approaches are evaluated in Sect. 5. Section 6 discusses the challenges and prominent open research issues and finally concludes the paper.

2   Related Work

The process of creating customized experiences for visitors to a website is the main function of web personalization. Personalization encompass several interdisciplinary techniques, with recommender systems being one of the most popular ones. Recommender systems are divided into online and offline systems. Offline recommendation systems [24] either content-based [29] or collaborative filtering based [34], they both have weaknesses. Offline line recommenders require significant training time; data updates usually require retraining the whole model and cannot take into account frequent changes in interests and profile of users.

An emerging approach in offline recommendation systems is session-based recommendation, which although was until recently a relatively unappreciated problem, in the last few years it has attracted increased interest [18]. This is because the behavior of users shows session-based traits, or users often have only one session. Recommendation systems widely use factor models [24] or neighborhood methods [34]. Factor models are hard to apply in session-based recommendation due to the absence of user profiles, while neighbourhood models, such as item to item similarity, ignore the information of the past clicks.

On the other, hand online recommender methods [41] need less processing power and do not require training, but they are less accurate than offline methods. As a result hybrid approaches [7] have been proposed that combine the advantages of online and offline recommendation methods. Preference elicitation is also a popular personalization technique. In the context of preference elicitation, questionnaires, reviewing pre-selected items, dynamic learning [32], entropy optimization [33] and latent factor models [19] have been employed. Nevertheless, preference elicitation is not always efficient and it is recommended only in specific problems [44]. Interactive systems are another popular group of methods relative to our case. In interactive systems users play an active role, they are usually based on reviews [8], constrains [14], and questionnaires [26]. A common method used in interactive systems, is when users are asked to review a predefined selection of items, in order to cope with the cold-start problem. These requirements may frustrate users.

Deep learning models, such as recurrent neural networks, have shown remarkable results [30] as they allow sequential data modeling fitting exactly to session-based date. Embedding deep learning techniques into recommender systems is gaining traction due to its state-of-the-art performance and high-quality recommendations that provide a better understanding of user's demands, item's characteristics, historical interactions and relationships between them than traditional methods do [43]. Especially recursive neural networks (RNNs) [16] model variable-length sequential data that scale to much longer sequences than other neural networks. A recurrent neural network can be thought of as multiple copies of the same network, each passing a message to a successor. In the last few years, there has been incredible success applying RNNs to a variety of problems: speech recognition, language modeling, translation, image captioning and session-based recommendations. To deal with the exploding and vanishing gradient problems that can be encountered when training traditional RNNs, long short-term memory (LSTM) units were developed, as well as GRU (Gated Recurrent Unit), a variation on the LSTM.

Another interesting field that attracts increased attention during the last years is personalized search which refers to search experiences that are tailored specifically to an individual's interests by incorporating information about the individual beyond specific query provided. Several item relevance signals such as users' general interests, their most recent browsing behavior, and current sales trends, lead to improved rankings of search results [20]. Recent behavior is also a strong indicator; Bennett et al. in [3] assessed that not only short-term behavior contributes the majority of gains in an extended search session, but also long-term behavior provides substantial benefits, especially at the start of a search session and that each of them can be used in isolation or in combination to optimally contribute to gains in relevance through search personalization.

On a different approach, Teevan et al. [37] investigated user intent, with the help of authors that examined its variability using both explicit relevance judgments and large-scale log analysis of user behavior patterns. Speretta and Gauch [35] explored the use of less-invasive means of gathering user information for personalized search, they built user profiles based on activity at the search site itself. According to their study, user profiles were created by classifying the information into concepts from the Open Directory Project concept hierarchy and then used to re-rank the search results by calculating the conceptual similarity between each document and the user's interests. Click-through data were used by Thorsten [21] for automatically optimizing the retrieval quality of search engines in combination with Support Vector Machine (SVM). Thorsten presented a method for learning retrieval functions that can effectively adapt the retrieval function of a meta-search engine to a particular group of users. Alternatives for incorporating feedback into the ranking process was also proposed [1], comparing user feedback with other common web search features showed that incorporating user behavior data can significantly improve ordering of top results in real web search setting.

Text mining techniques have also been proposed for personalized search. The use of LDA [5] models was proposed by Yu and Mohan [42] for discovering hidden user intents of a query, and then rank the user intents by making trade-offs between their relevance and information novelty. Based on Yu and Mohan's conclusions, the LDA model discovers meaningful user intents and the LDA-based approach provides significantly higher user satisfaction than other popular approaches.

Learning to Rank (LTR) [6] is a class of techniques that apply supervised machine learning to solve ranking problems. LTR solves a ranking problem on a list of items. The aim of LTR is to come up with optimal ordering of those items. As such, LTR doesn't care much about the exact score that each item gets, but cares more about the relative ordering among all the items. Several LTR algorithms, such as SVMRank, RankLib, RankNet, [6], XGboost [9] and BM25F [31], have been used for improving search engine results [28]. In any case, for a LTR algorithm to work, it is required building a judgment list which is a tedious and resourceful process. Moreover, extensive training and evaluation is required that need substantial computation power, thus frequent or sudden changes in data and/or user behavior may lead to decreased performance.

Using multiple learning algorithms (ensemble methods) to obtain better predictive performance have also been proposed. Wu, Yan and Si [23] proposed a stacking ensemble model that used different types of features, (i.e. statistic features, query-item features and session features) consisting of different models, such as logistic regression, gradient boosted decision trees, rank SVM and a deep match model. In a similar approach, Lie et al. [25] presented a cascade model in a large-scale operational e-commerce search application. Their approach modelled multiple factors of user experience and computational cost and addressed multiple types of user behavior in e-commerce search that provided a good trade-off between search effectiveness and search efficiency within operational environments in regular e-commerce environment.

Any web user would agree that there are few things more frustrating than a slow website, as performance plays a major role in customer satisfaction. A faster website means a better visitor experience, on the contrary a slow website will lead to a poor user experience. Providing improved speed was one of the reasons Elasticsearch [17] was built. Elasticsearch is a search engine based on the Lucene library [27]. It provides an open-source, distributed, multitenant-capable full-text search engine that can be used to search all kinds of documents. Elasticsearch is distributed, which means that indices can be divided into shards and each shard can have zero or more replicas. Each node hosts one or more shards, and acts as a coordinator to delegate operations to the correct shard(s).

According to our discussion in this Section, a lot of progress has been made in personalization systems, as well as in recommendation and search systems; nevertheless, in the case of recommendation applications, there is no integrated solution that can semantically understand user's intentions and dynamically evolve based on them, while in the case of personalized search there is still a great need for integrated solutions that are affordable in terms of human resources and processing requirements. These solutions should on the one hand deliver personalized search results that improve UX and on the other hand be flexible enough to quickly adapt to new trends and sporadic changes in user behavior, as well as be scalable and resource efficient in terms of processing power and memory consumption.

3   A Framework for the Conversational Web

At a first glance, from a user's point a view, there is little difference between a hyper-personalized website employing conversational web technologies and a conventional website. However, as one uses more and more a conversational website, somehow things get so much easier to use, everything seems simple and intuitive both in terms of UX elements and product search. On the contrary, from the system's point of view, creating a truly conversational website involves a rather complex multi-step procedure, as we will discuss in this Section.

3.1   A Use-Case Scenario

Next we present a use case scenario of how the conversational web can augment the personalized experience of a customer Zoe, who wants to buy the new brand X1 night face cream. Zoe visits her favorite e-commerce site and performs a search using the site's search form. She clicks the third result, although the first two results are about two very popular night face creams of brand X2, Zoe is only interested in brand X1. At this point the implicit conversation between the customer and the user has already begun. The website *"listens"* that a returning customer landed using direct access (direct traffic), searching for brand X1 night cream, and has a strong preference to brand X1, rather than brand X2, so it responds with recommendations about other night creams, as well as other products of brand X1 that are commonly bought together with night creams. In addition, the site recognizes that this is a returning user, so it displays a "welcome back" greeting together with a reminder about a coupon that is expiring in the next few days. Next, Zoe adds the product to her basket and then hovers for some time over a shampoo for oily hair, but finally clicks on a brand X1 serum she noticed in a banner of the main page. These actions alone comprise four discrete messages: as the user has stated that she is actually (a) very interested in the brand X1 night cream (with intent to buy), (b) she is also interested in general for brand X1 and (c) more specifically in serums, and (d) she may need a shampoo for oily hair.

The website once again *"listens"* and responds with even more personalized search results and customized recommendations as it quickly learns the interests of the user, for example it recommends cheaper shampoos for oily hair as the ones displayed before are considered premium products and are probably too expensive. In case Zoe clicks on a cheaper shampoo the website will probably classify Zoe as a customer interested in mid-level products (at least until she starts showing interest for premium products). This is a continuous and ever-lasting process; the website not only adapts to better serve Zoe's interest but also learns from her behavior and the behavior of other users, aggregating this collective wisdom into actionable insights for improving the overall e-commerce UX of the site.

3.2   A Framework for the Conversational Web

In this Section we propose the overall architecture for creating a conversational website that consists of discrete modules, the behavior analysis module; the user experience analysis module; big data warehousing and the personalization module. Figure 1 depicts the proposed architecture as well as the data exchange means between subsystems [38].

Dynamic analyses of user behavior is performed by the Behavior analysis module. Data from various interdisciplinary analytical sources along with click heatmaps, scroll maps and mouse gestures are used to train models that can identify different patterns and user segments. Classification and support vector machines have provided improved performance for similar tasks in the past [36], while recently deep learning models such as recurrent neural networks have shown promising results. Semantic analysis is also required, as topic modelling and latent dirichlet allocation are useful for analyzing user's interests.

Having multiple dimensions of data, such as user experience data are necessary to understand user perspective and effectively adapt to their needs. User

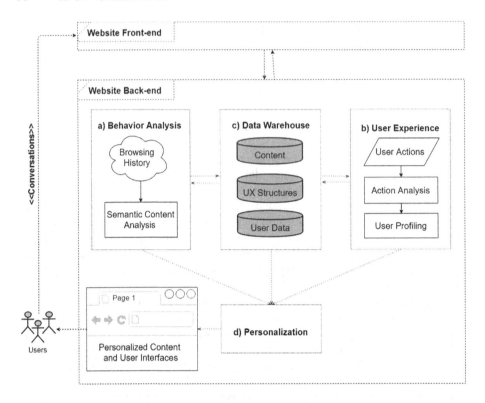

Fig. 1. System architecture in a conversational website.

experience is a multifactor parameter, as website structure, marketing, trust, interactive and information elements, colors and ease of use, all effect a person's perception about a website. All these factors are hard to be defined as they contain strongly subjective elements, key performance indicators, such as bounce rate, average time on site, conversion rate, and depth of search can provide accurate metrics for calculating user experience.

Big data warehousing is necessary for a conversational system. Due to the nature of *"conversations"*, which are unstructured, continuous, lengthy and heterogeneous, data warehousing should be able to cope with big volume and high velocity data, as well as heterogeneous information, including product data, user click history, mouse movements, scroll data, e-commerce data including buys, add to cart, and favorites, visual elements and statistics about their use. On the one hand, intelligent models are required for hyper-personalization that can only be trained in offline mode and on the other hand, real-time analysis is necessary for delivering personalized services and user interfaces.

Finally, the main component of the proposed framework is the personalization module which is responsible for adapting content to a particular user according to his or her personal preferences, needs and capabilities. The personalization module dynamically integrates information data and user actions recorded from past user experiences and behavior and provides user-tailored recommendations, website user interfaces and content. Volume, velocity, and variety are key factors for effectively providing personalized experiences, thus this module must integrated hybrid solutions combining both offline and online methods.

4 Personalization via Recommendations and Search in Conversational Web

4.1 Personalized Recommendations

The Conversational Web encompass a wide variety of applications and requirements, thus there is not a universally acceptable solution that fits in every circumstance and efficiently solves any problem in product recommendation. As a result, different approaches have to be adopted that depend on the dataset attributes and the target e-commerce site, such as volume that is mainly depending on the traffic of the e-shop and the number of orders and available products. For this reason we propose *PRCW* (Product Recommendations for the Conversational Web), a hybrid approach for product recommendations in e-commerce sites that combines offline $RFMG$ (Recency-Frequency-Monetary-Gender) analysis and online partial matching while we also apply a deep neural model.

A successful recommendation has two prerequisites: (1) be relevant (according to user interests) and (2) be provided on time. As discussed in Sect. 1, hybrid approaches are necessary in Conversational Web, as they can provide real-time recommendations as well as support intense data processing in offline-mode. Towards this goal, we introduce a new hybrid approach using offline and online processing that combines a clustering algorithm with a rule-based method. Clustering is applied to perform consumer segmentation based on consuming behavior, using $RFMG$, a modified version of RFM modeling that combines recency, frequency and monetary with gender, whereas the proposed rule based approach combines partial matching for dealing with the problem of limited user history.

Three are the main processes (Fig. 2) included in the offline phase: (a) data preprocessing, (b) clustering via $RFMG$ analysis and (c) post-processing analysis. First, transforming raw data into an understandable format is necessary, then data cleaning and transformation should take place for smoothing noisy data and resolving the inconsistencies and missing values in the data. Reduction of the number of values via discretization is also necessary, as well as outlier detection for discovering extreme deviations.

In the retail world usually 80% of a business comes from 20% of the customers, as loyal customers are the ones that produce most of the revenue. Based on that observation, RFM (recency, frequency, monetary) [4] analysis is used to determine quantitatively which customers are the best ones by examining how recently a customer has purchased (recency), how often they purchase (frequency), and how much the customer spends (monetary). RFM is widely used for customer segmentation and has received particular attention in retail and professional services industries [13]. One approach to RFM is to assign a score

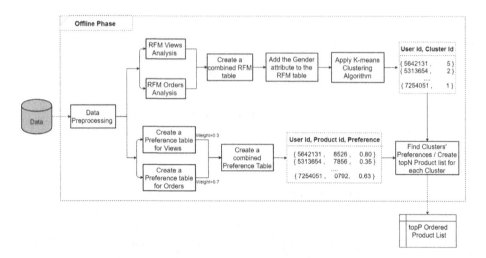

Fig. 2. Offline phase of PRCW.

for each dimension on a scale from 0 to 1. A formula could be used to calculate the three scores for each customer, for example, recency is the number of days that have passed since the customer last purchased (or viewed, clicked) a product, frequency is the number of purchases (or views/clicks) by the customer in the last d days and monetary is the summary of the value for all purchases (views/clicks) by the customer. In our work we also add the Gender attribute as it is highly related to e-commerce behavior (0/1 for males/females). After calculating the recency, frequency, monetary and gender values, normalization is applied.

Next, clustering is exercised on the $RFMG$ values through k-means. This leads to customer segments of similar users where customized information can be provided to them. Within-cluster sums of squares (WCSS) [40] can be used for determining the optimal number of clusters. Next for each consumer segment, a list of top-N most preferred (clicked/bought) items is fetched for every cluster.

Prediction by partial matching (PPM) [15] is an adaptive statistical data compression technique based on context modeling and prediction. PPM models use a set of previous symbols in the uncompressed symbol stream to predict the next symbol in the stream. PPM algorithms can also be used to cluster data into predicted groupings in cluster analysis. Figure 3 depicts our proposed online phase of our approach. The number of previous symbols, n, determines the order of the PPM model which is denoted as $PPM(n)$. Unbounded variants where the context has no length limitations also exist and are denoted as $PPM*$. If no prediction can be made based on all n context symbols a prediction is attempted with $n-1$ symbols. This process is repeated until a match is found or no more symbols remain in context. At that point a fixed prediction is made. Assuming that q_t is the state at time t, an R-order model is defined as in Eq. 1 [15], where in our problem each state is a product view. When a user views the product q_t, partial matching is applied in order to discover the pattern $<q_{t-1}, q_t>$ using data from all the users. Then the top-N products are calculated using the frequencies of the products matched. Naturally, when the order of the model R increases precision is increased but recall on the other hand is decreased.

$$P[q_t|q_{t-1}, ..., q_1] = P[q_t|t_{t-1}, ..., q_{t-R}] \tag{1}$$

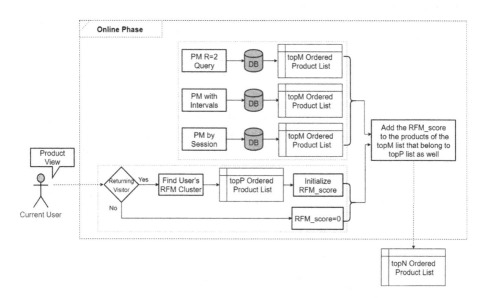

Fig. 3. Online phase of PRCW.

Due to the nature of the partial matching algorithm, datasets with limited data, originating from medium to small e-commerce site have an increased probability for non-matching patterns. Thus we use two variants of the partial matching procedure. The first one is called *"PM by intervals"* and looks for the pattern $<q_{t-1}, ..., q_t>$ within the history, with the restriction that the time interval between the product views q_{t-1} and $q\{t\}$ is less than a time period T. In this case, the top-N list is computed using the products that were viewed within the time period T and after the product view q_t. The second one is called *"PM by session"* and looks for the pattern $<q_{t-1}, ..., q_t>$ within the history, with the restriction that the product views q_{t-1} and q_t occur within the same session. In this case the top-N list is computed using the products that were viewed within the same session and after the product view q_t. For example, assume that a user u views the products $<p_9, p_1>$ and our history consist of 5 Sessions (Session1–Session5) as in Table 1. The top-N recommendation list using our PPM algorithm is presented in Table 2.

4.2   Personalized Search in Conversational Web

Another crucial application for providing a pleasant customer experience is personalized search that gains popularity as the demand for more relevant information is increased. Our approach for personalized search takes into consideration three sets of features, elicited from: (1) products, (2) users and (3) queries. The architectural diagram of our approach is depicted in Fig. 4. All data are integrated in json files, imported in Elasticsearch. For each product i, we calculate $popularity_i$ as in Eq. 2, where $buys_i$, $clicks_i$, $views_i$ are the number of buys, clicks and views for product i and $|buys|$, $|clicks|$, $|views|$ are the total number of buys, clicks and views respectively. Popularity score is usually affected more by buys, then by clicks and finally by product views, thus the use of w_b, w_c and w_v.

$$popularity_i = w_b \frac{buys_i}{|buys|} + w_c \frac{clicks_i}{|clicks|} + w_v \frac{views_i}{|views|} \tag{2}$$

The views, clicks and buys of each user for each product are important factors that encompass hints for the user-product relation. Time is also taken into account, as recent interactions naturally are more important than historic ones. So, in case user history is available, the user-product relevance is calculated by Eq. 3, where $buys_{d,u,i}$, $clicks_{d,u,i}$, $views_{d,u,i}$ are the number of buys, clicks and views of user u for product i at day d, x is the difference in days between day d and day of search, and $|buys_u|$, $|clicks_u|$, $|views_u|$ are the total number of buys, clicks and views of user i respectively.

$$relevance_{u,i} = w_b \frac{\sum \left(buys_{d,u,i} * \left(1 + \frac{1}{1-e^{-x}} \right) \right)}{|buys_u|}$$
$$+ w_c \frac{\sum \left(clicks_{d,u,i} * \left(1 + \frac{1}{1-e^{-x}} \right) \right)}{|clicks_u|} + w_v \frac{\sum \left(views_{d,u,i} * \left(1 + \frac{1}{1-e^{-x}} \right) \right)}{|views_u|} \tag{3}$$

Query-product relevance is also taken into account, meaning the similarity between the query tokens q and the product textual description d (usually the product name) tokens as described by the Elasticsearch score function:

$$qScore(q,d) = qNorm(q) * coord(q,d)$$
$$* \sum \left(tf(t \text{ in } d) * idf(t)^2 * norm(t,d) \right)(t \text{ in } q) \tag{4}$$

In Eq. 5 $qNorm$ is a measure for comparing queries when using a combination of query types, $coord$ is a measurement of matching on multiple search terms, where a higher value of this measurement will increase the overall score, tf is a measure of the number of occurrences of a t in d, idf is a measurement of how frequently the search terms occur across a set of documents, and $norm$ measures smaller field matches and gives these more weigh [16].

Finally, by integrating all the above mentioned signals, ranking depends on the weighted sums of product popularity, user past behavior, query-product similarity and the collaborative filtering recommendation, according to Eq. 5.

$$recommendationScore_{q,u,i} = w_p * popularity_i + w_r * relevance_{u,i}$$
$$+ w_q * qScore(q,d) \tag{5}$$

Table 1. Example of different products views in 5 sessions.

Sessions	
Session1:	$<p_3>$ $<p_5>$ $<\mathbf{p_1}>$ $<p_2>$
Session2:	$<p_4>$ $<\mathbf{p_9}>$ $<\mathbf{p_1}>$ $<p_3>$
Session3:	$<p_6>$ $<p_4>$ $<p_9>$ $<p_4>$
Session4:	$<p_4>$ $<\mathbf{p_1}>$ $<p_2>$ $<p_6>$
Session5:	$<\mathbf{p_9}>$ $<p_2>$ $<\mathbf{p_1}>$ $<p_4>$

Table 2. Example of top-N recommendation list using the different PM algorithms.

Method	Recall@1Next	Recall@AllNext	Precision R
PM R $=1$	i2 40%	i3 20%	i4 20%
PM R $=2$	i3 20%	–	–
PM by intervals	i3 20%	i4 30%	–
PM by session	i2 40%	i3 20%	i4 20%

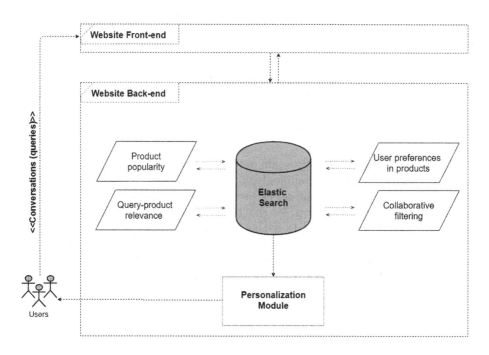

Fig. 4. The proposed architecture for personalized search.

5   Experimental Results

In this Section we evaluate the approaches described in Sects. 4.1 and 4.2 using two publicly available datasets, as well as a private dataset coming from an active e-commerce site.

5.1   Evaluation of the Recommendation Method

Our evaluation of the proposed hybrid recommendation method was performed on two different datasets. The first dataset originated from Pharm24.gr, a small-medium (in terms of traffic) retailer in Greece that provided a click stream containing data from a period of 9 months. Data from the first 7 months were used as the training set, whereas data from the last 2 months were used as the test set. Items with less than 5 views were filtered out from the training set, as well as sessions with less than two item views. Sessions with less than one item view were also removed from the test set, as well as item views that do not exist in the training set. After preprocessing, the training set contained 53,071 sessions of 875,366 events and 9,733 items, whereas the test set contains 86 sessions of 585 events and 244 items.

The second dataset is the RecSys dataset that was provided for the RecSys Challenge 2015 [2]. This dataset contains click-streams of a big e-commerce site, organized in sessions. The training set contains all but the last 10 days of the dataset, whereas the test set contains the sessions of the last 10 days. After the same preprocessing phase, the training set contains 7,802,137 sessions of 30,958,148 events and 37,331 items, while the test set contains 71,060 sessions of 217,014 events and 10,829 items. The evaluation was performed by providing the events of each session of the test set one by one and making recommendations applying the proposed algorithm to the training set.

Evaluation Metrics. To fully evaluate the effectiveness of our model we use precision and recall [12], two commonly used metrics in the field of recommender systems. Suppose that U is the set of users that are examined, $R(u)$ is the set of items recommended to user u, $V(u)$ is the set of items viewed by user u after the recommendation and $V(u, 1)$ is the first product that user u viewed after the recommendation. $PrecisionR$ (Eq. 6) is defined as the percentage of recommended items viewed by the user over the number of recommended products and $PrecisionV$ (Eq. 7) as the percentage of recommended items viewed by the user.

$$PrecisionR = \frac{\sum_u |R(u) \cap V(u)|}{\sum_u |R(u)|} \tag{6}$$

$$PrecisionV = \frac{\sum_u |R(u) \cap V(u)|}{\sum_u |V(u)|} \tag{7}$$

Recall is the percentage of users that viewed recommended items at next timestamps [12]. Three variants of recall were used: $Recall@1Next$ (Eq. 8), the strictest one, takes into account only the first next view after recommendation, $Recall@AllNext$ (Eq. 9), also considers all next views after recommendation, and $Recall@Positive$ (Eq. 10), considers only the cases where the recommendation list has at least one item.

$$Recall@1Next = \frac{\sum_u |R(u) \cap V(u,1)|}{|U|} \tag{8}$$

$$Recall@AllNext = \frac{\sum_u |R(u) \cap V(u)|}{|U|} \tag{9}$$

$$Recall@Positive = \frac{\sum_u |R(u) \cap V(u)|}{\sum_u |R(u) \neq 0|} \tag{10}$$

Recommendation Results. Next, we present the results achieved by the $PRCW$, the RNN and the combination of them using the Pharm24.gr and the RecSys dataset. Results are presented in Tables 3 and 4 accordingly [38]. For deep model evaluation we used a GRU-based RNN model [18] for session-based recommendations, while for partial matching we used the second order model. The input of the network was the actual state of the session represented by a $1 - of - N$ encoding, where N is the number of items (a vector with 1 to the active items and 0 elsewhere), and the output was the likelihood for each item to be part of the next session. Session-parallel mini-batches and mini-batch based output sampling were used for the output.

Table 3. Results of the Pharm24 dataset using the hybrid approach for product recommendation.

Method	Recall@1Next	Recall@AllNext	Prec.R	Prec.V	Pos.Recall
PRCW	0.2880	0.5247	0.0518	0.1414	0.5247
RNN	0.1993	0.3101	0.0348	0.0936	0.3101
PRCW+ RNN	0.3901	0.6065	0.0734	0.1737	0.6065

Table 4. Results of the RecSys dataset using the hybrid approach for product recommendation.

Method	Recall@1Next	Recall@AllNext	Prec.R	Prec.V	Pos.Recall
PRCW	0.0868	0.1711	0.0273	0.0229	0.1711
RNN	0.8120	0.8886	0.0998	0.6380	0.8886
PRCW+RNN	0.8366	0.9037	0.1139	0.7069	0.9037

According to results presented in Tables 3 and 4, the RNN model could not achieve good enough results in a smaller and sparse dataset, while the proposed approach not only demanded considerable less RAM and CPU recourses, but also performed better, as $PRCW$ achieved better results than RRN for the Pharm24 dataset, both in terms of Recall and Precision. On the other hand, the RNN has better performance in the RecSys dataset which contains more data both in terms of quantity and density. Nevertheless, the combination of both methods ($PRCW$+RNN) achieves improved performance in both datasets.

When looking into the results of Tables 3 and 4, one can better witness the differences between the algorithms and datasets. Bigger datasets have improved chances to get better recommendations, due to the larger amount of information that contain, and achieve worse results at the $PrecisionR$ metric, as there are too many products in the dataset. On the other hand, smaller datasets have shorter sessions and achieve worse results at the $PrecisionV$ metric. Deep learning can perform exceptionally well, as long as there are enough data and processing power to feed the neural network. Nevertheless, the proposed method $PRCW$ works better on smaller datasets. In any case combining both $PRCW$ and RNN delivers the best results in both datasets, which leads us to the conclusion that both methods deliver useful results that should be combined for optimal performance.

5.2   Evaluation of the Personalized Search Solution

The proposed personalized search approach is evaluated against a dataset provided by Diginetica[1] for the "CIKM Cup 2016 Track 2: Personalized E-Commerce Search Challenge", which contains information for more than 500,000 sessions, 1,000,000 clicks, 900,000 searches, 18,000 products and 1,000 categories (Table 5). The data are divided into two groups: (1) "query-less" data, that is search engine result pages in response to the user click on some product category; and (2) "query-full" interactions of search engine result pages returned in

Table 5. Dataset from CIKM Cup 2016 Track 2: Personalized E-Commerce Search Challenge.

Description	Number	Description	Number
Sessions	573,935	Searches	923,127
Clicks	1,127,764	Query-full queries	53,427
Buys	18,025	Query-less queries	849,700
Products	184,047	Registered users	232,817
Categories	1,217	Anonymous users	333,097
Views	1,235,380		

---

[1] http://diginetica.com/.

response to a query. Further information regarding the dataset and its characteristics is online available [11].

$nDCG$ measures ranking quality and is often used to measure effectiveness of web search engine algorithms or related applications [39]. In our case $nDCG$ is calculated by employing the ranking of products provided by Diginetica for each query, and then averaged over all test queries. There are three grades for relevance: 0 means irrelevant, that represents products with no clicks, 1 stands for somewhat relevant and corresponds to the products which were clicked by the user and 2 is relevant meaning products that were clicked and purchased by the user. In Eq. 11, p stands for the positions up to which we calculate $nDCG$, $rating(i)$ is the score for position i and $|REL|$ is the best score for p. Since we evaluate both types of queries, query-full and query-less, we followed the same evaluation procedure as CIKM: the final $nDCG$ value is a weighted sum of the query-full $nDCG_{qf}$ and query-less $nDCG_{ql}$ as: $nDCG = 0.2 * nDCG_{qf} + 0.8 * nDCG_{ql}$.

$$nDCG_p = \sum_{i=1}^{p} \frac{rating(i)}{log_2(i+1)} \left/ \sum_{i=1}^{|REL|} \frac{rating(i)}{log_2(i+1)} \right. \tag{11}$$

The evaluation results are available in Table 6. First, we randomly ranked the results, calculated the $nDCG$ values and used them as our baseline. Consequently we experimented only with the collaborative filtering algorithm to test different values of the weighting factors for interaction a. In [24] the optimal value for a was 40, so we tested for $a = 15, 30$ and 40. According to our experiments, $a = 40$ achieved the best results for the query-less case, while the best result for query-less came with $a = 30$, thus it makes sense to use different a values depending on the query type. Thereafter we tested different values for the weighting factors w_r, w_p, w_q and w_s (Table 6), according to our experiments, values $w_r = 1$, $w_p = 1.5$, $w_q = 1.5$ and $w_s = 0$ gave the best results improving $nDCG$ up to +42.42% when compared with the baseline. In all our experiments

Table 6. Evaluation results.

Description	nDCG	Impr.	nDCG$_{ql}$	Impr.	nDCG$_{qf}$	Impr.
Baseline	0.242	–	0.220	-	0.334	–
$w_p = 0, w_q = 0, w_s = 1, a = 15$	0.325	34.0%	0.313	42.5%	0.372	11.5
$w_p = 0, w_q = 0, w_s = 1, a = 30$	0.325	34.0%	0.313	42.6%	0.372	11.6%
$w_p = 0, w_q = 0, w_s = 1, a = 40$	0.325	34.0%	0.372	69.5%	0.313	−6.1%
$w_r = 1.5, w_p = 3, w_q = 3$	0.343	41.6%	0.336	52.7%	0.375	12.3%
$w_r = 3, w_p = 1.5, w_q = 1.5$	0.343	41.6%	0.336	52.8%	0.388	16.3%
$w_r = 1, w_p = 1.5, w_q = 1.5$	0.344	41.9%	0.335	52.3%	0.382	14.5%
$w_r = 1.5, w_p = 1, w_q = 1$	0.346	41.6%	0.335	52.6%	0.388	16.3%
$w_r = 1, w_p = 1, w_q = 1, w_s = 0$	0.345	42.4%	0.337	53.41%	0.379	13.5%
$w_r = 1, w_p = 1.5, w_q = 1.5$	0.344	41.9%	0.337	53.2%	0.375	12.3%

for calculating the *popularity*$_i$ we used the weights $w_b = 5$, $w_c = 3$ and $w_v = 1$, as naturally buys are more important that clicks which are more important than views.

6 Conclusion

Delivering individualized experiences is at the heart of converting a business's generic audience into loyal customers. Hyper-personalization helps organizations realize granularity of customer data to gain a deeper customer connection and build a loyal customer base. In order to do so, the application of qualitative tools and frameworks is needed, in order to collect meaningful omnichannel data in real-time. Hyper-personalization is possible only in a truly Conversation Web. The Conversation Web is far more than just chatbots and conversational web services, it is a new type on Web where implicit and explicit conversation between websites and users are continuous.

In this paper we presented a generic framework for the conversational web that can provide hyper-personalized services, such as product recommendation, personalized search, UI/UX personalization, as well as individual messages and promos per customer. We presented two methods for hyper-personalization, one for product recommendations and one for search. Finally, we evaluated these methods on different datasets.

Future work includes working on better integrating the various personalization methods in a way that they can interact and learn from each other. Deeper integration of our hybrid approach with RNNs is also worth investigating in the near future. Moreover, privacy concerns that arise from collecting such a large amount of customer data is an open issue. Finally, we plan to work on improving the integration of both our methods with Elasticsearch.

Acknowledgements. This work was partially funded by an IKY scholarship funded by the "Strengthening of Post-Academic Researchers" Act from the resources of the OP "Human Resources Development, Education and Lifelong Learning" with Priority Axes 6, 8, 9 and co-funded by the European Social Fund ECB and the Greek government. The authors would like to thank George Katsikopoulos for his valuable help with the personalized search experiments and Kostas Nikolaros for his useful feedback regarding user search behavior.

References

1. Agichtein, E., Brill, E., Dumais, S.: Improving web search ranking by incorporating user behavior information. In: Proceedings of the 29th Annual International ACM SIGIR Conference on Research and Development in Information Retrieval, SIGIR 2006, pp. 19–26. ACM, New York, NY, USA (2006). https://doi.org/10.1145/1148170.1148177
2. Ben-Shimon, D., Tsikinovsky, A., Friedmann, M., Shapira, B., Rokach, L., Hoerle, J.: RecSys challenge 2015 and the YOOCHOOSE dataset. In: Proceedings of the 9th ACM Conference on Recommender Systems, RecSys 2015, pp. 357–358. ACM, New York, NY, USA (2015). https://doi.org/10.1145/2792838.2798723

3. Bennett, P.N., et al.: Modeling the impact of short- and long-term behavior on search personalization. In: Proceedings of the 35th International ACM SIGIR Conference on Research and Development in Information Retrieval, SIGIR 2012. pp. 185–194. ACM, New York, NY, USA (2012). https://doi.org/10.1145/2348283. 2348312

4. Birant, D.: Data mining using RFM analysis. In: Knowledge-Oriented Applications in Data Mining, chap. 6. Funatsu, Kimito, Rijeka (2011). https://doi.org/10.5772/13683

5. Blei, D.M., Ng, A.Y., Jordan, M.I.: Latent dirichlet allocation. J. Mach. Learn. Res. **3**, 993–1022 (2003). http://dl.acm.org/citation.cfm?id=944919.944937

6. Burges, C., et al.: Learning to rank using gradient descent. In: Proceedings of the 22nd International Conference on Machine Learning, ICML 2005, pp. 89–96. ACM, New York, NY, USA (2005). https://doi.org/10.1145/1102351.1102363

7. Burke, R.: Hybrid recommender systems: survey and experiments. User Modeling User-Adap. Inter. **12**(4), 331–370 (2002). https://doi.org/10.1023/A:1021240730564

8. Chen, L., Pu, P.: Critiquing-based recommenders: survey and emerging trends. User Modeling User-Adap. Inter. **22**(1), 125–150 (2012). https://doi.org/10.1007/s11257-011-9108-6

9. Chen, T., Guestrin, C.: XGBoost: a scalable tree boosting system. In: Proceedings of the 22nd ACM SIGKDD International Conference on Knowledge Discovery and Data Mining, KDD 2016, pp. 785–794. ACM, New York, NY, USA (2016). https://doi.org/10.1145/2939672.2939785

10. Chen, Y.L., Kuo, M.H., Wu, S.Y., Tang, K.: Discovering recency, frequency, and monetary (RFM) sequential patterns from customers' purchasing data. Electron. Commer. Res. Appl. **8**(5), 241–251 (2009). https://doi.org/10.1016/j.elerap.2009.03.002. Special Issue: Marketing and Electronic Commerce

11. CIKM Cup organizing committee: Cikm cup 2016 track 2: Personalized e-commerce search challenge (2016). https://competitions.codalab.org/competitions/11161#learnthedetails-data2. Accessed 15 Jan 2019

12. Davis, J., Goadrich, M.: The relationship between precision-recall and ROC curves. In: Proceedings of the 23rd International Conference on Machine Learning, ICML 2006, pp. 233–240. ACM, New York, NY, USA (2006).https://doi.org/10.1145/1143844.1143874

13. Fader, P.S., Hardie, B.G., Lee, K.L.: RFM and CLV: using iso-value curves for customer base analysis. J. Mark. Res. **42**(4), 415–430 (2005). https://doi.org/10.1509/jmkr.2005.42.4.415

14. Felfernig, A., Friedrich, G., Jannach, D., Zanker, M.: Developing constraint-based recommenders. In: Ricci, F., Rokach, L., Shapira, B., Kantor, P.B. (eds.) Recommender Systems Handbook, pp. 187–215. Springer, Boston, MA (2011). https://doi.org/10.1007/978-0-387-85820-3_6

15. Gellert, A., Florea, A.: Web prefetching through efficient prediction by partial matching. World Wide Web **19**(5), 921–932 (2016). https://doi.org/10.1007/s11280-015-0367-8

16. Goodfellow, I., Bengio, Y., Courville, A.: Deep Learning. MIT Press, Cambridge (2016)

17. Gormley, C., Tong, Z.: Elasticsearch: The Definitive Guide, 1st edn. O'Reilly Media Inc., Sebastopol (2015)

18. Hidasi, B., Karatzoglou, A., Baltrunas, L., Tikk, D.: Session-based recommendations with recurrent neural networks. CoRR abs/1511.06939 (2015). http://arxiv.org/abs/1511.06939

19. Huang, S.L.: Designing utility-based recommender systems for e-commerce: evaluation of preference-elicitation methods. Electron. Commer. Rec. Appl. **10**(4), 398–407 (2011). https://doi.org/10.1016/j.elerap.2010.11.003

20. Jannach, D., Ludewig, M.: Investigating personalized search in e-commerce. In: FLAIRS Conference, pp. 645–650. AAAI Press (2017)

21. Joachims, T.: Optimizing search engines using clickthrough data. In: Proceedings of the Eighth ACM SIGKDD International Conference on Knowledge Discovery and Data Mining, KDD 2002, pp. 133–142. ACM, New York, NY, USA (2002). https://doi.org/10.1145/775047.775067

22. Saleh, K.: Online shopping personalization - statistics and trends (2018). https://www.invespcro.com/blog/online-shopping-personalization/. Accessed 15 Jan 2019

23. Kong, D.: Personalized feature based re-ranking method for ecommerce search at cikm cup 2016. Technical report, CIKM Cup (2016)

24. Koren, Y., Bell, R., Volinsky, C.: Matrix factorization techniques for recommender systems. Computer **42**(8), 30–37 (2009). https://doi.org/10.1109/MC.2009.263

25. Liu, S., Xiao, F., Ou, W., Si, L.: Cascade ranking for operational e-commerce search. In: Proceedings of the 23rd ACM SIGKDD International Conference on Knowledge Discovery and Data Mining, KDD 2017, pp. 1557–1565. ACM, New York, NY, USA (2017). https://doi.org/10.1145/3097983.3098011

26. Mahmood, T., Ricci, F.: Improving recommender systems with adaptive conversational strategies. In: Proceedings of the 20th ACM Conference on Hypertext and Hypermedia, HT 2009, pp. 73–82. ACM, New York, NY, USA (2009). https://doi.acm.org/10.1145/1557914.1557930

27. McCandless, M., Hatcher, E., Gospodnetic, O.: Lucene in Action, Second Edition: Covers Apache Lucene 3.0. Manning Publications Co., Greenwich (2010)

28. Palotti, J.: Learning to rank for personalized e-commerce search at CIKM cup 2016. Technical report CIKM Cup (2016)

29. Pazzani, M.J., Billsus, D.: Content-based recommendation systems. In: Brusilovsky, P., Kobsa, A., Nejdl, W. (eds.) The Adaptive Web. LNCS, vol. 4321, pp. 325–341. Springer, Heidelberg (2007). https://doi.org/10.1007/978-3-540-72079-9_10

30. Quadrana, M., Karatzoglou, A., Hidasi, B., Cremonesi, P.: Personalizing session-based recommendations with hierarchical recurrent neural networks. In: Proceedings of the Eleventh ACM Conference on Recommender Systems, RecSys 2017, Como, Italy, 27–31 August 2017, pp. 130–137 (2017). https://doi.acm.org/10.1145/3109859.3109896

31. Robertson, S., Zaragoza, H.: The probabilistic relevance framework: BM25 and beyond. Found. Trends Inf. Retr. **3**(4), 333–389 (2009). https://doi.org/10.1561/1500000019

32. Rubens, N., Kaplan, D., Sugiyama, M.: Active learning in recommender systems. In: Ricci, F., Rokach, L., Shapira, B., Kantor, P. (eds.) Recommender Systems Handbook, pp. 735–767. Springer, Boston (2011). https://doi.org/10.1007/978-0-387-85820-3_23

33. Salimans, T., Paquet, U., Graepel, T.: Collaborative learning of preference rankings. In: Proceedings of the Sixth ACM Conference on Recommender Systems, RecSys 2012, pp. 261–264. ACM, New York, NY, USA (2012). https://doi.acm.org/10.1145/2365952.2366009

34. Sarwar, B., Karypis, G., Konstan, J., Riedl, J.: Item-based collaborative filtering recommendation algorithms. In: Proceedings of the 10th International Conference on World Wide Web, WWW 2001, pp. 285–295. ACM, New York, NY, USA (2001). https://doi.org/10.1145/371920.372071

35. Speretta, M., Gauch, S.: Personalized search based on user search histories. In: The 2005 IEEE/WIC/ACM International Conference on Web Intelligence (WI 2005), pp. 622–628, September 2005. https://doi.org/10.1109/WI.2005.114
36. Sun, A., Lim, E.P., Ng, W.K.: Web classification using support vector machine. In: Proceedings of the 4th International Workshop on Web Information and Data Management, WIDM 2002, pp. 96–99. ACM, New York, NY, USA (2002). https://doi.acm.org/10.1145/584931.584952
37. Teevan, J., Dumais, S.T., Liebling, D.J.: To personalize or not to personalize: Modeling queries with variation in user intent. In: Proceedings of the 31st Annual International ACM SIGIR Conference on Research and Development in Information Retrieval, SIGIR 2008, pp. 163–170. ACM, New York, NY, USA (2008). https://doi.org/10.1145/1390334.1390364
38. Vavliakis, K.N., Kotouza, M.T., Symeonidis, A.L., Mitkas, P.A.: Recommendation systems in a conversational web. In: Proceedings of the 14th International Conference on Web Information Systems and Technologies, WEBIST 2018, Seville, Spain, 18–20 September 2018, pp. 68–77 (2018). https://doi.org/10.5220/0006935300680077
39. Wang, Y., Wang, L., Li, Y., He, D., Liu, T.Y., Chen, W.: A theoretical analysis of NDCG type ranking measures. CoRR abs/1304.6480 (2013)
40. Witten, D.M., Tibshirani, R.: A framework for feature selection in clustering. J. Am. Stat. Assoc. **105**(490), 713–726 (2010)
41. Ying, Y., Feinberg, F., Wedel, M.: Leveraging missing ratings to improve online recommendation systems. J. Mark. Res. **43**(3), 355–365 (2006). http://www.jstor.org/stable/30162410
42. Yu, J., Mohan, S., Putthividhya, D.P., Wong, W.K.: Latent Dirichlet allocation based diversified retrieval for e-commerce search. In: Proceedings of the 7th ACM International Conference on Web Search and Data Mining, WSDM 2014, pp. 463–472. ACM, New York, NY, USA (2014). https://doi.org/10.1145/2556195.2556215
43. Zhang, S., Yao, L., Sun, A.: Deep learning based recommender system: a survey and new perspectives. CoRR abs/1707.07435 (2017)
44. Zhao, X., Zhang, W., Wang, J.: Interactive collaborative filtering. In: Proceedings of the 22nd ACM International Conference on Information & Knowledge Management, CIKM 2013, pp. 1411–1420. ACM, New York, NY, USA (2013). https://doi.acm.org/10.1145/2505515.2505690

A Declarative Data Protection Approach: From Human-Readable Policies to Automatic Enforcement

Francesco Di Cerbo[1]([✉]), Alessio Lunardelli[2], Ilaria Matteucci[2], Fabio Martinelli[2], and Paolo Mori[2]

[1] SAP Security Research, Sophia Antipolis, France
francesco.di.cerbo@sap.com
[2] IIT-CNR, Pisa, Italy
{alessio.lunardelli,ilaria.matteucci,fabio.martinelli,
paolo.mori}@iit.cnr.it

Abstract. In recent years, almost any object we use in our lives is connected and able to generate, collect and share data and information. This leads to the need of having, on the one hand, legal regulations, such as the new General Data Protection Regulation, able to guarantee that privacy of humans is preserved within the sharing process, and on the other hand, automatic mechanisms to guarantee that such regulations, in addition to user privacy preferences, are applied. The goal of this work is to propose an approach to manage data protection policy, from their specification in a controlled natural language to their translation into an automatically enforceable policy language, UPOL, for access and usage control of personal information, aiming at transparent and accountable data usage. UPOL extends and combines previous research results, U-XACML and PPL, and it is part of a more general proposal to regulate multi-party data sharing operations. A use case is proposed, considering challenges brought by the new EU's GDPR.

Keywords: Personal data protection · GDPR · Privacy · Security

1 Introduction

The increased adoption of cloud solutions to store and share data among entities, companies and objects leads to the necessity of having a clear legal regulation for personal data protection, in place in a transnational environment to regulate the current practice for data exchanges among data producers, consumers and cloud providers. This awareness has driven the advent of the new European General Data Privacy Regulation (GDPR Regulation (EU) 2016/679) [8], entered in force in May 2018. This regulation has a deep impact on the legal framework and the requirements for data processing of European citizens because it is applicable to all entities, all over the world, aiming at processing personal data belonging to citizens of an European country.

© Springer Nature Switzerland AG 2019
M. J. Escalona et al. (Eds.): WEBIST 2018, LNBIP 372, pp. 78–98, 2019.
https://doi.org/10.1007/978-3-030-35330-8_5

To be compliant with this regulation, all such entities need to perform a deep revision of their data management processes and, consequently, of the software deputed to manage them in order to be compliant with the new prescriptions. In particular, we focus on a number of key requirements of GDPR formalised in Articles 5 - Principles relating to processing of personal data - and 25 - Data protection by design and by default - dealing with *"lawfulness, fairness and transparency"*, *"purpose limitation"* and *"data minimisation"*.

The principle of *"lawfulness, fairness and transparency"* deals with requirements on how data must be processed from the owner of the personal data prospective. The *"purpose limitation"* principle aims at linking the request of data processing with the purpose of use of them that has to be explicitly accepted by the data subject (explicit consent) with a contract prepared under the fairness and transparency principles. *"Data minimisation"* imposes to *data controllers*, such as, companies collecting personal data of customers, to reduce the amount of collected data to the strict minimal necessary to carry out the requested service, also reducing "the extent of processing, the period of their storage and their accessibility".

To guarantee these requirements, in this paper we propose a Data Protection approach able to regulate both access and usage of data with an eye to the GDPR regulation, i.e., to fulfill the data minimisation requirement in its part referring to computation purpose verification, data retention and data access. Access and usage of data are regulated by the definition of rules. In our approach, we consider to have a unique document that collects both legal requirements and user rules about access and usage control of a piece of data, i.e., we refer to the concept of *Data Sharing Agreement* (DSA) associated to the target data. It is an agreement among contracting parties regulating how they share data. A DSA represents a flexible mean to assure privacy, in terms of GDPR directive, of data exchanged on the Cloud. Here, we refer to the work in [11], in which the authors introduced a Controlled Natural Language for DSA aiming at lowering the barrier to adoption of DSA, and, at the same time, ensuring mapping to a chosen enforceable language.

Our activity identified two solutions, whose combination would allow a data controller to achieve a transparent usage of personal data. They are PPL [7,15] and U-XACML [10]. The novelty of our proposal consists of an approach (policy language and reference architecture) that unifies both benefits and allows to achieve new results, namely:

R1. to meet GDPR's transparency requirement by fully controlling information processing operations. This is achieved through the full support of the Usage Control model proposed by Park and Sandhu [13,16], achieved through our contribution as simple extension to a well-known access control standard, XACML [12].

R2. the control and tracking of processing purpose(s), for the operations requesting an access to the protected pieces of information, both at the moment of the access request and during their consumption. This aims at meeting GDPR's purpose limitation.

R3. the support for GDPR's data minimisation, considering for example data retention conditions.

R4. to ease compliance audit of a solution integrating our approach, also considering the different stakeholders' background involved in the audit process: lawyers, software architects, public bodies but also citizens (data subjects).

The concepts presented here appeared in an earlier form in [6], however this work extends them by:

- recalling the notion of Data Sharing Agreements as way to express and group all security and data protection constraints expressed at high abstraction level (human language) by different parties to regulate data sharing operations.
- recalling the CNL4DSA high level controlled natural language introduced in [11], functional to the expression of Data Sharing Agreements.
- introducing a novel architectural component, named DSA Mapper, in charge of automatically translating the security and data protection constraints expressed in CNL4DSA to enforceable UPOL policies.
- combining all previously mentioned extensions to present an extended architecture and a complete data flow for regulated data sharing operations, covering data provisioning and consumption operations.
- achieving a new result, a simplification for conducting audit given by the simplified understandability and transparency of the extended approach.

The paper is structured as follows: next section describes the motivation of this work that is mainly part of a EU FP7 project named Coco Cloud about the sharing of sensitive data through the Cloud, and how parts of this effort are continued in project C3ISP. Section 3 briefly recalls the existing access and usage control policy languages while Sect. 4 presents the new one, named UPOL able to integrate and enhance in a unique language the expressiveness of both languages. Section 5 presents a use case for an UPOL policy and finally Sect. 6 draws the conclusion of the paper and discusses about ongoing and future work.

2   Usage Control in Coco Cloud and C3ISP

The Confidential and Compliant Cloud (Coco Cloud) EU FP7 funded project [4] proposes a data centric approach to enhance data security on the cloud. In particular, the project is aimed at enabling its users to regulate the usage of the data they share on the cloud, in order to increase their trust in, and consequently their adoption of, cloud services. In the Coco Cloud scenario, multiple subjects are involved in the data sharing, including companies, public bodies, and citizens. Consequently, the data sharing must be automatically regulated by digital contracts, called Data Sharing Agreements (DSA) [2], defined by the sharing parties, which must be paired with the data when they are shared on the Cloud and must be enforced every time such data are accessed and used by the Cloud users [3]. A peculiar goal of the Coco Cloud project is to embed in the DSA also a further set of constraints to allow a legally compliant data sharing in the cloud. Hence, the project places an early emphasis on understanding and incorporating legal and regulatory requirements into the data sharing agreements. The European data protection legal framework has been one of the key legal focuses of our work.

To this aim, the first step consists in an automatic translation of both legal and sharing parties constraints in a policy format that can be directly enforced. In fact, DSA are automatically mapped into Usage Control Policies expressed through the *UPOL* language. The Usage Control model [13] is adopted because the factors that are taken into account to define constraints in the DSA are mutable, i.e., they can change over time. As a matter of fact, one of the main improvements introduced by the Usage Control model with respect to traditional access control ones is the management of those user and resource attributes which change their values over time, thus requiring the continuous evaluation of the usage control policy to promptly react to changes. In particular, attribute values could change in such a way that an access which was previously authorized according to the previous attribute values and is now in progress should instead be forbidden because of the new values of such attributes. Hence, the usage control policy is continuously evaluated during the data access time, and the access can be interrupted when the policy is not satisfied any more. For instance, the physical position of a person is one of these mutable attributes because, obviously, it changes when the person moves from one place to another. A DSA could state that a critical document produced by a company can be read only by the employees of such company when they are located within a given area (e.g., the building of a company). Hence, an employee could open the document on her mobile phone when she is located within the company building but, as soon as she exits the building, the usage control policy is violated and the countermeasure defined in the policy is taken. For instance the policy could require to close such document saving the unsaved changes in a temporary document copy).

Moreover, the Usage Control model also allows policy makers to express that some actions, called obligations, must be executed as a consequence of the execution of other actions or when certain events occur. For instance, the DSA of a piece of data could include an obligation which requires that the related file is deleted after a given date. This concept has clear application in expressing a personal data retention period, according to the GDPR. Another example of obligation recalling the previous DSA is the one that, when the user leaves her country, deletes the document from her mobile device.

The usage control model allows to define very expressive data sharing agreements which satisfies the requirements of many application scenarios. For example, we applied it to e-government, corporate and healthcare [2] solutions. Moreover, part of the described approach is used in C3ISP[1], an EU-funded H2020 project focussing on cyber security and in particular on the sharing of particularly critical pieces of information, that are necessary for organising an effective defense against online attacks but that may also be used, if in wrong hands, to conduct malicious activities. This is the case of information describing cyber

---

[1] Homepage: https://c3isp.eu/.

attacks trace logs: other defenders may tune up their countermeasures in order to identify the latest attacks (malware received per email, specially crafted web requests targeting a software's vulnerability etc.) but on the other hand, an attacker may get to know where and how a target system is vulnerable and may be successfully breached. Specific extensions are being studied and they will be discussed in the future.

This paper describes *UPOL*, the language we defined to express the enforceable version of the usage control policies representing the DSAs exploited in the Coco Cloud and C3ISP European projects. We also describe how we automatically obtain UPOL policies starting from DSAs in which the rules are expressed in a *Controlled Natural Language* [11]. Such language has been introduced to help the user to express in a natural language style yet controlled way not only her own constraints on data but also legal regulations [9] on them.

3   Background

In this section, we recall some background notions about languages used for expressing policies at both high level through a controlled natural language and low level trough XACML-based languages.

3.1   Controlled Natural Language

The core of Controlled Natural Language named CNL4DSA [11] (CNL4DSA) is the notion of *fragment*, a tuple $f = \langle s, a, o \rangle$ where s is the subject, a is the action, o is the object. The fragment expresses that "the subject s performs the action a on the object o", e.g., "the doctor reads the medical report". It is possible to express authorisations, obligations, and prohibitions by adding the *can/must/cannot* constructs to the basic fragment. Fragments are evaluated within a specific *context*. In CNL4DSA, a *context* is a predicate c that usually characterises factors such as users' roles, data categories, time, and geographical location. Contexts are predicates that evaluate either to *true* or *false*. To describe complex policies, contexts must be combined. Hence, we use the Boolean connectors *and*, *or*, and *not* for describing a *composite context* C which is defined inductively as follows (Eq. 1):

$$C := c \mid C \ and \ C \mid C \ or \ C \mid not \ c \tag{1}$$

The syntax of a *composite authorisation fragment*, F_A, is as follows:

$$F_A := nil \mid can \ f \mid F_A; F_A \mid if \ C \ then \ F_A \mid after \ f \ then \ F_A \mid (F_A) \tag{2}$$

with the following meaning:

- *nil* can do nothing.
- *can f* is the atomic authorisation fragment that expresses that f is allowed, where $f = \langle s, a, o \rangle$. Its informal meaning is *the subject s can perform the action a on the object o*.

- $F_A; F_A$ is a list of composite authorisation fragments.
- *if C then* F_A expresses the logical implication between a context C and a composite authorisation fragment: if C holds, then F_A is permitted.
- *after f then* F_A is a temporal sequence of fragments. Informally, after f has happened, then the composite authorisation fragment F_A is permitted.

The list of authorisations represents all the composite authorisation fragments that define the access rights on the data.

Also, CNL4DSA has a specific syntax expressing composite obligation and prohibition fragments. Similar to the authorisations, the obligation fragment indicates that *the subject s must perform the action a on the object o*, while, for the prohibition, *the subject s cannot perform the action a on the object o*.

of a composite obligation fragment, F_O, is inductively defined as follows:

$$F_O := nil \mid must\ f \mid F_O; F_O \mid if\ C\ then\ F_O \mid after\ f\ then\ F_O \mid (F_O) \qquad (3)$$

The intuition is the same as for F_A, except for *must f* that represents the atomic obligation: *the subject s must perform the action a on the object o*. The atomic obligation *must f* expresses that f is required.

Finally, the syntax of a composite prohibition fragment, F_P, is as follows:

$$F_P := nil \mid cannot\ f \mid F_P; F_P \mid if\ C\ then\ F_P \mid after\ f\ then\ F_P \mid (F_P) \qquad (4)$$

The atomic prohibition is represented by *cannot f*: *the subject s cannot perform the action a on the object o*. The atomic prohibition *cannot f* expresses that f is not permitted.

3.2 Enforceable Policy Languages

We identified the Usage Control model as the theoretical underpinnings for our objective but we observed a number of limitations in the current approaches. Essentially, we looked at a number of declarative solutions (i.e. controllable through a configuration policy) and we concentrated on three technologies that have available implementations:

- **XACML:** the eXtensible Access Control Markup Language [12] is a standard produced by the OASIS Consortium which defines an XML based language for expressing Attribute Based Access Control policies and a reference architecture for the enforcement of such policies. Several open source, academic and commercial implementations of the XACML standard are currently available on the market. The main limitation is that it only covers access control models and not usage control. XACML only partially fulfill R1, R2, and R3.
- **U-XACML:** the UCON XACML [10] is an extension of the XACML standard aimed at supporting usage control functionalities, most notably the continuous policy evaluation during the access to the requested resources. U-XACML extends both the XACML language, in order to introduce proper constructs to express which XACML conditions must be satisfied at access request time and which must be satisfied for the whole duration of the access,

and the reference architecture, in order to introduce further components devoted to the continuous policy evaluation and to the management of usage sessions. U-XACML fulfills R1, partially R2 but not R3.

- **PPL:** as well extends XACML with the possibility to verify resource processing purposes against a policy plus it caters the automatic execution of obligations defined by a resource owner. It can be used to implement R3 especially with respect to data retention, R2 but not completely R1.

In order to achieve the fulfillment of requirements **R1, R2, R3** starting from the previously listed technologies, we defined a new concept, UPOL. In other words, we extended the XACML standard by combining the advantages brought in by two other extensions, U-XACML and PPL.We also extended all previous approaches in order to fulfill **R4**, by designing a process for transforming a human-readable set of directives into an actionable policy; this allows an easier understandability of UPOL policies by non-technical stakeholders, considering for example legal experts and citizens.

From the combination of the mentioned technologies, UPOL achieves new capabilities as detailed in Sect. 4. It is the language we used to express DSAs terms and conditions in a machine-enforceable manner. UPOL policies therefore regulate the usage of the data they are paired with: following the sticky policy model [14], each policy (that regulates the access to a resource) get attached to a resource to form a *bundle*, normally protected by means of strong encryption. This imposes that data can be processed only by means of special mechanisms able to decrypt the bundle and to allow its access in accordance to the associated policy. Any attempt to consume arbitrarily a resource once it is protected by such bundle, is destined to fail. The UPOL language is based on the Usage Control model, which extends traditional access control model by dealing with attributes related to the subjects and of the objects which change their values over time. The Usage Control model allows to define policies which are continuously evaluated during the execution of an access, in order to revoke such ongoing access when the corresponding policy is not valid any longer. In particular, the usage control policies define authorization and condition rules which must be satisfied before and/or during the usage of such data (*pre-/ongoing-authorizations* and *pre-/ongoing-conditions*), along with obligations (similarly, *pre-/ongoing-obligations*). UPOL comprises all such categories, extending the XACML capabilities with two new contributions the *asynchronous* and *synchronous* obligations, normally implemented by a trusted third party. The asynchronous obligations are usage control obligations which have to be fulfilled when an event occurs. Events may used to model reactions to mutable attributes as in Park and Sandhu model but, extending it, they may not be connected to an access request, as such as when the retention period for a piece of data expires (as requested for GDPR's data minimization). The synchronous obligations are again usage control obligations. For instance banners that appears while one watches a streaming video, or logging of the exact consumption time of a resource, for accountability purposes. Such kind of obligations may also be considered as *session* obligations and can be used in order to pinpoint when an user starts and terminates to use a resource as well as when the user's access right to the resource is revoked.

In UPOL, the violation of pre-authorization or pre-condition rules prevents the access to the protected data. Instead, when pre-authorization and pre-condition rules are satisfied, the access to the data is allowed, and the ongoing-authorization and ongoing-condition rules are enforced continuously while the access is in progress. In this case, the violation of ongoing rules causes the interruption of the usage of the data. Session obligations may be associated to passed or failed checks, in order to model a desired behavior.

3.3   U-XACML

The U-XACML language is an extension of the XACML language which includes additional constructs to express Usage Control features. XACML is a standard developed by the OASIS consortium for expressing and managing access control policies in a distributed environment [12]. Briefly, the XACML standard defines a policy meta-model, syntax, semantics, and the related enforcement architecture. The top-level element of a policy is *<PolicySet>*, which includes a set of *<Policy>* elements (or other distinct *<PolicySet>*), each of which, in turn, includes a *<Target>*, which denotes the target of the policy, and a set of *<Rule>* elements which represent the authorization rules. A rule is defined by three main components: the *<Target>*, the *<Condition>*, and the effect of the rule which can be either Permit or Deny. The *<Target>* denotes the target of the rule, i.e., to which authorization requests the rule can be applied. The *<Condition>* elements are predicates evaluating the attributes. A rule can include the *<ObligationExpressions>* element, which, in turn, includes a set of *<ObligationExpression>* elements. Each *<ObligationExpression>* element includes the ID of the obligation and which effect will trigger its execution. A rule is applicable to an access request if the target of the access request matches the target of the rule and if all the conditions included in the rule are satisfied. If a rule is applicable to an access request, the effect declared for the rule concurs to determine whether the access request is permitted or denied, and the related obligation must be executed. As a matter of fact, the effects of all the applicable rule are combined to produce the effect to be actually enforced according to the combining algorithm specified at the beginning of the policy. For instance, the PERMIT OVERRIDE combining algorithm causes the policy to be evaluated to permit if at least one applicable rule has been assigned permit as effect.

XACML allows to express traditional attribute based access control policies dealing with immutable attributes and it does not have specific constructs to deal with mutable attributes and to express the continuity of policy enforcement. In particular, adopting a standard XACML system, the policy is evaluated at request time only, and no further policy evaluation are executed while the access is in progress. Consequently, once an access has been granted, if the attributes values change in such a way that the policy is not satisfied any more, no countermeasures are taken, and the ongoing access is not affected.

The U-XACML language extends XACML with usage control constructs as follows. To express the continuity of policy enforcement, the U-XACML language introduces in the *<Condition>* element a clause, called *DecisionTime*, which defines when the evaluation of this condition must be executed. The admitted values are *pre* and *on* denoting, respectively, *pre-decisions* and *on-decisions*. In this way, the conditions whose decision time is set to *pre* are the same as usual XACML conditions, since they are evaluated at access request time only. On the other hand, the conditions whose decision time is set to *on* must be continuously evaluated while the access is in progress. These conditions typically involve mutable attributes, because their values change over time thus requiring the re-evaluation of the condition. We recall that in U-XACML, XACML conditions are exploited to represent both UCON authorizations and conditions. In the same way, U-XACML extends the *<ObligationExpression>* element with the *DecisionTime* clause to define when the obligation must be executed. In this case too, the admitted values for the *DecisionTime* clause are: *pre* (*pre-obligations*, i.e., usual XACML obligations) and *on* (*on-obligations*), and *post* (*post-obligations*).

To deal with mutable attributes, U-XACML introduces a new element, *<AttrUpdates>*, which represents the attribute updates in the policy. This element includes a number of *<AttrUpdate>* elements to specify each update action. Each *<AttrUpdate>* element also specifies when the update must be performed through the clause *UpdateTime* which can have one of the following values: *pre* (*pre-update*), *on* (*on-update*), and *post* (*post-update*). U-XACML language, please refer to [5].

3.4 PPL

PPL (Primelife but also Privacy Policy Language) is another XACML extension that allows to express policies for personal data processing, also including specific credential capabilities. PPL directives refers to access and usage control security properties. In particular it was designed for modelling personal data exchanges between data subjects and data controller, according to definitions provided by the European Data Protection Directive 95/46/EC, very similar to those stated in GDPR. PPL adopts the "sticky policy" approach: a piece of data gets associated, for example in a bundle, to its policy and they form a unit, an atomic entity. Such approach is applied to regulate the exchange between a data subject and controller: once personal data handling terms (the "terms of use") have been agreed between the two actors, such terms become a PPL policy that gets associated to the personal data given to the data controller. By definition, this policy cannot be detached from the data and regulates each usage of the piece of information. One notable aspect is the expression of usage control obligations. Normally in XACML, an obligation must be fulfilled by the actor that issues an access request. In PPL, they are defined as *"a promise made by a data controller to a data subject in relation to the handling of his/her personal data. The data controller is expected to fulfill the promise by executing and/or preventing a specific action after a particular event, e.g., time, and optionally under certain conditions"* [1]. PPL obligations may also apply to data processors, i.e., entities authorized by data controller to carry out computations on the data, under the responsibility of the data controller.

PPL obligations are expressed as in the following Eq. 5:

$$\textbf{Obligation} = Do \ \textbf{Action} \ when \ \textbf{Trigger} \qquad (5)$$

where

$$\textbf{Trigger} = \textbf{Event} \wedge \textbf{Condition} \qquad (6)$$

Obligations modeled in this way may or may not be dependent on access requests and therefore, they differ from access control obligations. They can be used to express a data retention period, e.g., data must be deleted by the data controller after 30 days from their submission. As shown in [7], triggers may also depend on contextual conditions like geographic location.

4 Our Data Protection Approach

Our data protection approach can be described as follows:

- specification of data protection requirements using a controlled natural language, with CNL4DSA
- transformation of CNL4DSA directives in UPOL enforceable control policy
- association of the control policy to a piece of information
- enforcement of the policy by a dedicated UPOL-enabled mechanism

As part of our contribution, we propose a reference software architecture for the materialization of our approach. The present section describes our architecture.

Once a data subject and controller agree on usage terms, they can express them using CNL4DSA, for example by means of an authoring tool, such as, the one briefly described in [9]. CNL4DSA terms can also be defined with a negotiation-less model: the CNL4DSA terms may represent the requirements of a subject and a controller can only decide to accept them to process the personal data, or the terms with which a controller can process a subject's data. The enforcement of CNL4DSA directives (i.e., the DSA) relies on their transformation in a UPOL policy. Such transformation, for its complexity, is most effective if performed automatically: to this extent, we foresaw a mapping function implemented by a specific software component, the *DSA Mapper*, and this main functionality is described in Sect. 4.1. As already mentioned, the UPOL language originates from XAMCL but adding statefulness to its interaction model. To cater for that, a number of contributions are proposed, in terms of reference architecture and language syntax, explained respectively in Sect. 4.2 and by means of an example in Sect. 5.

As a first step, we describe the mapping function we implement to automatically transform rules expressed in CNL4DSA (that is, a simple controlled natural language) to the UPOL language. Then, we describe the UPOL reference architecture and a comparison with the existing UCON_ABC.

4.1   Mapping Function

As mentioned, the mapping function allows to convert DSA statements into UPOL directives. The software component in charge of its implementation, the DSA Mapper, takes as input am .xml file representing a set of DSA rules and translates them in the UPOL language. The outcome of this tool is an enforceable policy, that will be evaluated at each request to process the associated piece of information.

An initial formulation for a mapping function has been presented in [11]. In the current and newest version, presented in the following, we have updated and simplified the process. In order to describe the mapping function, it is useful to recall that CNL4DSA has been developed considering the design of XACML constructs, thus it is possible to identify in each CNL4DSA statement the main XACML elements:

- A subject element is the entity requesting the access. A subject has one or more attributes.
- The resource element is a data, service or system component. A resource has one or more attributes.
- An action element defines the type of access requested on the resource. Actions have one or more attributes.
- An environment element can optionally provide additional information.

The mapping function implemented by the DSA Mapper is the results of two sub-functions: the *mapping function* that considers all the rules in a DSA as policies of a policy set, as it is defined in the standard XACML, and translate it in UPOL language, and the *BuildUPOL* function that is able to build an actual enforceable UPOL policy starting from the single policies output of the mapper function.

The mapping function takes each basic fragment $\langle s, a, o \rangle$, where s identifies the subject, a the action, and o the object (mainly the data which the DSA is referred to), and puts each of this element into a UPOL policy by using the appropriate tag, i.e., $\langle subject \rangle \ldots \langle \backslash subject \rangle$, $\langle action \rangle \ldots \langle \backslash action \rangle$, and $\langle resources \rangle \ldots \langle \backslash resources \rangle$, respectively. These represent the elements of the UPOL target ($\langle Target \rangle$). All the contextual conditions expressed in CNL4DSA are mapped into the tag $\langle Condition \rangle$. It is worth noting that even the attributes related to both subject and resources are mapped into the tag $\langle Condition \rangle$, in such a way to put all the contextual conditions under the same tag. This choice was made because the executable policy structure reflects the one of the CNL4DSA statement in which the conditions on subject, object, and environment are specified all together into the context.

The BuildUPOL function takes in input the output of the mapping function, i.e., the UPOL specification of each rule composing the DSA, to build a valid UPOL policy. The *BuildUPOL* functionality is in charge of building the UPOL policy skeleton, that represents the constant part of the UPOL policy. It is made of:

- the header of the policy comprehensive of:
  - the namespace,
  - the XML schema (version 3)
  - name of the schema (XACML 3)
  - name of the schema according to which the UPOL has to be validated
  - the policy ID
  - the combining algorithm (fist-applicable)
  - version of the policy
- Three specific tags:
  - $\langle description \rangle$, e.g., $\langle xacml : Description \rangle$ UPOL Policy $\langle /xacml : Description \rangle$.
  - $\langle DSAID \rangle$, e.g., $\langle upol : DSA\_id \rangle$ DSA-d75b9cbf-5893-4779-baf9 $\langle /upol : DSA\_id \rangle$.
  - $\langle Target \rangle$, that is empty because each rule has its own target specification with also the conditions (see below), e.g., $\langle xacml : Target/ \rangle$.
- Default deny rule
- All the rules derived from the DSA. Note that rules are inserted into the UPOL policy. According to the choice of applying the "first-applicable" combining algorithm, the order in which rules are inserted into the UPOL policy can follow a strategy. For example business reasons, regulations, personal preferences.

4.2   UPOL Architecture

The UPOL reference architecture is depicted in Fig. 1. The figure shows how the UPOL architecture interacts with a business software that involves the processing of personal information, to offer its data protection functionalities. This business software has at two main stakeholders of interest:

- a *Data Owner* that submits her/his personal data together with a DSA in the controlled natural language CNL4DSA
- a *Requestor* that uses the functionalities of the business software and needs to process a piece of information from the Data Owner.

The business software is only represented in its essential parts for the interaction with the UPOL architecture:

- a *Storage* for storing personal information
- a component that is at the same time part of the business software and the UPOL architecture, the PEP (later described).

UPOL originates from the XACML standard thus it inherits the XACML main components for its reference architecture, however extending their functionalities:

PEP. Policy Enforcement Point is part of a software system that intercepts any requests to perform security relevant actions, thus triggering the authorization decision process and enforces the results. In our UPOL design, it is also in charge of retrieving the *sticky policy bundle* from the business software storage (or data base) and to submit it to the PAP for reading the contained policy.

CH. Context Handler coordinates the communication and information exchange among the components of the enforcement engine in order to execute the policy evaluation process triggered by the PEP. In order to deal with UPOL policies, this component has been enabled to manage also the policy re-evaluation process which, instead, is triggered by a PIP and involves also the SM component.

PDP. Policy Decision Point evaluates authorization requests according to the applicable UPOL policies.

PAP. Policy Administration Point is in charge of retrieving applicable policies for PDP evaluation. It is an important component especially when adopting the sticky policy approach, as it allows to read the policy included in a bundle to permit its evaluation against the PEP request. It does so by complementing the request, issued by the PEP, extracting the UPOL policy from the bundle, and sending it to the CH.

PIP. Policy Information Point(s) retrieves all the necessary attributes of any actor (subject, action, resource, environment) for enabling policy evaluation. In order to evaluate UPOL policies, PIPs have been enabled also to detect when the values of the attributes change for the purpose of calling the CH to trigger the policy re-evaluation process.

The UPOL architecture also requires specific components, that are:

SM. Session Manager is responsible for tracking the usage sessions: a session is established once an authorization request is permitted and the associated operation is started. The session captures information about the operation by storing all relevant meta-data. It allows the execution of the continuous authorization phase, because it determines which sessions need a re-evaluation of authorization policies as a consequence of an attribute mutation, thus enabling the PDP to operate continuously.

OE. Obligation Engine is responsible for keeping track of obligation triggers and executing the associated action(s).

MAP. The DSA Mapper is responsible for the transformation of a DSA expressed in CNL4DSA format into a UPOL policy that is then associated to a piece of information in the sticky policy bundle, and stored in the business software storage according to its logic. Such bundle is subsequently handled by the PAP when the piece of information is to be used in order to extract such UPOL policy.

In our UPOL architecture, CH also implements an information exchange between OE and SM, to enable the mentioned session obligations to be triggered. The UPOL architecture is instrumental to the implementation of its new obligations; they go beyond the capabilities of XACML/U-XACML and PPL.

Table 1 details the different types of obligations supported by our architecture: those defined by XACML/U-XACML, PPL and obviously, the newly defined UPOL obligations.

The first row describes U-XACML obligations: they derive directly from the standard XACML obligations and they are associated to an access request. They

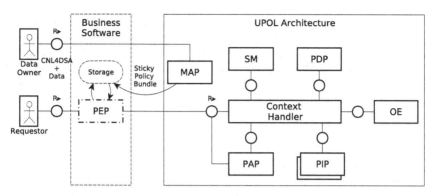

Fig. 1. The UPOL Reference Architecture, including the Mapper component to transform CNL4DSA documents in UPOL policies. Information can be provisioned by the Data Owner to the business software that uses the Mapper to obtain a sticky policy bundle to be persisted. When a Requestor asks for a resource, the PEP issues a request to the framework, in cooperation with the PAP that extracts the UPOL policy from that resource bundle.

Table 1. Obligations part of an UPOL policy, as presented in [6].

Obligation type	Reference event	Obligation action type	Obligation enforcement
U-XACML pre- or post-obligations	At the moment of the request	Punctual actions	PEP
PPL obligations	Dependent or independent from access request	Punctual actions	Trusted third party (through UPOL Mechanism)
UPOL session obligations	At the beginning, end or during data consumption	Punctual or continuous actions	Trusted third party (through UPOL Mechanism) or PEP

normally prescribe actions executed pre- or or post- an access request ("punctual actions" in the table) and for this reason, they are normally referred as pre- or post-obligations.

Second row is about PPL obligations. Differently from U-XACML, PPL obligations are not (necessarily) associated to an access request (see Formula 5). Their definition relies on triggers (see Formula 6) that may encompass a variety of situations. Expiration of a retention period but also proximity to a specific geographic location [7] are just initial examples of possible triggers. By definition, the enforcement of PPL obligations must take place reliably and certainly. Considering this requirement, PPL states that a trusted third party, different from Data Subject and Data Controller and trusted by both actors, is in charge of automatic obligation enforcement.

Lastly, the third row is about UPOL obligations. They can be defined using the notion of session: UPOL defines three new event types *StartAccess*, *EndAccess* and *RevokeAccess* that are part of UPOL triggers. Therefore, UPOL obligations consider the different stages of a usage session work-flow to prescribe the execution of specific actions. For example, a UPOL obligation can start at the beginning of a data consumption operation and terminate at its end. We recall that a (UPOL) session as managed by the Session Manager is created when an access request is approved and the requestor (or an agent) notifies the beginning of a resource consumption thus generating a session event *StartAccess*. *EndAccess* obligations are triggered when the requestor interrupts a resource consumption operation. *RevokeAccess* on the contrary occurs when a policy violation is detected and a session is interrupted by initiative of the UPOL mechanism (i.e., by initiative of the PDP).

As just presented, UPOL obligations differentiate from other obligations as they can be used to execute continuous actions; they result effective for example in streaming scenarios: showing banners during a video streaming, or to influence Big Data streaming analytics computation. One last consideration about the enforcement actor. XACML/U-XACML obligations are normally enforced at the requestor's end, by the PEP. PPL obligations, instead, are enforced by a third party (for example, a cloud provider) trusted by data subject and data controller. UPOL obligations are triggered by the Obligation Engine run by a trusted third party but they may be also executed by the PEP, according to the associated actions.

4.3   Comparison with the UCON$_{ABC}$ Model

The UCON model defined by Park and Sandhu in [13] presents a number of innovative features which enhances it with respect to traditional access control models, namely:

1. the factors taken into account to carry out the decision process, besides traditional authorizations (A), include also obligations (B) and conditions (C).
2. the continuity of the decision: the policy can state that the access control decision have to be made when the access request is received (like in traditional access control, *pre*), and/or have to be performed continuously during object consumption (typical trait of UCON, *ongoing*).
3. mutability of attributes: are subject or object attributes changing following to a decision? and when? This originates: *immutable, pre − update, ongoing − update* or *post − update* models respectively for models where no attribute changes are foreseen, updates takes place before, during or after an access takes place.

We claim that the UPOL language proposed in this paper is capable of implementing the typical features of the Usage Control model previously listed, by leveraging:

1. the native XACML constructs.
2. the constructs brought in by U-XAMCL.
3. the specific extensions offered by U-XACML combined with PPL: *pre* and *ongoing* conditions can originate specific events to trigger the newly defined UPOL obligations (*synchronous* and *asynchronous*).

Moreover, if used in conjunction with the sticky policy approach, UPOL spans its scope beyond access and usage control, as UPOL obligations can be triggered also without the reception of an access request. Such functionality is particularly helpful in cases like GDPR's data minimisation requirement, where a piece of data may reside on the Data Controller cloud only for a limited amount of time. Provided that a trusted third party runs a UPOL-aware enforcement mechanism to control the UPOL-regulated data on the cloud, such requirement may be fulfilled.

5   Use Case

Let us consider a simple e-commerce scenario involving three main actors: a company, *ACME*, that plays the role of the data controller, as it is defined in the GDRP, a customer of ACME, referred as *Customer*, that is the data subject, and a third-party, a *Marketing* service, that is able to produce profiles of customers and suggest marketing campaigns to ACME. The use case is depicted in Fig. 2. The customer submits a set of personal data, such as, address, credit card details, etc., needed by ACME to process her/his order. The treatment of such personal data is regulated by a DSA expressed in CNL4DSA, stating precisely data controller's rights and obligations as well as the customer's policies on her data. Data submission and consent recording take place through a specific service, called "Usage Control Service" (the proposed contribution, implementing the UPOL reference architecture) in the figure, that:

- associates to the personal data, using the sticky policy model, a UPOL policy, output of the DSA Mapper, that states in enforceable format the access and usage terms defined in the Data Sharing Agreement;
- enforces the UPOL policy upon incoming personal data access requests;
- monitors usage of personal data, through interactions with the ACME information systems, enforcing continuous authorizations as well as usage control obligations.

When the third party uses the ACME information systems, they interact with the enforcement system, creating requests to access the protected resources. Information systems cater for a number of attributes that allow their requests to be evaluated by the enforcement system, as well as providing indications about the beginning and the end of information processing operations. The interaction protocol between systems and enforcement also allows the interruption of an operation, in case of changes in the evaluation conditions.

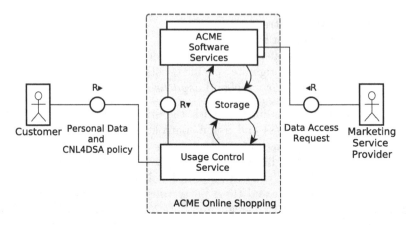

Fig. 2. An e-commerce use case, extended from [6].

It is out of the scope of the current work to include a detailed analysis of the interaction protocol and of the architecture of the enforcement system. Focusing instead on the policy expression, it can be modeled as a (sticky) UPOL *Policy* where a *Rule* with *Target: subject role = marketing-third-party, contractor = ACME* may access the data. The UPOL representation of (part of) such policy can be found at Listing 1.1. Two conditions (*pre* and *ongoing*) control the geographic location of the subject, provided by the information systems, before and during the access in order to protect against data export clauses, GDPR Article 49 (the UPOL policy in Listing 1.1 actually shows only the ongoing condition, since the other is identical except for the value of *DecisionTime* that would be *pre* instead of *ongoing*). In CNL4DSA, these two conditions are expressed through a CNL4DSA context `hasLocation` in case of *pre* condition and `hasContinuosLocation` in case the context condition needs to be checked *ongoing*. We can model the notification obligation by means of session obligations, triggered by *StartAccess*, *EndAccess* and *RevokeAccess*. In this way, the beginning and the end of sessions can be recorded for future use. Last but not least, each access of the third-party will trigger an email notification to the data subject, in order to fully meet the transparent processing requirements. In CNL4DSA, this rule is expressed as an obligation composed fragment in which the simple fragment has as subject `system` and as action `notifyByEmail`. It might be worth noting that other accesses performed by the data controller (as the trigger of this obligation is on the fulfillment of the Rule that applies only on requestors with role=marketing-third-party) will not trigger such notification. Data minimization (with respect to retention directives) is also enforced by means of a specific obligation to delete the data associated to the policy after 3 months from the moment when the personal data is received.

Listing 1.1. UPOL Use Case.

```
1   <!-- DETAILS OMITTED -->
2   <Rule RuleId="Permission:Marketing-Third-Party" Effect="Permit">
3     <!-- XACML Target: ABAC check for attribute 'marketing-third-party'
        ↪ of requestor
4       in the authentication system, i.e. role == 'marketing-third-party'
        ↪ -->
5   <Target>
6   <AnyOf>
7   <AllOf>
8     <MatchMatchId="urn:oasis:names:tc:xacml:1.0:function:string-equal">
9     <AttributeValue DataType="http://www.w3.org/2001/XMLSchema#
        ↪ string">
10        marketing-third-party
11    </AttributeValue>
12    <AttributeDesignator
13     AttributeId="urn:oasis:names:tc:xacml:2.0:subject:role"
14     Category="urn:oasis:names:tc:xacml:1.0:subject-category:access-
        ↪ subject"
15     DataType="http://www.w3.org/2001/XMLSchema#string"
16     MustBePresent="false" />
17    </Match>
18    </AllOf>
19    </AnyOf>
20   </Target>
21
22    <!-- Continuous Authorization: requestor must be in EU to process the
        ↪ information -->
23   <upol:Condition DecisionTime="ongoing">
24    <!-- Standard condition definition (with DecisionTime="pre") is identical
        ↪ and thus omitted -->
25    <xacml:Apply FunctionId="urn:oasis:names:tc:xacml:1.0:function:string-
        ↪ equal">
26      <xacml:Apply FunctionId="urn:oasis:names:tc:xacml:1.0:function:string-
27       one-and-only">
28          <xacml:AttributeDesignator
29            AttributeId="urn:oasis:names:tc:xacml:1.0:subject:subject-
        ↪ location"
30            Category="urn:oasis:names:tc:xacml:1.0:subject-category:
31          access-subject"
32            DataType="http://www.w3.org/2001/XMLSchema#string"
33            MustBePresent="true">
34          </xacml:AttributeDesignator>
35      </xacml:Apply>
36      <xacml:AttributeValue DataType="http://www.w3.org/2001/
        ↪ XMLSchema#string">
37          EU</xacml:AttributeValue>
38    </xacml:Apply>
39   </upol:Condition>
40   <ob:ObligationsSet xmlns:ob="http://www.primelife.eu/ppl/obligation">
41    <ob:Obligation>
42    <ob:TriggersSet>
43     <!-- UPOL Session Obligations: trigger on each session event if
```

```
44    evaluation result is "Permit"-->
45        <upol:TriggerRuleEvaluated FulfillOn="StartAccess" Effect="Permit
          ↪ " />
46        <upol:TriggerRuleEvaluated FulfillOn="EndAccess" Effect="Permit" /
          ↪ >
47        <upol:TriggerRuleEvaluated FulfillOn="RevokeAccess" Effect="Permit"
          ↪ />
48      </ob:TriggersSet>
49
50      <!-- Action : notify data subject to record an access for future
        ↪ reference -->
51      <ob:ActionNotifyDataSubject>
52        <ob:Media>Mail</ob:Media>
53        <ob:Address>customer.email@email.provider</ob:Address>
54      </ob:ActionNotifyDataSubject>
55    </ob:Obligation>
56    <!-- Obligation: delete after 3 months from information received -->
57    <ob:Obligation>
58      <ob:TriggersSet>
59      <TriggerAtTime>
60        <!-- the trigger is set in 3 months time-->
61        <MaxDelay>
62          <Duration>P0Y3M0DT0H0M0S</Duration>
63        </MaxDelay>
64      </TriggerAtTime>
65      </ob:TriggersSet>
66      <ob:DenyAllAndDeleteNow/>
67    </ob:Obligation>
68    </ob:ObligationsSet>
69  </Rule>
70  <!-- DETAILS OMITTED -->
```

6 Conclusion

The attention given by online service operators to data protection, especially for personal information, is constantly growing. Such trend can be explained also by some recent changes in the legal framework that bring new requirements for achieving full compliance. For example, the EU General Data Privacy Regulation require significant changes in the way entities collect and process personal data of EU citizens, anywhere in the world, but similar requirements are also requested for operating in markets like Australia, China and Russia.

In this work we presented our proposal to address such new requirements. It consists of an approach to data protection that uses data protection policies to achieve such compliance, using as technical means, a combination of access and usage control measures. Our approach foresees to facilitate the production and human understandability of the data protection policies, by allowing stakeholders to express them using a controlled natural language, subsequently transformed into a new and automatically enforceable policy. To this extent, we developed a new policy language, UPOL, as part of our commitments in the EU

FP7 Coco Cloud project. Its main aim is to obtain a unique language that is powerful enough to express legal, security, and privacy constraints in automatically enforceable policies, focussed on the sharing and management of (personal or otherwise sensitive) data over the Cloud. Now, our development continues in the EU H2020 C3ISP project, extending data protection also to Big Data analytics scenario, especially considering cyber security information sharing.

Our initial results count the implementation of a UPOL mechanism, capable of enforcing automatically obligations as trusted element by data subjects, processors and controllers. We managed to define UPOL policies that go towards the fulfillment of some data controller obligations as stated by the GDPR. We are currently working towards structuring and extending more our language, in order to support more data protection use cases, looking at personal data but also at more in general, confidential information especially in the cyber security domain.

Acknowledgements. This work was partly supported by EC-funded projects Coco Cloud [grant no. 610853] and by C3ISP [grant no. 700294].

References

1. Ardagna, C.A., et al.: Primelife policy language. In: W3C Workshop on Access Control Application Scenarios. W3C (2009)
2. Caimi, C., Gambardella, C., Manea, M., Petrocchi, M., Stella, D.: Legal and technical perspectives in data sharing agreements definition. In: Berendt, B., Engel, T., Ikonomou, D., Le Métayer, D., Schiffner, S. (eds.) APF 2015. LNCS, vol. 9484, pp. 178–192. Springer, Cham (2016). https://doi.org/10.1007/978-3-319-31456-3_10
3. Carniani, E., D'Arenzo, D., Lazouski, A., Martinelli, F., Mori, P.: Usage control on cloud systems. Fut. Gener. Comput. Syst. **63**, 37–55 (2016). https://doi.org/10.1016/j.future.2016.04.010
4. Coco Cloud Consortium: Coco Cloud website (2016). http://www.coco-cloud.eu
5. Colombo, M., Lazouski, A., Martinelli, F., Mori, P.: A proposal on enhancing XACML with continuous usage control features. In: Desprez, F., Getov, V., Priol, T., Yahyapour, R. (eds.) Grids, P2P and Services Computing, pp. 133–146. Springer, Boston (2010). https://doi.org/10.1007/978-1-4419-6794-7_11
6. Di Cerbo, F., Martinelli, F., Matteucci, I., Mori, P.: Towards a declarative approach to stateful and stateless usage control for data protection. In: Proceedings of the 14th International Conference on Web Information Systems and Technologies, WEBIST 2018, Seville, Spain, 18–20 September 2018, pp. 308–315 (2018). https://doi.org/10.5220/0006962503080315
7. Di Cerbo, F., Some, D.F., Gomez, L., Trabelsi, S.: PPL v2.0: uniform data access and usage control on cloud and mobile. In: Matteucci, I., Mori, P., Petrocchi, M. (eds.) 1st IEEE/ACM International Workshop on TEchnical and LEgal aspects of data pRIvacy and SEcurity, TELERISE 2015, Florence, Italy, 18 May 2015, pp. 2–7. IEEE Computer Society (2015). https://doi.org/10.1109/TELERISE.2015.9
8. European Parliament and Council: Regulation (EU) 2016/679 of the European Parliament and of the Council (General Data Protection Regulation) (2016). Accessed 27 Apr 2016. http://goo.gl/LfwxGe

9. Gambardella, C., Matteucci, I., Petrocchi, M.: Data sharing agreements: how to glue definition, analysis and mapping together. ERCIM News **106**, 28–29 (2016). http://ercim-news.ercim.eu/en106/special/data-sharing-agreements-how-to-glue-definition-analysis-and-mapping-together

10. Lazouski, A., Martinelli, F., Mori, P.: A prototype for enforcing usage control policies based on XACML. In: Fischer-Hübner, S., Katsikas, S., Quirchmayr, G. (eds.) TrustBus 2012. LNCS, vol. 7449, pp. 79–92. Springer, Heidelberg (2012). https://doi.org/10.1007/978-3-642-32287-7_7

11. Matteucci, I., Petrocchi, M., Sbodio, M.L.: Cnl4dsa: a controlled natural language for data sharing agreements. In: Proceedings of the 2010 ACM Symposium on Applied Computing SAC 2010, pp. 616–620. ACM, New York (2010). https://doi.org/10.1145/1774088.1774218. http://doi.acm.org/10.1145/1774088.1774218

12. OASIS: eXtensible Access Control Markup Language (XACML) Version 3.0 (2010)

13. Park, J., Sandhu, R.: The UCON ABC usage control model. ACM Trans. Inf. Syst. Secur. (TISSEC) **7**(1), 128–174 (2004)

14. Pearson, S., Casassa Mont, M.: Sticky policies: an approach for managing privacy across multiple parties. Computer **44**(9), 60–68 (2011)

15. Trabelsi, S., Njeh, A., Bussard, L., Neven, G.: PPl engine: a symmetric architecture for privacy policy handling. In: W3C Workshop on Privacy and Data Usage Control, vol. 4 (2010)

16. Zhang, X., Parisi-Presicce, F., Sandhu, R., Park, J.: Formal model and policy specification of usage control. ACM Trans. Inf. Syst. Secur. **8**(4), 351–387 (2005). https://doi.org/10.1145/1108906.1108908. http://doi.acm.org/10.1145/1108906.1108908

IUPTIS: Fingerprinting Profile Webpages in a Dynamic and Practical DPI Context

Mariano Di Martino[1(✉)] , Pieter Robyns[1] , Peter Quax[2] ,
and Wim Lamotte[1]

[1] Hasselt University/tUL - Expertise Center for Digital Media, Hasselt, Belgium
{mariano.dimartino,pieter.robyns,wim.lamotte}@uhasselt.be
[2] Hasselt University/tUL/Flanders Make - Expertise Center for Digital Media,
Hasselt, Belgium
peter.quax@uhasselt.be

Abstract. In this paper, we propose an extended overview of a novel webpage fingerprinting technique 'IUPTIS' that allows an adversary to identify webpage profiles in an encrypted HTTPS traffic trace. Our approach works by identifying sequences of image resources, uniquely attributed to each webpage. Assumptions of previous state-of-the-art methods are reduced by developing an approach that does not depend on the browser utilized. Additionally, it outperforms previous methods by allowing webpages to be dynamic in content and permitting a limited number of browser and CDN-cached resources. These easy-to-use properties make it viable to apply our method in DPI frameworks where performance is crucial. With practical experiments on social media platforms such as Pinterest and DeviantArt, we show that IUPTIS is an accurate and robust technique to fingerprint profile webpages in a realistic scenario. To conclude, we propose several defenses that are able to mitigate IUPTIS in privacy-enhanced tools such as Tor.

Keywords: Webpage fingerprinting · Social networks · Privacy · Traffic analysis

1 Introduction

Identifying Internet users is often the core business of large social media networks, advertising agencies and internet service providers (ISPs). Collecting this personal information is useful to construct user profiles in order to provide mass targeted advertisements. However, in the last 5 years, the businesses in question have come under scrutiny by the public, due to the way they handle the extracted information of their users. As a response, the research community has developed frameworks and tools to limit the leakages of such personal information in the form of ad-blockers [23] and hardened browsers [36]. It is clear that such businesses are constantly looking for novel techniques that are able to bypass these limitations, thus keeping the impact on their core business model to

© Springer Nature Switzerland AG 2019
M. J. Escalona et al. (Eds.): WEBIST 2018, LNBIP 372, pp. 99–124, 2019.
https://doi.org/10.1007/978-3-030-35330-8_6

a bare minimum. With a similar goal, we have cyber investigation departments and commercialized intrusion detection systems, that have expressed concerns with the steady rise of encryption on the Internet [18]. Tracking down criminal Internet actors such as malware authors or child predators was previously possible by utilizing Deep Packet Inspection (DPI) software to monitor and analyze network traffic. Nowadays, developing traffic classification algorithms to identify users or systems is is a considerable burden on DPI tools due to the large amount of encrypted network traffic on the Internet. In general, network forensics is a demanding field that requires new techniques to be able to cope with the widespread use of encrypted protocols.

In the late 90s, pioneers have shown that encrypted tunnels such as SSL can leak information that is critical for the construction of fingerprinting techniques, such as packet sizes and timing [8,40]. However, attacks based on these techniques were not feasible on a large scale. In late 2000, social networks have grown in popularity which quickly led to a collection of personal information given by the end users themselves. Due to the recent strict regulations, (such as the GDPR [17]) that have been put in place, the method of extracting personal information has shifted back towards more covert approaches, such as fingerprinting, where the explicit input from the end user is not necessary and detection is nearly impossible [35]. The concepts applied in fingerprinting techniques have also given rise to companies and government organizations that combine the analysis of public and intercepted data [2,19,37]. Regardless whether or not these analyses are legal, they are actively being used for predicting social media influence [28], personalized advertisements, assessing financial and health conditions [14] and forensic science [15]. However, additional encryption frameworks or tools such as Tor exist and can be (partially) utilized to protect the end user against these exposures. Despite their valuable capabilities, the performance of for instance, Tor networks, are suboptimal due to the bandwidth-hungry defenses and the long route that the data has to travel, to reach its destination. Therefore, when compared to users that use HTTPS only, the Tor network or other protocols that enhance privacy are adopted by a significantly lower number of users. This reminds us to focus ourselves on protocols and frameworks that are widely deployed and thus utilized by the average Internet user. Moreover, several studies have explored *website fingerprinting* (WFP) over various encrypted layers and tunnels [20,21,29,33,34] and several countermeasures have been developed that defend the end user against such attacks [4,13,34]. Juarez et al. [24] have shown that modern WFP attacks often have unpractical assumptions about the adversary or end user and therefore, limits the practicality of such attacks in a realistic environment. Hence in this paper, we propose an extended version of a HTTPS webpage fingerprinting technique called IUPTIS[1] that infers the webpage of an individual profile by finding a sequence of images in an encrypted network traffic trace, unique to each profile. Our method improves upon the practicality of previous work by introducing parameters that can be fine-tuned according to the adversary model and the targeted webplatform. Browser caching, dynamic

---

[1] IUPTIS stands for 'Identifying User Profiles Through Image Sequences'.

webpages and the generation of a single fingerprint per profile for all browsers and versions is incorporated in these parameters and thus can be balanced with the precision and sensitivity of our technique. We specifically focus on a practical attack in a realistic scenario for traffic communicated over HTTPS, without additional encryption tunnels such as Tor. To quantify the value of our attack, we have conducted an experiment on three popular online platforms while accomplishing favorable results.

We summarize the key elements of our original WFP attack [12]:

- A novel HTTPS webpage fingerprinting attack that infers profile webpages of an online platform by searching for a unique sequence of images that are associated to that online profile, in a network traffic trace.
- Our attack introduces a technique that integrates the ability for the end user to enable browser caching and utilizes different browsers by establishing parameters that can be fine-tuned according to the intended model of the end user and online platform. Additionally, it also takes care of Content Distribution Networks (CDN) inserted between the targeted platform and attacker. This directly relaxes numerous of the assumptions in previous state-of-the-art methods [24].
- We can perform our attack in an open world scenario without fingerprinting a selection of unmonitored webpages as was realized in previous work [20,29, 33,40].
- We show that, unlike previous work has claimed [33,40], dynamic webpages that undergo frequent changes such as social profile pages *can* be fingerprinted with promising results.
- In the context of the adversary model, three experiments on popular online platforms are performed to demonstrate the effectiveness of our method. Experiments on online platforms with similar properties were not yet explored in previous state-of-the-art techniques.
- To reduce the impact on the privacy of the end users, defenses have been proposed that are able to mitigate an IUPTIS attack in a realistic environment.
- The source code and dataset of the experiment, is provided to the research community.

In this paper, we first discuss the related work that has led to the development of our WFP attack. In Sect. 3, we introduce our intended adversary model in which we can successfully perform our IUPTIS attack and compare its abilities with several state-of-the-art techniques. In the next section, we provide in-depth details of the inner workings of our WFP method. To quantify the practicality of our technique, we show 3 experiments on popular online platforms (Pinterest, DeviantArt and Hotels.com) and discuss our findings in Sect. 4. To conclude our paper in Sects. 5 and 6, we examine existing countermeasures that are able to mitigate our attack in a Tor network and discuss future work that might enhance the overall performance.

2   Related Work

Early work have shown that it is feasible to fingerprint webpages over HTTPS by taking the size of web objects into account [8,40]. Nonetheless, some of the assumptions provided in these works, such as one TCP connection per web object, are not valid anymore in current modern browsers [34]. The introduction of classifiers to infer webpages over the SSL protocol [27] has lead to the construction of Hidden Markov models to utilize the link structure of a website in combination with supplementary features such as the sizes and order of HTTPS web objects to deduce the browsing path of the end user [6,31]. Furthermore, the ability to fingerprint webpages over encrypted tunnels such as SSH and Tor has been researched extensively [21,29,33,34].

Recent work and currently a state-of-the-art technique to fingerprint HTTPS webpages (originally developed for Tor hidden services) is k-fingerprinting [20]. Their work extends a previous approach [26] and is also suitable over HTTPS. The classification of webpages is implemented using random forests and their experiment produces a TPR of 87% with a world size of 7000 unmonitored HTTPS webpages and 55 monitored HTTPS webpages by using the ordering, timing and size of TCP packets without the need to identify the actual web objects. Nevertheless, defenses against WFP attacks have been designed to reduce or completely nullify the precision and sensitivity of these experiments. Different padding methods have been evaluated to avoid the possibility of selecting packet size as a main feature [13]. Specifically designed for HTTPS, HTTPOS is a defense in the form of a client-side proxy which implements several countermeasures to make it difficult for an adversary to use features such as timing, flow and size [30]. Their defense uses the HTTP Range header to request parts of the HTTP content multiple times instead of requesting the entire content at once. Furthermore, it injects junk data to the content in order to cover up the real traffic data. A countermeasure named Camouflage [34] is a method to confuse WFP attacks by randomly requesting existing dummy webpages during the request of a legit webpage coordinated by the end user. Such mitigation has the advantage of explicitly generating false positives and is generally easy to incorporate in existing client-side proxies. Other defenses are much more deceptive such as "Traffic Morphing" [45], in that they provide a theoretical approach to transform the distribution of packets of a traffic trace to another distribution in such manner that it resembles a different webpage. More recently, a defense called CS-BuFLO and an improved version has been devised [4,5,13]. This defense transforms a stream of original TCP packets to a continuous flow of fixed size packets to reduce the variance in timing and size of the original packets. Akin to the aforementioned defense, 'Walkie-Talkie' is a similar approach [42] where they greatly improve upon bandwidth and practicality by devising a method that sends packets in short bursts and is currently regarded as a state-of-the-art defense. More recently, instead of manually selecting features to design WFP attacks, deep learning algorithms have been utilized to develop a process that allows an adversary to automatically select features [38]. To conclude this section, we refer to an extensive and critical evaluation of the various WFP attacks and their countermeasures [24].

3 IUPTIS: Identifying User Profiles Through Image Sequences

3.1 Adversary Model

In the interest of a practical and reliable WFP attack, we would like to lay out some assumptions that are made:

– The adversary has a network traffic trace from the end user during the period in which they navigated to the webpage profile. Such traffic trace can be extracted with any passive MiTM, almost always incorporated in DPI frameworks.
– The recorded communication between the targeted online platform and the end user is handled by the HTTP/1.1 protocol encapsulated in TLS records. In other words, the end user is visiting the profile webpage over the HTTPS protocol.
– Each individual *profile* page may be accessed by an individual URL where distinctive and unique images are the main source of information on the webpage of that profile. A profile is associated with a person (e.g. social network pages) or unique entity (e.g. hotel pages). The images on each webpage profile have to be large enough (>8 Kb) and usually larger than other resources (for instance, stylesheets) on the same webpage, to achieve acceptable results.
– The headers of the TCP and IP layer of the traffic trace are not encrypted and thus may be analyzed by the adversary. Background traffic (noise) from other websites or protocols is therefore trivial to filter out, since they will not match the IP or domain name of the targeted server.

Adversaries that adhere to these assumptions come in many forms. Social Wi-Fi providers and government agencies may essentially hold a passive MitM position and can therefore apply these techniques. Moreover, the introduction of WiFi4EU [43] will boost the number of accessible Wi-Fi access points and in turn, increase the attack surface to perform MitM attacks. In a similar fashion, social networks such as Facebook may provide VPN tools like Onavo [35] that still have access to HTTPS payloads with the ability to correlate the data with their own collection of online profiles.

3.2 Fingerprinting Images

Profile pages often contain several images that are uploaded by the owner of the page. These images are often the largest part of the page content and are most likely unique over the whole platform. The uniqueness of these images is very convenient to select as a feature for WFP attacks. When visiting such a profile page in a browser over HTTPS, the images will be downloaded in several TCP connections. As we are using HTTP over TLS, the actual content of the images is encrypted and thus not visible. However, the HTTP request and response sizes are not encrypted and can therefore be calculated easily [8,29]. Extracting the absolute raw size of each image contained in a HTTP response is not trivial due to the addition of HTTP headers, which are often dynamic in length. HTTP headers are the largest overhead in size that we have to eliminate in order to get the absolute size of each image. However, it is possible to deterministically model the appearance of these headers in each request and response. For each image contained in a HTTP response, we formulate the following equation that defines the total size of such HTTP response:

$$\text{Out}_x = w_{\text{out}} + p_{\text{out}} + i_{\text{out}} \tag{1}$$

Here, w_{out} is the length of all HTTP headers (including the corresponding values) that are dependent on the webserver that issues the response to the browser. For instance, the header "Accept-Language" or "Server" is always added by the webserver (online platform) independent of the image that is requested or the browser that is used. Considering that we are targeting a specific webserver and leave out the presence of a *Content Distribution Network* (CDN) in the middle, the value of w_{out} can be calculated easily.

p_{out} is the length of all HTTP headers (including the corresponding values) that depend on the image requested. For instance, the "Content-Type" and "Content-Length" header can be different for each image requested from a given webserver and is independent of the browser that is used.

i_{out} is the length of the complete HTTP response body. In our case, this only contains the raw data of the image requested. In a similar fashion, we also formulate an equation that defines the total size of HTTP request of a web object image:

$$\text{In}_x = p_{\text{in}} + b_{\text{in}} \tag{2}$$

Similar to the response, the variable p_{in} is the total length of all HTTP headers that are dependent of each requested image. Examples are the GET path in the first request line and the "Referrer" header.

b_{in} is the length of all HTTP headers (including the corresponding values) that are dependent on the browser that issues the request. For instance, the "DNT" or "User-Agent" header may be different for each browser.

Since we would like to fingerprint webpage profiles based on the images that they contain, we have to determine the total size for each image. Then, based on the calculated values, we use the collection of all the images contained in a profile page to construct a fingerprint for the whole profile webpage.

We will extract the fingerprint of an image from the corresponding HTTP request and response sizes as follows:

$$\text{Img}_y = (\text{In}_x, \text{Out}_x) \tag{3}$$

To construct our fingerprint database for this preprocessing stage, we develop a fingerprint for each profile webpage x with n images where the approach is similar to the ordered sequence method [29]:

$$\text{Profile}_z = \langle (\text{Img}_0, \text{Img}_1, \ldots, \text{Img}_{n-1}, \text{Img}_n) \rangle \tag{4}$$

Unlike previous work [29], the order in which the images are added have no impact on the experimental results of our method.

A practical consideration that arises is the fact that the variable b_{in} is unknown and is most likely to be different for various browsers. It is therefore necessary to either figure out the browser that the end user is utilizing in order to estimate the variable [7,22] or to set the variable b_{in} to a fixed size. The latter option will result in a trade-off with a lower precision of the WFP attack as we will show in Sect. 4. Likewise, w_{out} may be hard to predict due to the variation of this variable within the same browser. More specifically, the usage of a CDN may introduce HTTP headers with irregular sizes, usually dependent on whether or not the requested image has been cached by the CDN. A possible solution for this concern is provided in Sect. 3.6 where we employ a single dimensional clustering method called 'Jenks optimization method'.

3.3 Constructing a Request/Response List

After our fingerprinting stage is finished, we have to build an ordered list of sizes that correspond to the HTTP requests and responses in our intercepted traffic trace, which we call a Request/response list (RRL).

A request/response list of length n is an ordered list that contains the timestamp of each HTTP request (T_n), the size of each HTTP request and HTTP response (request/response pair) *associated* with a web object image:

$$\text{RRL} = \langle (R_0, R_1, \ldots, R_{n-1}, R_n) \rangle \tag{5}$$

$$R_n = \langle (T_n, \text{Req}_n, \text{Resp}_n) \rangle \tag{6}$$

When the end user navigates to a profile webpage, several TCP connections to the webserver will download the resources located on that particular webpage. These resources consist of images, stylesheets, source files, etc. . . . Due to the encryption provided by HTTPS, an adversary cannot trivially identify the responses that contain images. Therefore, similar to the ordered sequence approach [29], we use the fair assumption that images are usually larger in size than other resources and filter out all other resources that are below a fixed threshold. Such threshold will effectively reduce the amount of noise associated with other resources. The value of this threshold is usually set to the fingerprinted image with the smallest size $(Resp_x)$. Other images (which we will also observe as noise) such as icons or banners are usually much smaller in size than the fingerprinted images and are often downloaded at the beginning or end of the HTML page. Interference of such noise with our method is therefore minimal.

3.4   Building a Profile Prediction List

At this stage, we have collected the necessary fingerprints and have constructed a RRL based on the intercepted traffic trace.

Subsequently, for each request/response pair (R) from our RRL, we evaluate whether this pair *matches* one or more Img_y fingerprints from any $\mathrm{Profile}_z$, where z denotes any fingerprinted profile and y denotes all image fingerprints from $\mathrm{Profile}_z$. The *matching* is performed i.f.f. the following equations hold:

$$\mathrm{Img}_y = (\mathrm{In}_w, \mathrm{Out}_w) \tag{7}$$

$$\mathrm{In}_w - \pi_{\mathrm{req}} < \mathrm{Req}_x < \mathrm{In}_w + \pi_{\mathrm{req}} \tag{8}$$

$$\mathrm{Out}_w - \pi_{\mathrm{resp}} < \mathrm{Resp}_x < \mathrm{Out}_w + \pi_{\mathrm{resp}} \tag{9}$$

In the equation above, we perform the matching if the request and response sizes lie within an interval defined by 2 newly introduced parameters, π_{req} and π_{resp}. Both parameters are defined as the statistical variance for respectively the request and response size and should be chosen with the intended platform and browser in mind. If the specific browser that is employed is known, b_{in} can be calculated to be very accurate and thus requires a low π_{req}. Similarly, π_{resp} depends on the accuracy of b_{out}. In the experiments discussed in Sect. 4, we show that a large π_{req} and π_{resp} are still sufficiently robust enough to achieve favorable results.

If the equations above (Eqs. 8 and 9) hold, the *matching* is then performed by passing the corresponding Req_x and Resp_x to construct a P_g^n which is finally appended to the *Profile Prediction List* (PPL):

$$P_g^n = \langle profileName, \epsilon_{\mathrm{req}}, \epsilon_{\mathrm{resp}} \rangle \tag{10}$$

$$\epsilon_{\mathrm{req}} = \mathrm{Req}_x - \mathrm{In}_w \tag{11}$$

$$\epsilon_{\mathrm{resp}} = \mathrm{Resp}_x - \mathrm{Out}_w \tag{12}$$

Subscript g denotes the index in the second dimension and superscript n denotes the index in the first dimension of the PPL. All elements in the PPL are chronologically ordered based on the timestamp of the matched request/response pair. The PPL is constructed as a 2D array with variable size in the second dimension. The first dimension defines each matched R element (ordered by the timestamp) and the second dimension defines all the newly constructed P_g^n:

$$\mathrm{PPL}[0] = \langle P_0^0, P_1^0, P_2^0, \ldots \rangle \tag{13}$$

$$\mathrm{PPL}[1] = \langle P_0^1, P_1^1, P_2^1, \ldots \rangle \tag{14}$$

$$\mathrm{PPL}[\ldots] = \langle P_0^{\cdots}, P_1^{\cdots}, P_2^{\cdots}, \ldots \rangle \tag{15}$$

$$\mathrm{PPL}[q] = \langle P_0^q, P_1^q, P_2^q, \ldots \rangle \tag{16}$$

In other words, for each intercepted request/response pair R_n (with a total of q pairs), we assign all image fingerprints (associated to a profile) that might belong to that pair and construct a P_g^n for each of them as shown in Fig. 1.

3.5   Finding a Valid Profile Sequence

After the creation of our PPL, we attempt to identify an uninterrupted sequence with length Φ in the PPL starting at any X such that $PPL[X]$, $PPL[X+1]$, $PPL[X+\ldots]$, $PPL[X+\Phi]$ in the sequence have respectively a P^X, P^{X+1}, $P^{X+\cdots}$, $P^{X+\Phi}$ such that they all have the same $profileName$:

$$P^X \in PPL[X] \tag{17}$$

$$P^{X+1} \in PPL[X+1] \tag{18}$$

$$P^{X+\cdots} \in PPL[X+\ldots] \tag{19}$$

$$P^{X+\Phi} \in PPL[X+\Phi] \tag{20}$$

$$profileName \in (P^X \cap P^{X+1} \cap P^{X+\cdots} \cap P^{X+\Phi}) \tag{21}$$

In other words, we have found a valid profile sequence if Φ request/response pairs in a row are all matched to at least one fingerprinted image of the same profile. We say that P^X, P^{X+1}, $P^{X+\cdots}$ and $P^{X+\Phi}$ form a valid sequence for that particular $profileName$. Multiple profile sequences may obviously exist. The introduction of the parameter Φ defines a balance between browser caching and resulting precision and sensitivity. When choosing this value, it's useful to look at the number of images that are exposed on each individual webpage. A large value for Φ will have a more accurate prediction but might reduce the effectiveness of the attack. For instance, if a profile webpage only has 2 images, then a Φ below 3 is necessary to identify that particular webpage. More importantly, the parameter is also utilized to reduce the impact of browser cached images. For instance, if the end user is visiting the webpage of a $Profile_z$ which has 10 images where 5 of those are already cached by the browser, we can still set Φ to a value below 6 in order to successfully find a valid sequence.

3.6   Evaluating a Profile Sequence

For a small collection of image fingerprints, the resulting profile sequences are already a valuable prediction. However, this is insufficient if multiple sequences for the same time range exist or when the variance between the fingerprinted images is too small. Therefore, we have to exclude profile sequences that have very different values for ϵ_{req} and ϵ_{resp}. The exclusion is accomplished by calculating the standard deviation σ_{req} and σ_{resp} over respectively all ϵ_{req} and ϵ_{resp} in that particular sequence. The mean over all ϵ_{req} and ϵ_{resp} for a sequence can be large if respectively b_{in} and w_{out} are inaccurate or unknown even though it should not influence our result and for this reason, the standard deviation is utilized. Afterwards, we evaluate whether the standard deviations are below a threshold H_{req} and H_{resp}. I.f.f. both deviations are above the thresholds, we can assume that the error differences in that sequence are too large and thus exclude that sequence. All other sequences are said to be 'complete'. A complete sequence will establish a prediction saying that the end user has navigated to the profile corresponding to the sequence. For instance, assume we have Φ profiles in our valid sequence – P_1, P_2, $P_{...}$, $P_{\Phi-1}$ and P_Φ, we can then calculate the following parameters:

$$\mu_{\text{req}} = \frac{\sum_{i=1}^{\Phi} \epsilon_{\text{req}}(P_i)}{\Phi} \tag{22}$$

$$\mu_{\text{resp}} = \frac{\sum_{i=1}^{\Phi} \epsilon_{\text{resp}}(P_i)}{\Phi} \tag{23}$$

$$\sigma_{req} = \sqrt{\frac{\sum_{i=1}^{\Phi}(\epsilon_{\text{req}}(P_i) - \mu_{\text{req}})^2}{\Phi}} \tag{24}$$

$$\sigma_{resp} = \sqrt{\frac{\sum_{i=1}^{\Phi}(\epsilon_{\text{resp}}(P_i) - \mu_{\text{resp}})^2}{\Phi}} \tag{25}$$

Jenks Optimization Method. Determining the standard deviations and then comparing it to a predefined threshold is relatively robust considering that b_{in} and w_{out} remains constant over all images of the same profile. Although, the presence of a CDN will essentially break that assumption by appending additional proprietary HTTP headers such as 'X-Cache' or 'X-Amz-Cf-Id', in case the requested image was cached by a CDN server. In the interest of distinguishing cached images[2] from uncached images or at least reduce the effect on the standard deviations, we employ the Jenks optimization method. This optimization method (also known as '*Goodness of Variance Fit*') clusters an 1D array of numbers into several classes with minimal average deviation from each class mean. For our IUPTIS attack, all ϵ_{resp} of each P_g^n (Eq. 10) in a valid sequence will be clustered into 2 classes (CDN-cached and uncached images). The integration of this method happens immediately after finding a valid sequence. Following the clustering, we compute σ_{req} and σ_{resp} for each class, which makes a total of 4 standard deviations. However, if one of the calculated classes only contain 1 element, we will have to assume that the single element is a false positive and therefore, fallback to the original method of computing the standard deviations for the whole sequence. Having multiple CDN of the same provider is not an issue, due to the responses not changing in size. When validating our experiments, we did not encounter an instance where multiple CDN of different providers were utilized on the same webpage. If it nevertheless does occur, the number of classes for the optimization method can be increased to compensate for this.

---

[2] Note the difference between browser-cached and CDN-cached images. We are talking about the latter here.

3.7 Recap

Our IUPTIS method is composed of the following steps [12]:

1. Intercept a network traffic trace from the end user.
2. Establish the collection of fingerprints by extracting the fingerprints of each targeted profile (Sect. 3.2).
3. Build an ordered Request/Response list (RRL) from the raw traffic trace as discussed (Sect. 3.3).
4. Construct a Profile Prediction List (PPL) by matching the elements from the RRL to one or multiple image fingerprints (Img_x).
5. Find a sequence of Φ elements in the PPL that all contain at least one image from the same $Profile_y$ (Sect. 3.5).
6. Evaluate the formed sequence by our IUPTIS algorithm which decides whether or not the sequence is classified as a valid profile prediction (Sect. 3.6).

Each attack is executed with the following tuneable parameters:

- b_{in}: The expected size of data (HTTP headers and corresponding values) in a request that is dependent on the webbrowser. If this value is unknown, an average value can be set albeit with a large π_{req} and π_{resp} to compensate for different browsers. It is for instance possible to extract this value by identifying the browser through the extraction of the User-Agent header from an unencrypted HTTP request.
- $useJenks$: Utilized if a CDN is employed on the targeted online platform.
- Φ: Minimum matching sequence or streak of images. This value can be freely set, although a long sequence results into an accurate prediction, but with a low accuracy for webpages that have cached images.
- π_{req}, π_{resp}: Request and response variance that allows matching to an image fingerprint. Calculate π_{req} by taking the difference between In_x and In_y where x defines the largest possible request size of any fingerprinted image and y defines the smallest possible request size of any fingerprinted image. Some manual fine-tuning is necessary for π_{resp} if a CDN is utilized. Creating a test case with several random profile fingerprints and then iteratively increasing π_{resp} with a constant size is recommended until the preferred results are achieved.
- H_{req}, H_{resp}: The threshold of the maximum standard deviation for respectively, the requests and responses. Both parameters are fixed for each online platform. Similar to π_{resp}, both parameters require manual fine-tuning by iteratively increasing the value.

The ideal combination of parameters depends on the adversary model, such as whether he wants to allow browser caching or a high precision in trade for a lower sensitivity. Possible combinations are provided in Sect. 4. In Fig. 1, we show an example of the IUPTIS method consisting of the first 5 steps. Starting from the bottom, the actual images are downloaded by the browser, resulting into a request and response, each with a specific size. Subsequently, the PPL is constructed by matching the request and responses to one or more profiles from our fingerprinting database. Then, we find an uninterrupted sequence of at least length Φ, which is 'Profile C' in our case. Finally, the sequence is evaluated to be fit for a valid profile prediction.

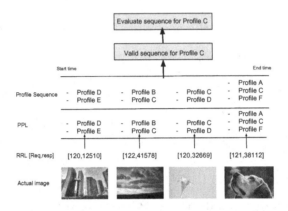

Fig. 1. Toy example with a visual 5-step overview of the IUPTIS method. Assume Φ is 3 and our fingerprint database consists of Profile A to Profile G. Originally demonstrated by Di Martino et al. [12].

3.8   Comparison to State-of-the-Art Techniques

In our original paper, we were the first to propose a WFP attack based on a sequence of images. Recent work from Brissaud et al. [3] have explored a similar concept applied on Google Images. Here they attempt to identify keywords in a Google search query based on applying kernel density estimations to a sequence of returned images. However, they did not consider the practical limitations of such attack as their method requires tampering of parameters in the browser to disable HTTP/2 and furthermore, they only target their attack to one browser with caching disabled.

Our attack also differs from state-of-the-art techniques like k-fingerprinting (k-FP) [20] and the Miller method [31], in the idea that we specifically target a subset of online platforms, and decouple browser caching and dynamic webpages by introducing several parameters that can be fine-tuned according to the demands of an adversary. In comparison to machine learning (ML) attacks [20,33,34] where we have to collect several traces from page loads, our fingerprinting stage only requires one page load for each profile. Numerous strong assumptions made in state-of-the-art methods are relaxed or completely removed in our IUPTIS attack [24]. For instance, the ability to perform our attack on different browsers and devices, without the need to collect session traces from each one individually, is an approach that is rarely proposed. Moreover as we will demonstrate in the experiments, our attack does not assume that we know the end and the beginning of a page load in a given trace, which is shown to be difficult to deduce [11,24]. Although due to such valuable properties, our attack is only applicable over TLS and thus it does not support anonymization services such as Tor. On the other hand, disadvantages of our attack can be found when applying mitigations. Due to the rather deterministic nature of our algorithm, existing defenses can be very effective to mitigate our attack as discussed in Sect. 5. Current state-of-the-art techniques are more resistant against defenses such as padding and have even defeated more advanced defenses such as HTTPOS, CS-BufLo or Tamaraw [5,6,20,25]. Although, as presented in the taxonomy *"I Know Why You Went To Clinic"* [31], most of these WFP methods need to fingerprint unmonitored webpages to make it feasible in an open world scenario [9,24] and almost all WFP attacks require browser caching to be turned off, which is less feasible nowadays. Furthermore, the flexibility of our attack parameters requires manual preliminary work which involves analyzing the HTTP request/responses and then tune these parameters in pursuance of an effective attack. In addition, we address the *base rate fallacy* [24,41] by carefully formulating our assumptions and adversary model and focussing on precision instead of sensitivity. Subsequently, the IUPTIS technique does not explicitly measure similarities between fingerprinted profiles and thus eliminates the necessity to create a separate collection of unmonitored webpages. As a result, our attack has the valuable property that whenever we increase the world size, only the precision will be affected and the sensitivity will remain relatively the same.

4   Experimental Validation

In this section, we perform our IUPTIS attack on the social platforms 'DeviantArt' and 'Pinterest' and the travel booking platform 'Hotels.com'. Our experiment is simulated by randomly selecting one of the following browsers (for each test): Firefox 56.0.2 (Linux), Google Chrome 62.0 (Linux) and Google Chrome 61.0 (Android). Nevertheless, in the context of our attack, there are no notable differences between different browsers except from the change in request size.

Each run in the experiments will result into a sensitivity (True Positive Rate), precision (Positive Predictive Value) and F1 score. We define these measurements as follows:

$$\text{TPR} = \frac{\text{TP}}{\text{TP} + \text{FN}} \quad \text{and} \quad \text{PPV} = \frac{\text{TP}}{\text{TP} + \text{FP}} \tag{26}$$

$$\text{F}_1 = \frac{2}{(\frac{1}{TPR} + \frac{1}{PPV})} \tag{27}$$

There are several accepted ways of defining what a *true positive* (TP), *false positive* (FP), *false negative* (FN) are. In the results of our own experiments[3], we utilize the following measurements:

---

[3] Previous work regarding fingerprinting often have slightly different ways of defining positives and negatives.

- True positive (TP): Correctly predict that the traffic belongs to fingerprint A in a specific timeframe.
- False positive (FP): Incorrectly predict the traffic to be from fingerprint A for a specific timeframe, while it is actually from fingerprint B.
- False negative (FN): Predict nothing while the intercepted traffic actually belongs to fingerprint B.

The platforms 'DeviantArt' and 'Hotels.com' discussed below were vulnerable to an IUPTIS attack at the time of writing the original paper [12], but are currently using HTTP/2 and thus are not affected anymore. We keep these experiments intact to show the conceptual method of an IUPTIS attack, which is still useful for many platforms today. Nevertheless, the platform 'Pinterest' is a new experiment and thus, vulnerable to an IUPTIS attack.

4.1   Pinterest

Pinterest is a social photo gallery with 175 million active users [1]. Users can search for images by providing keyword queries. We compile a list of 535 random Pinterest queries of popular categories[4]. To construct our traffic trace, we utilize the same approach as the DeviantArt experiment. However, instead of targetting the user profiles of Pinterest, we extend the concept of a profile to a *query*. Therefore, we try to predict the queries that a user has searched for, on Pinterest. Additionally, we removed queries that were very similar to other queries such as plural forms (for instance, 'car' vs 'cars'). The location of the dataset and source code of this experiment can be found in Sect. 6.

When comparing the results of Pinterest and DeviantArt, it is clear that the sensitivity in the Pinterest experiment is inferior. This behaviour can be attributed to the fact that Pinterest domain name that downloads the images, also downloads other resources in the same TCP connection. For instance, Javascript files. The additional resources are too large to ignore and the timing of these resources depends on the performance of that specific TCP connection. As a result, this will often break our image sequence.

Nevertheless, favorable results are still achieved with a sequence of 4 images and $H_{resp} = 1.0$, which indicates that a lower H_{resp} often has a slight advantage in this experiment. Moreover, the Jenks optimization method doesn't have much of a positive effect on small sequences due to the fact that only one HTTP header (Cache-tag) is being added depending on the status of the requested image. In a DPI context, where precision is more important due to the infinite many queries that are not contained in our dataset, we argue that the configuration with $\Phi=5$, $H_{resp} = 0.6$ is optimal to deploy (Table 1).

To show how browser-cached images affect our result, we have conducted an experiment where 50% of the images on the query were already visited and thus cached by the browser. Clearly, sensitivity is decreasing rapidly when the

---

[4] Categories: Movie, Sport, Travel, Music, Games, Clothing, Science, Food and Business.

Table 1. Experiment on Pinterest with parameters (π_{resp} = 600, $useJenks$ = no, b_{in}=Y, H_{resp} = 0.6) and a worldsize of 500 queries. b_{in} is set to any value, thus, browser is unknown. Sensitivity, precision and F1 score are presented as percentages.

Sequence (Φ)	Other parameters	Sensitivity	Precision	F1 score
3	H_{resp} = 0.3	98	83	89
3	/	99	71	82
3	H_{resp} = 2.0	99	42	58
4	/	97	92	94
4	H_{resp} = 0.3	91	95	93
5	H_{resp} = 2.0	95	98	96
5	/	95	99	97
5	$useJenks$ = yes	96	88	91
6	$useJenks$ = yes	93	96	94
6	/	91	99	94
7	$useJenks$ = yes	88	99	93
7	$useJenks$ = yes, H_{resp} = 1.6	90	98	93
7	H_{resp} = 1.6	86	99	92

minimum sequence is increasing. On average, there is a decrease in sensitivity of approximately 7% over each sequence and an average decrease of 4% compared to the experiment where caching is disabled. This is a vast improvement over state-of-the-art methods, where caching is often not incorporated in their methods and thus performs poorly when queries or webpages are revisited. The precision in our experiment is not affected and is even better in cases where false positives are being avoided with a very small sequence ($\Phi = 3$) (Table 2).

Table 2. Experiment on Pinterest with parameters (π_{resp} = 600, $useJenks$ = no, b_{in}=Y, H_{resp} = 0.6, $cache$ = 50) and a worldsize of 500 queries. b_{in} is set to any value, thus, browser is unknown. Parameter '$cache$=X' indicates that we pre-cache (browser based) the first X % of all the images located on the profile webpage. Sensitivity, precision and F1 score are presented as percentages.

Sequence (Φ)	Other parameters	Sensitivity	Precision	F1 score
3	/	97	77	85
4	/	91	93	92
5	/	85	99	91
6	/	78	99	87
7	/	70	99	82

4.2   DeviantArt

DeviantArt is an online art community that consists of 36 million users where artists can upload and view a substantial number of artworks. We randomly compile a list of 2150 DeviantArt profile webpages[5] that have at least 5 uploaded images. Our traffic trace is constructed by spawning each profile webpage separately after each other until all images are loaded with a minimum delay of 3 seconds before closing the previous page and opening the next webpage. *Lazy loading* is a concept that is applied on DeviantArt which means that only the images in the current viewport will be downloaded and thus visible in the traffic trace. With this generated traffic trace containing 2150 profiles, we run our IUPTIS attack and obtain the results in Table 3. The first test has set the parameter b_{in} which indicates that the adversary knows which browser the end user is using. Including this additional parameter has a considerable positive effect on the precision of the attack with an increase of 11% (ceteris paribus). It is also evident that a large sequence will increase the precision and decrease the sensitivity. We can attribute this due to the statistical probability that it is less likely for a profile to have the same size of several images in a row as another profile. Browser-cached images do influence the sensitivity since the request for those images will not lead to the image contained in a HTTP response. It is therefore possible that the number of images that are left on a particular profile do not meet the requirements to evolve into a valid sequence. Although, the precision is clearly not affected since browser-cached images do not generate any additional false positives due to the fact that those browser-cached images are often being requested at the start or end of the series of fingerprinted images.

Table 3. Original experiment from Di Martino et al. [12] on DeviantArt with parameters ($\pi_{req} = 300$, $\pi_{resp} = 40$, $useJenks = no$, $b_{in} = 252$, $H_{resp} = 3.6$ and $H_{req} = 0.4$) and a worldsize of 2150 profiles. Parameter '$cache = X$' indicates that we precache (browser based) the first X % of all the images located on the profile webpage. Sensitivity, precision and F1 score are presented as percentages.

Sequence (Φ)	Other parameters	Sensitivity	Precision	F1 score
2	$\pi_{resp}=10$, $b_{in} = X$	99	98	99
2	$\pi_{resp}=10$, $b_{in} = X$, $cache = 40$	94	98	96
2	/	99	88	93
3	/	98	93	95
4	$useJenks = yes$	97	97	97
5	$useJenks = yes$	96	99	98
5	$useJenks = yes$, $cache = 40$	87	99	92

4.3   Hotels.com

Hotels.com is an online travel booking platform with an average of 50 million visitors per month and currently has around 260 000 bookable properties.

We compile our profile list by randomly selecting 900 hotel profile webpages[6]. Our traffic trace is constructed by spawning each hotel webpage and then

---

[5] 'https://www.deviantart.com/[USER_NAME]/gallery'.
[6] https://hotels.com/ho[NUMBER]/?[GET_PARAMS].

opening 75% of all the images located on the webpage. Images are not loaded automatically and thus requires the end user to click on the image in the interest of downloading the full resolution image. We argue that the average end user does not open all images when browsing through the webpage.

In Table 4, we show the sensitivity, precision and F1 score based on the experiment run by altering parameter H_{resp}, the sequence length and whether or not we use the Jenks method. With the exception of 'Without Jenks($H_{resp} = 3.5$)', a consistent F1 score between 80–98% is achieved. For a sequence (Φ) of 8 images, 'With Jenks ($H_{resp} = 6.0, \Phi = 8$)' yields a F1 score of 98%. Overall, sensitivity is relatively constant in almost all tests and only decreases slightly when a longer sequence is necessary as shown in Figs. 2 and 3. On the contrary, the precision starts low and increases to a very convenient 99% in some cases. However, a low sequence length is preferred to incorporate the ability for the end user to use browser caching in trade for a lower precision. Fortunately, performing the attack without Jenks and $H_{resp} = 8.5$ already attains a sensitivity and precision of respectively 99 and 92% for a sequence of 6 images. Furthermore, applying the Jenks method to model the CDN cache behavior does show major improvements in sensitivity over different H_{resp} values (ceteris paribus) with only a nominal decrease in precision. For instance, 'Without Jenks ($H_{resp} = 3.5$)' has inferior sensitivity (below 55%) compared to the other tests due to the fact that some images are cached by the CDN server which makes the resulting responses very different in size. On the contrary, in the DeviantArt experiment, the CDNs employed did not had a significant impact on the response size. Ultimately, we argue that 'Without Jenks ($H_{resp} = 8.5$)' is ideal in this scenario due to the very advantageous precision (85% to 100%) and relatively high sensitivity (82% to 99%) over all possible sequence lengths. In conclusion, we determine that the combination of parameters to perform the attack will greatly depend on the adversary and end user model.

A timeframe of 14 days was created between generating the image fingerprints and performing our experiment to show the longevity of our fingerprints. Within this timeframe, several profiles of our targeted platforms had added and deleted several images. The results of our experiment demonstrates that the impact with such modifications is neglectable. Furthermore, we have conducted our tests on different hours and days in a week to get a decent statistical overview of all the requests. This is crucial due to the fact that a CDN is heavily dependent on the time of day which influences the responses and in turn our results.

4.4   Overview Notes

In all experiments, it is notable that the sensitivity and precision on a small sequence (Φ) is very volatile. As we increase our sequence, the sensitivity will decrease and the precision will increase, ultimately turning into more robust results. Focussing on precision will also allow us to use larger datasets since only that metric will decrease. The sensitivity will not be affected on larger datasets because we do not measure similarities between different fingerprints. Furthermore, if images are cached by the browser, the influence on the results will depend on the length of the sequence. The effect is neglectable on smaller sequences, but

Table 4. Original experiment from Di Martino et al. [12] on Hotels.com with a world-size of 900 hotel profiles and fixed parameters ($b_{in} = 250$, $\pi_{resp} = 100$, $\pi_{req} = 450$ and $H_{req} = 0.2$). Sensitivity, Precision and F1 score are presented as percentages. The underlined percentages represent the highest F1 score for that particular sequence Φ.

Parameters	Sensitivity	Precision	F1 score
Without Jenks ($H_{resp} = 3.5$, $\Phi = 5$)	55	86	67
Without Jenks ($H_{resp} = 3.5$, $\Phi = 6$)	27	97	43
Without Jenks ($H_{resp} = 3.5$, $\Phi = 7$)	9	99	16
Without Jenks ($H_{resp} = 3.5$, $\Phi = 8$)	3	99	6
Without Jenks ($H_{resp} = 3.5$, $\Phi = 9$)	1	100	2
Without Jenks ($H_{resp} = 8.5$, $\Phi = 5$)	99	85	<u>92</u>
Without Jenks ($H_{resp} = 8.5$, $\Phi = 6$)	99	92	<u>96</u>
Without Jenks ($H_{resp} = 8.5$, $\Phi = 7$)	91	95	83
Without Jenks ($H_{resp} = 8.5$, $\Phi = 8$)	90	99	94
Without Jenks ($H_{resp} = 8.5$, $\Phi = 9$)	82	100	<u>90</u>
With Jenks ($H_{resp} = 3.5$, $\Phi = 5$)	91	77	83
With Jenks ($H_{resp} = 3.5$, $\Phi = 6$)	91	91	91
With Jenks ($H_{resp} = 3.5$, $\Phi = 7$)	99	92	<u>96</u>
With Jenks ($H_{resp} = 3.5$, $\Phi = 8$)	83	99	90
With Jenks ($H_{resp} = 3.5$, $\Phi = 9$)	73	100	85
With Jenks ($H_{resp} = 6.0$, $\Phi = 5$)	97	71	82
With Jenks ($H_{resp} = 6.0$, $\Phi = 6$)	99	80	88
With Jenks ($H_{resp} = 6.0$, $\Phi = 7$)	99	85	89
With Jenks ($H_{resp} = 6.0$, $\Phi = 8$)	99	98	<u>98</u>
With Jenks ($H_{resp} = 6.0$, $\Phi = 9$)	82	99	89

will be substantial on higher sequences. More importantly, we are the first to show acceptable precision and sensitivity on browser-cached webpages.

Also note that our experiments are performed with limited assumptions, compared to previous state-of-the-art techniques. Some uncommon elements such as downloading other resources besides images in the same TCP connection or randomly added HTTP headers to responses, will affect the results on larger sequences. Moreover, the Jenks optimization method does only improve slightly on higher sequences with CDN-cached images.

To show the reproducibility of our results, we have released the source code and dataset for the new Pinterest experiment.

5   Defenses

Our results have shown that it is practically viable to perform an IUPTIS attack in a realistic scenario. Even though, DPI tools have a significant advantage with

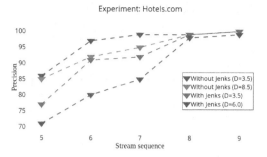

Fig. 2. Original figure from Martino et al. [12]. Hotels.com experiment consisting of various tests from Table 4 with different parameters, plotting the precision on the length of a valid sequence

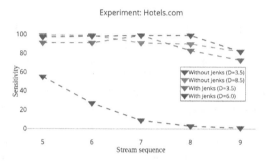

Fig. 3. Original figure from Di Martino et al. [12]. Hotels.com experiment consisting of various tests from Table 4 with different parameters, plotting the sensitivity on the length of a valid sequence.

our approach, we consider that the privacy of the end users can be severely affected when applying this method. Therefore, we analyze and discuss several defenses that might be able to mitigate IUPTIS. To limit ourselves to a practical context, we only consider defenses that are implemented or have ever been discussed to be implemented in the Tor Onion browser.

5.1   Padding

A basic defense that we consider is 'linear padding'. By applying this defense, we make sure that the length of every HTTP request and response is divisible by a specific number of bytes. Padding is still common on some older web platforms as it is applied to block ciphers (for instance, CBC) used in HTTP over TLS. Even if the adversary knows that padding is applied, HTTP requests and responses will look larger than they actually are, resulting into a large standard deviation σ. In this case, we cannot use a H_{req} and H_{resp} lower than $padding/2$ because our σ will likely overshoot both boundaries. So in order to compensate for this,

Table 5. Linear padding applied to the IUPTIS attack performed on DeviantArt with the following parameters: ($\pi_{\text{req}} = 300$, $\pi_{\text{resp}} = 40$, $useJenks = $ no, $b_{\text{in}} = X$, $H_{\text{resp}} = 3.6$ and $H_{\text{req}} = 0.4$). Sensitivity, precision and F1 score are shown as percentages. Padding is in bytes.

Sequence ($\varPhi$)	Padding	Sensitivity	Precision	F1 score
3	0	98	93	95
4	0	97	97	97
3	32	96	63	76
4	32	93	90	91
3	128	92	1	65
4	128	89	2	64

we increased both parameter H_{req} and H_{resp} to 16 and 64 for respectively 32 byte blocks and 128 byte blocks of padding applied.

With that in mind, we ran all tests on existing configurations from our original DeviantArt experiment (Sect. 4.2), with linear padding applied: The results are still acceptable for a small amount of padding, but the precision suffers substantially when applying padding to blocks of 128 bytes. Nevertheless, it is clear that a linear padding of 128 bytes (or more) is effective in generating many false positives. The sensitivity is obviously not affected which means that the adversary can still narrow down the number of possible webpages that the victim has visited if we would utilize a closed world scenario. It is also important to note that we modified our parameters of the attack with the prior knowledge that padding will be applied. This assumption is fair if the padding is part of the protocol standard. Although, if variable padding (without the fixed block size) is applied to the HTTP data itself, an adversary might have difficulties guessing which parameters he should use in order to successfully perform the attack (Table 5).

We conclude that padding does not completely mitigate our attack, but it certainly makes the preliminary work of the adversary much more cumbersome. Furthermore, such mitigation is often criticized for their performance intensive nature due to the extra bandwidth that is necessary [6,25]. Other padding schemes proposed by Dyer et al. [13] like Mice-Elephant or Exponential padding have a similar effect, depending of the number of bytes added.

5.2   Camouflage

Camouflage is a client-side defense (originally developed for Tor networks) that requests a random webpage whenever the victim is trying to visit the actual wanted webpage [34]. Requesting such unrelated webpage will actually add the concept of 'noise' to the traffic trace. Applied to our attack, this would mean that we request a random profile page Y when the victim requests a profile page X. Both profiles will be loaded simultaneously by opening multiple TCP connections

Table 6. Camouflage defense applied to the IUPTIS attack performed on DeviantArt with the following parameters: $H_{\text{resp}} = 3.6$, $H_{\text{req}} = 0.5$, $useJenks = no$, $\pi_{\text{req}} = 450$, $\pi_{\text{resp}} = 100$ and b_{in} is not set (unknown browser). Sensitivity, Precision and F1 score are shown as percentages.

Sequence (Φ)	Number of dummies	Sensitivity	Precision	F1 score
2	0	99	88	93
2	1	98	51	73
2	2	82	39	53
5	0	96	99	97
5	1	85	56	68
5	2	68	47	55

to the target server. Since our attack expects a sequence of HTTP responses that belong to the same profile, the camouflage method will interleave the responses and requests which makes it statistically much harder to find a valid sequence. As a result, the number of false positives will increase and will possibly point to the randomly requested webpage. We have performed tests where where apply the Camouflage technique to our attack (Table 6): As expected, Camouflage introduces many false positives due to the extra requests and responses. If we compare the results to the experiment without defenses applied (Sect. 4.2), we notice that the sensitivity has decreased substantially. This is the result of the interleaved HTTP requests and responses which makes a correct sequence less likely to occur. The same explanation can be given for the fact that the precision with 2 dummy requests is higher for a sequence of 5 compared to a sequence of 2 (ceteris paribus). Whether or not Camouflage mitigates the IUPTIS attack depends on the context in which the attack is performed. Does the adversary wants to know exactly which profile the victim visited or is he satisfied with several possible predictions? Generally, we can say that an adversary already has enough sensitive information to abuse when several predictions are given to him. It will also depend on whether or not the fingerprints that the adversary has, is a subset of the possible dummy requests. As a result, we conclude that Camouflage does not sufficiently protect the end user against an IUPTIS attack.

5.3 HTTP/2

HTTP/2 is the successor of the HTTP/1.1 protocol, standarized in 2015 and supported by 91% of the browsers in use today [39]. However, only 33% of all websites on the internet support HTTP/2. The major differences that affect webpage fingerprinting is the use of multiplexing over one TCP connection for each requested resource from the same domain, instead of a sequential approach for each connection. Since each request and response are not necessarily following up on each other, calculating the size of a HTTP request/response is not possible in HTTP/2, with the IUPTIS technique proposed in this paper. Fingerprinting techniques or traffic classification algorithms in general, often have difficulties in coping with this protocol [16,32]. Therefore, we conclude that HTTP/2 is indeed a solution to mitigate IUPTIS without the disadvantages discussed in the defenses above. In addition, applying this as a possible fingerprinting defense might not only be successful against many proposed fingerprinting techniques, it will also greatly improve upon bandwidth and performance in most scenarios [44].

5.4   Overview

Existing modern WFP defenses are highly effective against an IUPTIS attack. Primarily because mitigations such as CS-BufLo [4] and Walkie-Talkie [42] completely remove the ability for the adversary to deduce the exact size of a web object image, thus rendering our attack ineffective. Unfortunately, these defenses often have a considerably large burden on bandwidth and performance which is nevertheless one of the reasons why such defenses are not implemented in privacy enhancing tools. Additionally, many end users do not have the knowledge nor the ability to apply such defenses. We can argue that it is the responsibility of the online platform to protect the end users from any fingerprinting attack. Recent work has shown the demand for such a server-side countermeasure called ALPaCA [10]. Despite their promising results on a Tor network, it is not suitable for webpages serving over HTTPS. However, recent work has also demonstrated that a proper server-side implementation of HTTP/2 does make it troublesome for an adversary to infer the exact image sizes [32]. Even though this would defeat our current attack, it does not completely mitigate the risk for future WFP attacks that might enhance our method to discover new techniques that use a sequence of images as their main feature. To conclude, we think it is critical to educate the end user about the available tools that exist to protect themselves against fingerprinting attacks such as IUPTIS, on a wide scale.

6   Conclusion and Future Work

Fingerprinting individual webpages associated to unique profiles is possible on a large set of webplatforms. We have proposed a novel method called 'IUPTIS' to use the size of image resources as a practical feature for webpage fingerprinting on the HTTP/1.1 protocol. Our method has also diminished the limitations of previous state of the art techniques by being able to fingerprint webpages that are dynamic in content, can handle cached resources and is able to perform well on different modern browsers. To cope with the variety of webplatforms available today, we have introduced several accuracy-enhancing parameters that can be finetuned by an adversary, according to the context in which they perform the attack. Newly performed experiments that have been performed on the popular webplatform 'Pinterest', have shown that our results are accurate enough to be suitable in DPI frameworks. F1 scores between 90% and 97% are achieved in different configurations and settings to show the practicality of our technique. Moreover, it is clear that the impact on privacy is troublesome and have therefore, discussed defensive strategies that are able to mitigate IUPTIS for end users, by carefully analyzing their advantages and limitations in realistic environments. We argue that server side defenses such as ALPaCA [10] and an efficient implementation of the HTTP/2 protocol (with multiplexing) are sufficient to protect end users against our attack.

Improvements on our method can be constructed by automating the manual fine-tuning of the parameters (for instance, H_{req} and H_{resp}), and thus reducing the time to perform an IUPTIS attack. Machine learning is a suggestion that would fit our fine-tuning problem. Additionally, the calculation of the error (ϵ) for each fingerprintined image in Sect. 3.4 is simple and other metrics such as the mean squared error have not been discussed and thus might be able to produce an even higher F1 score for our experiments. Finally, the Jenks optimization method to handle CDNs has only been applied to 2 different CDN providers. A generalization of this optimization to more providers is suitable for future work.

Acknowledgements. We thank the anonymous reviewers for their insightful feedback.

Source Code and Dataset. The source code and dataset of the Pinterest experiment can be found here: https://github.com/M-DiMartino/IUPTIS.

References

1. Pinterest (2018). https://www.pinterest.com. Accessed 13 Nov 2018
2. Brandwatch: Brandwatch Peer Index (2017). https://www.brandwatch.com/p/peerindex-and-brandwatch. Accessed 14 Oct 2017
3. Brissaud, P.O., Francois, J., Chrisment, I., Cholez, T., Bettan, O.: Passive monitoring of HTTPS service use. In: 14th International Conference on Network and Service Management (CNSM 2018), Rome, Italy , p. 7, November 2018. https://hal.inria.fr/hal-01943936
4. Cai, X., Nithyanand, R., Johnson, R.: CS-BuFLO: a congestion sensitive website fingerprinting defense. In: Proceedings of the 13th Workshop on Privacy in the Electronic Society, WPES 2014, pp. 121–130. ACM, New York (2014). https://doi.org/10.1145/2665943.2665949
5. Cai, X., Nithyanand, R., Wang, T., Johnson, R., Goldberg, I.: A systematic approach to developing and evaluating website fingerprinting defenses. In: Proceedings of the 2014 ACM SIGSAC Conference on Computer and Communications Security, CCS 2014, pp. 227–238. ACM, New York (2014). https://doi.org/10.1145/2660267.2660362
6. Cai, X., Zhang, X.C., Joshi, B., Johnson, R.: Touching from a distance: website fingerprinting attacks and defenses. In: Proceedings of the 2012 ACM Conference on Computer and Communications Security, CCS 2012, pp. 605–616. ACM, New York (2012). https://doi.org/10.1145/2382196.2382260
7. Cao, Y., Li, S., Wijmans, E.: (Cross-)browser fingerprinting via OS and hardware level features. In: NDSS (2017)
8. Cheng, H., Cheng, H., Avnur, R.: Traffic analysis of SSL encrypted web browsing (1998)

9. Cherubin, G.: Bayes, not Naïve: security bounds on website fingerprinting defenses. In: PoPETs, pp. 215–231 (2017)
10. Cherubin, G., Hayes, J., Juarez, M.: Website fingerprinting defenses at the application layer. Proc. Priv. Enhanc. Technol. **2017**(2), 186–203 (2017)
11. Coull, S.E., Collins, M.P., Wright, C.V., Monrose, F., Reiter, M.K.: On web browsing privacy in anonymized NetFlows. In: Proceedings of 16th USENIX Security Symposium on USENIX Security Symposium, SS 2007, USENIX Association, Berkeley, CA, USA, pp. 23:1–23:14 (2007). http://dl.acm.org/citation.cfm?id=1362903.1362926
12. Di Martino, M., Robyns, P., Quax, P., Lamotte, W.: Iuptis: a practical, cache-resistant fingerprinting technique for dynamic webpages. In: WEBIST (2018)
13. Dyer, K.P., Coull, S.E., Ristenpart, T., Shrimpton, T.: Peek-a-boo, i still see you: why efficient traffic analysis countermeasures fail. In: Proceedings of the 2012 IEEE Symposium on Security and Privacy, SP 2012, pp. 332–346. IEEE Computer Society, Washington (2012). https://doi.org/10.1109/SP.2012.28
14. The Economist: Very personal finance (2012). http://www.economist.com/node/21556263. Accessed 10 Sept 2017
15. Ejeta, T.G., Kim, H.J.: Website fingerprinting attack on psiphon and its forensic analysis. In: Kraetzer, C., Shi, Y.-Q., Dittmann, J., Kim, H.J. (eds.) IWDW 2017. LNCS, vol. 10431, pp. 42–51. Springer, Cham (2017). https://doi.org/10.1007/978-3-319-64185-0_4
16. Estêvão, F.P.C.: Fingerprinting HTTP/2 web pages (2017)
17. European Commission: Data protection (2018). https://ec.europa.eu/info/law/law-topic/data-protection_en. Accessed 17 June 2018
18. Council of the European Union: Common challenges in combating cybercrime, p. 5 (2017). http://data.consilium.europa.eu/doc/document/ST-7021-2017-INIT/en/pdf
19. Gallagher, S.: Chinese government launches man-in-middle attack against icloud [updated]. Ars Technica (2014). https://arstechnica.com/information-technology/2014/10/chinese-government-launches-man-in-middle-attack-against-icloud/
20. Hayes, J., Danezis, G.: k-fingerprinting: a robust scalable website fingerprinting technique. In: 25th USENIX Security Symposium (USENIX Security 16), USENIX Association, Austin, TX, pp. 1187–1203 (2016)
21. Herrmann, D., Wendolsky, R., Federrath, H.: Website fingerprinting: attacking popular privacy enhancing technologies with the multinomial Naïve-bayes classifier. In: Proceedings of the 2009 ACM Workshop on Cloud Computing Security, CCSW 2009, pp. 31–42. ACM, New York (2009). https://doi.org/10.1145/1655008.1655013
22. Husák, M., Čermák, M., Jirsík, T., Čeleda, P.: HTTPS traffic analysis and client identification using passive SSL/TLS fingerprinting. EURASIP J. Inf. Secur. **2016**(1), 6 (2016). https://doi.org/10.1186/s13635-016-0030-7
23. InformAction: Noscript. https://noscript.net/. Accessed 18 Oct 2018
24. Juarez, M., Afroz, S., Acar, G., Diaz, C., Greenstadt, R.: A critical evaluation of website fingerprinting attacks. In: Proceedings of the 2014 ACM SIGSAC Conference on Computer and Communications Security, CCS 2014, pp. 263–274. ACM, New York (2014). https://doi.org/10.1145/2660267.2660368
25. Juarez, M., Imani, M., Perry, M., Diaz, C., Wright, M.: Toward an efficient website fingerprinting defense. In: Askoxylakis, I., Ioannidis, S., Katsikas, S., Meadows, C. (eds.) ESORICS 2016. LNCS, vol. 9878, pp. 27–46. Springer, Cham (2016). https://doi.org/10.1007/978-3-319-45744-4_2

26. Kwon, A., AlSabah, M., Lazar, D., Dacier, M., Devadas, S.: Circuit fingerprinting attacks: passive deanonymization of tor hidden services. In: 24th USENIX Security Symposium (USENIX Security 15), USENIX Association, Washington, D.C., pp. 287–302 (2015). https://www.usenix.org/conference/usenixsecurity15/technical-sessions/presentation/kwon
27. Liberatore, M., Levine, B.N.: Inferring the source of encrypted HTTP connections. In: Proceedings of the 13th ACM Conference on Computer and Communications Security, CCS 2006, pp. 255–263. ACM, New York (2006). https://doi.org/10.1145/1180405.1180437
28. Liu, L., Preoţiuc-Pietro, D., Riahi, Z., Moghaddam, M.E., Ungar, L.: Analyzing personality through social media profile picture choice. In: ICWSM (2016)
29. Lu, L., Chang, E.-C., Chan, M.C.: Website fingerprinting and identification using ordered feature sequences. In: Gritzalis, D., Preneel, B., Theoharidou, M. (eds.) ESORICS 2010. LNCS, vol. 6345, pp. 199–214. Springer, Heidelberg (2010). https://doi.org/10.1007/978-3-642-15497-3_13
30. Luo, X., Zhou, P., Chan, E.W.W., Lee, W., Chang, R.K.C., Perdisci, R.: HTTPOS: sealing information leaks with browser-side obfuscation of encrypted flows. In: Proceedings of the Network and Distributed Systems Symposium (NDSS). The Internet Society (2011). http://hdl.handle.net/10397/50561
31. Miller, B., Huang, L., Joseph, A.D., Tygar, J.D.: I know why you went to the clinic: risks and realization of HTTPS traffic analysis. In: De Cristofaro, E., Murdoch, S.J. (eds.) PETS 2014. LNCS, vol. 8555, pp. 143–163. Springer, Cham (2014). https://doi.org/10.1007/978-3-319-08506-7_8
32. Morla, R.: Effect of pipelining and multiplexing in estimating HTTP/2.0 web object sizes. ArXiv e-prints (2017)
33. Panchenko, A., et al.: Website fingerprinting at internet scale. In: NDSS (2016)
34. Panchenko, A., Niessen, L., Zinnen, A., Engel, T.: Website fingerprinting in onion routing based anonymization networks. In: Proceedings of the 10th Annual ACM Workshop on Privacy in the Electronic Society, WPES 2011, pp. 103–114. ACM, New York, (2011). https://doi.org/10.1145/2046556.2046570
35. Perez, S.: Facebook starts pushing its data tracking onavo vpn within its main mobile app (2018). https://techcrunch.com/2018/02/12/facebook-starts-pushing-its-data-tracking-onavo-vpn-within-its-main-mobile-app/
36. Project, T.T.: Tor. https://www.torproject.org. Accessed 17 June 2018
37. Rao, A., Spasojevic, N., Li, Z., Dsouza, T.: Klout score: measuring influence across multiple social networks. In: 2015 IEEE International Conference on Big Data (Big Data), pp. 2282–2289 (2015)
38. Rimmer, V., Preuveneers, D., Juarez, M., Van Goethem, T., Joosen, W.: Automated feature extraction for website fingerprinting through deep learning (2017, to appear)
39. Statcounter: Statcounter Global Stats (2018). http://gs.statcounter.com/. Accessed 06 Nov 2018
40. Sun, Q., Simon, D.R., Wang, Y.M., Russell, W., Padmanabhan, V.N., Qiu, L.: Statistical identification of encrypted web browsing traffic. In: Proceedings of the 2002 IEEE Symposium on Security and Privacy, SP 2002, pp. 19–30. IEEE Computer Society, Washington, (2002). http://dl.acm.org/citation.cfm?id=829514.830535
41. Wang, T.: Website fingerprinting: attacks and defenses (Doctoral dissertation), university of Waterloo, Canada (2015)

42. Wang, T., Goldberg, I.: Walkie-talkie: an efficient defense against passive website fingerprinting attacks. In: 26th USENIX Security Symposium (USENIX Security 17), USENIX Association, Vancouver, BC, pp. 1375–1390 (2017). https://www.usenix.org/conference/usenixsecurity17/technical-sessions/presentation/wang-tao
43. WiFi4EU: Free wi-fi for europeans (2016). https://ec.europa.eu/digital-single-market/en/policies/wifi4eu-free-wi-fi-europeans
44. Wijnants, M., Marx, R., Quax, P., Lamotte, W.: HTTP/2 Prioritization and its Impact on Web Performance. In: The Web Conference WWW 2018 (2018)
45. Wright, C.V., Coull, S.E., Monrose, F.: traffic morphing: an efficient defense against statistical traffic analysis. In: Proceedings of the 16th Network and Distributed Security Symposium, pp. 237–250. IEEE (2009)

Evaluation in Pilot-Based Research Projects: A Hierarchical Approach

Thomas Zefferer[✉]

Secure Information Technology Center Austria (A-SIT), 8010 Graz, Austria
thomas.zefferer@a-sit.at
https://www.a-sit.at

Abstract. The evaluation of project results is a crucial part of most research projects in the information-technology domain. In particular, this applies to projects that develop solutions for the public sector and test them by means of pilot applications. In these projects, involved stakeholders require meaningful evaluation results to derive lessons learned and to steer future research activities in the right directions. Today, most projects define and apply their own evaluation schemes. This yields evaluation results that are difficult to compare between projects. Sometimes, inconsistent evaluation schemes are even applied within a project. In these cases, even evaluation results of a single project lack comparability. In absence of coherent evaluation schemes, lessons learned from conducted evaluation processes cannot be aggregated to a coherent holistic picture and the overall gain of research projects remains limited. To address this issue, we propose and introduce an evaluation scheme for arbitrary pilot-based research projects targeting the public sector. The proposed scheme follows a hierarchical approach. Concretely, it organizes evaluation criteria on different layers of abstraction. Furthermore, the proposed scheme describes in detail necessary process steps to carry out evaluations using the defined criteria. This way, the proposed scheme enables in-depth evaluations of research projects and their pilot applications. At the same time, it assures that obtained evaluation results remain comparable anytime. The hierarchical evaluation scheme introduced in this article has been successfully applied to the international research project FutureTrust, demonstrating its practical applicability, and showing its potential also for future research projects.

Keywords: Evaluation scheme · Project evaluation · Hierarchical evaluation model

1 Introduction

During the past decades, advances in information technology (IT) have disruptively changed various parts of everyday life. While the impacts on the corporate and private sector are rather obvious, also the public-sector is increasingly

© Springer Nature Switzerland AG 2019
M. J. Escalona et al. (Eds.): WEBIST 2018, LNBIP 372, pp. 125–146, 2019.
https://doi.org/10.1007/978-3-030-35330-8_7

employing information technologies to save costs and to provide citizens a better service. Today, leveraging the use of information technology is on top of the agenda of most public-sector institutions. While this is a global phenomenon, especially the European Union (EU) has a long tradition in pushing the use of information and communication technologies in public administrations. Accordingly, the EU invests considerable financial resources in bringing forward its digital agenda on pan-European level [5]. One approach followed by the EU to achieve these goals is the funding of international research projects that develop innovative IT solutions for the public sector. The Large Scale Pilots (LSPs) STORK 2.0[1], PEPPOL[2], epSOS[3], or e-SENS[4] are just a few examples of recent research activities funded by the EU in this domain.

Many research activities funded by the EU follow a pilot-based approach. Accordingly, these activities develop new and innovative IT solutions and integrate them into one or more pilot applications. These pilot applications typically serve a concrete use case and satisfy a certain demand. Thus, pilot applications evaluate the applicability and the usefulness of the developed solution in practice. For instance, the EU-funded LSPs STORK and STORK 2.0 developed an interoperability layer for national electronic identity (eID) solutions [12]. This interoperability layer aimed to achieve an identity federation between different national eID systems, such as the Austrian Citizen Card [11], the Belgian BELPIC card [2], or the Estonian eID card [13]. In addition to the interoperability layer itself, STORK and STORK 2.0 have developed a series of pilot applications. They have all relied on the interoperability layer developed, and have enabled EU citizens to use their respective national eID to authenticate at electronic services provided by other EU member states. Details of these pilots have for instance been discussed by Knall et al. [10] and Tauber et al. [16].

The above example illustrates that the piloting phase constitutes an integral part of pilot-based research projects and activities. However, the piloting phase is usually limited to the respective research project's lifetime. As a consequence, even successful pilot applications typically need to be terminated at the end of a research project. Turning the pilot application into a productive and viable service is usually out of the project's scope. It is thus essential that all stakeholders involved in the project derive as many lessons learned from the piloting phase as possible. Involved stakeholders include researchers, funding bodies, and, of course, end users. After completion of a project, lessons learned from its piloting phase are crucial to turn a promising pilot into a successful productive service.

Both, researchers and funding bodies are well-aware of this fact. Thus, a sound evaluation of planned pilot applications is part of most proposals for pilot-based projects. In theory, a sound pilot evaluation appears to be an adequate method for the derivation of findings and lessons learned. Still, the current situation is often unsatisfying in practice. It can be observed that pilot

---

[1]   https://www.eid-stork2.eu/.

[2]   https://peppol.eu/.

[3]   http://www.epsos.eu/.

[4]   https://www.esens.eu/.

evaluations are often heterogeneous with regard to the concrete approaches followed and methods applied. This leads to a situation, in which evaluation results obtained are heterogeneous too. This heterogeneity can be observed within projects, i.e. between pilot applications, and also on a higher level between different projects. Ultimately, this leads to a situation, in which obtained evaluation results are hardly comparable. Consequently, lessons learned from conducted pilot evaluations cannot be aggregated to a coherent holistic picture. This, in turn, makes it difficult for responsible stakeholders to draw the correct conclusions from obtained evaluation results.

To address this issue, we propose a common evaluation scheme for pilot-based research projects targeting the public sector. The proposed evaluation scheme is project and pilot independent. Accordingly, it can be applied to a broad range of research projects and activities. The evaluation scheme introduced in this article relies on a hierarchical evaluation-criteria model and defines a common procedure to apply criteria based on this model. By providing a common basis for pilot evaluation, the proposed scheme ensures that obtained evaluation results are homogeneous enough to enable comparisons between different pilots. In this article, we introduce the proposed evaluation scheme in detail. Furthermore, we demonstrate its practical applicability by applying the scheme to pilot applications of the EU-funded research project FutureTrust[5].

This article is based on a paper presented at the 14th International Conference on Web Information Systems and Technologies [17]. Overall, this article is structured as follows. Section 2 defines in more detail the problem tackled by this work and briefly surveys related work. In Sect. 3, we introduce a simple project model, which also serves as basis for the proposed evaluation scheme. The evaluation scheme itself is then introduced and described in detail in Sect. 4. A first application of the proposed scheme is discussed in Sect. 5. Lessons learned from this application are sketched in Sect. 6. Finally, conclusions are drawn and an outlook to future work is provided in Sect. 7.

2   Problem Statement and Related Work

During the past years, the EU has invested significant financial resources to fund a series of research projects with the goal to improve IT services that are related to the public sector. A major driver behind these funding activities has been the aim to support the EU's strategy of a Digital Single Market [7]. According to this strategy, many funded research projects have focused on achieving cross-border interoperability between public-sector IT services of different EU Member States. Examples are the Large Scale Pilots STORK and STORK 2.0[6] focusing on eID interoperability, epSOS[7] targeting the e-health sector, or PEPPOL[8], which put an emphasis on e-procurement. Results yielded by all these LSPs have

---

[5] https://cordis.europa.eu/project/rcn/202698/factsheet/en.
[6] https://www.eid-stork2.eu/.
[7] http://www.epsos.eu/.
[8] https://peppol.eu/.

been consolidated by the research project e-SENS[9] . Leveraging the use of IT in public-sector use cases has also been the main goal of the international research project SUNFISH[10], funded under the EU's Horizon 2020 research and innovation programme, and of the project FutureID[11] funded under the ICT theme of the Cooperation Programme of the 7th Framework Programme of the European Commission. Scientific contributions of these projects have been discussed by Suzic et al. [15] and Rath et al. [14], respectively. This brief and by far not exhaustive overview shows that various research projects have been done during the past years aiming to bring forward the use of information technology in cross-border public-sector solutions.

Examining in more detail the surveyed projects' internal structure reveals that most of them follow a similar approach: solutions developed in the project are usually tested by means of one or more pilot applications. Furthermore, all projects foresee some sort of evaluation, where obtained results are assessed against defined criteria. However, the approaches followed by the various projects to carry out evaluations differ considerably from each other. In the worst cases, there is even no consistent evaluation method applied within a project, e.g. to evaluate different pilot applications of the project. Instead, each pilot application defines and applies its own evaluation method. This heterogeneity in applied evaluation methods has an impact on obtained evaluation results. While these results might be sufficient within the scope of a single pilot application, they cannot be assembled to a coherent big picture. This, in turn, renders the conclusive derivation of findings from available evaluation results difficult.

Of course, there are sometimes good reasons to divert from a common evaluation method and to rely on pilot-specific evaluation schemes instead. One reason can be the fact that pilot applications can undergo major redesigns during project lifetime. This can necessitate an adaptation of the planned pilot evaluation as well. Another reason to abandon a common evaluation method for all pilot applications within a project can be a high degree of heterogeneity between the pilot applications themselves, which makes it difficult to find an evaluation method that perfectly fits all pilots. Despite these valid reasons, incomparable evaluation results constitute a serious issue that threatens to decrease the overall gain of a research project for involved stakeholders.

This issue has also been recognized by the scientific community. Accordingly, interesting works exist that focus on the evaluation of research projects. For instance, Khan et al. [9] discuss the problem of evaluating a collaborative IT-based research and development project. While this work identifies relevant challenges to overcome, the proposed evaluation method has been mainly tailored to one specific project. This renders an application of the proposed method to arbitrary projects difficult. More generic evaluation methods have been introduced by Eilat et al. [4] and by Asosheh et al. [1]. Both proposals make use of the balanced scorecard (BSC) approach and data envelopment analysis (DEA).

---

[9] https://www.esens.eu/.
[10] http://www.sunfishproject.eu/.
[11] http://www.futureid.eu/.

However, they do not take into account the specifics of the type of projects targeted in this article, i.e. pilot-based projects aiming to improve public-sector solutions.

In summary, evaluation schemes proposed in literature usually focus on very specific types of projects or are even tailored to one single project. An evaluation scheme that can be applied to a broad range of pilot-based research projects from the public sector is currently missing. The evaluation scheme proposed in this article closes this gap.

3   Project Model

The basic aim of the work presented in this article is the development of a common evaluation scheme for pilot-based research projects. The main challenge in developing such an evaluation scheme, which is applicable to a broad set of research projects, lies in the trade-off between assuring general applicability and obtaining meaningful evaluation results. On the one hand, an abstract scheme enables a broad applicability to arbitrary research projects. However, an abstract evaluation scheme typically yields rather abstract evaluation results too, which complicates the derivation of concrete conclusions. On the other hand, a more specific evaluation scheme can consider peculiarities of a given research project or its pilot applications. However, such a specific scheme can usually only be applied to a limited set of projects or pilots. The demand for general applicability is not satisfied in this case.

To overcome this trade-off, we have based the proposed evaluation scheme on a well-defined project model. The proposed scheme can be applied to any research project complying with this model. The project model has been based on the following three assumptions, which define the scope of targeted project types:

- The proposed evaluation scheme targets pilots and projects that provide solutions for the public sector. Accordingly, the evaluation scheme assumes that an IT agenda is in place, from which goals for different projects under this agenda are derived.
- The proposed scheme targets pilot-based projects, which apply and test solutions developed in the project by means of one or more pilot applications.
- The proposed evaluation scheme assumes the research project to be carried out in multiple consecutive project phases, each comprising an own phase-specific pilot evaluation.

From these assumptions, a general project model can be derived, which serves as basis for the proposed evaluation scheme. This project model defines the general project structure as well as general project-execution and evaluation phases. The two aspects of the derived project model are detailed in the following subsections.

3.1   Project Structure

From the assumptions made above, the general project structure illustrated in Fig. 1 can be derived for the project model. As shown in Fig. 1, the project model does not make detailed restrictions regarding the project structure. There are only two requirements to be met by projects complying with the structure shown in Fig. 1 and thus with the general project model. First, the project needs to be defined under a given IT agenda. Second, the project must foresee development and operation of one or more pilot applications.

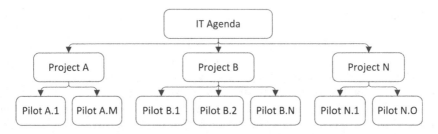

Fig. 1. The proposed evaluation scheme can be applied to all projects complying with the shown general structure (adapted from [17]).

By intention, the project structure of the general project model has been kept as abstract as possible. This assures a broad applicability of the general project model to concrete research projects. This, in turn, guarantees that the proposed evaluation scheme, which builds on the general project model defined in this section, can be applied to a broad set of research projects as well.

3.2   Project-Execution Phases

General project-execution phases constitute the second aspect of the general project model defined in this section. Similar to the project structure introduced in Sect. 3.1, also general project-execution phases can be derived from the three basic assumptions made above. Overall, the project model foresees three basic project-execution phases. In parallel, three evaluation phases are foreseen as well, covering evaluation-related tasks throughout the project.

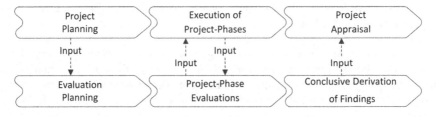

Fig. 2. The proposed evaluation scheme can be applied to all projects implementing the shown general project-execution phases (adapted from [17]).

Project-execution phases and related evaluation phases are shown in Fig. 2. According to this figure, the general project model considers the following three project-execution and evaluation phases:

- *Project Planning / Evaluation Planning*: During the Project Planning phase, the project's overall structure, contents, goals, and setup are defined. In parallel, the Evaluation Planning phase is executed, in which aspects related to evaluation activities within the project are defined. As shown in Fig. 2, relevant input from project planning needs to be considered during evaluation planning.
- *Execution of Project Phases / Project-phase Evaluations*: These two phases are executed after completion of the Project Planning and Evaluation Planning phases. According to the underlying assumptions of the general project model, the project is executed in consecutive project phases. Figure 2 shows that each project phase is accompanied by a corresponding evaluation phase. Figure 2 also shows that corresponding project-execution phases and evaluation phases influence each other. While conducted evaluations certainly depend on the respective project-execution phase and its goals and contents, project phases also should take into account available evaluation results (e.g. from previous phases). This supports a continuous improvement of the entire project.
- *Project Appraisal / Conclusive Derivation of Findings*: These phases are executed after completion of the last iterative project phase and corresponding project-phase evaluation. Hence, these phases are carried out at the end of the project to collect all lessons learned, draw the correct conclusions from these lessons, and to bring the project to a round figure. In the corresponding evaluation phase, findings are derived from conducted evaluations and serve as direct input to project appraisal. Figure 2 shows that the *Project Appraisal* phase needs to consider input from the *Conclusive Derivation of Findings* phase.

Similar to the project structure introduced in Sect. 3.1, also general project-execution phases have been defined on a rather abstract level. Together with the defined project structure, this yields a rather abstract general project model. As the general project model will serve as basis for the proposed evaluation scheme, its abstract nature assures that the proposed scheme is applicable to the majority of pilot-based projects targeting the public sector. Thus, the project model introduced in this section reasonably handles the trade-off between assuring general applicability and obtaining meaningful evaluation results.

4   Proposed Evaluation Scheme

Based on the defined general project model, we propose a generic evaluation scheme for the systematic evaluation of pilot-based public-sector research projects. The proposed evaluation scheme aims for two goals. On the one hand, the scheme aims to be abstract enough to be applicable to a broad range of pilots and projects, in order to ensure comparability within projects (i.e. between the project's pilots) and also on a higher level between different projects. On the other hand, the evaluation scheme should still enable in-depth evaluations that take into account specifics of pilots and projects. The proposed scheme deals with this obvious trade-off by following a hierarchical approach.

In general, the evaluation scheme introduced in this section relies on the general project model defined above. If a research project complies with this general model, the proposed evaluation scheme defines in detail how to carry out evaluation-related activities throughout the project.

Essentially, the proposed evaluation scheme is composed of two building blocks. The first building blocks specifies an evaluation-criteria model. Evaluation criteria are crucial for any type of evaluation. Choosing adequate evaluation criteria turns out to be a challenging task, especially with regard to the given trade-off between general applicability and desired in-depth evaluations. The evaluation-criteria model, which is part of the proposed evaluation scheme, assists in overcoming this challenge by providing a framework for the definition of adequate evaluation criteria. Details of the proposed scheme's evaluation-criteria model are provided in Subsect. 4.1.

The second building block of the proposed evaluation scheme specifies the detailed evaluation process, which represents a step-by-step procedure to evaluate pilots using evaluation criteria that have been defined using the provided evaluation-criteria model. The proposed evaluation process builds up on the general project model introduced in Sect. 3 and further refines the various project and evaluation phases defined by this model. Details of the proposed scheme's detailed evaluation process are presented in Subsect. 4.2.

4.1   Evaluation-Criteria Model

The evaluation-criteria model constitutes the first major building block of the proposed evaluation scheme. It provides a framework that supports evaluators in defining and structuring evaluation criteria that are used during evaluation processes.

In principle, evaluation criteria used for pilot evaluation need to meet the same requirements as the overall evaluation scheme. Concretely, evaluation criteria should ideally be the same for all pilots in all evaluated projects. Only in this case, direct comparisons between different pilots and even between different projects are feasible. At the same time, evaluation criteria should be concrete enough to consider specifics of different pilots and projects. Obviously, these are contradictory requirements, which cannot be met by a simple one-dimensional list of evaluation criteria. Therefore, the proposed evaluation scheme follows a more complex approach and relies on a hierarchical evaluation-criteria model. This hierarchical model defines multiple layers, to which evaluation criteria can be assigned to. This is illustrated in Fig. 3.

The evaluation-criteria model shown in Fig. 3 considers the fact that evaluation criteria are typically closely related to project and pilot goals. Concretely, evaluation criteria are used to assess a pilot's or project's compliance

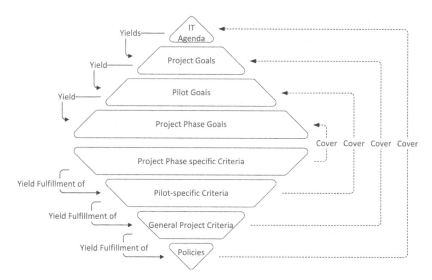

Fig. 3. The proposed evaluation-criteria model enables the definition of goals and related criteria on multiple layers of abstraction (adapted from [17]).

with defined goals. This close relation is also reflected by the evaluation-criteria model depicted in Fig. 3. The upper pyramid shows the different layers, on which relevant goals can be defined. Note that the pyramid's structure complies with the general project model defined in Sect. 3. The pyramid's topmost level represents the relevant IT agenda defining the very basic goals to consider. This agenda yields project-specific goals for concrete projects executed under this agenda. Within a concrete project, pilot-specific goals can be derived for each of the project's pilots from the overall project goals. Finally, pilot-specific goals can be further detailed by defining pilot-specific goals separately for each project phase. Overall, the proposed evaluation-criteria model defines relevant goals to be defined on four different layers of abstraction.

Once all goals have been defined according to the four layers, relevant evaluation criteria can be derived. The proposed model foresees evaluation criteria to be defined on four layers of abstraction as well, yielding the lower pyramid shown in Fig. 3. When deriving evaluation criteria for the four layers, two aspects need to be considered. First, defined evaluation criteria must cover the relevant goals defined before. This applies to all layers and is indicated in Fig. 3 by arrows between the upper and the lower pyramid. Second, evaluation criteria defined in neighboring layers must be related. In particular, given the fulfillment degree of criteria in one layer, it must be possible to derive the fulfillment degree of criteria in the subjacent layer.

Together the different layers for project-related goals and for evaluation criteria constitute the evaluation-criteria model shown in Fig. 3. Note that the proposed evaluation-criteria model deliberately does not define concrete evaluation criteria, in order to ensure a broad applicability of the proposed evaluation model. Instead, the evaluation-criteria model merely defines a framework for the definition and classification of relevant goals and for the derivation of related evaluation criteria. The provided framework enforces a systematic derivation process for relevant goals and evaluation criteria on different layers of abstraction, supports the modeling of relations between goals and criteria defined on different layers, and assures a precise mapping between goals and evaluation criteria. This enables a systematic evaluation process, where the fulfillment of higher-level criteria can be derived automatically from the fulfillment of lower-level requirements.

4.2 Evaluation Process

Once relevant goals have been defined and evaluation criteria have been derived using the evaluation-criteria model introduced above, the actual evaluation process can be carried out. This evaluation process constitutes the second building block of the proposed evaluation scheme and is illustrated in Fig. 4. In principle, the shown process can be regarded as a detailing of the general project and evaluation phases introduced in Sect. 3. Thus, the proposed evaluation process implicitly complies with the defined general project model introduced in that section.

Figure 4, which illustrates the proposed evaluation process by means of a flow chart, is subdivided into six areas. First, the entire chart is split into two halves. The left half describes process steps to be carried out during project execution. Hence, this half of the flow chart corresponds to the upper part of Fig. 2. In contrast, the right half describes necessary steps to be carried out during project evaluation. Accordingly, this half of the chart corresponds to the lower part of Fig. 2. Second, the two halves of the flow chart are further split into three horizontal areas. This reflects the three general execution phases defined in Sect. 3. In summary, this yields six areas, each representing a project or evaluation phase, and each containing relevant process steps to be carried out in that phase.

Figure 4 shows that the proposed evaluation scheme comprises 18 processing steps to be carried out in total. For the first project-execution and evaluation phase, i.e. *Project Planning* and *Evaluation Planning*, the evaluation scheme foresees execution of the following steps:

- **Step (1) - Identification of Relevant IT-agenda Goals:** In this first step in project planning, general goals from relevant IT agendas, under which the project is executed, are identified. This step yields the most high-level goals to be considered during project execution. In the end, the overall success of the project is assessed against the goals identified in this step.
- **Step (2) - Definition of Project Goals:** From the general goals identified in Step (1), concrete project goals are derived in this step. Project goals detail higher-level goals by applying the respective project's specific context to them. Hence, the project's context and its defined contents are a relevant input during execution of this processing step.

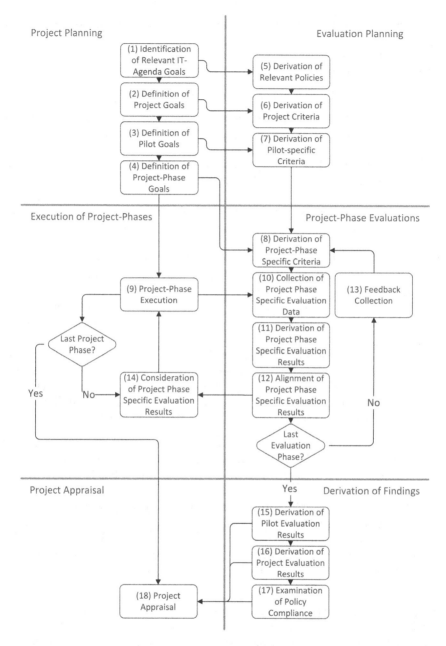

Fig. 4. The evaluation scheme specifies process steps to be carried out in the shown order (adapted from [17]).

- **Step (3) - Definition of Pilot Goals:** Once the overall project goals have been fixed in Step (2), pilot-specific goals need to be derived. Pilot-specific goals of course need to comply with the higher-level project goals, but additionally take into account the specifics of the project's different pilot applications. Accordingly, the definition of pilots and their foreseen role in the project are relevant inputs to this processing step.

– **Step (4) - Definition of Project-phase Goals:** Pilot-specific goals obtained in Step (3) can again vary between different project phases. For instance, concrete goals of a pilot can vary between project phases, in which the pilot is developed, and phases, in which the pilot is operated. To consider possible phase-specific variations, pilot-specific goals are further detailed to project phase specific goals in this step.

– **Step (5) - Derivation of Relevant Policies:** This is the very first step to be taken in evaluation planning. In this step, relevant policies to be considered are derived from general goals extracted from relevant IT agendas. Hence, results of Step (1) are a relevant input to this step. In the end, the overall evaluation process will tell whether the project complies with the policies identified in this step.

– **Step (6) - Derivation of Project Criteria:** By taking into account the policies derived in Step (5) and the general project goals obtained in Step (2), evaluation criteria are defined on project level in this step. These criteria must be defined such that their degree of fulfillment can tell whether the project meets its goals defined in Step (2).

– **Step (7) - Derivation of Pilot-specific Criteria:** From the project criteria obtained from the previous step, pilot-specific criteria are derived in this step. Pilot-specific goals obtained in Step (3) are a relevant input to this step. Derived pilot-specific criteria must be defined such that their degree of fulfillment can tell whether the respective pilot meets its goals defined in Step (3).

After completing the process steps described so far, all relevant goals and (almost) all evaluation criteria have been defined and set in relation according to the evaluation-criteria model introduced in Sect. 4.1. What is still left to be done is the derivation of project phase specific evaluation criteria (Step (8)). This task is intentionally shifted to the subsequent project-execution/evaluation phase (i.e. the next horizontal area shown in Fig. 4), as the proposed evaluation model foresees a dynamic and iterative adaption of these criteria during the entire project life-cycle. Overall, the next project-execution and evaluation phase (i.e. *Execution of Project Phases* and *Project Phase Evaluations*) comprise the following processing steps:

– **Step (8) - Derivation of Project-phase Specific Criteria:** In this step, project phase specific evaluation criteria are derived for each pilot, taking into account the respective pilot's pilot-specific criteria from Step (7) on the one hand, and project phase specific goals derived in Step (4) on the other hand. For all but the first project phase, feedback collected during the previous project phase is another relevant input to this step and must be considered for the definition of criteria for the current project phase. This way, project phase specific criteria can be dynamically adapted during the entire project life-cycle to consider changing circumstances and requirements.

– **Step (9) - Project-phase Execution:** This step covers the execution of a project phase according to the project setup. Note that this is a rather complex and time-consuming step in most cases, as it covers all project-related activities assigned to a specific project phase. However, details of this processing step are usually irrelevant for the proposed evaluation scheme. Hence, these details are not modeled in the flow chart shown in Fig. 4.

– **Step (10) - Collection of Project Phase Specific Evaluation Data:** This step is executed in parallel to Step (9), i.e. in parallel to the execution of a certain project phase. During this step, evaluation data is collected. This can be achieved e.g. through interviews, questionnaires, or through the automated measuring or logging of data. The proposed evaluation scheme leaves the choice of the most suitable method to the respective project evaluators. This ensures a broad applicability of the proposed evaluation scheme, as the best tool choice can depend on the nature of the project to be evaluated. In any case, Step (9) provides relevant input to this processing step.

– **Step (11) - Derivation of Project Phase Specific Evaluation Results:** In this step, evaluation data collected in Step (10) are analyzed in order to derive evaluation results for the current project phase. The concrete analysis process depends on the type of evaluation data collected. Hence, the proposed evaluation scheme again does not apply any restrictions here. In any case, project-phase specific criteria derived in Step (8) are a prerequisite for this step.

– **Step (12) - Alignment of Project Phase Specific Evaluation Results:** Evaluation results of the current project phase obtained in Step (11) are subsequently aligned with other relevant stakeholders involved in the project. Depending on the respective project setup, this can be e.g. pilot developers or pilot operators. This step gives involved stakeholders the chance to comment on results obtained, in order to prevent misunderstandings early and to ensure a consensual overall evaluation process.

– **Step (13) - Feedback Collection:** In case there is at least one more project phase (and hence also one more evaluation phase) to come, feedback on the applied evaluation process is collected from all involved stakeholders. Again, the method applied to collect feedback is left open to the respective evaluators. Also in this context, the best choice can depend on the actual project setup. Independent of the chosen method, collected feedback serves as input for the definition of project phase specific criteria for the next project phase (Step 8). If no further project phase is foreseen, i.e. the project has just completed its last phase, this step is omitted.

– **Step (14) - Consideration of Project Phase Specific Evaluation Results:** After completion of a project phase, and if there is another project phase to come, this step is carried out by the project executors. In this step, evaluation results of the just completed project phase are analyzed. If possible, lessons learned are derived and considered as input for the execution of the next project phase. This way, the project is continuously improved based on intermediate evaluation results. In case the last project phase has already been completed and no further phase is to come, this step is omitted.

After completion of the final project phase, the last two overall phases, i.e. *Project Appraisal* and *Derivation of Findings* are carried out. Relevant processing steps of these phases are described in the following:

- **Step (15) - Derivation of Pilot Evaluation Results:** This step is executed after completing the last iterative project and evaluation phases. In this step, project phase specific evaluation results collected iteratively in Step (10) and analyzed in Step (11) are combined for each pilot to derive overall pilot-specific evaluation results. If evaluation criteria have been defined according to the proposed evaluation-criteria model, this step can be carried out efficiently, as pilot-specific evaluation results can be derived directly from project phase specific results. After completion of this step, project evaluators know if and to what extent pilot-specific criteria defined at the beginning of the project in Step (7) are met.
- **Step (16) - Derivation of Project Evaluation Results:** Once all pilot-specific evaluation results have been derived in Step (15), this step combines them to overall project evaluation results. Again, this is an efficient process, if evaluation criteria have been defined such that the degree of fulfillment can be derived from the lower layer of the evaluation-criteria model. After completion of this step, project evaluators know if and to what extent project criteria defined in Step (6) are met.
- **Step (17) - Examination of Policy Compliance:** This step finally checks derived project evaluation results against relevant policies identified at the beginning of the project (Step 5). This way, stakeholders can assess whether the project and its results comply with IT agendas, from which these policies have been derived. This process step concludes evaluation-related activities within the project. All evaluation results (pilot evaluation results, project evaluation results, and policy compliance) serve as input for the final project-appraisal phase (Step 18).
- **Step (18) - Project Appraisal:** In this final step, all evaluation results stemming from different layers of abstraction are combined to derive the most valuable lessons learned. Due to the multi-layered approach followed, detailed analyses of evaluation results can be conducted, including specific results as well as comparisons between pilots and even between different projects.

4.3 Configurability

Although the proposed evaluation scheme specifies in detail necessary steps to be carried out, it deliberately remains flexible and abstract in certain aspects and gives evaluators, who apply the scheme in practice, room for configuration. This makes the proposed evaluation scheme more flexible and applicable to a broader range of projects. In particular, it ensures that the evaluation scheme can be applied to all pilot-based research projects complying with the general project model introduced in Sect. 3. Concretely, the proposed evaluation scheme can be configured and adapted to the respective project, to which it is to be applied, by means of the following aspects:

- **Number of Iterative Project Phases:** The evaluation scheme supports an arbitrary number of iterative project phases and corresponding evaluation phases. Not that this does not require the project to define multiple project phases. The evaluation scheme works with one single project phase (and corresponding evaluation phase) as well. However, it is not limited to that but supports 1 to N phases.
- **Evaluation Criteria:** The proposed evaluation scheme comprises an evaluation-criteria model. While this model provides a hierarchical framework for the definition and classification of evaluation criteria, it does not define concrete evaluation criteria. Instead, concrete evaluation criteria can be defined by the respective project evaluators, taking into account the specifics of the project and pilots to be evaluated.
- **Relation between Evaluation Criteria:** The proposed evaluation-criteria model enables the definition of evaluation criteria on multiple layers of abstraction. Criteria on neighboring layers should be set in relation to each other. This way, the fulfillment degree of higher-level criteria can be derived systematically from the fulfillment degree of lower-level criteria. The model does not impose any restrictions regarding the definition of relations between criteria. For instance, evaluators can follow a rather simple approach, which assumes each criterion to be equally important. Alternatively, more complex relations can be defined between different layers of the evaluation-criteria model. While this enables a more fine-grained modeling of dependencies between criteria on different layers of abstraction, it potentially complicates the derivation of evaluation results. However, evaluators are free to choose the approach that fits best the requirements of the respective project.
- **Method for Evaluation-Data Collection:** In each iterative project phase, evaluation data needs to be collected by evaluators. In principle, different approaches can be followed to carry out this task. For instance, data can be collected with the help of questionnaires, by means of personal interviews, by doing project-internal audits, or by collecting and analyzing generated data such as log files. The proposed evaluation scheme is flexible enough to support all these (and also other) approaches. Hence, evaluators can choose the method that fits best the characteristics of the project to be evaluated.
- **Method for Deriving Evaluation Results from Evaluation Data:** In each iterative project phase, evaluation results need to be derived from collected evaluation data. The proposed evaluation scheme does not specify this step and the methods to be applied in this step in detail. Hence, it is up to the executing evaluators to agree on an appropriate method that enables comprehensible derivation of evaluation results from collected evaluation data. Of course, the method applied needs to be aligned with the type of collected evaluation data. For instance, if this data is available in structured form, automated methods can be applied to derive evaluation results from it. In case evaluation data has been collected e.g. by means of telephone interviews, manual methods may be necessary.
- **Method for Alignment of Project Phase Specific Evaluation Results:** The proposed evaluation scheme gives involved stakeholders such as

pilot developers or pilot operators the opportunity to comment on intermediate evaluation results in each project and corresponding evaluation phase.
However, the scheme does not define a concrete method to be applied for carrying out this task. Also for this aspect of the evaluation process, evaluators
are free to choose their preferred approach to align intermediate evaluation
results with other involved stakeholders.
- **Provision of Feedback:** Finally, the proposed evaluation scheme also defines
a feedback channel from involved stakeholders to the project evaluators.
Again, the scheme does not define a concrete implementation of this feedback
channel but leaves this decision to the executing evaluators. This way, evaluators can choose the approach fitting best the characteristics of the respective
project.

Of course, leaving certain aspects unspecified imposes an additional task on
the evaluators of a project. They need to parametrize the evaluation scheme, in
order to adapt it to the specifics of the respective project. However, we believe
the gain in flexibility and applicability definitely compensates for the additional
effort. In the following section, we show one possible parametrization by dis-
cussing the application of the proposed evaluation scheme to the EU-funded
research project FutureTrust and its pilots.

5   Evaluation

Future Trust Services for Trustworthy Global Transactions (FutureTrust) is an
international research project funded by the EU under the programme *H2020-
EU.3.7. - Secure societies - Protecting freedom and security of Europe and its
citizens*. The project consortium consists of 16 partners from 10 countries, including EU member states as well as third-party countries. The overall aim of
FutureTrust is to support the practical implementation of the EU eIDAS Regulation [8] in Europe and beyond. Software components developed by FutureTrust
are applied to real-world use cases by means of several pilots and demonstrators.

FutureTrust fully complies with the general project model described in
Sect. 3. The project has a focus on the public-sector domain and is motivated
by an EU agenda, as described in the project's funding programme [6]. Furthermore, FutureTrust develops and operates a series of demonstrators and pilots.
Thus, the evaluation scheme proposed in this article is well suited for carrying
out pilot evaluations in FutureTrust. First experiences gained during application
of the proposed evaluation scheme in FutureTrust are discussed in this section.

5.1   Configuration

The proposed evaluation scheme introduced in Sect. 4 intentionally remains
generic in several aspects and hence needs to be configured and parametrized
before being applied to a concrete research project. In the case of FutureTrust,
the following parameters have been chosen for configurable aspects listed in
Sect. 4.3:

- **Number of Iterative Project Phases:** In principle, the evaluation scheme supports an arbitrary number of iterative project phases and corresponding evaluation phases. For FutureTrust, three phases have been defined. Evaluations are carried out before piloting (ex-ante evaluation), during piloting (mid-term evaluation), and after piloting (ex-post evaluation). This complies with FutureTrust's overall project setup as defined in FutureTrust's project description.
- **Evaluation Criteria:** While the proposed evaluation scheme provides a hierarchical evaluation-criteria model for the definition and classification of evaluation criteria, it does not define concrete evaluation criteria. For FutureTrust, relevant evaluation criteria have been extracted from relevant agendas and project-definition documents. Details on chosen evaluation criteria are provided in Subsect. 5.2.
- **Relation between Evaluation Criteria:** According to the proposed evaluation-criteria model, evaluation criteria assigned to neighboring layers of abstraction should be set in relation to each other. This way, the fulfillment degree of higher-level criteria can be derived systematically from the fulfillment degree of lower-level criteria. The model does not impose any restrictions regarding the definition of relations between criteria. For the sake of simplicity, we have followed a rather simple approach in FutureTrust. This approach assumes each criterion to be equally important and to have the same impact on related criteria in neighboring layers of abstraction.
- **Method for Evaluation-data Collection:** The proposed scheme requires evaluators to collect evaluation data in each iterative project phase. As FutureTrust piloting partners are distributed all over Europe, questionnaires have been prepared and sent out to piloting partners to collect necessary evaluation data. Where necessary, telephone calls have been organized to clarify open issues in a bilateral way.
- **Method for Deriving Evaluation Results from Evaluation Data:** In each iterative project phase, evaluation results need to be derived from collected evaluation data. In FutureTrust, evaluation data has been collected by means of questionnaires. As these questionnaires contain answers in prose, i.e. in unstructured form, an automated processing and analysis of evaluation data has not been feasible. Thus, the analysis of questionnaires and the derivation of intermediate evaluation results has relied on manual processes.
- **Method for Alignment of Project Phase Specific Evaluation Results:** The proposed evaluation scheme gives all involved stakeholders the opportunity to continuously comment on intermediate evaluation results. Due to the local dispersion of stakeholders within the project, FutureTrust follows again a document-based approach for this task. Evaluation results are compiled into intermediary evaluation reports. These reports are sent out to all involved stakeholders in order to give them the opportunity to provide feedback in written form.
- **Provision of Feedback:** The proposed evaluation scheme defines a feedback channel from involved stakeholders to the evaluators. FutureTrust organizes regular meetings (online and face-to-face) that bring together involved

stakeholders. These meetings can be used to bilaterally provide feedback on the overall evaluation process as defined by the proposed evaluation scheme.

5.2 Results

After applying the configuration as described in Sect. 5.1, the proposed evaluation scheme has been applied to the FutureTrust project and its pilots. In particular, the scheme has been applied twice, once for the evaluation of FutureTrust pilots and demonstrators, and once for analyzing their impact. The applied evaluation process has been exactly the same for pilot evaluation and impact analysis. However, different (hierarchical) evaluation criteria have been defined to reflect the different scopes of pilot evaluation and impact analysis.

Based on EU agendas relevant for FutureTrust, the following general project criteria have been defined for pilot evaluation:

- *Security and Data Protection*
- *Functionality*
- *Usability*
- *Interoperability*
- *Reusability and Sustainability*
- *Legal Compliance*
- *Compliance with Project Goals*

Accordingly, the following general project criteria have been defined for impact analysis:

- *Demonstration of Positive Business Case*
- *Empowerment and Protection of Users*
- *Increase of Use of Trust Services*
- *Reduction of Administrative Overhead*
- *Adherence to Sufficient Technology Readiness Level (TRL)*

From these general project criteria, pilot-specific evaluation criteria have been derived for each FutureTrust pilot and demonstrator. For each pilot and demonstrator, 24 pilot-specific criteria have been defined for pilot evaluation. In addition, 9 pilot-specific criteria have been defined for impact analysis for each pilot and demonstrator. Finally, project phase specific evaluation criteria have been derived. In total, 33 criteria for pilot evaluation and 9 criteria for impact analysis. To assure meaningful evaluation results, pilot-specific evaluation criteria have been defined based on the SMART approach described by Doran [3]. Accordingly, all defined criteria are Specific, Measurable, Achievable, Relevant, and Time-bound.

Based on the derived project phase specific evaluation criteria, questionnaires have been prepared and sent out to pilot developers and operators. By analyzing returned filled questionnaires, the fulfillment degree of project phase specific evaluation criteria could be determined. Where necessary, ambiguities have been clarified in bilateral calls.

From the obtained project phase specific evaluation results, the fulfillment of higher-layer criteria could be derived automatically. As an illustrative example, Figs. 5 and 6 show first results of the conducted pilot evaluation and impact analysis. Obtained results demonstrate the applied evaluation scheme's capability to yield evaluation results that are comparable among different FutureTrust pilots.

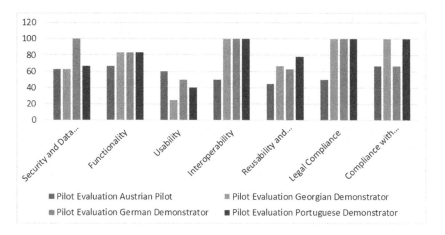

Fig. 5. Results of FutureTrust pilot evaluation (adapted from [17]).

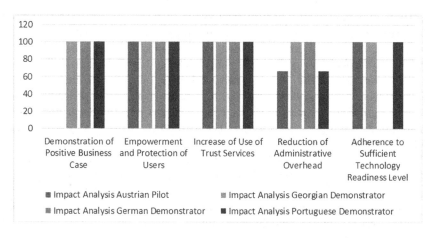

Fig. 6. Results of FutureTrust impact analysis (adapted from [17]).

Overall, the successful completion of the described evaluation steps in the context of FutureTrust demonstrates the practical applicability of the proposed evaluation scheme. The FutureTrust project was still ongoing when obtaining the evaluation results described above. Accordingly, the entire project evaluation was not finished at that time. However, most processing steps of the proposed evaluation scheme (including the most challenging ones like the definition of evaluation criteria) could already be applied and completed successfully. The proposed scheme can hence be regarded suitable for application in practice.

6   Lessons Learned

Although the FutureTrust project was not completed at the time of writing this article, several useful findings and lessons learned could be obtained during a first application of the proposed evaluation scheme to FutureTrust pilots and demonstrators in the first project phases.

The probably most important lesson learned is the finding that the proposed scheme can by applied successfully to a concrete research project. All concepts and processing steps defined by the proposed scheme could be applied and carried out as foreseen. Furthermore, the proposed scheme is able to meets its basic goal, i.e. yield comparable evaluation results while still taking into account specific characteristics and properties of different pilots.

Another positive lesson learned is the finding that the proposed scheme is rather flexible with regard to changes in the overall project structure. As pilots are treated independently to a large extent, varying schedules of different pilots caused by unexpected delays, or even the inclusion of new pilots during the project lifetime does not cause severe problems.

A less positive lesson learned concerns the scheme's evaluation-criteria model. It turned out that some assumptions made when designing this model were too optimistic. Concretely, the proposed evaluation scheme assumes that pilot-specific criteria are defined once at the beginning of the project. Although project phase specific criteria are derived from these pilot-specific criteria in each project phase, the pilot-specific criteria are assumed to be stable. FutureTrust has shown that this is not always the case in practice. Indeed, a minor extension of pilot-specific criteria was necessary after the first project phase, in order to achieve necessary alignments with other evaluation-related tasks in the project. While this was no show stopper in practice, the evaluation scheme should probably consider such necessities.

Overall, first lessons learned from applying the proposed evaluation scheme in FutureTrust are predominantly positive. While minor room for improvement has been identified, the scheme has passed its practical test so far. FutureTrust will continue to rely on the proposed evaluation scheme for the remaining project lifetime to obtain valuable evaluation results.

7   Conclusions and Future Work

In this article, we have proposed and introduced an evaluation scheme for pilot-based research projects. Based on the awareness that project evaluations of past research projects have not always been as good as they could be, the proposed scheme aims to support the systematic derivation of both comparable and detailed evaluation results.

To meet this apparently contradictory goal, the proposed scheme follows a hierarchical approach. Concretely, it defines evaluation criteria on different layers of abstraction and provides a detailed process description for carrying out evaluations against these criteria. Its successful application within an international research project shows that the proposed scheme indeed is able to meet its goal. The scheme's hierarchical nature enables in-depth evaluations of specific pilots, while still guaranteeing comparability of obtained evaluation results on a higher level of abstraction. Ultimately, the proposed scheme yields more valuable evaluation results, from which all stakeholders involved in a research project can benefit in the end. Especially funding bodies such as the EU can take advantage of more homogenous evaluation results, which supports them in steering research activities into the right directions, and in complying with relevant IT agendas.

Lessons learned from applying the proposed evaluation scheme to the research project FutureTrust still show some room for improvement. We continuously consider new findings to further improve the scheme. Applied improvements are continuously tested and evaluated by applying the scheme in the remaining project phases of FutureTrust. For the future, we also plan to apply the scheme to other projects, to further evaluate its project-independent applicability and to test the comparability of evaluation results obtained from different projects. At the same time, we aim to extend the scope of the proposed evaluation scheme. While its current focus lies on pilot-based projects from the public sector, we plan to make it applicable to other project types as well. This way, an even broader set of research projects could benefit from the proposed scheme.

Acknowledgments. This work has been supported by the FutureTrust project (N.700542) funded under the programme H2020-EU.3.7. - Secure societies - Protecting freedom and security of Europe and its citizens (2013/743/EU of 2013-12-03).

References

1. Asosheh, A., Nalchigar, S., Jamporazmey, M.: Information technology project evaluation: an integrated data envelopment analysis and balanced scorecard approach. Exp. Syst. Appl. **37**(8), 5931–5938 (2010). https://doi.org/10.1016/j.eswa.2010.02. 012. http://www.sciencedirect.com/science/article/pii/S0957417410000515
2. De Cock, D., Wouters, K., Preneel, B.: Introduction to the Belgian EID card. In: Katsikas, S.K., Gritzalis, S., López, J. (eds.) EuroPKI 2004. LNCS, vol. 3093, pp. 1–13. Springer, Heidelberg (2004). https://doi.org/10.1007/978-3-540-25980-0_1
3. Doran, G.T.: There's a SMART way to write managements's goals and objectives. Manag. Rev. **70**(11), 2 (1981). EBSCOhost. http://web.a.ebscohost.com/ehost/pd fviewer/pdfviewer?sid=c62fb711-f4fb-4a4e-9f6e-62de080316e0%40sessionmgr4006 &vid=1&hid=4101

4. Eilat, H., Golany, B., Shtub, A.: R&d project evaluation: an integrated dea and balanced scorecard approach. Omega **36**(5), 895–912 (2008). https://doi. org/10.1016/j.omega.2006.05.002. http://www.sciencedirect.com/science/article/ pii/S0305048306000442

5. European Commission: Digital Agenda for Europe (2018). https://eur-lex. europa.eu/legal-content/EN/TXT/HTML/?uri=LEGISSUM:si0016&from=DE. Accessed 05 July 2018

6. European Commission: H2020-EU.3.7. - Secure societies - Protecting freedom and security of Europe and its citizens (2018). https://cordis.europa.eu/programme/ rcn/664463_en.html. Accessed 05 July 2018

7. European Commission: Shaping the Digital Single Market (2018). https://ec.eur opa.eu/digital-single-market/en/policies/shaping-digital-single-market. Accessed 05 July 2018

8. European Union: Regulation (EU) No 910/2014 of the European Parliament and of the Council of 23 July 2014 on electronic identification and trust services for electronic transactions in the internal market and repealing Directive 1999/93/EC (2018). https://eur-lex.europa.eu/legal-content/EN/ TXT/?uri=CELEX:32014R0910. Accessed 05 July 2018

9. Khan, Z., Ludlow, D., Caceres, S.: Evaluating a collaborative it based research and development project. Eval. Prog. Planning **40**, 27–41 (2013). https://doi.org/10. 1016/j.evalprogplan.2013.04.004. http://www.sciencedirect.com/science/article/ pii/S0149718913000347

10. Knall, T., Tauber, A., Zefferer, T., Zwattendorfer, B., Axfjord, A., Bjarnason, H.: Secure and privacy-preserving cross-border authentication: the STORK pilot 'SaferChat'. In: Andersen, K.N., Francesconi, E., Grönlund, Å., van Engers, T.M. (eds.) EGOVIS 2011. LNCS, vol. 6866, pp. 94–106. Springer, Heidelberg (2011). https://doi.org/10.1007/978-3-642-22961-9_8

11. Leitold, H., Hollosi, A., Posch, R.: Security Architecture of the Austrian Citizen Card Concept. In: 18th Annual Computer Security Applications Conference, 2002. Proceedings, pp. 391–400 (2002). https://doi.org/10.1109/CSAC.2002.1176311

12. Leitold, H., Posch, R.: STORK - technical approach and privacy. In: Bus, J., Crompton, M., Hildebrandt, M., Metakides, G. (eds.) Digital Enlightenment Yearbook 2012, pp. 289–306 (2012)

13. Martens, T.: Electronic identity management in Estonia between market and state governance. Identity Inf. Soc. **3**(1), 213–233 (2010). https://doi.org/10.1007/ s12394-010-0044-0

14. Rath, C., Roth, S., Bratko, H., Zefferer, T.: Encryption-based second authentication factor solutions for qualified server-side signature creation. In: Kő, A., Francesconi, E. (eds.) EGOVIS 2015. LNCS, vol. 9265, pp. 71–85. Springer, Cham (2015). https://doi.org/10.1007/978-3-319-22389-6_6

15. Suzic, B., Reiter, A.: Towards secure collaboration in federated cloud environments. In: 2016 11th International Conference on Availability, Reliability and Security (ARES), pp. 750–759, August 2016. https://doi.org/10.1109/ARES.2016.46

16. Tauber, A., Zwattendorfer, B., Zefferer, T.: Stork: pilot 4 towards cross-border electronic delivery. In: Verlag, T. (ed.) Electronic Government and Electronic Participation - Joint Proceedings of Ongoing Research and Projects of IFIP EGOV and ePart 2011, pp. 295–301 (2011)

17. Tou, J.T.: Information systems. In: von Brauer, W. (ed.) GI 1973. LNCS, vol. 1, pp. 489–507. Springer, Heidelberg (1973). https://doi.org/10.1007/3-540-06473-7_52

Personalized Review-Oriented Explanations for Recommender Systems

Felipe Costa$^{(\boxtimes)}$ and Peter Dolog

Aalborg University, Selma Lagerløfs Vej 300, 9220 Aalborg, Denmark
{fcosta,dolog}@cs.aau.dk

Abstract. Explainable recommender systems aim to provide clear interpretations to a user regarding the recommended list of items. The explanations present different formats to justify the recommended list of items such as images, graphs or text. We propose to use review-oriented explanations to help users in their decision since we can find crucial detailed feature in the reviews given by users. The model uses advances of natural language processing and incorporates the helpfulness score given in previous reviews to explain the recommended list of items provided by a latent factor model prediction. We conducted empirical experiments in the Yelp and Amazon datasets, proving that our model improves the quality of the explanations. The model outperforms baselines models by 13% for NDCG@5, 83% for HitRatio@5, 13% for NDCG@10, and 55% for HitRatio@10 in the Yelp dataset. For the Amazon dataset, the observed improvement was 9% for NDCG@5, 83% for HitRatio@5, 9% for NDCG@10, and 22% for HitRatio@10.

Keywords: Explainability · Recommender systems · Matrix factorization

1 Introduction

Recommender systems research area experienced extensive improvements in the past years regarding its accuracy. The current recommender systems models are reasonably capable of predicting items close to the user's preferences. The most well-known recommender system model is collaborative filtering, which predicts items based on the user's or item's similarities. Figure 1 illustrates a user rating and reviewing a product according to different features. Further, the recommender system predicts a list of the most preferred items based on the previous historical information. However, the majority of the current models neglect the explanations of the recommendations, making the online systems less trustworthy and dropping the user's fidelity to those systems.

Recently, researchers have proposed different models to explain recommendations such as based on graphs or text. However, they do not consider the quality of explanations presented to a user. The interpretation given to a user is either in a modular way "You like the item i because you previous liked the item j

© Springer Nature Switzerland AG 2019
M. J. Escalona et al. (Eds.): WEBIST 2018, LNBIP 372, pp. 147–169, 2019.
https://doi.org/10.1007/978-3-030-35330-8_8

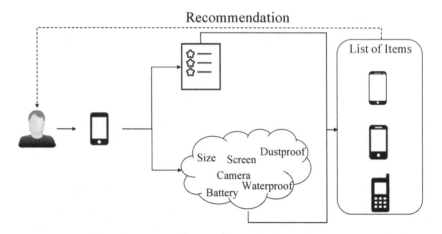

Fig. 1. Example of an online shopping system.

and they have the same feature f." or only the list of features previously liked by the user.

We propose an extension of the NECoNMF model [2] which uses collective matrix factorization to predict user's preferences and a neural interpretation model to explain the recommendations. NECoNMF succeeds in providing accurate recommendations, but it does not present good quality the generated text to describe the predicted list of items.

NECoNMF collectively factorizes ratings, item's content features, contextual information, and sentiments. Furthermore, it provides an explainable neural model based on users' previous reviews and ratings. We extend the NECoNMF model in two directions: (1) adding the user's influence score to the factorization model and (2) adding the helpfulness score to the explainable model. The users have a stronger influence on their friends' decisions, so by jointly decomposing the influence score, the model improves its accuracy. The reviews are written in online systems present helpfulness to qualify the information about a specific item, which can influence other users to decide if they would like or not to interact with the described item.

We conducted experiments in Yelp and Amazon benchmark datasets to measure the accuracy of the recommendations based on two metrics Hit Ratio and NDCG. Furthermore, we present examples of explanations given by our model.

This paper presents the contributions listed below:

- Collective factorization of five information: ratings, item's content features, contextual information, sentiments, and user's influence score;
- Text generation model using neural networks and helpfulness score;
- Results given by the empirical experiments in the Yelp and Amazon datasets.

2   Related Works

The top-N task in recommender systems aims to predict the N preferable items given the user's previous interest. The Popular Items (PopItem) model [3] recommends the most popular items to a user. It is a simple implementation due to the natural understanding of its logic. The PageRank [6] model is another simple model with reasonable results which rank a list of items according to the user's previous preferences. Another well-known technique for collaborative filtering is named matrix factorization (MF). This technique became popular with the accurate results given by the SVD model [9] presented on the Netflix contest. Later, NMF model [11] received attention in the recommender systems researchers' community, due to its clear interpretability for matrices decomposition.

Collective matrix factorization (CMF) is an extended version of MF aiming to jointly factorize features to improve the accuracy in predicting the list of items. Liu *et al.* proposed MultiNMF for multiview-clustering [12], which divides the objects into clusters based on multiple representations of the object. Likewise, He *et al.* proposed a co-regularized NMF (CoNMF) [8], which formalizes comment-based clustering as a multi-view problem using pair-wise and cluster-wise CoNMF. Saveski & Mantrach proposed Local Collective Embeddings (LCE) model [14] to identify a common latent space for user-document and document-term matrices. Costa & Dolog proposed an extended version of LCE, named CHNMF [1]. CHNMF decomposes the input matrices using a hybrid regularization term. Costa & Dolog improved CHNMF model [2] by adding the sentiment feature to its factorization model.

The matrix factorization models, generally, do not provide clear explanations for their recommended list of items. Recently, researchers have given attention to the explainability of recommendations models to improve the transparency, effectiveness, scrutability, and user trust [15] in online systems. The explanations can receive different presentation format, for example, text, graph or table. In this paper, we selected three baselines using textual information due to fairly compare the review-oriented explanations given by our model. Zhang *et al.* proposed the Explicit Factor Model (EFM) [15] based on a sentiment lexicon construction technique to extract the most relevant features from the reviews. He *et al.* proposed a review-aware recommendation named TriRank [7], which applies a tripartite graph algorithm to improve accuracy for top-N recommendations. Costa & Dolog proposed the NECoNMF [2], which uses a neural model to generate textual explanations.

We propose to extend NECoNMF model in two directions: adding influence score to improve the accuracy in the recommendation model and adding the helpfulness score to enhance the explainable model.

3   Problem Formulation

This section defines the preliminaries, our model, and formulate our problem.

3.1   Preliminaries

Definition 1. *An **item** is an entity (for example, book, place, movie) which the user can interact with. A set of items is denoted by* I.

Definition 2. *A **user** is a person that interacts with items. A set of users is denoted by U.*

Definition 3. *A **rating** refers to an interaction of a user $u \in U$ with an item $i \in I$. The set of all ratings over U and I is denoted $R(U, I)$.*

Definition 4. *A **contextual information** over U and I consists of context which the user was during the interaction with item $i \in I$. The set of all contexts over U and I is denoted $C(U, I)$.*

Definition 5. *An **attribute** denotes the attributes belonging to the items I preferred by a user $u \in U$. The set of all attributes over U and I is denoted $A(U, I)$.*

Definition 6. *A **sentiment** denotes the sentiment which the user $u \in U$ had while reviewing an item $i \in I$ belonging to the items I preferred by a user $u \in U$. The set of all sentiment over U and I is denoted $S(U, I)$.*

Definition 7. *A **helpfulness score** denotes how helpful a review was.*

3.2   Our Model

We utilize five features to predict the top-N items recommended to a user u: (i) ratings of user u to item l, (ii) interactions of user u with items having similar attributes as i, (iii) interactions of user u at context c (iv) sentiment s of user u for item i given its review, and (v) influence of u on friends. Next, we describe the scores for each of these features.

Ratings. Users tend to interact with items of their interests. We set the preference of a user u in an item i based on the *ratings*, given by:

$$X_u(u, i) = \begin{cases} 0, & \text{if } R_{ui} = unk \\ \{1, 2, 3, 4, 5\}, & \text{otherwise} \end{cases} \tag{1}$$

Items' Category Score. Users like to interact with items of their general interest, identified by a items' attribute, such as "crime" and "romance". To incorporate this effect, we compute the *item category score*, given by the following equation.

$$X_a(u, a) = \frac{\sum_{i | a \in i.A} |R(u, i)|}{|R(u)|} \tag{2}$$

where $i.A$ is the set of categories of i.

Items' Context Score. Users like to interact with items in a specific context, such as "alone" and "weekend". To incorporate this effect, we compute the *item context score*, given by the following equation.

$$X_c(u,c) = \frac{\sum_{i|c \in i.C} |R(u,i)|}{|R(u)|} \tag{3}$$

where $i.C$ is the set of context of i.

Sentiment Score. Users tend to present a specific sentiment when interacting with an item. We set the sentiment of a user u for an item i based on the *sentiment score*, given by:

$$X_s(u,s) = \begin{cases} 1, & \text{if the user has positive sentiment} \\ -1, & \text{otherwise} \end{cases} \tag{4}$$

Users Influence. Users tend to follow the activities of their friends [13]. Based on this statement we compute the influence score of users on their friends.

The influence score assumes that a user u influences his/her friend v if u interacts with item i and v interacts with the same item after u within a particular timeframe.

We consider a user v to be influenced by his friend u if u visits a location l and v visits the same location after u within a particular time. The influence score is computed based on the Bernoulli distribution proposed by Goyal *et al.* [5]. The Bernoulli distribution defines the influence score as the ration of the number of successful tentative to persuade the influenced user to follow another user's activities over the total number of trials. Considering that a user can affect another only in a specific timeframe, we set the time window $\omega = 1$, as we capture the interaction times in hours. Equation 5 gives the formal definition of the influenced friends of a user u [13].

$$X_i(u,v) = \{v|p(u,v) \geq \xi \wedge (u,v) \in F\} \tag{5}$$

where $p(u,v)$ is the influence probability of u on v. ξ is a threshold representing minimum influence to persuade a user to follow an activity. F is the set of all friends in the dataset.

Next, the factor model factorize the input matrices into a low-rank approximation matrices, where the latent features decomposed into in five low-rank matrices: ratings as $W \times H_u$; content features as $W \times H_a$; context as $W \times H_c$; sentiment as $W \times H_s$; and influence score $W \times H_i$. H_u denotes the latent features for user u. Similarly, H_a denotes the content's latent features a, H_c denotes the context's latent features c, H_s denotes the sentiment's latent features, and H_i denotes the influence latent feature. Finally, W denotes the common latent space.

Explainable Model. The latent factor models do not provide a straightforward explanation about the predicted list of items. Our model aims to generate natural language review-oriented explanations based on previous user reviews, ratings and review's helpfulness score.

The formal definition of review-oriented explanation mode is: given an input ratings vector $r_{ui} = (r_1, \ldots, r_{|r_{ui}|})$ and an input helpfulness score vector $s_{ui} = (s_1, \ldots, s_{|s_{ui}|})$ we aim to generate item explanation $e_i = (w_1, \ldots, w_{|t_i|})$ by maximizing the conditional probability $p(e|r,s)$. The rating r_{ui} is a vector of the user's overall rating for a target item i. The helpfulness score s_{ui} is a vector of the review's quality. The review t_i is considered a sequence of characters of variable length. The model learns to compute the likelihood of generated reviews given a set of input ratings. This conditional probability $p(e|r,s)$ is represented in Eq. 6 [2].

$$p(e|r,s) = \prod_{b=1}^{|e|} p(w_b | w < b, r, s) \tag{6}$$

where $w < b = (w_1, \ldots, w_{t-1})$

3.3 Problem Statement

We define the problem statement as follows:

Problem 1. Given a user u, an item l, the attribute a of i, a context c, a sentiment s, and the influence score X_i, predict the top-N items preferred by user u.

We can explain the recommended list of items based on the features of the items and the explicit features preferences of the user.

4   Methodology

Our model extends the NECoNMF model in two directions: (1) adding the influence score to the factorization step, and (2) adding the helpfulness score to the explainable model.

4.1   Collective Matrix Factorization

The collective non-negative matrix factorization aims to jointly decompose the ratings, items' attribute, context, sentiment, and user's influence score into a common latent space.

Consider the online shopping system as illustrated in Fig. 2, where a user may rate a specific product (here defined as an item) according to his/her preferences. Furthermore, the user may write a review giving particular information about the feature are most relevant in his/her opinion. Considering this scenario, we model the information into: rating matrix X_u, user-attribute matrix X_a, user-context matrix X_c, user-sentiment matrix X_s, and user-influence matrix X_i. The

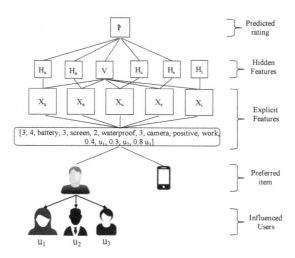

Fig. 2. Our model.

factorization of X_u retrieves the item's hidden features preferred by a user u. Factorizing X_a gives us the content features according to the user's preferences. The factorization of X_c allow us to identify the hidden contextual features related to the item. Factorizing X_s lead us to find the sentiment from a user u given an item i. Likewise, the decomposition of X_i computes the potential influence scores among the users.

The independent factorization of each matrix represents a different latent space with no correlation among the features. Applying the collective non-negative matrix factorization allows us to represent the decomposed features in a common latent space. We aim to solve the following optimization problem:

$$
\begin{aligned}
min : f(W) = \frac{1}{2}[\alpha \|X_u - WH_u\|_2^2 \\
+\beta \|X_a - WH_a\|_2^2 + \gamma \|X_c - WH_c\|_2^2 \\
+\omega \|X_s - WH_s\|_2^2 + \eta \|X_i - WH_i\|_2^2 \\
+\lambda(\|W\|_2 + \|H_u\|_2 + \|H_a\|_2 \\
+\|H_c\|_2 + \|H_s\|_2 + \|H_i\|_2)] \\
s.t. W \geq 0, H_u \geq 0, H_a \geq 0, H_c \geq 0, H_s \geq 0, H_i \geq 0
\end{aligned}
\tag{7}
$$

where the first five terms correspond to the factorization of the matrices X_u, X_a, X_c, X_s, and X_i. The matrix W denotes the common latent space, and H_u, H_a, H_c, H_s, and H_i are denote the hidden factors for each item-user interaction feature. The hyper-parameters α, β, γ, ω, and η control the importance of each factorization with values between 0 and 1. Setting the hyper-parameters as 0.2 implies equal importance to the matrices factorization, while values of α, β, γ, ω, and η set as > 0.2 (or < 0.2) give more importance to the factorization of X_u (or X_a, or X_c, or X_s, or X_i), respectively. To avoid overfitting and guarantee the smoothness of the solution, we use the hyper-parameter λ to control the common latent space W.

Optimization. Our model minimizes the objective function by applying the alternating optimization proposed in [2] which assumes that the user and item data has a joint distribution to exploit a better low-dimensional space. For example, u_i and v_j are close to each other in the low-dimensional space if they are geometrically close in the data distribution. The literature describes this assumption as the *manifold assumption*, and it has been applied in algorithms for dimensionality reduction and semi-supervised learning [2].

The optimization assumes the local geometric structure using the nearest neighbor graph on a scatter of data points as proposed in [14]. Our goal is to find the k nearest neighbors for each node n and later connect these nodes in the graph. The edges in the graph may have a binary or weights representation. Considering the binary representation, 1 denotes a neighbor and 0 otherwise. The weights representation use methods to capture the correlation among the nodes, such as Pearson correlation or cosine similarity. The graph results in an adjacency matrix A to find the local closeness of two data points u_i and v_j.

The collective factorization reduces the data point u_i from a matrix X into a common latent space W as w_i. Then, we calculate the distance between two low-dimensional data points using the Euclidean distance $\|w_i - w_j\|^2$ and map them into the adjacency matrix A. We repeat the computation until the pre-defined number of iterations or a stationary point as formally defined in Eq. 8 [2].

$$
\begin{aligned}
M &= \frac{1}{2} \sum_{i,j=1}^{n} \|w_i - w_j\|^2 A_{ij} \\
&= \sum_{i=1}^{n} (w_i^T - w_i) D_{ii} - \sum_{i,j=1}^{n} (w_i^T - w_i) D_{ii} \\
&= Tr(W^T DW) - Tr(W^T AW) = Tr(W^T LW),
\end{aligned}
\tag{8}
$$

where $Tr(\bullet)$ denotes the trace function. D denotes the diagonal matrix whose entries are row sums of A (or column, as A is symmetric). We define the Laplacian matrix as $D_i i = \sum_i A_i j$; $L = D - A$ to guarantee the non-negative constraints required by non-negative matrix factorization.

We may re-write the optimization problem of function $f(W)$ as:

$$
\begin{aligned}
min : f(W) &= \frac{1}{2} [\alpha \|X_u - WH_u\|_2^2 + \beta \|X_a - WH_a\|_2^2 \\
&+ \gamma \|X_c - WH_c\|_2^2 + \omega \|X_s - WH_s\|_2^2 + \eta \|X_i - WH_i\|_2^2 \\
&+ \varphi Tr(W^T LW) \\
&+ \lambda (\|W\|_2 + \|H_u\|_2 + \|H_a\|_2 + \|H_c\|_2 + \|H_s\|_2 + \|H_i\|_2)] \\
s.t. W &\geq 0, H_u \geq 0, H_a \geq 0, H_c \geq 0, H_s \geq 0, H_i \geq 0
\end{aligned}
\tag{9}
$$

fwhere φ the hyper-parameter controlling the objective function. The hyper-parameters α, β, γ, ω, η, and λ have the same semantics as in Eq. 7.

4.2 Multiplicative Update Rule

Our model follows the hybrid regularization proposed by Costa and Dolog [2]. The Multiplicative Update Rule (MUR) method is the regularization term of W. MUR updates the scores in each iteration until finding the stationary point. We fix W while minimizing $f(W)$ over H_u, H_a, H_c, H_s, and H_i. We formally define the partial derivatives of W based on Eq. 10 before calculating the update rules.

$$\nabla f(W) = \alpha W H_u H_u^T - \alpha X_u H_u^T + \beta W H_a H_C^T - \beta X_a H_a^T$$
$$+\gamma W H_c H_c^T - \gamma X_c H_c^T + \omega W H_s H_s^T - \omega X_s H_s^T \qquad (10)$$
$$+\eta W H_i H_s^T - \eta X_i H_i^T + \lambda I_k$$

where k denotes the number of factors. I_k represents the identity matrix with $k \times k$ dimension.

The Eq. 11 formalizes the update rules, after computing the derivatives of $f(W)$, $f(H_u)$, $f(H_a)$, $f(H_c)$, $f(H_s)$, and $f(H_i)$ from Eq. 10.

$$W = \frac{[\alpha X_u H_u^T + \beta X_a H_a^T + \gamma X_c H_c^T + \omega X_s H_s^T + \eta X_i H_i^T]}{[\alpha H_U H_U^T + \beta H_a H_a^T + \gamma H_c H_c^T + \omega H_s H_s^T + \eta H_i H_i^T + \lambda I_k]} \qquad (11)$$

where $\frac{\bullet}{\bullet}$ corresponds to left division.

Each iteration of Eq. 11 returns the solution of the pair-wise division. The objective function and δ decrease in each interaction of Eq. 11 to guarantee the learning convergence. Due to the principle of non-negative values from non-negative factorization, we map any negative values from W matrix to zero after each update.

4.3 Barzilai-Borwein

The Brazilai-Borwein optimization method regularizes the hidden factor matrices H_u, H_a, H_c, H_s, and H_i. For simplicity, we denotes the hidden factor matrix H as a representation of the input matrices X_u, X_a, X_c, X_s, and X_i, due to equal computation of H_u, H_a, H_c, H_s, and H_i. The problem is formaly defined in Eq. 12 [2].

$$\min_{W \geq 0} : f(H) = \frac{1}{2}\|X - WH\|_F^2 \qquad (12)$$

We map the negative values from each update into zero utilizing $P(\bullet)$ for any $\alpha > 0$. The Eq. 13 denotes the formal definition of $P(\bullet)$ [2].

$$\|P[H - \alpha \nabla f(H)] - H\|_F = 0. \qquad (13)$$

We apply ϵ_H in Eq. 13 as [2]:

$$\|P[H - \alpha \nabla f(H)] - H\|_F \leq \epsilon_H, \qquad (14)$$

where $\epsilon_H = max(10^{-3}, \epsilon)\|P[H - \alpha \nabla f(H)] - H\|_F$ [2]. The stopping tolerance is decreased by $\epsilon = 0.1\epsilon_H$

The Algorithm 1 describes the steps to solve Eq. 12 [1].

Algorithm 1. Barzilai-Borwein.

1: **procedure** BB
2:     $\sigma \in (0,1), \alpha_{max} > \alpha_{min} > 0;$
3:     $L \leftarrow \|W^T W\|_2$
        $H_0 \leftarrow H^k; \alpha_0 \leftarrow 1; t \leftarrow 0;$
4:     **if** H_t is a stationary point of (1) **then return** H_t
5:     *loop:*
6:     **if** $t/2 \neq 0$ **then return** $Z_t \leftarrow H_t;$
7:     **else**
        $Z_t \leftarrow P \left[H_t - \frac{1}{L} \nabla f(H) \right];$
8:     $D_t \leftarrow P \left[Z_t - \alpha_t \nabla f(Z_t) \right] - Z_t$
9:     $\delta \leftarrow \langle D_t, WW^T D_t \rangle$
10:    **if** $\delta_t = 0$ **then return** $\lambda_t \leftarrow 1$
11:    **else**
12:        $\lambda_t \leftarrow min\{\tilde{\lambda}_t, 1\}$ *where*
13:        $\tilde{\lambda}_t = -\frac{(1-\sigma)\langle \nabla f(Z_t), D_t \rangle}{\delta_t}$
14:        $H_{t+1} \leftarrow Z_t + \lambda_t D_t$
15:    $S_t \leftarrow H_{t+1} - H_t$
16:    $Y_t \leftarrow \nabla f(H_{t+1}) - \nabla f(H_t)$
17:    **if** $\langle S_t, Y_t \rangle \leq 0$ **then**
        $\alpha_{t+1} \leftarrow \alpha_{max}$
18:    **else**
19:        **if** $t/2 \neq 0$ **then**
        $\alpha_{t+1}^{BB} \leftarrow \frac{\langle S_t, S_t \rangle}{\langle S_t, Y_t \rangle}$
20:        **else**
        $\alpha_{t+1}^{BB} \leftarrow \frac{\langle S_t, Y_t \rangle}{\langle Y_t, Y_t \rangle}$
21:        $\alpha_{t+1} \leftarrow min\{\alpha_{max}, max\{\alpha_{min}, \alpha_{t+1}^{BB}\}\}$
22:    $t \leftarrow t + 1$
23:    **goto** *loop*.

The gradient $\nabla f(W)$ of $f(H)$ is the Lipschitz term with constant $L = \|W^T W\|_2$. L. Due to the optimization problem defined in Eq. 9 defines $W^T W$ with dimensions $k \times k$ and $k \ll min\{m, n\}$, the gradient is not expensive to obtain For a given $H_0 \geq 0$ [2]:

$$\mathcal{L}(H_0) = \{H | f(H) \leq f(H_0), H \geq 0\}. \tag{15}$$

Following the definition of Eq. 15 we have the stationary point of the Barzilai-Borwein method [2].

4.4   Top-N Recommendation Process

The decomposition of the input matrices X_u, X_a, X_c, X_s, and X_i results in the trained matrices W, H_u, H_a, H_c, H_s, and H_i, which gives us the hidden features to predict the list top-N items. We can predict the preferable items according to the user's previous interest v_u given the new items' vector v_i [2]. We project the new items' vector v_i into the common latent space by solving the formal definition $v_i = wH_u$ applying the least square method. The vector w is responsible for identifying the features in the common latent space that explain the preferable items v_i. To infer the missing part of the query $v_u \leftarrow wH_t$, we use the low dimensional vector w. H_t denotes the concatenation of attributes, context, sentiment, and influence score matrices $H_t = H_a||H_c||H_s||H_i$. Each element of v_u denotes the score of how strong is the user preference given the item. We may sort the list of items based on the given scores.

Based on the sorted list of items and their rating scores, we can explain the predicted ratings by applying the neural language generation model. An attention model composes the explanation model to generate the personalized sentences according to the user's writing style. The model can identify positive and negative sentiment according to the user's previous reviews.

4.5 Natural Language Explanation

The explanation model has the context encoder, the LSTM network, the attention layer, and the generator model [2]. To generate the explanations the model uses the review text and the concatenated character embeddings of the user, item, rating, and helpfulness score as the input sources. Figure 3 illustrates the architecture of the explanation model. We apply *doc2vec* model [10] to learn the users and items embeddings. We concatenate the output vectors with the ratings given by the users. We split the reviews into characters and convert them to one-hot vectors. The input data for the time-step of the LSTM network has the one-hot vectors, the embedded vector, and the helpfulness score. The output from the LSTM network and the embedded vector are the input for the attention layer. The output from our attention layer become the input of our generator model, which produces sentences based on the input data. The following paragraphs describe the explainable model's components in detail.

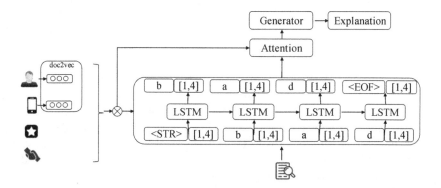

Fig. 3. Our model.

Context Encoder. The goal of the context encoder is to encode the inputted characters into one-hot vectors. Then we concatenate the ratings given by a user according to her/his preferences with the encoded characters. To encode the characters during the training step and decoding during the generating step, we previously created a dictionary to define the characters positions. For each character in the reviews, we generate the one-hot vector based on its position in the dictionary. Furthermore, we concatenate the encoded vector with the ratings with values varying from 0 to 1 and the helpfulness score. The Eq. 16 denotes the formal definition of the context encoder.

$$X'_t = [onehot(x_{char}); x_{rating}; x_{helpfulness}]$$ (16)

LSTM Network. The LSTM network improves the recurrent neural network (RNN) model by solving the vanishing gradient problem present in the last model. The LSTM model improves the computation of long-short term dependencies. Figure 3 presents the LSTM network as a sequential connection cell. Each cell has the forget, input, and output gates. The forget gate decides which old information should be forgotten, the input gate updates the current cell state, and the output gate selects which information goes to the next layer and cell as illustrated in Fig. 4.

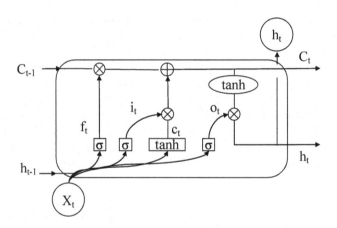

Fig. 4. LSTM cell

The LSTM network receives the input data x_t at time t and the cell state C_{t-1} from previous time step $t-1$ [2]. The forget gate receives the inputted data and discard the ones which are not useful. The Eq. 17 defines the LSTM network, where f_t denotes the forget fate in time t, where W_f is the weight matrix and b is the bias. Once the forget gate discards the not useful information, it set which information should be stored in cell state by the input gate i_t. Later, the current cell creates a candidate state C'_t by a *tanh* layer. The LSTM network updates the current state C_t according to the candidate state, the previous cell state, the forget gate, and the input gate. Finally, the LSTM network transfers the data to the output gate, which applies the *sigmoid* function to define the output and multiply the *tanh* with the current cell state C_t to return the next character with the highest probability [2].

$$
\begin{aligned}
f_t &= \sigma([x_t, C_{t-1}] \odot W_f + b_f) \\
i_t &= \sigma([x_t, C_{t-1}] \odot W_i + b_i) \\
C'_t &= \tanh([x_t, C_{t-1}] \odot W_c + b_c) \\
C_t &= f_t \odot C_{t-1} + i_t \odot C'_t \\
o_t &= \sigma([x_t, C_{t-1}] \odot W_o + b_o) \\
h_t &= o_t \odot \tanh(C_t)
\end{aligned}
\tag{17}
$$

Attention Layer. The goal of the attention layer is to learn soft alignments h_t between the character dependencies c_t and the *attention* inputs [2]. Equation 18 formally describes the character dependencies using attention layer $h_t^{attention}$ as explained by Dong *et al.* [4].

$$
\begin{aligned}
c_t &= \sum_i^{attention} \frac{\exp(\tanh(W_s \odot [h_t, attention_i]))}{\sum \exp(\tanh(W_s \odot [h_t, attention_i]))} attention_i \\
h_t^{attention} &= \tanh(W_1 \odot c_t + W_2 \odot h_t)
\end{aligned}
\tag{18}
$$

Generator Model. The generator model is responsible for generating sentences based on character-level. First, the explanation model maximizes the *softmax* function to compute the conditional probability p among the characters. Equation 19 presents the formal definition of the generator model. The generator model receives a *prime* text as the *start* symbol in each generated review-based explanation according to different item's content features [2]. The network feeds the *softmax* layer with its output data, as shown in Eq. 19 [2].

$$
p = \mathrm{softmax}(H_t^{attention} \odot W + b), \quad char = argmax\, p
\tag{19}
$$

where $H_t^{attention}$ is the output of the LSTM network. W is the weight, and b denotes the bias of the *softmax* layer.

This procedure generates a character *char* recursively for each time step until it finds the pre-defined *end* symbol, which defines the length of the generated explanation.

5   Empirical Evaluation

The empirical evaluation aims to answer the following research questions:

RQ1. Does the proposed method outperforms the state-of-art methods for item recommendations?

RQ2. Does the proposed method present a clear explanation for the recommended items?

5.1 Datasets

We utilize two datasets to conduct our experiments: Yelp and Amazon.

The Yelp dataset is an essential source for the recommender systems community due to containing users' reviews. The dataset has 45,981 users, 11,537 items, and 22,907 reviews. The dataset is sparse due to the few numbers of users evaluating the items. We applied the strategy recommended by [7,15] to filter the users with more than ten reviews since the dataset contains 49% of the users with only one review. The Amazon dataset is larger than Yelp containing more than 800k users, 80k items and 11.3 M reviews. To avoid the sparseness, we applied the same strategy from Yelp dataset in the Amazon dataset. Table 1 summarizes statistics of each dataset information [2].

Table 1. Dataset summarization.

	Yelp	Amazon
#users	3,835	2,933
#items	4,043	14,370
#reviews	114,316	55,677
#density	0.74%	0.13%

We used a Unix server with 32 GB of RAM and 8 core CPU Intel Xeon with 2.80 GHz to perform the experiments. The parameters for collective matrix factorization were set as defined in [2]: *learning rate* = 0.001; $k = 45$; *iterations* = 50 (to ensure the convergence point); and $\lambda = 0.5$. The LSTM network has two hidden layers with 1024 LSTM cells per layer. The input data was devided into 100 batches with size equal to 128 and each batch has a sequence length equal to 280 [2]. For this experiment, we applied k-fold cross-validation to avoid overfitting with $k = 5$.

5.2 Evaluation Metrics

The effectiveness of the top-N recommendation task follows the information retrieval ranking metrics: NDCG and Hit Ratio (HR). The HR compared the recommended list of top-N items with the ground-truth test dataset (GT). A *hit* denotes when an item from the test dataset appears in the recommended list. The Eq. 20 gives the formal definition for HR metric [2].

$$Hit@N = \frac{Number\,of\,Hits@N}{|GT|} \tag{20}$$

The NDCG measures the ranking quality as defined by Eq. 21. NDCG set a higher score to the items at the top rank, and lower scores to the items at the low-rank [2].

$$NDCG@N = Z_N \sum_{i=1}^{N} \frac{2^{r_i} - 1}{log_2(i + 1)} \qquad (21)$$

where Z_N normalizes the values to guarantee that the perfect ranking has a value of 1. r_i is the graded relevance of item at position i. We define $r_i = 1$ if the item is in the test dataset, otherwise 0.

N defines the number of listed item in the trained dataset. Therefore, we set $N = 5$ and $N = 10$, due to large values of N would result in extra work for the user to filter among a long list of relevant items [2].

5.3   Comparison Baselines

We use the following state-of-art methods as the baselines to evaluate our model's performance. Two baselines are popular techniques for top-N recommendations, and the three others are recent techniques applying review-oriented explanations.

Top-N Recommendation

- *ItemPop.* The ItemPop method ranks items by their popularity given by the number of ratings [2]. The method usually has a good performance when compared to others baselines, because the users tend to consume popular items.
- *PageRank.* The Personalized Pagerank recommends the top-N items based on the user's previous interest. We applied the configuration proposed by [7], where the authors set the user-item graph and the damping parameter to 0.9 for the Yelp dataset and 0.3 for the Amazon dataset.

Explainable Recommendation

- *EFM.* The model applies a phrase-level sentiment analysis of user reviews for a personalized recommendation. It extracts the most relevant features from the reviews using a sentiment lexicon construction technique. EFM incorporates the user-feature, the item-feature, and user-item ratings into a hybrid matrix factorization framework. The method has k as hyper-parameter to define the number of most cared features, which we define $k = 45$ as reported in [15] to have the best performance in the Yelp dataset.
- *TriRank.* The model ranks the vertices of user-item-aspect tripartite graph by regularizing the smoothness and fitting constraints [2]. The authors assure that setting the $item - aspect$, $user - aspect$, and $aspect - query$ as 0 results in poor performance [7]. The experiments performed in this paper use the default settings $\alpha = 9$, $\beta = 6$, and $\gamma = 1$ given by the authors.
- *NECoNMF.* The model jointly factorizes the ratings, items' attribute, contextual information, sentiments, and user's influence into a common latent space to predict the preferred list of items given the user's interest. The model uses an explainable neural model to explain the recommended items resulted from the joint factorization.

6   Results and Discussions

In this section, we describe the results regarding the overall performance of our
model in comparison to our baselines for top-N recommendation and discuss the
generated review-oriented explanations.

6.1   Performance Comparison (RQ1)

Tables 2 and 3 summarize the performance comparison for top-N recommendation in the Yelp and Amazon datasets. The analysis considers $N = 5$ and
$N = 10$ list of items as they are generally used to express the effectiveness of
item recommendation.

Table 2. NDCG and Hit Ratio results for our model and compared methods at rank 5
and 10 for Yelp dataset.

Dataset	Yelp			
Metric	NDCG@5	HIT@5	NDCG@10	HIT@10
Top-N Algorithms				
ItemPop	0.0110	0.0136	0.0185	0.0306
PageRank	0.0235	0.0278	0.0313	0.0452
Explainable Recommendation				
TriRank	0.0258	0.0313	0.0353	0.0527
EFM	0.2840	0.0448	0.2955	0.0678
NECoNMF	0.3366	0.0503	0.3461	0.0763
Our Model	**0.3805**	**0.0925**	**0.3910**	**0.1190**

Table 3. NDCG and Hit Ratio results for our model and compared methods at rank 5
and 10 for Amazon dataset.

Dataset	Amazon			
Metric	NDCG@5	HIT@5	NDCG@10	HIT@10
Top-N Algorithms				
ItemPop	0.0077	0.0082	0.0136	0.0238
PageRank	0.0978	0.1070	0.1029	0.1200
Explainable Recommendation				
TriRank	0.1033	0.1127	0.1086	0.1266
EFM	0.3615	0.1284	0.3670	0.1429
NECoNMF	0.3892	0.1301	0.3962	0.1486
Our Model	**0.4264**	**0.1640**	**0.4344**	**0.1815**

Our model outperforms the naive ItemPop model by 33× for the Yelp dataset and 54× for the Amazon dataset considering the NDCG@5 as shown in Tables 2 and 3, respectively. Analyzing the HIT@5 score the relative improvement is 5× for the Yelp dataset and 19× for the Amazon dataset. Both ItemPop and our model presented a better performance for NDCG@10 and HIT@10. However, comparing ItemPop with the others baselines, we observe it shows the poorest overall performance, due to not assume the personalization during its prediction task.

Personalized PageRank presented a good performance due to considering the users' previous preferences in its top-N prediction task. However, page rank does not consider the latent information to predict the recommended list of items, such as the features considered in our model, for example, item's content features, context, sentiment, ratings, and user's influence.

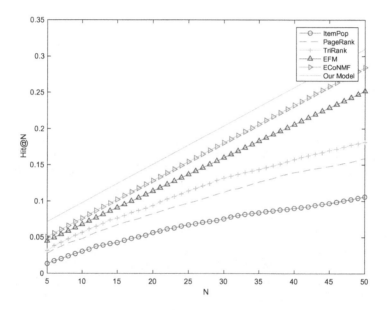

Fig. 5. Hit Ratio evaluation on Yelp dataset for N from 5 to 50.

Not considering hidden features may explain why our model outperforms PageRank model for the Yelp dataset in 15× for NDCG@5 and 3× for HIT@5. We further observed the better performance in the Amazon dataset in 4× for NDCG@5 and 53% for HIT@5. Assuming $N = 10$ shows an improvement of our model and PageRank when compared to $N = 5$.

Analyzing the NDCG@5 and HIT@5, we observe our model had a better performance than TriRank for both Yelp and Amazon datasets. Our model has a relative improvement of 14× for NDCG@5 and 2× for HIT@5 in the Yelp dataset. Considering the Amazon dataset, the increase was 4× for NDCG@5 and 45% for HIT@5. The poorer performance of TriRank when compared to our

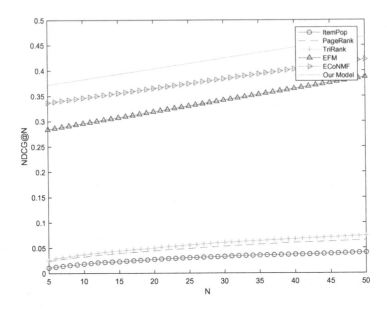

Fig. 6. NDCG evaluation on Yelp dataset for N from 5 to 50.

model due to TriRank inability of identifying hidden features, since it uses a tripartite graph approach. Moreover, TriRank and PageRank have close scores in the performance comparison. However, TriRank outperforms PageRank due to incorporate the *aspect* feature during the learning step for the prediction of the top-N items.

EFM has a close performance from our method considering the NDCG and HIT metrics for top-N recommendation. However, analyzing the results in Table 2, our model presents a relative improvement of 33% in NDCG@5, 13% in HIT@5, 32% in NDCG@10 and 75% in HIT@10 for the Yelp dataset. Likewise, the relative improvement in the Amazon dataset was 18% in NDCG@5, 27% in HIT@5, 18% in NDCG@10, and 27% in HIT@10. Our model has a better performance than EFM due to factorize more features such as items' attributes, contextual information, sentiment, and user's influence. The factorization of those features allows a better user modeling in the vectorial space and improves the accuracy for top-N recommendation task. EFM, on the other hand, uses only the ratings and aspects to model the user's behavior. However, observing the results, we conclude that the features used by our model play an essential role in the accuracy of the recommender systems as shown by the NDCG and HR metrics. The contextual information has a significant impact on the prediction task due to its contribution in prediction when the user-item interaction should happen. EFM factorizes its input feature matrices into four different latent spaces, while our model jointly factorizes into one common latent space. Hence, we conclude that jointly factorizing the input matrices may retrieve hidden features not identified by EFM model during the learning step.

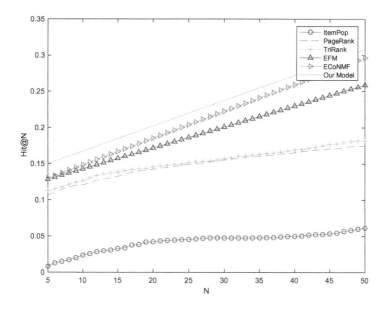

Fig. 7. Hit Ratio evaluation on Amazon dataset for N from 5 to 50.

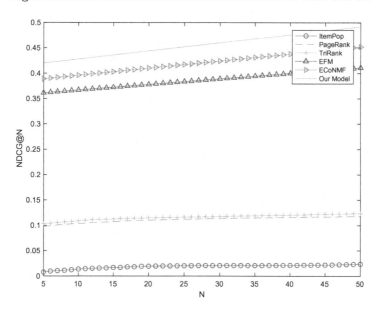

Fig. 8. NDCG evaluation on Amazon dataset for N from 5 to 50.

NECoNMF presents the closest performance of our model due to applying a similar approach. The difference between NECoNMF and our model is because our model factorizes the user's influence, which improves the prediction for top-N recommendation task. The assumption of a user receiving recommendations based on her/his friend has a good impact on the user's decision. We observe in Table 2 that our model outperforms NECoNMF in 13% for NDCG@5 and 83% for HIT@5 considering Yelp dataset. Similarly, the relative improvement for Amazon dataset was 9% for NDCG@5 and 22% for HIT@5.

We measured the effectiveness of our model in comparison to the others baselines for top-N recommendation for N varying from 5 to 50. Figures 5, 6, 7 and 8 shows the performance has a linear increase for a larger value of N. This result is due to the decrease in error when the system has a higher number of items.

6.2   Explainability

The evaluation of the quality of the explanations given by our model is not easy to measure. To assess its effectiveness, we apply the method proposed by Zhang *et al.* [15], where the authors computed the quality of the explanation via examples generated by the explanation model.

Table 4. Example explanations produced by our model on the Amazon dataset.

User	Item	Rating	Generated Explanation
A	X	1	It is disappointed . The screen is too small and low brightening . The camera is bad . I can't recommend this phone for everyday use .
A	Y	3	It is a good phone . I am happy with its screen and the camera . I would recommend it for work purpose.
B	X	5	I really like this phone . I it is awesome for work purpose, because the battery can last for more than two weeks. I can strongly recommend it.

Table 4 presents the explanations given the predicted user's ratings for different products. The generated texts offer an interpretation according to the user's writing style. The dark gray fragments in the table denote a negative sentiment, while the light gray denotes a positive sentiment for different item's features. The mid-gray mark denotes the contextual feature, for example *every day*, *leisure* and *work*. The explanations follow the review-oriented writing style

Table 5. Example explanations produced by ECoNMF on the Amazon dataset.

User	Item	Rating	Generated Explanation
A	X	1	i am disappointed , the screen is small and small . the camera is worse . the camera is worse . i don't recommend it everyday use .
A	Y	3	i am satisfied with phone . it has good screen and camera . it has good screen and camera . i can recommend it it for work .
B	X	5	it is a great phone . its battery lasts more than two weeks. more than two weeks. it is waterproof i can use it under the rain without care too much. i recommend it for work purpose. i recommend it.

due to reviews play an important role in helping the user's decision. The readability observed in Table 4 has better readability in comparison with TriRank and EFM due to apply natural language text generation to build the sentences. Furthermore, the review-oriented explanation has a good impact in persuading the user's next decision since the generated text has a similar structure of the previous user's reviews.

Comparing the explanations generated by ECoNMF in Table 5 with the explanations from our model in Table 4, we observe our model creates better readability than ECoNMF model. ECoNMF was not able to recognize the punctuation properly, making it start sentences with lowercase characters. Furthermore, the text repeats some words or phrases, making the quality of the explanation lower than our model. ECoNMF may not perform better than our model due to not applying the helpfulness score during the learning step to generate the explanations. The helpfulness score collaborates on the confidence of the trained reviews, doing the best reviews with higher scores having a better quality and consequently best readability.

7   Conclusions

We proposed personalized review-oriented explanations for recommender systems. Our model jointly factorizes ratings, item's attributes, contextual information, sentiment, and user's influence score in a common latent space. Moreover, we introduced an interpretable neural model to explain the predicted top-N recommendation. The interpretable model generates the explanations based on the user's previous ratings and the reviews' helpfulness score. Finally, we presented the empirical evaluation to observe the performance of our model in comparison with our baselines. The results show that our model outperforms the state-of-art methods.

We improved the top-N recommendation task by using five different input features into a collective non-negative matrix factorization model. The alignment of the items' attribute, contextual information, ratings, sentiment, and user's influence score contribute significantly to the effectiveness of our model.

Moreover, the interpretable model presented effectiveness for the review-oriented explanation task. The ratings and helpfulness score improved the quality of the review-oriented explanations by generating a readable personalized text. The explanations may help users during their decisions in interacting with different items. Consequently, enhancing users' trust in the online system.

We want to improve the interpretable model in two directions: (1) applying different neural models such as convolutional neural network or RestNet for text generation and (2) developing an agnostic model to explain any recommender system. Furthermore, we would like to improve our model effectiveness when dealing with the cold-start problem.

The LSTM network presented good performance in generating character-level sentences, however training the LSTM has high computational complexity, because it requires memory-bandwidth-bound computation. It means that the LSTM requires four linear layers per cell to perform each sequence in the time-step. The linear layers require large amount computations for the memory bandwidth. However, they cannot compute many units because the system has not enough memory bandwidth to feed the computational units. On the other hand, it is easy to add more computational units than add more memory bandwidth. Moreover, advances in neural network models presented better results for memory management, such as convolutional neural networks (CNN). Hence, applying others neural network models may improve the performance of our model.

Acknowledgements. The authors wish to acknowledge the financial support and the fellow scholarship given to this research from the Conselho Nacional de Desenvolvimento Científico e Tecnológico - CNPq (grant# 206065/2014-0).

References

1. Costa, F., Dolog, P.: Hybrid learning model with barzilai-borwein optimization for context-aware recommendations. In: Proceedings of the Thirty-First International Florida Artificial Intelligence Research Society Conference, FLAIRS 2018, Melbourne, Florida USA, 21–23 May 2018, pp. 456–461 (2018)
2. Costa, F., Dolog, P.: Neural explainable collective non-negative matrix factorization for recommender systems. In: Proceedings of the 14th International Conference on Web Information Systems and Technologies - Volume 1: WEBIST, pp. 35–45. INSTICC, SciTePress, Setúbal (2018). https://doi.org/10.5220/0006893700350045
3. Cremonesi, P., Koren, Y., Turrin, R.: Performance of recommender algorithms on top-n recommendation tasks. In: Proceedings of the Fourth ACM Conference on Recommender Systems, RecSys 2010, pp. 39–46. ACM, New York (2010)

4. Dong, L., Huang, S., Wei, F., Lapata, M., Zhou, M., XuT, K.: Learning to generate product reviews from attributes. In: Proceedings of the 15th Conference of the European Chapter of the Association for Computational Linguistics, CECACL 2017, pp. 623–632. Association for Computational Linguistics (2017)
5. Goyal, A., Bonchi, F., Lakshmanan, L.V.: Learning influence probabilities in social networks. In: WSDM (2010)
6. Haveliwala, T.H.: Topic-sensitive pagerank. In: Proceedings of the 11th International Conference on World Wide Web, WWW 2002, pp. 517–526. ACM, New York (2002)
7. He, X., Chen, T., Kan, M.Y., Chen, X.: Trirank: review-aware explainable recommendation by modeling aspects. In: Proceedings of the 24th ACM International on Conference on Information and Knowledge Management, CIKM 2015, pp. 1661–1670. ACM, New York (2015)
8. He, X., Kan, M.Y., Xie, P., Chen, X.: Comment-based multi-view clustering of web 2.0 items. In: Proceedings of the 23rd International Conference on World Wide Web, WWW 2014, pp. 771–782. ACM, New York (2014)
9. Koren, Y., Bell, R., Volinsky, C.: Matrix factorization techniques for recommender systems. Computer **42**(8), 30–37 (2009)
10. Le, Q., Mikolov, T.: Distributed representations of sentences and documents. In: Proceedings of the 31st International Conference on International Conference on Machine Learning - Volume 32, ICML 2014, pp. II-1188-II-1196 (2014). JMLR.org
11. Lee, D.D., Seung, H.S.: Algorithms for non-negative matrix factorization. In: Proceedings of the 13th International Conference on Neural Information Processing Systems, NIPS 2000, pp. 535–541. MIT Press, Cambridge (2000)
12. Liu, J., Wang, C., Gao, J., Han, J.: Multi-view clustering via joint nonnegative matrix factorization. In: Proceedings of the 2013 SIAM International Conference on Data Mining, pp. 252–260. SIAM (2013)
13. Saleem, M.A., da Costa, F.S., Dolog, P., Karras, P., Calders, T., Pedersen, T.B.: Predicting visitors using location-based social networks. In: MDM, pp. 245–250 (2018)
14. Saveski, M., Mantrach, A.: Item cold-start recommendations: Learning local collective embeddings. In: Proceedings of the 8th ACM Conference on Recommender Systems, RecSys 2014, pp. 89–96. ACM, New York (2014)
15. Zhang, Y., Lai, G., Zhang, M., Zhang, Y., Liu, Y., Ma, S.: Explicit factor models for explainable recommendation based on phrase-level sentiment analysis. In: Proceedings of the 37th International ACM SIGIR Conference on Research & Development in Information Retrieval, SIGIR 2014, pp. 83–92. ACM, New York (2014)

Web Semantic Technologies in Web Based Educational System Integration

Géraud Fokou Pelap[1,2,3]($\boxtimes$) ⓘ, Catherine Faron Zucker[1] ⓘ, Fabien Gandon[1] ⓘ,
and Laurent Polese[3]

[1] University Côte d'Azur, CNRS, INRIA, I3S, Nice, France
{geraud.fokou-pelap,fabien.gandon}@inria.fr, faron@unice.fr
[2] University of Dschang, Dschang, Cameroon
geraud.fokou@univ-dschang.org
[3] Educlever, Paris, France
{ge.fokou,laurent.polese}@educlever.com

Abstract. Web based e-Education systems are an important kind of information systems that benefited from Web standards for content, implementation, deployment and integration. An e-Education system requires the collaboration of many actors in a complete ecosystem: public authorities (e.g. Ministry) and knowledge engineers, who build official reference standards; teachers and pedagogical engineers, who build digital pedagogical resources; and IT engineers who build digital platforms for e-Learning. In this article we propose and evaluate a Semantic Web approach to support the features and interoperability of a real industrial e-Education system in production. We show how ontology-based knowledge representation supports the required features, their extension to new ones and the integration of external resources (e.g. official standards) as well as interoperability with other systems and knowledge sharing between different actors. Our proof of concept is entirely based on Semantic Web technologies and complies with the industrial constraints; we qualitatively and quantitatively evaluated it and performed a benchmark of different alternatives on real data and real queries. We present an in-depth evaluation of the quality of service and response time in this industrial context that shows on a real-world testbed that Semantic Web based solutions can meet the industrial requirements, both in terms of services and efficiency compared to existing operational solutions.

Keywords: e-Education information system · e-Education model · Semantic Web · Ontology · Benchmarking · Web API · REST · SPARQL

This work is supported by the EduMICS Innovation Inria Lab between the Wimmics team and the Educlever company, e-Education solutions provider.
This article is an extended version of an article published in the Proceedings of the 14th International Conference on Web Information Systems and Technologies, WEBIST 2018, Seville, Spain, September 18–20, 2018.

M. J. Escalona et al. (Eds.): WEBIST 2018, LNBIP 372, pp. 170–194, 2019.
https://doi.org/10.1007/978-3-030-35330-8_9

1   Introduction

Modern e-Education systems are always at the intersection of information systems and Web based systems. They leverage state of the art results of information sciences and technologies (IST) as well as the Web architecture and resources to support educational processes including: the management of their users (learners and teachers), the pedagogical resources (courses, exercises, etc.), the regulations (e.g official reference standards), etc. While they often integrate different systems, heterogeneous resources and contributions from various actors, they must ensure compatibility and a seamless user experience.

Since education is under the responsibility of public authorities, educational solutions developed by public or private organizations must comply with the public authorities specifications. Taking the example of France, as part of the Education Code [18], the Ministry of Education has defined and published in the French Official Journal a common reference base of knowledge and skills[1]. It standardizes the content of courses by specifying knowledge and skills that a student must acquire at each step of his school curriculum. Additionally, the French Ministry of Education specifies a format for digital pedagogical resources description called ScoLOMFR [21]. It is based on the IEEE standard Learning Object Metadata (LOM) [6] and its French version, LOMFR[2]. ScoLOMFR specifies a description schema and a common vocabulary for all online pedagogical resources for their indexing and sharing among different e-Education actors in France. As a result, any learning environment developed by public institutions or private companies have to meet these standards and norms to ensure a wide dissemination, whatever the educational context. Moreover, they must have updating capabilities to adapt to the possible evolution of these standards. Semantic Web technologies stand as a solution to achieve these goals, offering open standards for ontology-based knowledge representation, with extensible schemata, and data integration and interoperability. They also provide the possibility to make e-Education services accessible through Web API invoked over the HTTP/HTTPS protocols where service arguments are passed as regular parameters of a HTTP request [17]. We designed such Web APIs to provide access services to our ontology-based knowledge representation. These Web services implement real industrial use cases using SPARQL protocol and execute SPARQL queries onto triplestores.

In this article, we show the benefits of semantic Web Information systems and technologies in the e-Education context. We present the results of an ontology-based educational knowledge modelling and management experience in a real e-Education environment: the learning solution developed by the Educlever company.

We address the following questions: (1) Can an industrial educational system in production rely on semantic Web technologies? (2) Does semantic Web ontology-oriented modelling effectively support educational system integration?

---

[1] Original name: *Socle commun de connaissance, de compétences et de culture.*
[2] http://www.lom-fr.fr.

(3) Does a semantic Web educational system support additional features when compared to traditional RDB or graph based solutions?

In order to answer these questions, we provide a proof of concept by implementing an ontology-based integration and augmentation of different systems and sources. We show that semantic technologies allow us to address use cases with fine-grained and loosely coupled semantic Web services building up a flexible and adaptable system. We benchmark our approach in the industrial real-world context of the Educlever company with their data and use cases.

Our proposed solution relies on the EduProgression ontology [22] which is modelling the official common base of knowledge and skills, and which we extended to meet the specific needs of the Educlever solution. The original technical solution adopted by Educlever is mainly based on a relational database of educational resources and a graph database of educational concepts and skills indexing these resources. We developed an alternative Semantic Web based solution with (1) an ontology of educational concepts and skills, (2) a repository of semantic annotations of pedagogical resources, and (3) a base of Web services implementing services offered by the existing solution and additional ones, using SPARQL queries on these repositories. We show the feasibility of our solution in a real industrial context by implementing it within four off-the-shelf triplestores: *Allegrograph*, *Corese*, *GraphDB* and *Virtuoso*. We benchmark the existing and new services on real data and queries and perform evaluation of the quality of service and response time. The results of our evaluation show that the semantic Web based solution meets the industrial requirements, both in terms of service and efficiency. Moreover, we show that our ontology-based modelling opens up new opportunities of advanced services.

This article is organized as follows: Sect. 2 presents state-of-the-art Educational ontologies and triplestores. Section 3 presents our proposed Semantic Web based modeling of educational systems which meets public standards. Section 4 proposes a Semantic Web architecture for educational systems and shows how we implemented the use cases, how this solution is compliant with the actual Educlever architecture and how it improves the Educlever services. Section 5 evaluates and compares Web based integration propositions. Section 6 summarizes our contributions and provides several perspectives.

2   Related Work

2.1   Educational Ontologies

The interest of ontologies in the domain of e-Education has been repeatedly pointed out during the last decade. In [13], the author analyses the reasons and ways to use ontologies in e-Education and for which goals. Many ontologies have been proposed and designed for dedicated applications. Among them CURONTO [1] is an ontological model dedicated to curriculum management and to facilitate program review and management.

In [20] the authors propose an e-Learning management system based on an ontology modelling all the dimensions of the system. Other works on ontology modelling deal with the production of pedagogical resources: [10] and [22] propose ontologies built from French official texts describing curriculum and populate such ontology. Finally, ontology engineering can support the management of the learning process. In [8], the authors use an ontology to describe the learning material that compose a course, to provide adaptive e-learning environments and reusable educational resources. In a similar way, [5], [11] and [12] have as primary objective to develop an ontology-based learning support system which allows the learners to build adaptive learning paths through the understanding of curriculum, syllabuses, and course subjects. In OntoEdu [9], the authors propose to use Semantic Web technologies to implement a service layer which will allow an automatic discovery, invocation, monitoring and composition of learning paths. In these contributions only specific tasks are based on semantic Web technologies, but not the whole system.

[2] and [3] presented a review and overview of works on ontologies in the domain of e-Education. They map works to different needs that ontologies can address. [2] classify ontologies in E-learning context into four categories: (1) curriculum modelling and management, (2) describing learning domains, (3) describing learner data and (4) describing e-Learning services. But, to the best of our knowledge, none of the ontologies reported in the literature has been used in an industrial context, or evaluated on the data of an EdTech company. Moreover, the proposed ontologies do not integrate public authority recommendations or standards model. This is precisely what we will focus on in this paper. We propose an ontology-based solution modeling public recommendations by representing knowledge and skills referential. Our solution relies on the Eduprogresion [22] ontology which models the *Common base of knowledge, skills and culture* published by the French ministry of national education in 2016. It specifies the set of knowledge and skills that must be mastered by students to build their personal and professional future and succeed in life in society. It also specifies the positioning of knowledge and skills in the different cycles of primary and secondary school, and therefore the learning progression.

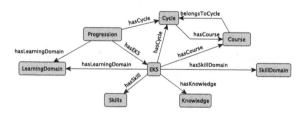

Fig. 1. Ontology eduprogression [7].

Figure 1 presents the main concepts of the Eduprogression ontology. The key concept is that of element of knowledge and skill (EKS), which should be acquired by a learner in his curriculum in a given course at a given cycle. Each element has at least one learning domain among the five defined by French ministry of education: languages for thinking and communicate, methods and tools to learn, formation of the person and the citizen, natural systems and technical systems, representation of the world and the human activities. The concept of Progression is another key concept which represents the program of study for a subject (*course*) at a particular level (*cycle*). In the last version of the recommendation, a progression is defined for an EKS and a learning domain. Our ontologies in this article will start from the Eduprogression ontology and extend it to cover the needs of a specific actor of e-Education.

2.2   Off-the-shelf Triplestores

Triplestores or RDF store systems are software solutions to store data represented in RDF format. These last years, development of triplestores has flourished. Today there are more than 20 systems available[3]. In order to help developers make the right choice among all these systems, many benchmarks have been designed [19,24]. But these benchmarks have some limitations: most of them rely on artificial data and/or hypothetical use cases while using target data improves benchmarking and helps for the right choice [14].

In order to conduct a comparative evaluation on the Educlever use cases and data, we first choose several triplestores by distinguishing between native RDF triplestores, designed and dedicated to store RDF data, and non native RDF triplestores, designed for another type of data (e.g. relational data) but adapted to store RDF data. Among native RDF triplestore, we distinguished between in-memory triplestores and triplestores with persistent storage. As a result, we choose the four following triplestores: *Corese* is an in-memory triplestore; it loads all the ontologies and RDF data when starting the application and saves it in an RDF file when exiting it. *Allegrograph* and *GraphDB* (*OWLIM*) both are native RDF triplestores with persistent storage capabilities. Finally, *Virtuoso* which is a non native RDF triplestore.

As detailed latter in this article, for the benchmarking of these triplestores we translated the Educlever dataset into RDF, relying on a dedicated ontology and we implemented the Educlever requirements with SPARQL queries deployed within Web services. In the next section we present our Semantic Web based modeling of the Educlever data and needs.

3   Ontology Based Modelling of Skills, Knowledge and Pedagogical Resources

In this section, we present our proposed ontology-based model to represent knowledge and skills referential and also pedagogical resources. Beforehand, the Educlever solution relied on relational and graph databases to store them and had limitations to integrate heterogeneous data without losing information and to infer new information from it. They also need to share data and collaborate with others actors of e-Education ecosystem, mainly to meet public recommendations, and perform update when it is needed. The ontology-based model of

---

[3] https://fr.wikipedia.org/wiki/Triplestore and https://db-engines.com/en/ranking/rdf+store.

skills, knowledge and pedagogical resources presented in the following has been setup in the Educlever software infrastructure.

Our solution relies on two linked datasets. The first one is called *Referential*, it describes and contains all the elements of knowledge and skill available through the e-Education solution, Educlever for our case study. The main concept is *Cocon*, which stands for *"COmpétences et CONnaissances"* in French (skills and knowledge). This ontology is an explicit description of knowledge and skills available in Educlever system. It is linked to ontology Eduprogression which model recommendations of the French ministry of national education, such that referential ontology meet these recommendations.

The second dataset is called *Corpus*, it describes and stores all pedagogical resources available through the e-Education solution, and ready for sharing with others actors. *Corpus* is described using a specific vocabulary, with *OPD* as key concept, which stands for *"Objet Pédagogique"* in French (Pedagogical Object). We formalized this vocabulary and underlying concepts into an ontology which reuses and extends EduProgression.

3.1   Knowledge and Skills Modelling

The concept of *Cocon* is the keystone of the *Referential* modelling. It represents an element of knowledge or skill learnt by students on the e-Education solution. We formalize the *Cocon* concept as a class equivalent to *EKS* from the ontology Eduprogression, thus integrating public standards description. Therefore, each *Cocon* can be described by indicating its learning domain(s), course and cycle using respectively properties *hasLearningDomain, hasCourse* and *hasCycle* defined on class *EKS* in ontology Eduprogression. For instance, the *Cocon Write A Fraction As The Sum Of An Integer And A Decimal Fraction Lesser Than One* (cf. Fig. 3), has for learning domain *Languages for thinking and communicate*, its course is *Mathematics* and its cycle is *Second cycle*.

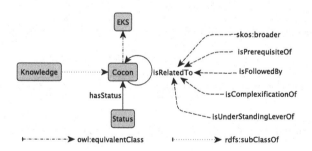

Fig. 2. Referential ontology [7].

Figure 2 presents the Educlever *Referential* ontology. In addition to *Cocon*, there are two other classes in the *Referential* ontology: *Knowledge* and *Status*. *Knowledge* specializes *Cocon*, and represents an high level abstract element of knowledge. For instance, *Mathematics*[4] or *French* are instances of *Knowledge* while *PluralizeAMasculineAndSingluarAdjective* or *WriteAFractionAsThe-SumOfAnIntegerAndADecimalFractionLesserThanOne* are instances of *Cocon*. The granularity of cocons is captured through property *skos:broader*. Figure 3 presents several instances of *Cocon* (in blue) and *Knowledge* (in green) and their relationships.

Status specifies the current state of an instance of *Cocon* in its life cycle in an e-Education solution; some of its instances are *inCreation*, *submitted*, *approved*, *inProgress*, *valid*, *inProduction* and *deleted*.

Referential comprises two mains properties: *hasStatus* to associate a status to a cocon, and *isRelatedTo* to link two cocons. The latter is specialized into five properties specifying the nature of the relation: *skos:broader* (in particular any instance of *Knowledge* is related to other cocons representing more specific elements of knowledge or skill), *isComplexificationOf* states that a *Cocon* goes more in depth than another, *isFollowedBy* expresses a progression between two instances of *Cocon*, *isPrerequisiteOf* and *isUnderstandingLeverOf* states that a *Cocon* helps to understand another.

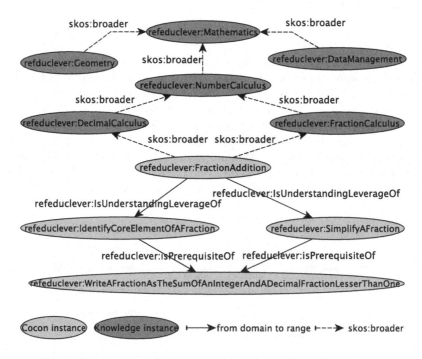

Fig. 3. Population of the referential ontology. (Color figure online)

The usefulness of the *Referential* ontology in the Educlever platform is twofold: (1) It enables to describe the knowledge and skills developed by the company for learners and to link them to the standard published by the French

---

[4] In namespace refeduclever: http://www.educlever.fr/edumics/refeduclever#.

education ministry. (2) When used in combination with the ontology of pedagogical resources described in the following, it enables to evaluate the acquisition of elements of knowledge or skills by learners and to recommend them relevant pedagogical resources. Moreover, by relying on semantic Web models and technologies we can reuse, extend and align with existing vocabularies to increase interoperability. The adopted solution is compliant with linked data Web architecture and principles such as derefenceable URIs.

3.2   Pedagogical Resources Modelling

Once we setup the referential ontology and its data instances, we need resources to help learner to get knowledge and skills and to be evaluated for these knowledge and skills. To reach to this goal we propose Corpus ontology for pedagogical resources. Figure 4 presents the *Corpus* ontology. The concept of *pedagogical object (OPD)* is the keystone of *Corpus*. It represents a pedagogical resource created to learn and acquire knowledge or skills. It is formalized as a class which is the range of all the properties declared in the ontology.

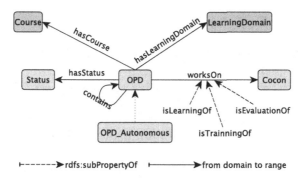

Fig. 4. Corpus ontology [7].

There are two key properties: Property *worksOn* enables to link an instance of *OPD* and an instance of *Cocon* from the *Referential* ontology, representing an element of knowledge or skill tackled in the pedagogical resource. It is specialized into three properties specifying the nature of the relation, the role of the *OPD* relatively to the *Cocon*: *isLearningOf*, *isTrainingOf*, and *isEvaluationOf*). The other key property is *hasOPD*, linking two *OPD*s. It represents composition, expressing how some pedagogical resources are composed as a combination of other resources, which may be reused for composing different other pedagogical resources. *Autonomous OPD* is the subclass of *OPD* gathering the resources which do not need any other resources to be used. Three other properties enable to associate a pedagogical resource to a course, a learning domain and a status in the life cycle of Educlever resources.

Figure 5 presents an example description involving several Corpus instances. Cocon *Write A Fraction As The Sum Of An Integer And A Decimal Fraction Lesser Than One* can be evaluated thanks to the pedagogical resource

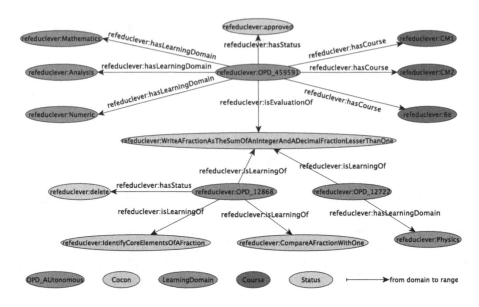

Fig. 5. Population of the Corpus ontology.

refeduclever:OPD_459591. Pedagogical resources *refeduclever:OPD_12868* and *OPD_12722* are used to learn this *Cocon*. It is important to observe that pedagogical resources (*refeduclever:OPD_12722* and *refeduclever:OPD_459591*) are linked to several learning domains (Physics and Mathematics) and can be used to learn a same *Cocon*. We can also note that a same pedagogical resource *refeduclever:OPD_12868* can be used to learn a *Cocon Write A Fraction As The Sum Of An Integer And A Decimal Fraction Lesser Than One* and its prerequisite *Identify Core Elements Of A Fraction*. All these observations will be useful to recommend a learning path to a learner.

Thanks to *Corpus* model, e-Education company could provide pedagogical resources annotated on public standards and so could be evaluated by the public authority. Moreover, based to this model, private companies could share pedagogical resources mainly when theses pedagogical resources allow to learn or evaluate many different skills and knowledge.

4   Semantic Web Based Architecture for e-Educational System

In this section we propose a Semantic Web based architecture, relying on triple-stores, SPARQL Endpoint and Web services to manage the above described ontology-based modelling of skills, knowledge and pedagogical resources. The proposed architectures follow three mains goals: (1) in some cases (partnership) allow sharing of Referential dataset (*Cocon instances*) and also Corpus dataset (*OPD instances*), (2) propose a less strong coupling data and process in order to allow data processing by different actors of e-Education ecosystem, (3) make available some basic process available on the Web through Web service API.

We use these architectures to upgrade the existing software architecture of the Educlever solution. We first briefly describe the initial industrial architecture and present one process example before explaining the proposed architectures.

4.1 Case of a Real e-Education Information System in Production: The Educlever Solution

The first version of the Educlever system was built on top of a relational database storing the pedagogical resources. Two tables were used: the first one storing *OPD*'s attributes like *status*, *title*, *author* and *type*; the second one storing the *course* and *cycle* of each *OPD* and the partonomy relations between them. Based on this relational database, the three main services implemented are: (i) find *OPDs* relative to a particular *course* and/or *cycle*, (ii) find *OPDs* contained in a given *OPD* and (iii) find *OPDs* by combining the two previous criteria. The *tree* structure storing the partonomy of *OPDs* is also useful for interactive exploration of the dataset of *OPD* by users through a dedicated web interface.

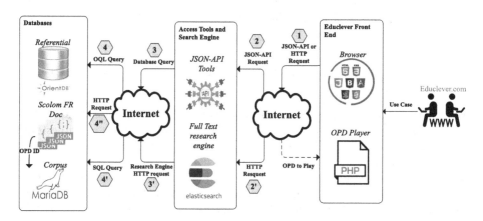

Fig. 6. Existing architecture of the Educlever solution.

A second version of the Educlever platform was built to enable the implementation of new services using *Cocons*, to support the construction of learning paths and the evaluation of learners, e.g. the computation of the accessibility of a *Cocon* by a learner, based on the evaluation of the acquisition of prerequisite *Cocon*, or the computation of the degree of understanding of a *Cocon* by a learner. To represent property chains on *Cocons* a relational database was not efficient, obliging to perform joins between table *Cocon* and itself. Then, Educlever upgraded its platform by adding a graph database (*OrientDB*) to represent the relations between *Cocons*. Its architecture is depicted in Fig. 6.

To ensure interoperability between the Front end of the solution (the presentation layer of the Web application) and its back end (the data access layer), JSON-API [23] services have been implemented, in PHP, to receive queries encapsulated into HTTP requests and turn them into SQL or OQL (*OrientDB query language*) queries to be executed on the dedicated database. JSON-API is also used to convert the answers to these queries into a JSON format adapted to the data model which was previously integrated into JSON-API. A service is defined for each concept of the model, in the form of a HTTP request. For instance, considering the Referential's URI `http://hostname/edumics/referential/` and the Corpus's URI `http://hostname/edumics/corpus/`, the HTTP request `http://hostname/edumics/referential/cocon/IdentifyCoreElementsOfA Fraction` enables to retrieve the description of cocon *Identify Core Elements Of A Fraction* (described in Fig. 5) and store it in a PHP variable. By using JSON-API and a graph database, the Educlever solution implements several services like finding all the prerequisites of a given Cocon, or finding all narrower Cocons of all direct prerequisites of a given Cocon. However, due to the limitations of JSON-API and the current architecture of the solution depicted in Fig. 6, services requiring queries on both datasets cannot be implemented. For instance, considering again the description in Fig. 5, the whole description of `refeduclever:OPD_12868`, which is a learning pedagogical resource for a *Cocon* and its prerequisite, cannot be retrieved. Moreover, what this architecture of a real industrial system also stresses is that there is a need for approaches taking into account the existence of legacy information systems and their integration, extension and evolution.

4.2   e-Education System Architecture Based on Semantic Web Technologies

We propose two architectures based on Semantic Web technologies and Web services to design an e-Education system. They are built on top of triplestores to store and process RDF data from the *Referential* and *Corpus* datasets: after mapping the Educlever relational and graph databases into RDF datasets, we chose to materialize the RDF data (and not only offer a virtual access to it). Our aim is to provide a basis for future versions of the Educlever solution natively based on semantic Web models and technologies.

In the simple architecture we used a triplestore to store both *Referential* and *Corpus* datasets into a single graph. As depicted in Fig. 7, the Educlever solution relies on a SPARQL endpoint queried with SPARQL queries conveyed by HTTP requests. We built a set of basic Web services using business settings as input - since the Educlever developers do not have SPARQL skills yet -, and outputting HTTP requests conveying the corresponding SPARQL queries according to the SPARQL Protocol. Then, in this architecture we upgraded the Educlever JSON-API component to invoke these Web services. This workflow is depicted in Fig. 7 (1-2-3-3'-4-5). While in the current architecture depicted in Fig. 6 some services are implemented by combining the results of several queries from different database systems, with different query languages, the implementation of Web service layer, with REST or SOAP technologies, allows us to avoid JSON-API limits and implement each service as a single SPARQL query answered using both datasets (workflow 1-2'-3'-4-5). For instance, to retrieve

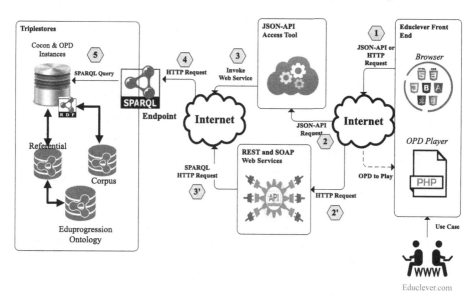

Fig. 7. Semantic web based architecture of e-Education solution (1).

all the pedagogical resources with a learning relation to cocon *Write A Fraction As The Sum Of An Integer And A Decimal Fraction Lesser Than One* and its prerequisite, a solution based on a Web service requires a single SPARQL query while a solution based on JSON-API first requires to retrieve the description of the prerequisite using a `http://hostname/edumics/referential/` request and then to retrieve the description of the pedagogical resources using a `http://hostname/edumics/corpus/` request, and finally to combine both results.

In the current solution (Fig. 6), the Educlever data relative to *Cocons* and *OPDs* are separated in two databases. This decision was motivated by the fact that these two databases can support different services and are used in different processes implemented in JSON-API. The graph database on *Cocons* is used for learning path design and *Cocon* evaluation while the relational database on *OPDs* is used for *OPD* creation by the pedagogical team and for learners training, learning and evaluation. So, a failure of one database does not affect the processes exploiting the other one which continue their execution. With this architecture, the impact of a failure online is limited on one database. However, it does not allow to querying both databases with a same JSON-API service.

In order to add this flexibility in the semantic Web based architecture, while allowing to query both databases with a single Web service, we proposed a federated architecture relying on a *SPARQL federated Endpoint*. As depicted in Fig. 8 this federated endpoint allows us to separate the two datasets, *Referential* and *Corpus*, thus preventing failure while continuing to query them as a single dataset. Moving into a federated architecture does not impact the Web service layer. The SPARQL Federation endpoint will take care of the execution of the

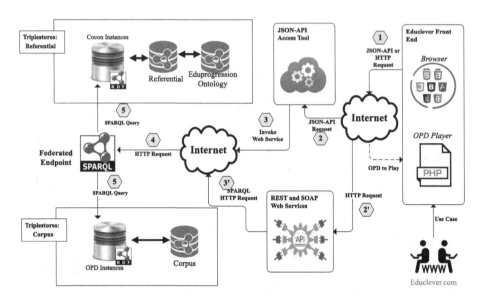

Fig. 8. Semantic web based architecture of e-Education solution (2).

appropriate SPARQL query for SOAP and REST services as well as JSON-API services. Moreover, this architecture enables to open the Referential dataset for public access, since it meets public standards, while keeping a limited access for the Corpus dataset. This context and scenario is typical of the need to take into account legacy software, information system and organizational constraints from real industrial contexts as well as the service quality constraints.

5   Evaluation of the Semantic Web Integration Efficiency

We conducted several experiments to evaluate the proposed e-Education solution based on Semantic Web technologies and Web service technologies (REST, SOAP, JSON-API). For this evaluation we implemented real use cases from the Educlever company, with its real data stored in the *Referential* and *Corpus* datasets. Here we report the results of (i) a qualitative evaluation of the proposed semantic Web based solution consisting in comparing the number of use cases that can be implemented within this solution to the number of them that are implemented in the current Educlever solution (Sect. 5.1); and (ii) a quantitative evaluation of the proposed solution, focusing on the execution cost time of the services implementing the use cases (Sect. 5.2).

5.1   Qualitative Evaluation: Implementability of the Use Cases

The existing Educlever system, based on JSON-API services, has been designed to address the company use cases. Here we present these use cases classified into four categories: (i) use cases exploiting dataset *Referential* only, from R_1 to R_6, (ii) use cases exploiting dataset *Corpus* only, from R_7 to R_9, (iii) use cases exploiting both datasets, from R_{10} to R_{12}, and (iv) use cases requiring querying property paths between *Cocons* on dataset *Referential*, from R_{13} to R_{15}.

1. **Find Information about a *Cocon* c with its ID:** this is used to retrieve all information concerning a *Cocon* identified by its ID.
2. **Find All Direct Prerequisites of a Given *Cocon* c:** this is used to check whether a learner is ready to work on c or if he needs to work on some prerequisites before.
3. **Find All Direct Narrower Cocons of a Given *Cocon* c:** this is mainly used for the exploration of the *Referential* dataset, starting with high level *Cocons* and iteratively going down by following the *broader/narrower* relations.
4. **Find All the *Cocons* Such That a Given *Cocon* c is in their prerequisites:** this is used to identify the candidate *Cocons* for the next learning step after working on *Cocon* c.
5. **Find All Direct Prerequisites of a Given *Cocon* c and All Direct Prerequisites of Its Direct Narrower Cocons:** this is used to score all these *Cocons* when a learner has successfully validated c.
6. **Find All Direct Prerequisites of All the *Cocons* Which are Understanding Levers of a *Cocon* c_i Which is a Complexification of a Given *Cocon* c:** this is used to find alternative (longer) learning paths to learn a *Cocon* c which seems to be complex.
7. **Find All Information about an *OPD* Identify with a Given ID:** this is used to retrieve information about a pedagogical resource.
8. **Find All *OPDs* Which Evaluate a given *Cocon* c:** this is used to build an evaluation *OPD* of c.
9. **Find All *OPDs* Which Are All Useful to Evaluate and Learn a Given *Cocon* c:** recommend evaluation *OPDs* for learning. The goal of this use case is used to prepare the learners to an evaluation session by using evaluation *OPDs* during learning stage.
10. **Find All *OPDs* Useful to Evaluate Both a Given *Cocon* c and all its prerequisites:** this supports the recommendation of *OPDs* in order to speed up the study.
11. **Find All Evaluation *OPDs* More Simpler than a Given *OPD* o,** considering the complexification relations between the *Cocons* these *OPDs* are related to: this is used to recommend *OPDs* to evaluate a learner.
12. **Find All *OPDs* Useful to Understand a Given *Cocon* c:** these *OPDs* are related to c with an instance of relation *isTrainingOf* or linked to *Cocons* c_i related to c with relation *isUnderstandingLeverOf*.
13. **Recursively Find All Direct and Indirect Prerequisites of a Given *Cocon* c:** this involves evaluating learning paths of property *isPrerequisiteOf*.
14. **Find All *Cocons* within a Prerequisite Path between Two *Cocons* c_1 and c_2.**
15. **Infer Implicit Prerequisite Paths between Two *Cocons* c_1 and c_2:** find the simplest *Cocons* associated to more complex *Cocons* in the path.

As Table 1 shows it, the semantic Web based proposed solutions implement all of the use cases while the current version of the Educlever solution implements

Table 1. Implementation of the use cases depending on the tested architectures.

	Referential						Corpus			Both datasets			Path queries		
	R1	R2	R3	R4	R5	R6	R7	R8	R9	R10	R11	R12	R13	R14	R15
Educ-V2	✔	✔	✔	✔	✘	✘	✔	✔	✘	✘	✘	✘	✘	✘	✘
Web Semantic	✔	✔	✔	✔	✔	✔	✔	✔	✔	✔	✔	✔	✔	✔	✔

only six of them due to the limits of its architecture. The services which are difficult or impossible to be implemented are those requiring to jointly exploit the two databases, and those requiring a recursive traversal of the graph base. These can seamlessly be implemented with semantic Web models. For instance in use case 13, the retrieval of all prerequisites of a given *Cocon* requires a recursive process with many query executions in the current Educlever architecture when it needs only a single SPARQL query then a single Web service invocation in the semantic Web based architecture:

```
SELECT ?prerequis
WHERE { ?prerequis refeduclever:isPrerequisiteOf+ <cocon> . }
```

Similarly, the implementation of use case 5 in the current Educlever architecture requires many JSON-API queries to (one query to retrieve prerequisites and childs, and several other queries to retrieve the prerequisites of each child) while it can be achieved with a single SPARQL query in the semantic Web based architecture:

```
SELECT ?prerequisite ?child ?childPrerequisite
WHERE {
    ?prerequisite referential:isPrerequisiteOf <cocon> .
    <cocon> referential:isParentOf ?child .
    ?childPrerequisite referential:isPrerequisiteOf ?child . }
```

5.2   Quantitative Evaluation: Analysis of the Query Execution Times

The Educlever solution has approximately 500,000 student user accounts and 25,000 teacher user accounts. Half of them use their account frequently and half of the connections to the system are concentrated on Wednesdays between 2 pm and 6 pm. As a result, in average, during these weekly 4 hours periods, more than 7,100 requests are sent to the system. These metrics show the high performance architecture needed by Educlever. To be adopted, the semantic Web based solution must provide acceptable query execution times.

For the evaluation of the implementation of the use cases, we first evaluated the current Educlever architecture (Fig. 6) with a set of data stored in OrientDB (*Referential*) and MariaDB (*Corpus*) databases. These datasets are depicted in Table 2, column 2 and 3. They are small datasets since the data in the first

Table 2. Datasets statistics.

	Educlever V2 dataset		Triplestores dataset	
	Referential	Corpus	Referential	Corpus
Number of instances	17	211	17 127	334 711
Number of triples	–	–	68 000	2 396 836

version of the Educlever solution has not been migrated yet in the (V2) current architecture.

Then we evaluated the semantic Web based architecture deployed in the Educlever industrial environment. We compared the execution times on this architecture depending on the chosen triplestore (Allegro, Corese, GraphDB, Virtuoso) and middleware (JSON-API, SOAP, REST). Since the current architecture of Educlever uses JSON-API in PHP, we implemented a JSON-API layer, in Java, which reuses REST Web services for querying the triplestores. This was done to measure the impact of each software layer on the overall system efficiency. Then, we measured the execution time of querying a triplestore directly with a SPARQL query on its SPARQL endpoint, when querying the SPARQL endpoint through SOAP and REST Web services (1 layer) and finally when using REST Web services through JSON-API tools (2 layers). For this evaluation we used the dataset depicted in Table 2, column 4 and 5. This dataset is the result of the migration of the data from the first version of the Educlever solution into RDF. In the following, we describe the experimental environment, protocol and results.

Experimental Environment and Protocol

Hardware: We perform experimentation on a virtual Linux server host on a remote machine. The remote VMWare virtual machine has a processor 4386 (x64) AMD Opteron 3.1 GHz, 8 GB of RAM and 96.6 GB for hard disc. We deploy triplestores and Tomcat 9 server as host of Web services.

DataSet: We used the exploitation data of Educlever for the experiments. Tables 2 summarizes the characteristics of datasets *Corpus* and *Referential*: the number of triples and the number of instances of *Cocon* in *Referential* and of *OPD* in *Corpus*. Let us note that the size of *Corpus* is much greater than that of *Referential*, therefore the execution times of queries on *Corpus* may be higher than that of queries on *Referential*.

Queries: We implemented the Educlever use cases, presented in Sect. 5.1, by writing a base of fifteen SPARQL queries.

Triplestores: We tested four triplestores: (i) *Allegrograph (Allegro-cent)*, (ii) *Corese (Corese-cent)*, (iii) *GraphDB (Graphdb)* and (iv) *Virtuoso (Virtuoso)* where we stored together the *Referential* and *Corpus* datasets, as described in the first proposed architecture, Fig. 7. We also setup two SPARQL Federated Endpoints with *Allegrograph (Allegro-fed)* and *Corese (Corese-fed)* storing *Referential* and *Corpus* datasets separately as proposed in the second proposed architecture, Fig. 8. The *Allegrograph* SPARQL Federated Endpoint uses two SPARQL Endpoints, each built with an *Allegrograph* repository. Similarly, the *Corese* SPARQL Federated Endpoint uses a *Corese* server for each SPARQL Endpoint.

Protocol: We evaluate two indicators: (i) the SPARQL query execution times and (ii) the SPARQL query answers themselves. The first one measures the performance of the solution and the second one checks its correctness. Since all the configurations returned the same sets of answers, in the following we focus on the evaluation of the performance. For each tested triplestore, we executed each query ten times and stored all the execution times. For each evaluation only concerned triplestore is on service, the others are stopped. For a deep analysis of the query execution behaviours, we considered two indicators: (i) the average execution time *(Av)* and (ii) the median *(Med)* execution time of the last nine times.

Results

Evaluation of the current Educlever architecture. We first measured the execution time of queries on the current Educlever architecture with the small dataset described in Table 2.

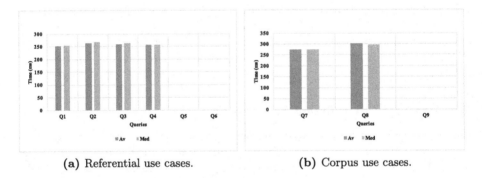

(a) Referential use cases.   (b) Corpus use cases.

Fig. 9. Evaluation of the Educlever architecture. Execution times of queries on referential and on Corpus.

Figure 9 shows the results of this evaluation. It must be noted that there is no evaluation of use cases requiring both datasets or path queries. This is due to the limits of this architecture. Indeed, in Table 1 we see that these use cases cannot be implemented with JSON-API (and therefore are not available online yet). For some of these use cases Educlever implemented dedicated functions and/or dedicated database connections. This brings heterogeneity in the system and makes it more complex. For example, use case 13 is implemented by a dedicated function using a dedicated connection to OrientDB with the following query:

```
SELECT FROM (TRAVERSE in('Prerequis') FROM <cocon>)
WHERE $depth >= 0.
```

We can observe that the average execution time of queries on Referential is less than 250 ms and the one for queries on Corpus is slightly greater. This difference can be explained by the size difference between the two datasets and is not significant. Most importantly, we can observe that the execution time remains greater than 200 ms, where 200 ms stands as reference threshold for acceptable response times for a Web application [15]. However, these execution times meet the service level agreement of 5 s [16].

Evaluation of the Semantic Web based Architecture. We evaluated the semantic Web based architecture, while distinguishing the access mode to the triplestores: with a SPARQL query directly submitted to the endpoint, or by using REST or SOAP Web services outputting the SPARQL query to be submitted to the endpoint, or by using an additional JSON-API layer. In [7], we reported on the evaluation of the four targeted triplestores deployed locally. But remoteness drastically impacts on the evaluation. This is why our aim here is to (i) show that a semantic Web based solution can meet the industrial requirements and eventually (ii) to choose among on the shelf triplestores, but also to (iii) highlight the impact of the different layers on the architecture (network latency, triplestore endpoint, communication between Web services and SPARQL endpoint) in order to choose the most appropriate solution.

For readability and an easy comparison between the architectures, we depict the results in stacked area diagrams. Each diagram represents an architecture. In each diagram, the query response time for a triplestore is represented by the width of a band and triplestores can be compared through the width of their bands. To compare architectures the whole stacked areas representing them must be compared. We distinguish between the four categories of use cases (queries on Referential, on Corpus, on both datasets and with property paths).

Use Cases on the Referential Dataset. Figure 10 shows the execution times of SPARQL queries on the *Referential* dataset with the four targeted triplestores deployed in a remote server in our three proposed architectures and the one adding a JSON-API layer (inline with the architecture of the solution currently deployed). First, we can observe that the query execution time with JSON-API (Fig. 10b) is high for Allegrograph and Allegrograph federation. We also confirm that this architecture does not implement R_5 and R_6. In general, GraphDB, Virtuoso, and Corese have similar performances in each of the three proposed architecture (SPARQL Endpoint (Fig. 10a), REST (Fig. 10c) and SOAP (Fig. 10d) Web services). We observe that the REST architecture gets the best query response time while the JSON-API based architecture gets the worst. This was expected since it stacks up a SPARQL endpoint, a REST Web service and a JSON-API adapter. Except the query implementing use case R_6, for our proposed architecture the query response time is under 1 s which is acceptable according to service level agreement [16]. For the specific case of R_6, its execution time is very high for Allegrograph Federation (3 s whatever the proposed architecture) because of network latency since this configuration uses two SPARQL endpoints.

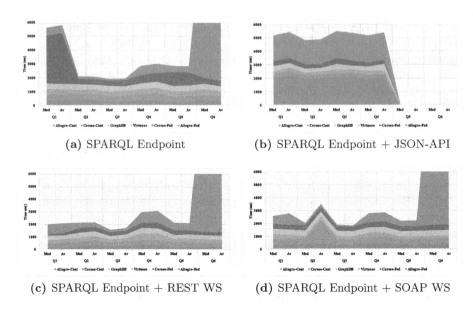

(a) SPARQL Endpoint

(b) SPARQL Endpoint + JSON-API

(c) SPARQL Endpoint + REST WS

(d) SPARQL Endpoint + SOAP WS

Fig. 10. Evaluation of the semantic web based architecture on referential use cases.

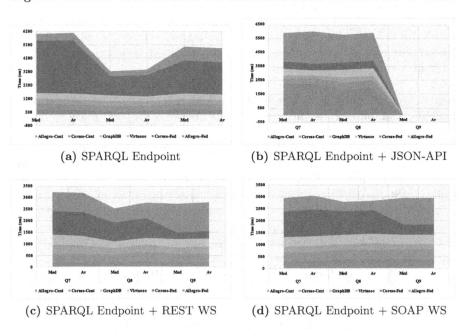

(a) SPARQL Endpoint

(b) SPARQL Endpoint + JSON-API

(c) SPARQL Endpoint + REST WS

(d) SPARQL Endpoint + SOAP WS

Fig. 11. Semantic web architecture evaluation with Corpus use cases.

Use Cases on the Corpus Dataset. Figure 11 shows the query execution time of SPARQL queries on *Corpus* for the four chosen architectures deployed with a remote server. The results confirm our previous comparative analysis on *Referential*: GraphDB, Virtuoso, and Corese have a same behaviour in our three proposed architectures (SPARQL Endpoint (Fig. 11a), REST (Fig. 11c) and SOAP (Fig. 11d) Web services); the query execution time in the JSON-API based architecture (Fig. 11b) is high for Allegrograph and Allegrograph federation, and this architecture does not enable to implement all use cases. The architectures with REST and SOAP Web services show the best performances, especially with *GraphDB* or *Virtuoso* as triplestore. We also observe that architectures with federated triplestores (Corese and Allegrograph federation) get worse execution time. As reported in [7], they get good results when deployed locally, so the results in a remote deployment must be explained by network latency and services stack. When comparing Figs. 10 and 11, we can note that the execution time of queries on *Corpus* are much lower than those of queries on *Referential* whereas the size of the *Corpus* dataset is much greater than that of the *Referential* dataset (see Table 2). This can be explained by the fact that the queries on *Corpus* have simple star patterns while the queries on *Referential* have heterogeneous and more complex patterns [4]. All the execution time remain below 1 s which is acceptable for a response time of a Web application [15].

Use Cases on Both Datasets. Figure 12 shows the execution times of the queries on both *Referential* and *Corpus*, for the four chosen architectures deployed with a triplestore deployed in a remote server. The trends are the same as in the above described use cases. The performances of the architectures are the same for SPARQL Endpoint (Fig. 12a), REST (Fig. 12c) and SOAP (Fig. 12d) associated to triplestores GraphDB, Virtuoso and Corese. Figure 12b shows that the JSON-API based solution does not enable to implement the uses cases requiring to jointly query both datasets. The execution times are all below 1 s, for all queries on all triplestores except for query 12 on Corese federation. Here is the query:

```
@service <http://host:8081/sparql>
@service<http://host:8082/sparql>
SELECT ?uri ?opd ?hasStatut
WHERE {
 {?opd referential:isTrainingOf referential:IdentifyAFirstGroupVerb .
  OPTIONAL { ?opd referential:hasStatus ?hasStatut . }}
 UNION
 {?isUnderstanding referential:isUnderstandingLeverageOf
    referential:IdentifyAFirstGroupVerb .
  ?opd referential:isEvaluationOf ?isUnderstanding .
  OPTIONAL { ?opd referential:hasStatus ?hasStatut .}}
```

The result of query 12 on Corese federation can be explained firstly by network latency, secondly by the query structure (UNION, OPTIONAL, number of triples) and thirdly by the cost of the merging operation of the federator.

Use Cases Implemented by Queries with Property Paths. Property paths are a key feature for implementing high value use cases for Educlever. Figures 13 shows the execution times of such queries on the four architectures deployed.

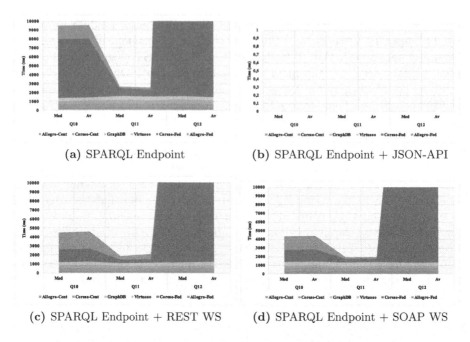

(a) SPARQL Endpoint

(b) SPARQL Endpoint + JSON-API

(c) SPARQL Endpoint + REST WS

(d) SPARQL Endpoint + SOAP WS

Fig. 12. Semantic web architecture evaluation with both datasets use cases.

For readability, we use the logarithmic scale to draw the chart in Fig. 13. Figure 13b confirms once again the limitations of a JSON-API based solution: it does not enable to implement path query. Figures 13a, c and d confirm that with *Corese-cent, GraphDB, Allegro-cent* or *Virtuoso* in the Educlever industrial context, the execution time of queries with a few property paths in the graph pattern, like it is the case for Q_{13}, remains under 1 s in average, which is acceptable for a Web application. But, for more complex queries, like Q_{14} and Q_{15}, the execution time can reach up to to 55000 ms (55 s), on Corese federated or Allegrograph federated, which is not acceptable in the Educlever industrial context. This is among our next challenges to find a convenient solution to handle such queries, probably with pre-processed results.

These evaluations show the feasibility of deploying a semantic Web based solution in the Educlever industrial context. The proposed architecture meets the performance needs and makes SPARQL skills optional by adding a Web service layer (REST or SOAP) on top of the triplestore. Finally, not surprisingly it performs better than a JSON-API based solution which introduces an additional layer in the architecture and is limited to use cases that can be implemented with a single query (or requires additional developments).

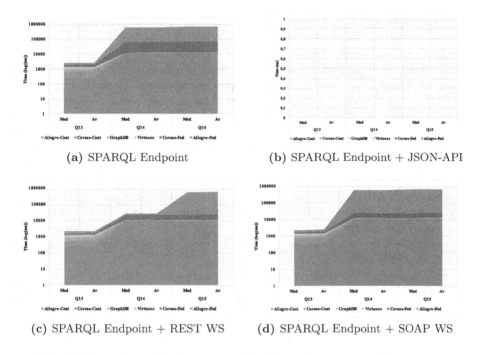

(a) SPARQL Endpoint   (b) SPARQL Endpoint + JSON-API

(c) SPARQL Endpoint + REST WS   (d) SPARQL Endpoint + SOAP WS

Fig. 13. Semantic web architecture evaluation with property path use cases

6   Conclusions

The work described in this article, is a proof of concept and a feasibility study for a knowledge-based solution providing, in an industrial context, an e-Education solution compliant with public education specifications. Moreover our study show that the maturity of semantic Web methods and standards supports the development and deployment of a scalable and operational application in a real-world scenario.

From the ontological and semantic Web schemata point of view, we showed how existing vocabularies can be reused, extended and integrated in an existing industrial platform to become a keystone of application and data integration. More precisely, we extended the ontology Eduprogression which describes a shared conceptualization of knowledge pieces and skills in the educational context. This extension models the specific needs of a company (Educlever) for the E-Education solution they develop and acts as a bridge between a public schema and a private one.

We also detailed the architecture and technical choices we made in developing and deploying a semantic Web operational platform in the real industrial context of Educlever. Again, the solution relies on two ontologies, (1) *Referential* populated by all the elements of knowledge and skills (*Cocons*), and (2) *Corpus* populated by all the pedagogical resources. Both the instances of these ontologies are obtained by lifting the data of the legacy stores of the Educlever learning platform. In this article, we briefly showed, through examples, how these ontologies were populated and how they were interlinked in order to meet Educlever requirements and support application-level integration.

To meet the industrial requirements and benchmark the proposed solutions, we developed a base of SPARQL queries capturing information retrieval needs from the Educlever use cases and we proposed four software architectures based on Semantic Web technologies designed for an e-Education systems. We upgraded the Educlever software architecture following these propositions and implemented them with four state-of-the-art triplestores: *Corese, Allegrograph, GraphDB* and *Virtuoso*. We specially detailed the way resources have to be available and sharable over the Web and we addressed that requirement by providing a dedicated SPARQL Endpoint with the required availability and quality of service. In order to be able to deal with existing systems and to provide a generic solution to the specific scenario of Educlever, we designed and implemented the entire architecture as a RESTful and SOAP compatible set of Web services and API on top of a generic SPARQL Endpoint.

Subsequently, we designed and performed a complete evaluation campaign to assess the quality of service and response time in an industrial context. We built a real-world testbed showing that the Semantic Web based solutions meet the industrial constraints, both in terms of functionalities and efficiency compared to existing operational solutions. These evaluations also allowed us to observe the impact on performance of different software layers (SPARQL endpoint, Web Services) and technologies (REST, SOAP or JSON-API). Moreover, we showed that by relying on semantic Web we can reuse, extend and align existing vocabularies to increase interoperability. In particular we demonstrated how the introduction of a standard such as ScolomFR can be performed by linking and aligning to the in-house Educlever ontologies. The semantic Web approach to interoperability is also illustrated by the ability we have to share *OPD*s and integrate *Cocon*s with other e-Education or guidance institutions like ONISEP[5], provided that they can be aligned with the Eduprogression model.

Finally, we identified new opportunities that an ontology-oriented modelling opens up. One of the next challenges for us is the modeling of learner profiles as an additional populated ontology integrated with *Referential* and *Corpus*. A motivation for that, is the modeling and support of SPARQL queries and rule-based reasoning mechanisms for resource recommendation and adaptive learning. We also intend to further demonstrate the application-level integration provided by (semantic) Web hypermedia architectures by linking pedagogical resources from several educational organizations in order to build an integrated educational solution offering the learner a coherent learning path across a set of educational systems, based on dynamically federated endpoints.

---

[5] http://www.onisep.fr.

References

1. Al-Yahya, M., Al-Faries, A., George, R.: Curonto: an ontological model for curriculum representation. In: Proceedings of the 18th ACM Conference on Innovation and Technology in Computer Science Education, ITiCSE 2013, pp. 358. ACM, New York (2013)
2. Al-Yahya, M., George, R., Al-Faries, A.: Ontologies in e-learning: review of the literature. Int. J. Softw. Eng. Appl. **9**, 67–84 (2015)
3. Alsultanny, Y.A.: e-learning system overview based on semantic web. Electron. J. e-Learning **4**, 111–118 (2006)
4. Arias, M., Fernández, J.D., Martínez-Prieto, M.A., de la Fuente, P.: An empirical study of real-world SPARQL queries. CoRR abs/1103.5043 (2011)
5. Brusilovsky, P., Peylo, C.: Adaptive and intelligent web-based educational systems. Int. J. Artif. Intell. Educ. **13**(2–4), 159–172 (2003). http://dl.acm.org/citation.cfm?id=1434845.1434847
6. Committee, I.L.L.: IEEE Standard for Learning Object Metadata. IEEE Standards Association, September 2002. https://standards.ieee.org/findstds/standard/1484.12.1-2002.html
7. Fokou Pelap, G., Faron-Zucker, C., Gandon, F.: Semantic models in web based educational system integration. In: Proceedings of the 14th International Conference on Web Information Systems and Technologies, WEBIST 2018, Seville, Spain, 18–20 September 2018, pp. 78–89 (2018). https://doi.org/10.5220/0006940000780089
8. Gascueña, J.M., Fernández-Caballero, A., González, P.: Domain ontology for personalized e-learning in educational systems. In: IEEE International Conference on Advanced Learning Technologies, (ICALT), pp. 456–458, July 2006
9. Guangzuo, C., Fei, C., Hu, C., Shufang, L.: Ontoedu: a case study of ontology-based education grid system for e-learning. In: GCCCE 2004 International conference, Hong Kong (2004)
10. Gueffaz, M., Deslis, J., Moissinac, J.C.: Curriculum data enrichment with ontologies. In: Proceedings of the 4th International Conference on Web Intelligence, Mining and Semantics, WIMS 2014, pp. 441–446. ACM, New York (2014)
11. Hyun-Sook, C., Jung-Min, K.: Ontology design for creating adaptive learning path in e-learning environment. In: Proceedings of International MultiConference of Engineers and Computer Scientists, IMECS 2012, pp. 585–5886 (2012)
12. Chung, H.-S., Kim, J.-M.: Semantic model of syllabus and learning ontology for intelligent learning system. In: Hwang, D., Jung, J.J., Nguyen, N.-T. (eds.) ICCCI 2014. LNCS (LNAI), vol. 8733, pp. 175–183. Springer, Cham (2014). https://doi.org/10.1007/978-3-319-11289-3_18
13. Jaffro, L.: Les objets de l'éducation: quelle ontologie? Revue de métaphysique et de morale 4(56), 429–448 (Septembre 2007)
14. Jean, S., Bellatreche, L., Fokou, G., Baron, M., Khouri, S.: OntoDBench: novel benchmarking system for ontology-based databases. In: Meersman, R., et al. (eds.) OTM 2012. LNCS, vol. 7566, pp. 897–914. Springer, Heidelberg (2012). https://doi.org/10.1007/978-3-642-33615-7_32
15. Khan, R., Amjad, M.: Performance testing (load) of web applications based on test case management. Perspect. Sci. **8**, 355–357 (2016). Recent Trends in Engineering and Material Sciences
16. Khan, R., Amjad, M.: Performance testing (load) of web applications based on test case management. Perspect. Sci. **8**, 355–357 (2016). https://doi.org/10.1016/j.pisc.2016.04.073. http://www.sciencedirect.com/science/article/pii/S2213020916300957. Recent Trends in Engineering and Material Sciences

17. Michel, F., Zucker, C.F., Gargominy, O., Gandon, F.: Integration of web apis and linked data using SPARQL micro-services-application to biodiversity use cases. Information **9**(12), 310 (2018). https://doi.org/10.3390/info9120310. http://www.mdpi.com/2078-2489/9/12/310

18. Ministère de l'éducation nationale: Code de l'éducation, Version consolidée au 1 janvier 2018 (Janvier 2018). https://www.legifrance.gouv.fr/affichCode.do?cidTexte=LEGITEXT000006071191

19. Mironov, V., Seethappan, N., Blondé, W., Antezana, E., Lindi, B., Kuiper, M.: Benchmarking triple stores with biological data. CoRR abs/1012.1632 (2010). http://arxiv.org/abs/1012.1632

20. Rani, M., Srivastava, K.V., Vyas, O.P.: An ontological learning management system. Comput. Appl. Eng. Educ. **24**(5), 706–722 (2016)

21. Réseau Canopé: ScoLomFR : Outil de description des ressources numériques de l'enseignement scolaire (Janvier 2011). https://www.reseau-canope.fr/scolomfr/accueil.html

22. Rocha, O.R., Faron-Zucker, C., Pelap, G.F.: A formalization of the french elementary school curricula. In: Knowledge Engineering and Knowledge Management - EKM and Drift-an-LOD, Bologna, Italy, Revised Selected Papers, pp. 82–94 (2016)

23. Klabnik, S., Yehuda Katz, D.G.T.K., Resnick, E.: A specification for building apis in json. https://jsonapi.org/format/. Accessed 20 Dec 2018

24. Wu, H., Fujiwara, T., Yamamoto, Y., Bolleman, J.T., Yamaguchi, A.: Biobenchmark toyama 2012: an evaluation of the performance of triple stores on biological data. J. Biomed. Semant. **5**(1), 32 (2014)

Affordable Voice Services to Bridge the Digital Divide: Presenting the Kasadaka Platform

André Baart[1](✉), Anna Bon[2,3], Victor de Boer[2], Francis Dittoh[4],
Wendelien Tuijp[2,3], and Hans Akkermans[2]

[1] Amsterdam Business School, Universiteit van Amsterdam,
Amsterdam, The Netherlands
a.h.j.baart@uva.nl

[2] The Network Institute, Vrije Universiteit Amsterdam,
Amsterdam, The Netherlands
{a.bon,v.de.boer,w.tuijp,j.m.akkermans}@vu.nl

[3] Centre for International Cooperation, Vrije Universiteit Amsterdam,
Amsterdam, The Netherlands

[4] University for Development Studies, Tamale, Ghana
fdittoh@uds.edu.gh

Abstract. Despite its global reach, the World Wide Web still fails to
serve about 3 billion people, the majority living in the Global South,
especially in poor, low-resource regions, where broadband internet is not
expected to be rolled out in the foreseeable future. Yet, to bring the
advantages of ICTs at the reach of communities in low-resource development regions, lightweight, affordable and context-aware ICT solutions
are needed, that fit local needs and context. To this end the *Kasadaka*
platform was developed. This platform supports easy creation of local-
content and voice-based information services, targeting currently 'unconnected' populations, taking into account contextual and infrastructural
requirements, and matching local ecosystems. The Kasadaka platform
and its Voice Service Development Kit support the development of decentralized voice-based information services, to serve local populations and
communities in their own local languages, in regions where Internet and
Web are absent and will continue to be for the foreseeable future.

Keywords: Digital Divide · Low literacy · Sub-Saharan Africa ·
Voice-based services · Low-resource hardware · Services development
software kit

1 Introduction

The World Wide Web is a public open space for knowledge sharing, content
creation and application service provisioning for billions on this planet. Despite
its global reach, the Web is not yet accessible for three billion people in the world,

© Springer Nature Switzerland AG 2019
M. J. Escalona et al. (Eds.): WEBIST 2018, LNBIP 372, pp. 195–220, 2019.
https://doi.org/10.1007/978-3-030-35330-8_10

the majority of whom live in the Global South, often in remote rural regions, under low-resource conditions and with poor or even absent infrastructures [11]. Obviously, the right to share knowledge and access relevant content should not be denied to people who live at the "other side of the Digital Divide".

Omnipresence of internet connectivity and large scale transfer of technologies from the Global North to poor regions, is generally assumed to be the best solution to this global problem. To this end large funds are made available by international development donors[1].

For example in Mali, one of the poorest countries in the world, around 80% of the population depend for their livelihood on work in small subsistence agriculture in remote rural regions where there is no Internet, very limited electricity, and low levels of literacy in the population (around 35% on average, for women even lower).[2] Under these conditions it is unlikely that technology transfer for Internet roll-out will take place in the foreseeable future.

An alternative approach to large-scale technology-transfer is an approach focusing on development of light-weight community-centered ICT services, based on locally expressed needs and embedded in local ecosystems. In this research we focus on the co-creation of new, context-aware services for information exchange and knowledge sharing support targeting specifically farmer communities in the West African Sahel.

In this paper we show that services can be developed that enable access to information and knowledge exchange in low-resource contexts, in the absence of Internet connectivity. This requires thorough field investigation to assess conditions, requirements and specific conditions. Context analysis leads to new insights and gives technical directions, which cannot be derived from advanced but far-away technology considerations alone. This approach stands in contrast to the one-size-fits-all technology transfer approach that is common in international development projects [21,22,24].

In this paper we present *Kasadaka*, a platform that intends to support the hosting and development of locally relevant voice-based information services, targeting 'unconnected' populations and meeting the harsh conditions at the "other side" of the Digital Divide.

The Kasadaka platform and its Voice Service Development Kit aims to serve local communities and small businesses, by facilitating the formation of a local ecosystem of decentralized voice-based information services, analogous to the services of the Web, but without need for high speed infrastructure or Internet connectivity.

This paper is an extended version of the paper presented at the 14th International Conference on Web Information Systems and Technologies (WEBIST18) [2]. This publication extends the preceding paper by including three additional evaluations of the Kasadaka platform, a description of an additional feature of the VSDK, a revised introduction and a revised and extended section on methodology and approach.

---

[1] https://webfoundation.org/our-work/projects/alliance-for-affordable-internet/.
[2] http://uis.unesco.org/en/country/ML.

This paper is structured as follows: Sect. 2 describes the methodology and approach used to elicit the requirements for designing and building the the platform. Section 3 present the resulting requirements from the requirements analysis, Sect. 4 describes the architecture and technical implementation, and Sect. 5 describes various evaluations of the platform. Section 6 discusses related work and Sect. 7 summarizes our main conclusions.

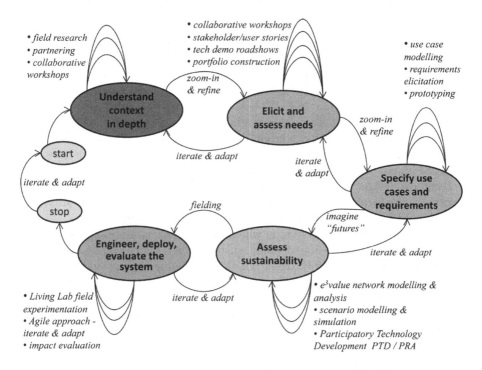

Fig. 1. ICT4D Field research methodology, from [2,9].

2 Methodology and Approach

Whereas, in a high-tech environment in the Global North, setting up the requirements for a new ICT service platform can be considered a well documented business-as-usual task, in which technical specifications are balanced against costs and expected revenues, this is less straightforward for platform design that targets low resource environments such as e.g. rural Africa. While adaptation to local contextual conditions is to be expected, these conditions are often initially unknown to the platform designers. In this section we present an adaptive, iterative field-based approach and methodology, on how to elicit platform requirements for complex low resource contexts. This task must be performed in close collaboration with local envisaged users of the platform, to ensure matching local needs.

For the whole life cycle of Information Systems engineering in the context of ICT for Development (ICT4D), we use an iterative, adaptive and collaborative field research methodology, based on extensive field piloting. This is depicted in Fig. 1, in the form of an intention-strategy map [20]. The methodology, dubbed ICT4D 3.0, has been extensively tested in low-tech low-resource environments, in the period 2012–2018 in rural regions of West Africa [9]. The methodology consists of various stages, not necessarily to be performed in a fixed order:

- An analysis of the local context: a through field-based analysis of local livelihoods, to find out local conditions with respect to technical infrastructure, environmental conditions, availability of technical support, etc;
- A collaborative needs assessment to find out the platform requirements, as also derived from the service use cases, elicited from local users during extensive user workshops;
- In-depth use case and requirements analysis in collaboration with local users, during workshops with focus group discussions and group assignments. This consists of elicitation of user and business requirements for the services, and technical, contextual and business requirements for the platform.
- Technical design, prototyping, engineering, piloting, deployment of the platform in the local environment; iterative testing and doing user evaluations; this may lead to new requirements and second cycle improvements.
- Analysis of the local ecosystem in which the platform is supposed to function; this is necessary to predict economic sustainability, which can be determined by analysis of the network of agents that exchange objects and services of value with each other, in order to deliver a service to the envisaged end users/customers. This analysis can be done in an early stage, before the actual implementation/deployment of the platform, and must involve data on the expected service (size and cost of the services, number of users, all expected costs involved).

3   Platform Requirements Analysis

The development of a system that is intended for people at the "other side of the Digital Divide", has to deal with circumstances and issues that are rarely encountered in technology development projects in the developed world. Therefore, finding requirements for a service platform is done in a iterative approach in which analyzing the requirements for the use cases and the service platform requirements go hand in hand. Figure 2 shows the various sources where requirements have been derived in the case of the Kasadaka platform.

3.1   Requirements Related to the Local Context

Voice-based access to information is an essential requirement for bridging the Digital Divide, and reaching the world's rural poor.

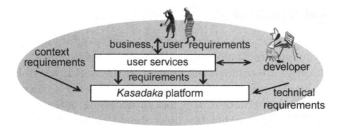

Fig. 2. Different sources for platform requirements: (i) contextual requirements related to e.g. cultural and language, (ii) technical requirements related to e.g. infrastructure, (ii) user and business requirements, derived from use case and requirements analysis that lead to the design and deployment of local user services.

In these populations, literacy rates are low, which disqualifies any service that is text-based. In several sub-Saharan African countries (such as Niger, Mali and Burkina Faso) the literacy rates are below 40%, which puts the vast amounts of textual information on the Internet out of reach for a major part of the population in these regions [23]. Furthermore, many indigenous cultures have a strong oral tradition in communication, so that voice-based services have a natural fit with the locally existing means of communication.

Voice services for the world's rural poor have to support under-resourced languages, which implies that they can not use advanced speech technologies.
While many developing countries have a technologically well-supported official language (often a remnant of colonial times), this language is not necessarily spoken by the entire population. Rather, the local population speaks their own indigenous language which is tied to their local region. Africa has around 2000 local languages, which each often have local dialects [14]. The majority of these languages are *spoken languages*, meaning that there exists little to no literature in these languages. Furthermore, due to the populations speaking these languages being poor and relatively small, these populations do not provide a profitable market for the development of Text To Speech, Automatic Speech Recognition and Natural Language Processing technologies in these languages. Most of the recently developed voice assistants that offer complex information services (e.g. Apple's Siri, Amazon Alexa, etc.) rely on the use of these technologies. While these technologies are in widespread use around the world, they require research and a substantial financial investment in order to support a language at a level that is sufficient for usage in voice services [4,6,7,10,17,25]. The number of languages that has well-developed speech technologies is rising, but these do not include any of the indigenous languages found in the developing world. This situation is not likely to change, as there is little (financial) incentive to develop technologies for these languages. Taking into account these restrictions, these languages are referred to as under-resourced languages [5].

3.2   Technical Requirements

Information services for the world's poor should be affordable and accessible through locally adopted technologies, i.e., mobile (dumb-)phones.
Developing countries are some of the poorest in the world, where large parts of the population live on less than €2 per day.[3] In order for a voice service to be of use to the general population, the cost of accessing and using it thus have to be very low. This implies that the users should be able to access the service without having to purchase a new device or service, but rather by using a device they already own or have access to. The initial costs and running costs of a voice service should also be low enough to be affordable (and to provide sufficient return on investment) for the rural poor.

The voice-service platform should function with limited infrastructure.
The (digital) infrastructure in these countries is often unreliable and expensive, especially in the rural areas. While some villages have access to electricity, it is often unreliable and black-outs often happen multiple times per day (even in cities). The majority of the population does not have (direct) access to electricity[4]. The ownership and usage of smartphones that can access the Internet is slowly becoming more common [19], but internet connections are still very expensive and unreliable[5], due to a lack of local hosting and limited international (backbone) connections. While Internet adoption is low, mobile phones have become a successful means of communication in much of the developed world, and has become the main means of telecommunication in sub-Saharan Africa [12]. The coverage of mobile telephony networks is often quite good, covering a large part of the population (also rural areas).

3.3   Business Requirements, Financial Sustainability and the Local Ecosystem

The platform should be able to provide financially sustainable voice services.
This can be achieved by reducing the cost of voice services –which consist of hardware costs, development costs and maintenance costs– as far as possible. This has consequences for all elements in the architecture of the platform, which have to be chosen and designed in such a way that costs are minimized. Financial sustainability assures that the services are accurately targeted at the needs of local communities and thus provide sufficient value to offset their cost.

The platform should facilitate development by local developers with limited programming skills. The development process of voice services should thus be simple,

---

[3] Sub-Saharan   Africa: https://data.worldbank.org/indicator/NY.GDP.PCAP.CD? locations=ZF.

[4] https://data.worldbank.org/indicator/EG.ELC.ACCS.ZS?end=2014& locations=ML&start=2014&view=map.

[5] As an illustration to this point, a group of Malian entrepreneurs launched a media initiative to persuade local Internet Service Providers to provide better services: http://100mega.ml/.

flexible, not require advanced programming skills and should take place in a graphical interface.

A very small amount of the population in developing countries owns (or has access to) a computer, let alone a connection to the Internet. As a consequence, there are few local software developers and technicians available for the development and maintenance of local infrastructure, systems and applications. From this small pool, the amount of software developers that have experience with voice services will thus likely be extremely low. Hiring foreign developers is not an option, as the cost of foreign labor is extremely high (in the financial context of these countries), conflicting with the above requirement of financial sustainability. Ensuring local development is thus essential for the formation of a voice service ecosystem targeted at the unconnected, as it keeps development costs at a minimum. In order to increase the size of the potential pool of voice service developers, the process of development should be accessible to users that do not have programming skills. This simplification of the development process should allow for people with a basic understanding of using computers to be trained in the development of voice services. Besides the financial aspect of local voice service development, an additional benefit of sourcing developers locally is that local developers have a smaller distance to the end-user of the voice service, not only in a spatial sense but also in social and cultural sense. This further aids in ensuring the local relevancy of the services as well as the understanding of the end-user's needs. The platform should facilitate the founding of small businesses and entrepreneurs that are specialized in developing and hosting voice services, enabling them to make a living from selling customized voice services to local companies and communities.

The platform should run on low-resource hardware and be based on Free/Libre and Open Source software.

In order to keep the costs of running voice services as low as possible—and thus contribute to the financial sustainability—the hardware used in the platform should be cheap, robust, and consume little energy. Another aspect that influences the cost of the platform is the cost of software licenses. The prices of commercial telephony products and other software are at a level that is acceptable in the Global North, which translates to "not affordable" in the developing world. Furthermore, the liberating nature of open-source software allows for the practice of *bricolage*: tinkering with existing technologies in new and innovative ways, which allows for the formation of successful innovations [1]. Accepting that the usage of technology cannot be tightly controlled and that successful innovations often come from unexpected directions, can be a determining factor of success. By explicitly granting the general population the freedom to use the technology in any way they see fit, practicing *bricolage* is facilitated and the available technology is more likely to be applied in a way that is most relevant and innovative to the local context.

3.4   Example Use Cases of Voice Services

Below we outline two examples of the types of voice services that the platform should be able to facilitate. These use cases have been elicited and analyzed during our various field visits to Mali, Burkina Faso and Ghana.

Foroba Blon, a system for village reporting
We briefly describe here the case of Radio Sikidolo, a small radio station in Konobougou, a village in the south of Mali several hours from the capital Bamako. It reaches up to 80,000 listeners in the region. According to its director, Adama Tessougué, this radio works with free-lance village reporters who collect news and announcements in the surrounding villages for broadcasting. Example topics are wedding announcements, funerals, lost animals, interviews and interesting stories. In the absence of Internet in these remote areas, village reporters use simple GSM mobile phones to send news to the radio. For this, the program maker at the radio station had to be available in person on the phone, and then write down the incoming information on paper for broadcasting. Evidently, this task is time consuming and inefficient. Foroba Blon is a voice-based system allowing village reporters to phone in and to submit spoken news items that are off line stored in the system [13]. Messages can then be accessed and managed by the radio journalist through a web interface on his laptop, without the need for Internet. The radio station uses the messages for interactive programming, or receives (financial) compensation for the spreading of advertisements and announcements. The Bambara name Foroba Blon refers to the Malian village square where everyone is allowed to speak out, though respectfully.

The Foroba Blon use case has been used during the evaluation of the platform, which is covered in Sect. 5.5.

Weather information
Many farmers and families in sub-Saharan Africa depend on rain-fed agriculture. The rainy season is short (three months) and so pertinent information on actual and forecast rainfall is extremely important, for example, to better plan cropping calendars and improve harvests. During recent collaborative use-case and requirements workshops in Gourcy, Burkina Faso, organized by local NGO Réseau MARP, regional radio stations, the association of innovative farmers in the Yatenga province, and the W4RA team of authors, it became abundantly clear that important weather information never reaches local farmers in Burkina Faso. Global weather information is in principle available through the Web, but it is not accessible to farmers that face the familiar issues of lack of electricity, of digital infrastructures, and issues of language and literacy. Furthermore this information is often inaccurate, due to a lack of measurement infrastructure and accurate weather models. The Burkina Faso weather voice service allows farmers to receive data on the amount of rainfall, as measured by fellow farmers that have a measurement bucket on their land. These farmers call in their measurements periodically. Besides providing other farmers with essential information, the information is also used to accurately track historical rainfall in the region.

The request of weather information has been repeated in many of the communities visited by members of the W4RA team. A similar variant (although with a slightly different context) of the use-case was elicited in Guabuliga, a village in the Northern Region of Ghana. Farmers in the community, upon understanding the broad concept of voice-services; providing information in their own language, immediately suggested weather forecast information. In Ghana, accurate seasonal (regional) rainfall forecast is available from the National Geological Services mostly online and during Television Weather Reports (in English). Less accurate, but usable daily and weekly local forecasts are also available through a combination of satellite data and local weather stations which feed open weather sources online. The lack of access to these sources of information, due to the lack of internet and low literacy (inability to read and write in English) results in this information not reaching members of these communities despite the fact that it remains relevant to them, for similar reasons as covered in the example of Burkina Faso. The Ghanian version of the weather information voice-service –dubbed *Mr. Meteo*– makes use of open-weather data APIs to source it's weather data.

The Mr. Meteo service was built with the VSDK and was used in an evaluation of the Kasadaka platform, see Sect. 5.4.

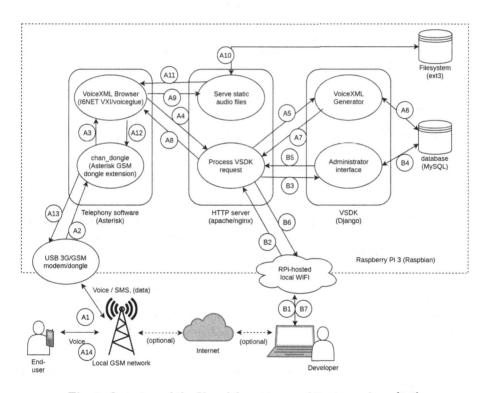

Fig. 3. Overview of the Kasadaka system architecture, from [2,3].

4   Kasadaka Technical Implementation

The platform that we propose is called *Kasadaka* (*talking box* in a number of northern Ghanaian languages). The platform consists of a combination of hardware and accompanying software. Figure 3 is a visual representation of the architecture of the system and highlights the interactions between the components.

4.1   Hardware

The hardware forming the foundation of the KasaDaka platform is the Raspberry Pi, which is a low-resource computer based on an ARM processor (like found in many smart phones). The main advantages of the Raspberry Pi are it's low power consumption (and subsequently no need for cooling), good on-board connectivity and the low price[6] (and thus also a low replacement cost). As the Raspberry Pi does not include a Real Time Clock (RTC), it cannot accurately keep time when the power is lost. To solve this problem, a small and cheap battery powered RTC is connected to the Pi's general connector. The Raspberry Pi is a very popular product for experimentation and many projects, and is thus widely available, making it easy to replace should hardware problems arise.

To provide the Raspberry Pi with connectivity to the local mobile phone network, a USB 3G modem (which can also connect to 2G networks) is used. The exact make and model of this modem can differ, as long as it is on the supported hardware list[7] of the `chan_dongle` Asterisk extension.

4.2   Software

Several applications run on top of the Raspbian Operating System, that work together to provide the voice-service functionality. Almost all applications used are open-source and thus free to use.

Telephone exchange software: Asterisk
Asterisk is a very popular open-source Private Branch Exchange (PBX) telephony application. It is used for the routing of incoming calls to its destination using Voice-over-IP technologies. In the implementation of the KasaDaka platform, Asterisk provides the connection between the phone network (3G dongle) and the VoiceXML interpreter. To enable Asterisk to interface with the 3G dongle an extension is required. Kasadaka uses `chan_dongle`[8], which is an open-source Asterisk extension that provides connectivity between GSM/3G modems and Asterisk. It enables Asterisk to receive and place calls using the connected modem, as well as send and receive SMS messages and USSD codes.

---

[6] A Raspberry Pi 3 (including case, power supply and SD card) costs around €60 at the time of writing.

[7] https://github.com/bg111/asterisk-chan-dongle/wiki/Requirements-and-Limitations.

[8] https://github.com/bg111/asterisk-chan-dongle.

Voice application document standard: VoiceXML
VoiceXML[9] is a document standard for voice applications, based on XML. It is a standard designed by the World Wide Web Consortium and is used for creating documents that describe voice-based interactions. It supports interactive voice dialogues between the computer and the user and usually contains text (in written form) that is later processed by a TTS engine. Responses by the user can happen through pressing a number on the phones keypad of by speaking (for this ASR needs to be available). As the voice applications that use the Kasadaka framework mainly focus on under-resourced languages, TTS and ASR are not used (nor available). Fortunately VoiceXML also supports the playback of audio files, much alike embedding images in an HTML page. This allows the use of pre-recorded fragments to build up spoken sentences, but restricts the way of interaction to using the phone's keypad. A VoiceXML document is 'rendered' for the user in a way that is comparable to the rendering of a HTML file in a web-browser, but in this case is done by a voice browser.

VoiceXML interpreter: VXI
The software component that is used for 'rendering' VoiceXML files is VXI[10], a closed-source VoiceXML interpreter built by the company I6NET[11]. VXI connects with Asterisk as an end-point for incoming calls. When a call is redirected to VoiceXML a pre-configured URL is passed on to VXI, which it loads and 'displays' to the user as initial voice interaction. Normally this is the principal document belonging to a voice service. VXI currently is the only closed-source component used in the KasaDaka platform. While the goal is to use only open-source software, there is no currently maintained open-source alternative.

HTTP server: Apache
VXI loads the VoiceXML files it interprets over a HTTP connection, just like loading a HTML page on the web, but locally. In order to serve these files (and the audio files that are referenced in the VoiceXML files), a web server is required. There are many open-source web-servers, one of the most used is Apache 2.

VSDK development framework: Django (Python)
In order to make the VSDK easy to extend by developers, Python is a programming language of choice as it is a popular language that is well supported and has several popular web-frameworks. As VoiceXML documents are comparable to HTML documents, most web-frameworks can also be used to generate VoiceXML files. Django[12] was chosen as the Python-based web-framework, as it has very good and extensive documentation, is well-supported and follows a Model-View-Controller (MVC) methodology [16]. Django is open-source and has a rich collection of projects and libraries that can be used to extend it's functionality. Django has a good implementation of internationalization functionalities, which enable the interface of the administrator interface to be translated to different languages (Fig. 4).

---

[9] https://www.w3.org/TR/voicexml21/.
[10] http://www.i6net.com/technology/voicexml-ivr/.
[11] http://www.i6net.com/.
[12] https://www.djangoproject.com/.

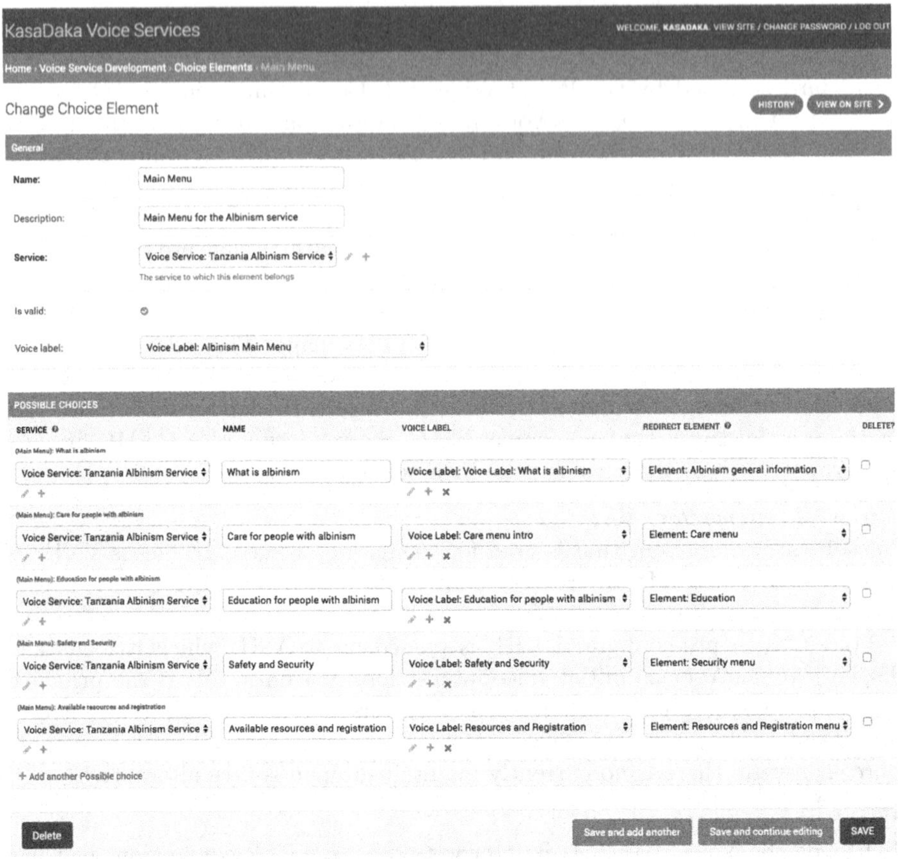

Fig. 4. An example screen shot of the voice-service development interface of the VSDK. Shown is an example of a choice interaction element. A voice service developer uses this GUI to develop voice-based applications on the Kasadaka platform.

4.3   Voice Service Development Kit

The Voice Service Development Kit is the main software component in the Kasadaka platform. The main goal of the VSDK[13] is to support the development of voice-services in the context of the developing world. As the voice services are hosted on a Raspberry Pi and Internet connectivity is not to be expected, the development of voice services happens off line. Using a web-based interface is preferable to running a development environment on a computer because it solves problems with compatibility (different devices, operating systems) and reduces complexity (does not require installation of software). Another advantage of this approach is that the development and hosting of voice services are

---

[13] The VSDK's code can be found on GitHub. See: https://github.com/abaart/KasaDaka-VSDK.

integrated, allowing for instantaneous results (and testing) of changes made to the application. The VSDK is hosted on the Raspberry Pi, which also hosts a local wireless network, through which it is accessible. Local entrepreneurs can use the VSDK to develop voice applications on the Kasadaka platform, without the requirement of programming skills.

The structure of the voice-application is stored in the database, using Django's model functionality. When an element in the voice-application is requested by the user in a phone call, the VoiceXML interpreter (VXI) requests the element through an HTTP call. Django then retrieves the information about this element from the database, and uses a view to 'render' the element in VoiceXML. The VoiceXML interpreter then interprets this VoiceXML file and 'displays' it to the user. In Fig. 3 a visual representation of the data flows in the Kasadaka platform is shown.

While the interactions in voice services are always different, most of them can be generalized to a small set of interaction types, such as making a choice, playing back an audio message, or recording (voice) input of the user. The VSDK provides a set of these *building-blocks*, which consist of a VoiceXML template, view and an administrator interface to use and customize them. The current set (which will be expanded in the future) consists of a menu-based interaction, recording of user voice input and the playback of messages. While this set is limited, it offers sufficient functionality for many voice services and serves as a demonstration of the method of voice service development.

Voice-services in the developing context have to support under-resourced languages, for which there are no speech technologies available. The VSDK supports different languages in voice services by utilizing pre-recorded audio fragments that are relevant for the use-case domain. During the development of the service, all the necessary voice-fragments are recorded in the different languages in which the service has to be accessible. These voice-fragments are stored in the file system and referenced in a "voice label" element that is stored in the database. This voice label refers to voice-fragments that represent a fragment of text, spoken in different languages [8].

4.4   Bip Recognition

In order to support certain use-cases, it is required that the Kasadaka system is able to recognize so-called *bips*, which can be compared to missed calls. In order to support the use-case as described in Sect. 5.2, the authors implemented the recognition of missed calls into the Kasadaka. The implementation consists of some elements in the Asterisk configuration which –instead of immediately accepting an incoming call– add some delay before accepting an incoming call. The time of the initial "first ring" is recorded in a logging file. Then the line will keep ringing for approximately 5 s, after which the call is accepted and the user will hear the configured voice-service. When the call is "picked up" by the system, another entry in the log file is made. By periodically parsing the log file, and recognizing the instances where a call was received, but was cancelled before the system established the connection, bips (missed calls) can be recognized by the Kasadaka. The periodical job that recognizes the bips can be configured to request a customize-able URL when a new bip has been recognized. This URL can be set to an endpoint in a VSDK application, which can then further process the bip according to a specific use-case.

5 Evaluations

There have been several evaluations of the VSDK, with varying degrees of sophistication. The first evaluation was done in the Netherlands with inexperienced users of the VSDK, which was used to further refine the VSDK. Subsequent evaluations enriched our understanding of the limitations of the current state of the VSDK, and how it could be extended to support more complex and more varied use cases.

5.1 Evaluation by Development of Several Use Case Prototype Services

The VSDK was evaluated with 10 student groups during the ICT for Development (ICT4D) course at the Vrije Universiteit Amsterdam [3]. The groups each developed a voice service for one of several use cases, which were co-created with rural communities and relevant in the context of the developing world and provided to the students in written form. The choice to evaluate with students was made because of the ease of communication with the students, which is significantly less complex and expensive than traveling to a developing country. While the level of computer literacy of the students is higher than that of the intended voice service developers in developing countries and the evaluation took place in the Netherlands, feedback of the students is still very relevant for verifying the underlying concepts and ideas of the VSDK's development work flow. The VSDK proved to be sufficient in providing the required functionality for the creation of basic voice-service services, and can be used for rapid-prototyping purposes. Using a graphical interface, voice-services consisting of simple choices with associated options and messages can be designed without having to write any code. These prototypes can be made quickly and without extensive knowledge of the underlying technologies, which is useful for rapid prototype development and evaluation; After set-up, a simple service can be developed and tested in under 30 min, however the development of complex use-cases takes more time. During the course, 80% of the student groups had successfully built a working voice service using the VSDK. These 8 applications were developed for 5 distinct use cases. The included interaction templates allowed the students to quickly build demonstration prototypes of their voice services. In order to provide more complex functionality in their voice services, 78% of the student groups had extended the functionality of the VSDK with data models specific to their use case and 67% of the groups extended the VSDK with additional interaction templates.

At the end of the course the students were asked to fill in a survey on their experience with creating a voice service and using the VSDK. The goal of this survey is to learn about the process that the students went through as they developed their first voice service. The survey consisted of statements about the usefulness of the VSDK, which had to be answered in a Likert scale. There were also qualitative questions about VSDK features, improvements and suggestions, as well as questions about their perceptions during the development process.

This evaluation has shown that the methodology of building-blocks that is used in the VSDK allows for the development of simple voice services by inexperienced users, which was the goal. It also provided insight in the limitations and problems of the VSDK. The main limitation lies in the area of user generated data management. The VSDK does not yet allow the creation of custom data models from the development interface. Other limitations were the limited set of user interactions provided and the lack of support for the integration of external data sources. These limitations prevent the VSDK of being suitable for more complex voice-services, as 'traditional' voice-service development skills are still required to extend the included features of the kit. In the case of a custom extension to the VSDK, the functionality of this extension can be reused throughout the application and shared with the rest of the development community. Furthermore the administrator interface can easily utilized by these custom extensions, which allow voice-service maintainers (without programming knowledge) to change settings and other elements of the extension's functionality. Thus after the development of the extension is completed, maintenance can still be performed by others without knowledge of the inner workings, maintaining the advantage of ease of use offered by the VSDK.

5.2   Case Study: BipVote, a Voting System for Rural Mali

During the successive edition of the ICT4D course at the Vrije Universiteit Amsterdam (see Sect. 5.1) in 2018, students received additional guidance on using the Django framework, prior to learning to develop voice services using the VSDK. This adjusted approach resulted in many student groups developing more complex applications that had both voice and web-based interfaces, extending significantly on the basic included functionalities of the VSDK. We will cover one of the applications here in depth, which showcases the creative uses and the diverse potential of voice services.

We present the case of the BipVote application [15], which was designed and built by ICT4D students at the VU University Amsterdam: Hans-Dieter Hiep, Roy Overbeek and Paweł Ulita. BipVote is a system that allows for polls to be held, in which votes can be cast by sending so-called *bips*. A bip a word used in several French speaking west-African countries, to describe what could be considered a missed call. More specifically, a bip is a call that is cancelled quickly, before the recipient has had the chance to pick up. This is registered as a missed call on the recipient's phone. Because there has not been a phone connection, sending a bip is free of charge. Sending bips is common practice when one does not have enough money for a call, or when someone wants to send a signal; For instance, it can be a request to the recipient of the bip, to call the sender back.

During our visits and collaborations with local radio presenters, an additional usage of bips emerged, being that radio stations use bips in interactive radio programming, allowing listeners to cast votes without cost. These polls are held to gauge the public's opinion on social issues, but also as small quizzes that are aimed to estimate whether (in the case of educational programming) listeners have gained a sufficient understanding of the subject matter.

The way radio organizers organize the votes, is that they broadcast 2 phone numbers –one for voting yes, one for no– that listeners can send bips to.[14] Because programming is usually recorded and broadcast several times during a week –allowing listeners to tune in when convenient– the votes usually run for a week's time. At the end of the week –during the next episode of the program– the number of missed calls on the phones are manually counted and the results broadcast and used in future programming, for example to explain a subject in further detail. In the case of Radio Sikidolo (see Sect. 5.5) during a one-week poll, usually around 800 votes are cast.

BipVote streamlines this work-flow by providing both a web-interface and a voice-interface[15] to allow for managing polls and viewing (past) results. Radio presenters are able to set up new polls, entering the time-frame in which the poll will run. During and after the vote, the votes are counted and plotted on a graph. The presenters are able to see the results of polls develop in real-time. These same features are available through a voice interface, to allow management of polls when a computer is not available.

In order to realize the features of the BipVote system, the students significantly extended the VSDK with additional functionality to support the handling of bips (using the bip recognition feature outlined in Sect. 4.4), the management of polls through the web interface, as well as through the voice interface. The included *building-blocks* of the VSDK were extended with elements that tell how much time is remaining in a poll, that allow for setting the time duration of a new poll, creating new polls and removing polls. The element that informs the user of the results of a poll, includes a custom-built algorithm that allows for the programmatic conversion of numbers into their spoken representations, in multiple languages (English, French and Bambara are supported). This is achieved by combining samples to compose larger numbers. "For example 152 becomes *one-hundred-fifty-two* (4 samples) in English, and *cent-cinquante-deux* (3 samples) in French, and *keme-ni-bi-duuru-ni-fila* (6 samples) in Bambara" [15].

The BipVote use-case is an example of a service that enables creative use of older technologies (*bricolage*, see Sect. 3.3) that is prevalent across developing countries. One could imagine several other possibilities that bips could offer in other use-cases, such as: letting the Kasadaka call back an user (shifting the costs of calling to the owner of the Kasadaka), or low-cost signalling applications.

---

[14] For this use-case a Kasadaka can be equipped with two dongles, providing two telephone lines.

[15] A demonstration of the BipVote application is available on YouTube: https://www.youtube.com/watch?v=mxtRCMht0qg.

5.3   Case Study: Tanzania Albinism Society

The VSDK's suitability as a rapid prototyping tool has additionally been evaluated in Tanzania with the cooperation of Tjitske de Groot (Vrije Universiteit Brussels) and Gamariel Mboya (Tanzania Albinism Society). Tjistke approached the authors with the wish of a voice-based system that could be used to educate people about albinism and collect contact information of people with albinism. Tjitske's research is centered around designing effective stigma reduction interventions for albinism in Tanzania. Gamariel and Tjitske had been looking into the possibility of running an experiment with a voice service that could educate the general public about albinism, and provide an alert system for those with albinism. Because of the costs associated with setting up a voice service at established companies –for which they did not have sufficient funding– they asked the authors whether it would be possible to build a low-cost prototype of the service.

The authors were sent a short overview of the intended functionalities of the voice service, which was processed into a tree that describes the structure of the voice service. From this tree a list of voice fragments was compiled, which were subsequently translated to Swahili by Gamariel. As Tjitske and the authors were both in the Netherlands at the time of developing the prototype, it was not possible to set up a session with Gamariel to record the voice fragments for the service, as the authors often do during the process of voice service development. This was resolved by resorting to Gamariel sending us recordings of each of the voice fragments through the smartphone messaging app Whatsapp. These recordings were transferred and corrected for volume and background noise using Audacity, an open-source audio editing application. After the quality of the recordings was sufficient, the voice service prototype was developed using the VSDK web-interface, based on the structure of the voice-service tree. The authors showed Tjitske around the interface of the VSDK, explained the properties of the *building-blocks* available in the interface and created the main elements of the voice-service structure. Using the explanation and examples, Tjitske was able to learn developing voice-services using the VSDK by doing; By finishing the voice-service prototype herself.

Tjitske acquired a Raspberry Pi and dongle, on which the Kasadaka software stack was installed. The authors explained how to set up the system, and how to troubleshoot in case of problems. Tjitske took the Kasadaka to Tanzania, and was able to demonstrate the voice service to Gamariel without any issues.

In this evaluation the Kasadaka platform was used to develop and demonstrate a voice-service prototype with a low investment of time and capital. The nature of the intended voice-service made the Kasadaka unsuitable for a roll out. This is because the service targets the whole of Tanzania and thus should be able to support a high number of concurrent calls, which is not achievable on the Kasadaka, as it runs on low-resource hardware which supports only one concurrent call. The development cooperation with Tjitske has shown the potential for voice-service development training using the VSDK, and that the recording of voice fragments does not require a native speaker to be physically present, but can also be done remotely through sending voice messages (Fig. 5).

Fig. 5. Gamariel Mboya calling the Tanzania albinism voice-service prototype, running from the Kasadaka on the table.

5.4   Case Study: Mr. Meteo

The Mr. Meteo voice-service (see Sect. 3.4), provides community-specific weather forecast/information via voice prompts in local Ghanian languages. The system was deployed using the Kasadaka platform in a test phase in December 2018 at Bolgatanga in the Upper East Region of Ghana, to a cross-section of animal and crop farmers, gathered from 4 local communities. The deployment was in collaboration with Cowtribe[16], a company that provides veterinary services with the use of ICT-driven technologies, and was received with overwhelming enthusiasm.

The Mr. Meteo use case in Ghana, provides an evaluation of the Kasadaka platform in a real developing world context. The system was built using the VSDK, at the University for Development Studies in Tamale, Ghana by a team with programming backgrounds who had previously been involved in the development and student evaluation process of the VSDK. The validation session was done within the local community, with no internet access and using a power-bank as source of power. This is because Cowtribe –whose clientele tested the system– require a model where it is possible to host devices within the communities; hosted by trained community members. Development of the service however was done with the availability of electricity and internet (although internet access was not directly required). The audio fragments were recorded locally (in Gurune, the major language in Bolgatanga, for which no TTS and ASR exists) using a normal Android-based smartphone in a quiet environment and sent via internet to Tamale where it was converted to the appropriate formats and integrated into the VSDK. An additional language (Dagbani, also without available

---

[16] https://www.cowtribe.com/.

TTS and ASR) was recorded in Tamale, also using a smartphone and integrated into the system to provide a control test case in terms of language. The VSDK prompts were set up to create a voice system that would welcome the user to the service and then proceed to the weather forecast for the current day as well as the subsequent day.

A total of roughly 5 h was needed to completely develop the application. One minor challenge faced was the need for interfacing external data (weather forecasts in this case) which must be accessed daily and parsed to indicate the appropriate voice fragments to play to the user. For the test phase this was not necessary, but a future implementation will require a minor extension to the VSDK to include this functionality. The resulting system was tested using a local Ghanaian Network Provider (MTN) and further piloted to farmers from 4 communities in the Upper East Region of Ghana. Farmers were of the opinion that this was very useful and would be something they would use (some regularly, others occasionally) and also inquired of the availability of other types of information such as; disease outbreaks, human and animal health, farming practices and information on their children's schooling. The system is currently being further developed to cater for these 4 communities. This will therefore require a prompt to select the appropriate community, or will require pre-registration of numbers with assigned communities. This evaluation shows the potential of the rapid prototyping and deployment of locally relevant voice-services using the Kasadaka platform. While the decentralized nature of the Kasadaka platform offers advantages in communities' ownership of the services, it also poses challenges, such as the lack of availability of an internet connection, if the service requires frequent information retrieval from the internet (Fig. 6).

Fig. 6. Francis Dittoh, the Cowtribe team and the farmers that participated in the testing of the Mr. Meteo voice-service in Ghana.

5.5   Case Study: Radio Sikidolo

The Foroba Blon use-case was built using the VSDK, and has been evaluated in collaboration with Adama Tessougué, the director of Radio Sikidolo in Konobougou, Mali (for more information see Sect. 3.4). While the other evaluations were sufficient for a general validation of the methodology of the VSDK, they did not evaluate the VSDK in the intended context of a developing country, with a user that had limited experience in voice-service development. This evaluation addresses these limitations: it evaluates the VSDK and the Kasadaka hardware and software as a whole, in the intended developing world context, with users that match the intended user profile. This validation session was done at Radio Sikidolo, which has electricity and a relatively stable Internet connection, the latter of which is however not used in the Foroba Blon use case. While Adama is relatively comfortable in the usage of a computer, he does not have any advanced technical skills, such as programming. However as he runs the radio station, he is familiar with processing audio fragments (using the open-source application Audacity).

This evaluation has shown that it is possible for a local agent to develop and change elements in a voice service on the Kasadaka platform, achieving the goal of enabling locally owned and developed voice services. During the session Adama has been instructed by the authors in the usage of the VSDK's development interface. Together we walked through the process of changing properties in the interface, adding new elements (such as new languages), recording and adding new voice fragments to the system and various other aspects. After this short training of about an hour, we asked Adama to go through the process again by himself, in order to verify that he was able to now use the VSDK on his own to change the properties of the voice service. Adama found the methodology and functionality of the VSDK to be well set up, and was satisfied with the way in which he was able to develop and maintain voice services through the development interface. The VSDK was a significant improvement over the prototypes that the authors had previously tested in cooperation with Adama.

During the evaluation, Adama has successfully used the VSDK to apply and adapt the included voice service interaction templates to the Foroba Blon use case. Support for the Malian language Bambara (for which no TTS and ASR exists) was added to the system by recording voice fragments and adding them through the development interface. The resulting service was tested using the local phone network and will be evaluated further during future visits of the authors to Radio Sikidolo. The combination of the Kasadaka's hardware and the VSDK allow for the off line development and maintenance of voice services by Adama, who falls in the intended user group for the VSDK and the Kasadaka platform and thus does not have any programming knowledge or advanced computer skills (see Fig. 7). During this case study the combination of hardware and software in the Kasadaka platform was successful in enabling the hosting and development of voice based information services in the context of the developing world. While it is still a case study and the outcomes are not guaranteed to be generalize-able, the outcomes show significant potential in allowing non-software developers to maintain voice-services that are hosted at a remote location.

Adama's level of computer literacy is around that of the targeted user group for the development of voice services on the Kasadaka platform. These voice service developers do not need to have programming skills, but some knowledge of using computers is required such as being able to use more complex web-based interfaces (such as a web-based e-mail client). In the future these users could then be trained (over several days) in the process of designing and developing voice services for local use cases. The design and set-up of such training sessions is to be determined in future work.

5.6   Discussion of Results

The general results from the evaluations of the VSDK and the Kasadaka as a whole show potential. The VSDK has been proven to successfully allow the maintenance and development of simple voice-services in the ICT4D context. Developing voice-service prototypes can be done in a matter of hours, which is invaluable during workshops and requirements analyses in the field.

The Kasadaka platform is affordable and is suitable for deployment in remote locations. While Kasadaka is also able to host more complex applications, the development process of such applications still requires programming skills and more time. In order to be able to realize the goal of facilitating local entrepreneurship in the development of voice-services (without software developers), these limitations will have to be overcome.

While the current version of the VSDK proves the potential of web-based voice-service development, this functionality is still limited to simple use-cases only. More complex use-cases can be supported by the VSDK's foundations, but still require software development skills to extend the VSDK with features that are specific to the use-case. Future work on the platform will focus on further expanding the voice service development functionality as well as more sophisticated data management, to allow for the development of more complex voice services. Furthermore, the hardware of the platform is to be made more robust to better withstand the conditions in the developing context. Other ideas on further expansion include the implementation of a TTS system that is suitable for under-resourced languages, solving the dependency on the closed source VoiceXML browser and allowing for the inclusion of external data sources that are available on the Internet.

6   Related Work

This section covers existing efforts in the development of Web-extensions in the developing context, as well as tools and applications that facilitate the development of information services in low-resource environments (Fig. 8).

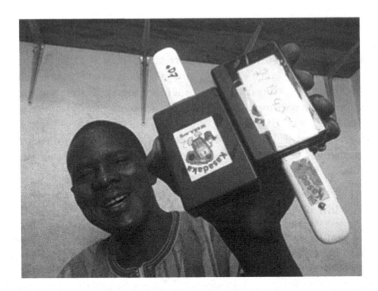

Fig. 7. Adama Tessougué of Radio Sikidolo shows the Kasadaka on which the Foroba Blon voice service now runs with its Bambara language interface [2].

Fig. 8. André Baart and Adama Tessougué evaluating the VSDK running on the Kasadaka platform, at Radio Sikidolo in Mali [2].

Large-Scale Voice Services. Voice based information systems that use the local (2G) mobile telephony network have already proven to be effective in reaching the rural population of the developing world. To support development of voice-based, mobile micro-services Orange Labs developed the *Emerginov*[17] platform

---

[17] See: https://emerginov.ow2.org/.

in 2012, targeting users in low resource environments such as e.g. rural Africa. It includes support for generation of voice-content in local languages, such as Wolof, a local language spoken in Senegal. Emerginov is normally hosted in the cloud, i.e. in a data center, connected to the Internet and the local phone network. Its hardware allows for 32 concurrent (in- or outbound) calls. Emerginov was technically promising, but the service has been discontinued by the operator after a successful pilot [13].

The company Viamo[18] runs several voice-based information services in many African countries. Viamo develops voice services for companies and NGOs. The company has contracts with several African telecommunication companies, allowing the local population to call these services without cost, using a toll-free number. The services Viamo develops are mainly aimed at large populations, with a very large number of concurrent calls. Although these services are able to reach a large amount of people, the large scale of the organization and the infrastructure that is required to run these large scale services, causes services targeted at the rural poor to be financially unsustainable.

Twilio Studio[19] is a web-based application that allows graphical voice-service development by dragging and dropping interaction elements into a call flow, which are the components in a voice service. However the deployment of voice-services created in Twilio Studio is limited to the Twilio platform, which does not offer local phone numbers in many of the developing countries where voice-services could be relevant. This severely restricts the availability of the voice services on the Twilio platform. Twilio Studio seems to not be usable without an Internet connection, which can not be assumed to be available. Furthermore, just like the previous examples Twilio makes intensive usage of TTS and ASR technologies, which are not available in the languages spoken by the local population.

SMS-Based Data Gathering Tools. In contexts where a connection to the Internet is not available, SMS can be used as a medium to exchange information with an automated system.

RapidSMS[20] is a tool set that allows for the development of SMS-based services for data collection and other work flows. RapidSMS is developed by UNICEF and has been used for various use cases, including remote health diagnostics and nutrition surveillance. RapidSMS is open-source and very scale able to suit large deployments, but can also run on a low-end server with a GSM modem [18].

DataWinners[21] is a data collection platform that is developed by Human Network International[22] (HNI). DataWinners enables the development of SMS and smart phone based data surveys. These surveys are primarily aimed at the

---

[18] See https://viamo.io.

[19] https://www.twilio.com/docs/api/studio.

[20] https://www.rapidsms.org/.

[21] https://www.datawinners.com/.

[22] http://hni.org/.

context of NGOs that need to retrieve data from their extension workers. By using SMS data can be collected without a need for an Internet connection, while the data can be still be entered through a user-friendly graphical interface on a smart phone. In the DataWinners web-based environment, new data surveys can be developed in a graphical interface.

Discussion. There exist several platforms for the development and hosting of large-scale voice services. These platforms allow for services that handle many concurrent calls and are thus well suited to services that aim to reach the general population. The drawback is that the infrastructure and development processes required for these services, are very expensive and thus out of reach of the local population.

While SMS-based services provide data exchange in contexts with limited Internet connectivity, it is only usable by the literate that have knowledge about the usage of SMS. Large populations in the developing world are illiterate or do not know how to use SMS. Thus while SMS-based services work well for data exchange without the Internet, these services are not accessible for the general population in the developing world.

Still, the existing solutions for the hosting and development of voice services and SMS based information services are not capable of providing benefits that are comparable to those of the Internet, at a cost that allows for financially sustainable voice services in the developing context. Besides the issue of cost, other problems for the application of these solutions in the context described in this article are in the area of support of under-resourced languages, the centralized nature of these solutions and the requirement for a reliable connection to the Internet.

7   Conclusion

The wider aim of the presented Kasadaka platform and its Voice Service Development Kit is to allow people at the "other side of the Digital Divide" to share knowledge and create content, analogous to the advantages provided by the Web. It takes into account the information needs of the local population, by enabling the hosting and development of voice services that cater to local use-cases. The Kasadaka platform is lightweight, tailored to the harsh circumstances that are found in the Global South, and enables the formation of a network of decentralized voice services. Such a network has the potential to provide the benefits of the Web to the world's rural poor.

Despite the moderate size and outreach of our research project, the Kasadaka platform evaluations have shown, as an alternative to high speed internet solutions and technology transfers, the potential of easy-to-learn, lightweight, affordable and context-aware ICT solutions that do more right to complex realities, context and needs of people "at the other side of the Digital Divide". The Kasadaka is targeted at the low-resource context as found in many developing countries. Kasadaka's main software component, the Voice Service Development Kit, enables to-be voice-service administrators to develop and maintain voice-services in the field. It overcomes the lack of skilled software developers by reducing the skill-set required for voice-service development. Evaluations of the VSDK have shown it's potential in providing the foundation for the development of creative voice-services, catered to the needs of communities in sub-Saharan Africa. Voice-service prototypes can be created with little effort, which enables rapid prototyping and demonstrations in the field.

Acknowledgements. The authors thank Christophe Guéret for the original idea and his initiative in the first steps towards the Kasadaka platform. Additionally, the authors would like to thank Adama Tessougué, Amadou Tangara, Gossa Lô, Julien Ouedraogo, Matthieu Ouedraogo, Hans-Dieter Hiep, Roy Overbeek, Paweł Ulita, Tjitske de Groot and Gamariel Mboya for their invaluable contributions to this research.

References

1. Ali, M., Bailur, S.: The challenge of sustainability in ICT4D-Is bricolage the answer. In: Proceedings of the 9th International Conference on Social Implications of Computers in Developing Countries, pp. 54–60. Citeseer (2007)
2. Baart, A., Bon, A., de Boer, V., Tuijp, W., Akkermans, H.: Ney yibeogo - hello world: a voice service development platform to bridge the web's digital divide. In: Proceedings of the 14th International Conference on Web Information Systems and Technologies WEBIST, vol. 1, pp. 23–34. INSTICC, SciTePress (2018). https://doi.org/10.5220/0006893600230034
3. Baart, A.: Master thesis - KasaDaka: a sustainable voice services platform. Technical report (2017). https://www.kasadaka.com/img/master-thesis-andre-baart.pdf
4. Bagshaw, P., Barnard, E., Rosec, O.: VOICES deliverable D3.1: report on state of the art and development methodology. Technical report, September 2011
5. Berment, V.: Méthodes pour informatiser les langues et les groupes de langues «peu dotées». Ph.D. thesis, Université Joseph-Fourier-Grenoble I (2004)
6. Besacier, L., Barnard, E., Karpov, A., Schultz, T.: Automatic speech recognition for under-resourced languages: a survey. Speech Commun. **56**, 85–100 (2014). https://doi.org/10.1016/j.specom.2013.07.008. http://www.sciencedirect.com/science/article/pii/S0167639313000988
7. Black, A.W., Lenzo, K.A.: Limited domain synthesis. Technical report, Carnegie-Mellon University (2000)
8. de Boer, V., Gyan, N.B., Bon, A., Tuyp, W., Van Aart, C., Akkermans, H.: A dialogue with linked data: voice-based access to market data in the Sahel. Seman. Web **6**(1), 23–33 (2015). http://www.few.vu.nl/~vbr240/publications/swj2013_deboer_dialogue.pdf
9. Bon, A., Akkermans, H., Gordijn, J.: Developing ICT services in a low-resource development context. Complex Syst. Inf. Model. Q. **9**, 84–109 (2016)
10. Farrugia, P.J.: Text to speech technologies for mobile telephony services. In: Pace and Cordina [PC03] (2005)
11. Fuchs, C., Horak, E.: Africa and the digital divide. Telemat. Inform. **25**(2), 99–116 (2008). https://doi.org/10.1016/j.tele.2006.06.004
12. GSMA: GSMA Report: The Mobile Economy: Africa (2016). https://www.gsmaintelligence.com/research/?file=3bc21ea879a5b217b64d62fa24c55bdf&download

13. Gyan, N.B., et al.: Voice-based web access in rural Africa. In: Proceedings of the 5th Annual ACM Web Science Conference on WebSci 2013, pp. 122–131 (2013). https://doi.org/10.1145/2464464.2464496. http://0-dl.acm.org.oasis.unisa.ac.za/citation.cfm?id=2464464.2464496

14. Heine, B., Nurse, D.: African Languages: An Introduction. Cambridge University Press, Cambridge (2000)

15. Hiep, H.D., Overbeek, R., Ulita, P.: BipVote: a radio-based mobile voting system for rural Mali. Technical report, June 2018. https://w4ra.org/wp-content/uploads/2018/08/Bipvote.pdf

16. Krasner, G.E., Pope, S.T., et al.: A description of the model-view-controller user interface paradigm in the smalltalk-80 system. J. Object Oriented Program. **1**(3), 26–49 (1988)

17. McTear, M., Callejas, Z., Griol, D.: Creating a conversational interface using chatbot technology. In: McTear, M., Callejas, Z., Griol, D. (eds.) The Conversational Interface, pp. 125–159. Springer, Cham (2016). https://doi.org/10.1007/978-3-319-32967-3_7

18. Ngabo, F., et al.: Designing and implementing an innovative SMS-based alert system (RapidSMS-MCH) to monitor pregnancy and reduce maternal and child deaths in Rwanda. Pan Afr. Med. J. **13**, 31 (2012)

19. Poushter, J.: Smartphone ownership and internet usage continues to climb in emerging economies. Pew Res. Cent. **22**, 1–44 (2016)

20. Rolland, C.: Capturing system intentionality with maps. In: Krogstie, J., Opdahl, A.L., Brinkkemper, S. (eds.) Conceptual Modelling in Information Systems Engineering, pp. 141–158. Springer, Heidelberg (2007). https://doi.org/10.1007/978-3-540-72677-7_9

21. Schmida, S., Bernard, J., Zakaras, T., Lovegrove, C., Swingle, C.: Connecting the Next Four Billion: Strengthening the Global Response for Universal Internet Access. USAID, Dial, SSG Advisors (2017)

22. The World Bank Group: Digital dividends, world bank development report. Technical report, The World Bank, Washington, US (2016). https://doi.org/10.1596/978-1-4648-0728-2

23. UNESCO: UNESCO report: regional overview: Sub-Saharan Africa (2011). http://en.unesco.org/gem-report/sites/gem-report/files/191393e.pdf

24. USAID: Closing the access gap: innovation to accelerate universal internet adoption. Technical report (2017)

25. de Vries, N.J., et al.: A smartphone-based ASR data collection tool for under-resourced languages. Speech Commun. **56**, 119–131 (2014). https://doi.org/10.1016/j.specom.2013.07.001. http://www.sciencedirect.com/science/article/pii/S0167639313000915

Torwards Flexible Multi-factor Combination for Authentication Based on Smart-Devices

Thomas Lenz[✉] and Vesna Krnjic

eGovernment Innovation Center - Austria, Inffeldgasse 16a, Graz, Austria
{thomas.lenz,vesna.krnjic}@egiz.gv.at

Abstract. The number of transactions that are performed electronically between coupled smart-devices increases rapidly. These devices are not only sensors nodes that collect the non-private data, but also are devices that process sensitive information that has higher requirements into security and privacy. Unique and qualified identification and high-secure authentication are essential basics to facilitate these requirements in security and privacy. While security and privacy are widely described and examined for applications used on personal computers, the situation is more demanding for smart-devices. Due to the steadily increasing number and the continuous enhancement of smart-devices, there will be no stable technology over the years. In consequence, new agile and secure methods become necessary to bring identification and high-secure authentication on smart platforms in a proper way. We propose a model for agile smart-device based multi-factor authentication combination to close this open gap and to provide secure authentication on mobile devices only. By using our proposed model, a user can combine multiple authenticators by using a cryptographic protocol on client-side only to increase the assurance into authentication. One significant advantage of our model is that it is transparent to existing eID validation infrastructure and can be used without modifications on the verification side. We proof the practical applicability of our model by implementing all components in combination with Austrian eGovernment infrastructure components. A first evaluation was done by a small group of users in conjunction with real eGovernment components on the testing stage.

Keywords: Authentication · Multi-factor · Aqile · Distributed signatures · Reliable · Identity management

1 Introduction

Electronic identity and secure authentication of entities is indispensable for a variety of Internet services or electronically coupled devices that perform electronic transactions to protect private data. Such transactions can include social

© Springer Nature Switzerland AG 2019
M. J. Escalona et al. (Eds.): WEBIST 2018, LNBIP 372, pp. 221–243, 2019.
https://doi.org/10.1007/978-3-030-35330-8_11

network interactions or sensor-node communication, but also more security-sensitive services such as a tax declaration or IoT based eHealth application that protects personal medical data. Figure 1 illustrates an assumption from Strategy Analytics[1] there will be 30 billion smart-devices connected together for electronic interactions.

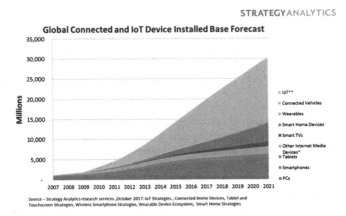

Fig. 1. Base forecast of installed and connected smart-devices. *Source:* https://www.strategyanalytics.com/strategy-analytics/news/strategy-analytics-press-releases/2017/10/26/smart-home-will-drive-internet-of-things-to-50-billion-devices-says-strategy-analytics

Consequently, the importance for a high level of assurance by secure means of authentication linked to a qualified identity is rising sharply to protect personal data and to keep the privacy of users. In each case, authentication is indispensable to prove a claimed identity to be authentic. In more detail, the authentication step links the identity information to an entity be using an *Authenticator* to prove that he or she is the owner of that identity information.

One of the first and still common forms of authentication is the simple provision of user name and password. However, as shown in [17] passwords are not reliable to provide adequate protection for security relevant applications. Taneski, Heričko, and Brumen [38] shows that users and their passwords are still considered the weakest link in a process-flow for entity authentication. One of the most promise approaches to increase the security and reliability of entity authentication-process is to use more than one authentication factors. This concept to combine more than one authentication factor is called multi-factor authentication. To increase the reliability, these authentication factors have to be from different categories, like *Something a user is* or *Something a user knows* as two examples. More and more Internet services and Web-based applications offer their users authentication by using a multi-factor approach.

---

[1] https://www.strategyanalytics.com.

Multi-factor authentication is mandatory for state-of-the-art implementations of security-sensitive Internet services like eHealth applications or transactional eGovernment services.

Maintaining a sufficient level of security, implemented authentication processes and involved entity devices have to keep in pace with technological changes and implementations have to be react immediately on changing threat scenarios. This requirement can become challenging in practice, as many technologies are often not flexible enough to keep pace with evolving requirements. The smart or mobile sector is a very illustrative example of an area that evolves very fast. In more detail, devices with new functional possibilities are published by different manufacturers at short intervals. Due to the fast increasing usage of different devices, a smooth interaction between systems and solutions that interact with these devices get necessary. These interaction must not only fulfill requirements on usability, but also are privacy and data protection that requires identification and secure authentication of entities. Especially in the smart or mobile sector, we face the challenge of providing secure, usable, and agile authentication methods, because it is not possible to define an authentication method or in general, a technology that is stable over the years. Consequently, a new usable and agile but also secure authentication method becomes necessary for these platforms.

While identification and secure authentication are widely described and examined, in respect to Web applications and services that are used on personal computers (PC) or similar devices, the situation is more demanding on smart or mobile devices. Typically, smart cards are in use for identification and high-secure authentication that implements two-factor authentication approach. The smart cards are inserted into a card reader connected to the personal computer. However, many smart or mobile devices, like smart phones or tablets, cannot connect to card readers. To overcome this issue, server-based solutions, like the Austrian Mobile-Phone Signature, are evolved. Nevertheless, there are also problems on some devices, because they could not have a sufficient user-interface to handle the identification and authentication process, or they need cellular radio to receive short messages (SMS) for mobile tan (mTAN) to implement authentication by using two authentication factors. Especially about mTAN based solutions, there were many security incidents in the last couple of years [22,23].

To overcome this issue, different solutions are proposed. One solution is to use wireless communication to interact with a contactless smart card. Such approach can be used on smartphones or tablet computers and was already described in [15]. However, sufficient contactless communication interface, like NFC is not available on every device. Such solutions are implementable in a secure way but lacks interoperability or usability. Therefore, another approaches are desirable.

One possible approach is the transfer of entity information from one device to another device that relies on an already existing strong authenticated method. In more detail, an entity authenticate a session on a personal computer by using an existing eID that facilitates qualified identification and secure authentication, like smart-card based solution. After this initial identification and authentication step, the identification information can be transferred and cryptographically bind to an entity and its smart or mobile device. This cryptographically binded eID can be reused for identification and authentication later. Such transfer of an already authenticated session to a smart or mobile device is similar to the guidelines for derived personal identity verification (PIV) credentials, which was published in the NIST Special Publication 800-157 [14]. There, the NIST describes guidelines and requirements for derived PIV credentials, which are based on the general concept of derived credentials in NIST Special Publication SP 800-63-2 [7]. Corella and Lewison [9,10] and the Entrust Datacard company [12] already published some examples of a derived credential architecture. However, these already existing solutions are focusing on specific requirements in enterprise ID systems that are often used by companies but describe no general process or architecture. Therefor, there exists no sufficient solution to use already existing qualified eID by using secure authentication methods on smart or mobile devices for identification and authentication on any other service providers or eID consumers in general.

One example to solve these problems was already proposed by [30]. This solution uses a generic concept for cross-device identity-management. By using these, identification and secure authentication can be provided to almost all service provider by using security features that are shipped with current smart or mobile devices. However, smart or mobile devices are different to smart-cards regarding to its security features because most of them are open or semi-open platforms that facilitate the execution of different applications. So, the current security features provided on smart devices, like as Sandboxing[2] for separating of running applications or hardware-based cryptographic elements[3] to manage cryptographic keys provide an obvious higher security level than simple password-based authentication or two-factor authentication by using password and mTAN. However, the missing security certification and the design-related semi-open platform of mobile devices limits the reliability into a mobile device as a single authenticator.

To antagonize this lack of reliability into a single mobile-device based authenticator, we propose an advanced multi-factor based approach for entity authentication. In more detail, our proposed approach cryptographically combines at least two cryptographic key-pairs that are located on different authenticators on entity side only. Therefor, this cryptographic combination can be accomplished on the smart or mobile device itself without influencing already existing services that rely on entity identification and authentication. This approach does not require any implementation update on identity-provider side or eID-consumer side. Consequently, our proposed solution still fulfills the requirements for modular and flexible identity management systems described in [32]. Furthermore, we can increase the security into authentication on the client side only by combining different cryptographic keys that are located on different devices or tokens. In other words, an attacker that compromises one smart or mobile device can not its authenticator functionality anymore. Consequently, our approach decreases

---

[2] https://techterms.com/definition/sandboxing.

[3] https://source.android.com/security/keystore/.

the likelihood to successfully attack an authentication significantly, because it is not enough for an attacker to compromise one single device. Additionally, there are no additional or special requirements into the second authenticator. Therefore, also the second authenticator must only fulfill the requirements defined in [30]. Consequently, our proposed solution perfectly fits into the already existing concept of cross-device eID and increases the reliability into entity authentication significantly. In a nutshell, we propose an extension to the idea of personal, derived credentials (PIV) by adding multi-factor authentication on client side to the concept of cross-device eID. By using this approach, we can increase the reliability into authentication significantly without influence the eID consumer server.

This paper is structured as follows. Section 2 defines some terms, like eID, authentication, authentication factor that are used in this paper. In Sect. 4, we shortly present the architectural concept of cross-domain eID. After this, we give technical details on our proposed model for multi-factor combination on entity device-side to increase the entity authentication assurance and illustrate the integration into the concept of cross-domain eID. Section 5 gives detail information about the practical implementation of the proposed model. Finally, evaluation-related aspects are detailed in Sect. 6. Finally in Sect. 7 we give a short conclusion.

2   Definitions

The aim of this section is to define some terms regarding eID and authentication to build up a basis for all further concepts discussed in this paper. We start with the definition of electronic identity (eID). After this, we define the term *authentication* and finally, we illustrate additional aspects, like multi-factor authentication.

2.1   EID

A precise definition of electronic identity (eID) or identity in general is hard to give because a verity of definitions exists. Every of this definition has a different meaning according to the semantic context and the applied environment. As an example, a social scientist defines identity as an: *"Identity is an umbrella term used throughout the social sciences to describe an individual's comprehension of him or herself as a discrete, separate entity."*[4] A common aspect of all definitions is that identity means the presentation of an entity in a particular domain. So, an electronic identity is the digital representation of an identity [25,27,36,40]. This reference to a particular domain is also part of the ISO/IEC FDIS 24760-1 specification [3] for Identity. The digital representation consists of an identifier, attributes which characterize additional properties of the entity, and credentials that provide evidence claims of the digital entity. As an example, the Commission Implementation Regulation (EU) 2015/1501 on the eIDAS interoperability

---

[4] http://ezinearticles.com/.

framework [13] published at 8 September 2015 a minimum data set of attributes, that has to be included to an eID. However, the eIDAS interoperability framework defines a minimum set of attributes. The identifier and consequently the digital identity had not been unique and persistent in general, as it could only be valid within a certain time frame or in a specific context. Concisely, the term identity or its electronic representation describes the distinct and non-ambitious properties and characteristics of an entity.

2.2   Authentication

Authentication is the process to provide evidence for a claimed digital identity with a certain level of assurance. In more detail, authentication means a formal technical or organizational process to get evidence that the digital identity, which is shown by an entity, is authentic and that the entity is the owner of the digital identity. The formal process uses one or more authentication factors to get evidence into the identity. If this formal authentication process is successfully finished, it results in an authenticated identity [3, 20, 24].

2.3   Authentication Factor

An authentication factor is a piece of information or a part of the authentication process that is used to authenticate or verify the identity of an entity. Many related work and standards [20, 24, 29, 35] defined different types of authentication factors. These authentication factors are grouped into three different categories:

- **Something a user knows:** Secrets such as a password or a PIN.
- **Something a user is:** Biometric factors such as a fingerprint or an iris recognition.
- **Something a user has:** Devices such as tokens or smart cards dedicated to an entity.

So, an authentication factor is the technical or organizational implementation of specific authentication sub-process. This implementation is called *Authenticator* and implements at least one authentication factor [19].

2.4   Multi-factor Authentication

Multi-factor authentication is an authentication that uses two or more authentication factors from different categories. Multi-factor authentication can be performed by using a single authenticator that provides more than one factors from different categories or by a combination of different authenticators that provides one factor [19].

3   Cryptographic Preliminaries

The aim of this section is to introduce the cryptographic building blocks that are used to fulfill the requirements in our proposed model. We illustrate the general concept of Digital signatures and give details about Elliptic-curve based Schnorr signatures that are used in the proposed model. Finally, we introduce a mathematical proof to verify the knowledge of the discrete logarithm of an elliptic-curve point.

Digital Signatures

In a nutshell, a digital signature scheme uses a message M and an asymmetric key-pair $key(sk^{sig}, pk^{sig})$ to produce a digital signature σ by using M and the private key sk^{sig} from asymmetric key-pair. A verifier can use the signature σ, the message M and the public key pk^{sig} from asymmetric key-pair to check the integrity (σ has been issued for M) and the authenticity (σ was produced by the holder of the corresponding signing key sk^{sig}) of the signature.

In a more formal way, a digital signature scheme (DSS) is a set (K, S, V) of poly-times algorithms. The first algorithm DSS_K takes a security parameter k to generate an asymmetric key-pair $DSS_K(sk^{sig}, pk^{sig})$ where the private key is sk^{sig} and the public key is pk^{sig}. The second algorithm DSS_S is the signing algorithm. This signing algorithm uses a message $M \in \{0,1\}^*$ and a private key sk^{sig} as input data and outputs a signature $\sigma = DSS_S(sk^{sig}, m)$. The third algorithm DSS_V is the verification algorithm. This verification algorithm uses the message $M \in \{0,1\}^*$, a public key pk^{sig}, and a signature σ as input data and outputs a single bit $b = RS_V(\sigma, M, pk^{sig})$, $b \in \{true, false\}$ that indicates if the signature σ is valid for M or not. Also, in a practical implementation the message M is not directly used as input data in DSS_S and DSS_V but rather $H(M)$, where H is a cryptographic hash function.

Elliptic-Curve Based Schnorr Signatures

Briefly, Schnorr signatures are a digital signature scheme that based on the Schnorr algorithm for identification and signature creation. The Schnorr approach was proposed by Schnorr in 1990 as a lightweight algorithm for identification and signature creation on smart cards [37]. The signing algorithm uses an asymmetric key-pair $key(sk^{sig}, pk^{sig})$ to produce a digital signature $\sigma = (R, s)$ by using an input message M and the private key sk^{sig} from asymmetric key-pair. A verifier can use the signature $\sigma = (R, s)$, the public key pk^{sig}, and the message M

In a more formal way, a elliptic curve base Schnorr digital signature scheme (ECSDSA) is a set (K, S, V) of poly-times algorithms. The first algorithm $ECSDSA_K$ chooses an elliptic curve E over a finite field F_q. Next, the algorithm randomly selects a elliptic curve point $G \in E(F_q)$, where G is the generator in the following steps. In the last step, the algorithm $ECSDSA_K$ takes a security parameter k to generate an asymmetric key-pair $ECSDSA(sk^{ECSDSA}, pk^{ECSDSA})$ where the private key is $sk^{ECSDSA} \in [1, r]$, where r is the order of P and the public key is $PK^{ECSDSA} = sk^{ECSDSA} \cdot P$. The full public key pk_{set} is the set (PK^{ECSDSA}, P) if the generator P was randomly chooses. The second algorithm

ECSDSA_S is the signature algorithm. The signature algorithm generates random number $k \in [1, r]$, where r is the order of P. After this, a new elliptic curve point R is calculated, where $R = k \cdot P$, and P is the generator select in ECSDSA_K. In the next step, cryptographic hash value e is calculated by using a cryptographic hash function $H()$ and the message M and the point P as input data. These means that $e = H(M||R)$, where $H : 0 : 1^* \to [1, r]$ and r is the order of the generator P, and $||$ is a concatenation of M and R. At last, the signature $\sigma_M = (R, s)$ is generated, where R is the point generated before and s is calculated from $s = k + sk^{\mathrm{ECSDSA}} \cdot e \mod r$. The third algorithm $mboxECSDSA_V$ is the verification algorithm. This verification algorithm used the public key PK^{ECSDSA}, the generator R, the message M and the signature $\sigma_M = (R, s)$ and outputs a single bit $b_M \in \{true, false\}$ that indicates if the signature σ_M is valid for M, otherwise not. At first, the algorithm $mboxECSDSA_V$ calculates the hash value e using a cryptographic hash function $H()$ and the message M and the point P, which is part of the signature σ_M. The single bit $b_M \in \{true, false\}$ is the proof, if $R + e \cdot PK^{\mathrm{ECSDSA}} = s \cdot P$, where R and s are part of the signature σ_M, and P is the generator [5,33,37].

Proof of Knowledge of the Discrete Log of an Elliptic-Curve Point

Briefly, a proof of knowledge of the discrete log of an elliptic-curve point means the follows. For a given elliptic curve E over a finite field F_q, a generator $G \in E/F_q$, and an elliptic curve point $P \in E/F_q$, a prover wants to prove that he knows a value x such that $B = x \cdot G$, without revealing x. In respect to the elliptic curve discrete logarithm problem (ECDLP) it is very hard for an attacker to calculate a valid proof without knowing x. There exists different interactive and non-interactive zero-knowledge schemes that provide functionality to proof the possession of x [8,21]. In this work, use a non-interactive zero-knowledge proof based on the Schnorr protocol; because it is lightweight, that means that it can be well integrated into smart or mobile devices. Therefore, we will give more details on this specific zero-knowledge proof.

More formally, the non-interactive zero-knowledge proof based on the Schnorr protocol consists of the following steps. In the initialize phase, a prover and a verifier agree on an elliptic curve E over a finite field F_q and a generator $G \in E/F_q$. The prover and the verifier knows an elliptic curve point $B \in E/F_q$ and the prover claims that he knows a value x such that $B = x \cdot G$. This fact should be proven to the verifier without revealing x.

1. The prover generates a random number $r \in F_q$ and computes the corresponding elliptic curve point $A = r \cdot G$.
2. The prover sends the elliptic curve point A to the verifier
3. The verifier computes a value c by using a cryptographic hash function $H()$, where $H : 0 : 1^* \to [1, r]$ and r is the order of the generator G. The value c is generated by $c = H(G, B, A)$, where G, B and A are the hash input data.
4. The verifier sends the value c to the prover
5. The prover computes the proof m as $m = r + c * x \mod q$
6. The prover sends the proof m to the verifier

7. The verifier can check that $P = m \cdot G - c \cdot B = (r + c * x) \cdot G - c \cdot B = r \cdot G + c \cdot x \cdot G - c \cdot x \cdot G = r \cdot G = A$. If $m \cdot G - c \cdot B = A$ than the prover knows x, otherwise the proof fails.

From a security point of view, a dishonest prover has a tiny chance for cheating as he would have to fix the value of $P = m \cdot G - c \cdot B$ before receiving the hash value c from the verifier. However, under the assumption that the cryptographic hash function $H()$ is secure, a prover that does not know x cannot cheat in respect to the discrete logarithm of B.

4   Model

This section illustrates the concept of cross-domain eID [30] and gives detail information about our model to facilitate user-centric eID and secure authentication on semi-trusted smart or mobile devices. In Subsect. 4.1, we shortly describe the concept of cross-domain eID and define the stakeholders that are involved in the eID lifecycle in this architecture. Afterward, Sect. 4.2 gives more detailed information about the authentication process-flow that is used in the concept of cross-domain eID. In Subsect. 4.3, we describe our proposed advanced multi-factor combination model for semi-trusted smart devices that facilities high secure authentication and user-centric eID.

4.1   Concept of Cross-Domain eID

Figure 2 shows the concept of cross-domain eID that mainly focus on qualified eID in a privacy preserving and user-centric model. The entities or stakeholders, which are involved into the eID processing, are partially similar to the stakeholders involved in a classic identity management system [4], however the interactions between the stakeholders and the assignments regarding trust relationships are different. The following itemization gives a short description of the stakeholders illustrated in Fig. 2.

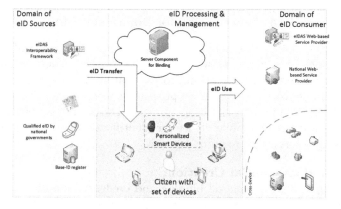

Fig. 2. High-level idea of cross-domain eID [30].

- **eID Source:** The area on the left side represents a so-called set of eID sources that provides an electronic identity in a specific context. This provision of identity information is based on an already existing authentication approach. In case of qualified eID, the eID source can be a registration authority (RA), like a national register that acts as a trusted third part for eID attributes and issues qualified eID attributes to the entity or other stakeholders. In case of an RA, the already existing authentication approach can be done by validating passport that is provided by an entity.
- **eID Consumer:** The stakeholders on the right side represent applications, services, or other devices that depend on the identification information. Consequently, the eID consumer has to be in confidence into the eID information that was provided by an entity in a user-centric approach. In the concept of cross-domain eID, such eID consumer can be located in different domains, and therefore, the eID consumer needs eID information for a specific context. For example, there can be a legal requirement that eID consumer services need different identifiers of an entity concerning the domain of the eID consumer for privacy reasons.
- **Entity:** A user or in general an entity wants to access a protected resource of an eID consumer, like a service provider. Therefore, the eID consumer consumes the eID information selective revealed by the entity to grant or deny access. The eID information, which was issued by an eID source, is stored on a personalized smart device in this model.
- **Personalized Smart Devices:** The personal smart device that is illustrated in the bottom area is a subtotal set of devices used by an entity to interact with eID consumer services by using identification information issued from an eID source. In our model, these set of devices are modeled as semi-trusted. There is a basic trust relationship according to the security features and there implementation of the smart or mobile device, like Sandboxing or hardware-based cryptographic elements. However, there is less confidence due to high-secure authentication by using these features on the same level as expressed for example by smart cards.

4.2 Agile Mobile Authentication for Smart and Mobile Devices

In respect to the high-level model illustrated in Fig. 2, the proposed process for agile mobile authentication consists of two sub-processes. The first sub-process is the binding and credential creation-process that transfers eID information to a smart or mobile device by using cryptographic operations. The second sub-process is the eID and credential usage-process. During the eID usage process, an entity uses a smart or mobile device for identification and authentication on an eID consumer service in a secure manner.

- **Binding and Credential Creation:**
  Figure 3 illustrates the generic binding and credential-enrollment process of the agile mobile authentication algorithm. This process generates crypto-graphic keys to binds an eID that is derived from an existing entity eID

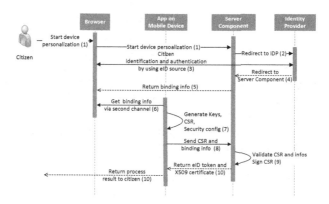

Fig. 3. Generic process to create a cryptographic binding for device personalization [31].

to a user and his smart or mobile device. The process shown in Fig. 3 consists of the following steps.

1. An entity wants to personalize its smart or mobile device by using an existing eID. For this purpose, the entity requests the Server Component that provides a binding service to personalize devices.

2. The Server Component redirects the entity to an Identity Provider (IDP) for initial identification and authentication. This identification and authentication use an existing eID that is provided by an eID source.

3. The entity execute the identification and authentication process by using its existing eID. This step satisfies the first requirement to support of any eID source.

4. If the initial identification and authentication is finished, the IDP sends the existing eID information to the Server Component. After this step, the eID derivation process is almost finished.

5. The Server Component starts the cryptographic binding process. Therefore, the Server Component provides generic binding info that contains all information that is required to initialize the binding part of the agile mobile authentication process. This binding info is provided to the entity and the smart or mobile device by using a second channel that is not fixed to a specific technical solution in general.

6. The entity uses a binding application on its smart or mobile device to receive the initial binding info over the second channel.

7. If the application receives the initial binding info than the cryptographic part of the binding process starts. At first, the application generates a public/private key pair by using security features provided by the smart or mobile device. After this, the application build a certificate-signing request (CSR) [39] by using the pubic key generated before. At last, additional security measures can be set by the entity to restrict the use of the private key on the smart or mobile device. This restriction can be

a PIN/password in the simplest case, but also some biometric factors like fingerprint, if it is supported by the smart or mobile device.

8. In the next step, the application connects to the Server Component and sends the CSR and the binding info.
9. The Server Component validates the CSR and the binding info. If both are valid, then the Server Component signs the CSR to generate an X509 certificate. The X509 certificate is attached to the eID information, which was received from the IDP in step four. The Server Component also signs the extended eID information. After this, the eID derivation process is completed.
10. In the last step of the binding process, the derived eID information is sent to the smart or mobile device and can be stored by the application. The result of the binding process is shown to the entity.

– **eID Usage Process:** If the binding process was successfully finished than the entity can use the smart or mobile device for authentication. Figure 4 illustrates the generic usage process of the agile mobile authentication algorithm. This generic process flow shows the usage of a derived eID that is cryptographically bound to a smart or mobile device for authentication on a Service Provider. A detailed description of this process is given in the following.

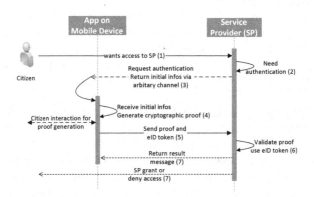

Fig. 4. Generic process to use a personalized device for authentication [31].

1. An entity wants access to a Service Provider. This Service Provider is not fixed to a specific type, as a Web-based application as an example, but could be any service that requires identification and secure authentication.
2. The Service Provider validates the access request and request authentication from the entity if it is needed.
3. To start the proposed agile mobile authentication process, the Service Provider provides all information that is necessary to initialize the algorithm over an arbitrary channel. This arbitrary channel is not fixed to a specific technology to satisfy the requirement to support almost all eID consumer services.

4. The entity can use its smart or mobile device to receive the information from the Service Provider. The application generates a cryptographic proof, by using the private key that was generated in the binding phase. If the entity has restricted the access to the private key in the binding phase, then also additional entity related information is necessary to complete this cryptographic proof.

5. The application sends the cryptographic proof and the derived eID information to the Service Provider.

6. The Service Provider can validate the derived eID information and the proof by using the X509 certificate that is attached to the derived eID information. If the validation is successful than the agile mobile authentication process is finished and the derived eID information can be used to identify the entity.

7. The Service Provider returns the result of the validation to the application, and after this, the entity can access the restricted area on the Service Provider.

4.3 Multi-factor Combination on Semi-trusted Smart and Mobile Devices

In this subsection, we illustrate our proposed model which cryptographically combine at least two authenticators that implement different authentication factors on a semi-trusted smart or mobile device to increase the reliability into the authentication process describe in Sect. 4.2. In more detail, the proposed model enhances the management of cryptographic keys and increases the trust into cryptographic keys that are created during the cryptographic binding process (see Fig. 3, Step 7) or are used during the authentication process (see Fig. 4, Step 4). Consequently, our advanced model for multi-factor combination on client side perfectly fits into the existing cross-domain eID approach, because these improvements do not influence other stakeholders besides the entity and the personalized smart device.

From a cryptographic point of view, threshold cryptography is used to cryptographically combine different multiple authentication factors that are implemented as authenticators on different smart or mobile devices. While threshold cryptography itself is no new cryptographic scheme, and a large body of research was done around the problem in most general form [6,11,16,18,33,34,37], the interest on threshold cryptography has been renewed for the purpose of key protection or distributed signatures schemes on semi-trusted devices such as mobile phones or any other smart device. For example such key protection approaches by using threshold cryptography can be used in bitcoin to protect the private signing key. However, our proposed model uses threshold cryptography to distribute the signature generation capabilities to different authenticators, which means that more than on cryptographic key is needed to generate a valid signature.

Threshold cryptography schemes for distributed signature generation exists for a wide variety of digital-signature schemes like RSA signing, digital signature schemes (DSA) based on RSA or elliptic curves (ECDSA), or other signature schemes like Schnorr signatures [37]. While it is more complex to build a distributed signature scheme on ECDSA signatures as it is more difficult to find a scheme to compute k and k^{-1} without knowing the private key k, it is much easier to define a distributed signature for other signature schemes. Schnorr signatures based on elliptic curves are one well example for such a signature scheme that facilitate distributed signature generation without complex and time expensive cryptographic operations. Consequently, the elliptic curve version of Schnorr signature schemes is used to integrate distributed signature schemes in our proposed model of cross-domain eID, as the signature generation can be easily integrated into lightweight smart or mobile devices.

According to the concept of cross-domain eID, our proposed model for multi-factor combination on semi-trusted mobile or smart devices can be split into three phases. The first phase is the distributed key generation, which can be integrated into Step 7 of Fig. 3, that generates a virtual asymmetric public/private key-pair $key(PK^{\mathrm{binding}}, sk^{\mathrm{binding}})$ used for the cryptographic binding described in Step 7. We called this key pair virtual, because the private key k^{binding} does not exist on one single device, as it is generated dynamically from more than one device specific private keys sk^{device_i}, $i \in (1, ..., n)$ where n is the number of devices. In more detail, this generation of the public part of the virtual binding key PK^{binding} can be formal described as $PK^{\mathrm{binding}} = \sum_{i=1}^{n} sk^{\mathrm{device}_i}) \cdot G$, where G is the generator of the group. Figure 5 illustrates a virtual binding-key generation by using two smart devices.

In the following, we describe this key generation process in a generic form for more than two devices.

1. The smart or mobile device that should be personalized by using an already existing eID and the authentication should be done by the virtual binding key $key(PK^{\mathrm{binding}}, sk^{\mathrm{binding}})$.
2. The personalization device sends a request to every authenticator to start the key generation process.
3. Every smart or mobile device that should be used as an authenticator generates its own asymmetric private key-pair $key(PK^{\mathrm{device}_i}, sk^{\mathrm{device}_i})$. The elliptic curve point that represents the public key PK^{device_i} is generates as $PK^{\mathrm{device}_i} = sk^{\mathrm{device}_i} \cdot G$, where $G \in E/F$ is the generator. This device specific asymmetric key-pair can be located in a hardware-based cryptographic element that is available on the authenticator.
4. Every authenticator generates a second random number $r_i \in F_q$ and a corresponding elliptic curve point $A_i = r_i \cdot G$, where $G \in E/F_q$ the generator is. The point A is required for the authenticator to knows the private key sk^{device_i}.
5. The authenticator sends the set $(PK^{\mathrm{device}_i}, A_i)$ to the smart or mobile device that should be personalized.
6. The smart device calculates the hash value c_i by using a cryptographic hash function H from input data $c_i = H(G, PK^{\mathrm{device}_i}, A_i)$.
7. The smart device sends the hash value c_i to the authenticator i to get a proof of possession of the private key sk^{device_i}.

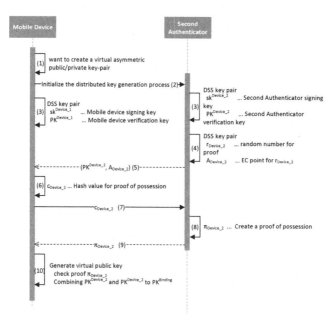

Fig. 5. Generation of a virtual public/private key-pair by using two devices [31].

8. By using c_i, every authenticator calculates a proof $\pi_i = r_i + c_i \cdot sk^{\text{device}_i}$ mod q, where q is modulo of the field F_q.
9. Every authenticator send its prove π_i back to the smart or mobile device that should be personalized.
10. The personalization device checks every proof π_{P_i}. If it is valid, the personalization device adds the authenticator public key PK^{device_i} to PK^{binding}. This simple elliptic curve addition operation can be done because: $PK^{\text{binding}} = \left(\sum_{i=1}^{n} sk^{\text{device}_i}\right) \cdot G = \sum_{i=1}^{n}\left(sk^{\text{device}_i} \cdot G\right) = \sum_{i=1}^{n} PK^{\text{device}_i}$. If all public keys are added the virtual public binding key PK^{device_i} can be used for the binding process.

The second phase is the distributed signature generation, which can be integrated into Step 4 of Fig. 4 that uses the virtual binding key $key(PK^{\text{binding}}, sk^{\text{binding}})$ to sign a challenge which is equivalent to a cryptographic proof. Additionally, this second phase is also required in Step 7 in Fig. 3 to sign the CSR in the binding process. Figure 6 illustrates this distributed signature generation process by using two devices.

In a generic form and with more detail, a distributed signature generation consists of the following steps:

1. The personalized smart or mobile device is requested by an eID consumer server to generate a cryptographic proof, by using the virtual private key sk^{binding} that was generated in the first phase. This cryptographic proof can be a digital signature which uses an elliptic curve Schnorr signature scheme on an input message m that was sent by the eID consumer service.

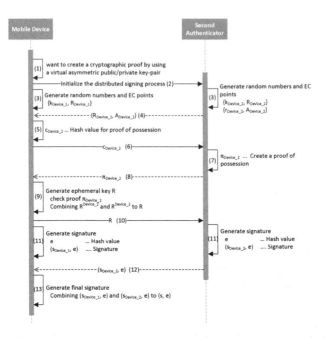

Fig. 6. Distributed signature creation by using two devices [31].

2. The personalized smart or mobile device generates a distributed signature initialization requests.

3. Every authenticator receives the signature initialization request and generates new random $k_i \in F_q$ where F_q is the field over the elliptic curve E. By using k_i, the authenticator can calculates a new random point $R_i = k_i \cdot G$, where $R_i \in E/F$ and G is the generator.
   In addition, every authenticator generates a second random number $r_i \in F_q$ and a corresponding elliptic curve point $A_i = r_i \cdot G$, where $G \in E/F_q$ is the generator. The point A is one step of the proof that the authenticator knows the random value k_i.

4. Every authenticator send the set (R_i, A_i) to the personalized smart device.

5. The smart device calculates the hash value c_i by using a cryptographic hash function H from input data $c_i = H(G, R_i, A_i)$.

6. The smart device sends the hash value c_i to the authenticator i to get a proof of possession of the private key k_i.

7. By using c_i, every authenticator calculates a proof $\pi_i = r_i + c_i \cdot k_i \mod q$, where q is modulo of the field F_q.

8. Every authenticator sends its prove π_i back to the smart or mobile device that should be personalized.

9. The personalized smart device checks every proof π_i. If it is valid, the personalization device adds the random points R_i to R. This is a simple elliptic curve addition operation as: $R = (\sum_{i=1}^{n} k_i) \cdot G = \sum_{i=1}^{n} (k_i \cdot G) = \sum_{i=1}^{n} R_i$.

10. The personalized smart device generates a distributed signature creation request that contains the message m and the sum of the randomly generates points R.

11. Next, every authenticator generates a cryptographic hash e from input message m and the random point R by calculating $e = H(m||R)$, where H is the cryptographic hash function. At last, the authenticator computes the signature value s by calculating $s = k - sk^{\text{device}_i} \cdot e \mod q$, where k is the random number, e hash value, and sk^{device_i} is the private key of a specific authenticator.

12. Every authenticator sends the signature $\sigma_i(s_i, e)$ back to the personalized device.

13. If all signatures $\sigma_i(s_i, e)$ are received, the personalized smart device can aggregate the single signature $\sigma_i(s_i, e)$, by simple adding the single signature values s_i to $s = \sum_{i=1}^{n} s_i \mod q$. This sample add operation is possible, because s_i was created only by linear operations. After this, the process of signature creation is completed and the signature $\sigma_m(s, e)$ for message m can be used as a proof of possession for the virtual secret key sk^{binding}.

The third phase is the signature verification phase in which an eID consumer service can verify the cryptographic signature that is used to authenticate the entity. This signature verification step is part of Step 6 in Fig. 4. From an eID consumer point of view, this verification phase is equal to the verification of an elliptic curve Schnorr signature by using the virtual public key PK^{binding} from the personalized smart or mobile device. More details on cryptographic building blocks for the Schnorr signature scheme and other basic cryptographic primitives that we used in our proposed model for multi-factor combination on mobile or smart devices are described in Sect. 3.

We have evaluated the practical applicability of the proposed model for multi-factor combination on mobile or smart devices by realizing two applications for smart devices that implement our proposed model.

5 Implementation of Multi-factor Combination on Client-Side

We used our proposed model of client-side multi-factor combination for entity authentication to implement and demonstrate the practical applicability in practice. This implemented solution consists of two applications for smart devices. The first application is a mobile-phone application that stores and manages the eID information in a secure way and implements the first authenticator regarding our proposed model. This mobile phone application can be used as personalized smart device regarding the concept of cross-domain eID. We implement a mobile-phone applications for the Android Operation System (Android OS)[5] that provides all functionality for binding and usage of eID information, by implementing our multi-factor combination approach.

---

[5] https://www.android.com/.

The second one is a smart-watch application that implements a second authenticator for our proposed model. For the second authenticator different smart watches were used, for example, a SmartWatch 3 from Sony[6], but every device runs on the Android Operation System. We implement an application for smart watches that perform all cryptographic operations, which are required in our model. Also, this application has a simple user interface to protect the secret key by using a PIN approach.

From a cryptographic point of view, we use the elliptic curve P-256 from [28] to implement our proposed model of a multi-factor combination. The basic implementation of the Schnorr signature scheme, which is used in our model, was done according to the recommendations from *BSI TR-03111* [2]. However, we modify the signature creation described in *BSI TR-03111* according to Sect. 4.3 to facilitate distributed signature creation. To implement the proof of possession, which is used in Sect. 4.3, we use the Schnorr NIZK Proof over Elliptic Curve from RFC 8235 [21]. By using these cryptographic schemes, we implement a communication protocol based on JSON [1] to transfer the payload between authenticators.

The communication interfaces used in our implementation are similar to the REST approach and defines service endpoints and payload. Therefore, we define two service endpoints to distinguish between the first and the second phase of the multi-factor combination approach described in Sect. 4.3. In more detail, the second authenticator provides a communication endpoint for virtual public/private key-pair generation and a communication endpoint for distributed signature generation. These technical endpoints are used by the mobile-phone application to interact with the smart-watch application. According to the sequence illustrated in Fig. 5, the generation of virtual public/private key-pair requires two communication steps between mobile-phone application and the smart-watch application. The first request (see Step 2, Fig. 5) has no payload and starts the virtual key-generation only. Listing 1.1 illustrates the result of Step 5 as JSON structure. The *type* element holds the current process step, like *keyGeneration* for a result of a virtual key-generation step, the *pubKey* holds the public-key of the device PK^{device_i}, and the parameter A is a random EC point required for the proof-of-possession. The JSON Web Key format [26] is used to encode EC points.

Listing 1.1. JSON Payload to initialize key generation.

```
1  {"type" : "keyGeneration",
2   "pubKey" : {
3    "kty":"EC",
4    "crv":"P-256",
5    "x":"oB4rYUsC62ulnQss8ExrenokShKQFwh...",
6    "y":"1LFDdZ_cn_K3klWhvCdJjUjXlLp9P3Q..."
```

---

[6] https://www.sonymobile.com/global-en/products/smart-products/smartwatch-3-swr50.

```
 7    },
 8    "A" : {
 9      "kty":"EC",
10      "crv":"P-256",
11      "x":"dfKnB0In_jPFuO5alg-ukPKPGEZssEHafe...",
12      "y":"5NQ4Gu8pZiKvujN8PvzwmVuLAMRXrELpHE..."
13    }
14  }
```

The second request (see Step 7, Fig. 5) requests the proof-of-possession of a private key. Therefore, the mobile-phone application sends hash $H(G, PK^{\text{device}_i}, A_i)$ as a nonce to the smart-watch application. The technical request is illustrated in Listing 1.2 and the response that contains the cryptographic proof is depict in Listing 1.3.

Listing 1.2. JSON Payload to request proof-of-possession of a private key.

```
1  {"type":  "generationProof",
2    "nonce":   "EjU528JZvHfH_gLdUoprj59tjCtbxE"
3  }
```

Listing 1.3. JSON Payload that contains the proof-of-possession of a private key.

```
1  {"type":  "generationProof",
2    "proof":   "j7wYn1JzdSsydVDio5
        vWMQFLZIwxjjtPOhehSBrNE"
3  }
```

The payload that is transmitted by using the second communication endpoint for the distributed signature generation (see Fig. 6) has the same format and data structure as described before. Therefore, we will not illustrate it in detail. By using these interfaces and communication channels, we implement two authenticators to illustrate the practical applicability of our proposed model. The implemented authenticators facilitate all functionality that is necessary to use them as authentication in eGovernment infrastructure during the evaluation phase.

6 Evaluation

The successful implementation of two authenticator prototypes for multi-factor combination on client-side has shown the feasibility of the proposed model. In order to evaluate the capabilities of our solution in a real-world scenario, we have deployed and tested the implementation with test deployments of real eGovernment infrastructure components. We deployed the server component of the already existing cross-domain eID infrastructure that was used during some evaluation phases in 2016 and 2017 [30]. By using this deployment, Austrian citizen can use there national eID cards to personalized there mobile phones. To evaluate the use of proposed model for multi-factor combination, we have deployed some demo service-provider that can be used by entities to test the advanced authentication process, which is illustrated in this paper. First internal tests shows practical applicability of our proposed model and illustrates the smooth integration into the existing cross-domain eID infrastructure. Currently, we are in the starting phase of a pilot to evaluate the proposed model in a bigger group of entities to get more detailed information on usability aspects regarding our model.

7   Conclusion

Due to the increasing number of smart devices, the processing and transfer of data between these devices rapidly rise. As these smart devices become closer and closer to the user, like smartphones, smart homes, eHealth sensors, the protection of private information moves into focus. This protection of sensitive data based on basic security concepts, like unique identification and high-secure authentication, to protect private data against unauthorized access. While processes and security models for identification and authentication are widely examined for Web-based applications and laptops, the situation is more demanding on smart devices. The continuous enhancement of smart devices leads to changing interfaces, functionality, and user expectations that also influence the security and privacy concepts. Divers researches and agencies already have a focus on this open problem. A first approach to tackle this known problem brings the idea of agile authentication to smart or mobile devices. While this first approach brings flexible authentication on these devices, it lacks in respect to high-secure authentication. The main disadvantage was the reliability regarding authentication because it relies on the trustworthiness of a single semi-trusted smart-device. Our proposed model antagonized this lack into the credibility of entity authentication. We use a flexible approach to combine multiple authentication factors on client side only cryptographically. This combination facilities high-secure entity authentication and increase the reliability into the trustworthiness significantly and thus strengthen the protection of private data. We implement our proposed model for the Android operation system to demonstrate the practical applicability of our approach. The Android apps were used in combination with Austrian eGovernment components to illustrate the integration of our model into existing infrastructure components. A first evaluation was done in a small pilot by using a study group of experts as users and real Austrian eGovernment components on testing level.

References

1. The JavaScript Object Notation (JSON) Data Interchange Format. RFC 7159 (2014). https://rfc-editor.org/rfc/rfc7159.txt

2. Bsi tr-03111: Elliptic curve cryptography, version 2.1 (2018)
3. International Journal of Security: Information technology – Security techniques – A framework for identity management – Part 1: Terminology and concepts. Technical report 24760-1, ISO/IEC, December 2011
4. Bertino, E., Takahashi, K.: Identity Management: Concepts, Technologies, and Systems. Artech House Inc., Norwood (2010)
5. van Tilborg, H.C.A., Jajodia, S. (eds.): Encyclopedia of Cryptography and Security. Springer, Boston (2011). https://doi.org/10.1007/978-1-4419-5906-5
6. Boyd, C.: Digital multisignatures. In: Cryptography and Coding, pp. 241–246 (1986)
7. Burr, W.E., et al.: Electronic authentication guideline. Technical report, 800-63-2, National Institute of Standards and Technology (NIST), August 2013. http://nvlpubs.nist.gov/nistpubs/SpecialPublications/NIST.SP.800-63-2.pdf
8. Chatzigiannakis, I., Pyrgelis, A., Spirakis, P., Stamatiou, Y.: Elliptic curve based zero knowledge proofs and their applicability on resource constrained devices, July 2011
9. Corella, F., Lewison, K.: Techniques for implementing derived credentials. Technical report, Pomcor Research in Mobile and Web Technology (2012). https://pomcor.com/whitepapers/DerivedCredentials.pdf
10. Corella, F., Lewison, K.: An example of a derived credentials architecture. Technical report, Pomcor Research in Mobile and Web Technology (2014). https://pomcor.com/techreports/DerivedCredentialsExample.pdf
11. Croft, R.A., Harris, S.P.: Public-key cryptography and reusable shared secrets. In: Cryptography and Coding, pp. 189–201 (1989)
12. Entrust, E.A.: Mobile derived PIV/CAC credential - a complete solution for NIST 800-157. Technical report, Entrust Datacard (2014). https://www.entrust.com/wp-content/uploads/2014/10/Mobile-Derived-Credential-WEB2-Nov15.pdf
13. European Union: Commission Implementing Regulation (EU) 2015/1501 of 8 September 2015 on the interoperability framework pursuant to Article 12(8) of Regulation (EU) No. 910/2014 of the European Parliament and of the Council on electronic identification and trust services for electronic transactions in the internal market. European Union (2015)
14. Ferraiolo, H., Cooper, D., Francomacaro, S., Regenscheid, A., Mohler, J., Gupta, S., Burr, W.: Guidelines for derived personal identity verification (PIV) credentials. Technical report, 800-157, National Institute of Standards and Technology (NIST), December 2014. http://nvlpubs.nist.gov/nistpubs/SpecialPublications/NIST.SP.800-157.pdf
15. Ferraiolo, H., Regenscheid, A., Cooper, D., Francomacaro, S.: Mobile, PIV, and authentication. Technical report, Draft NISTIR 7981, National Institute of Standards and Technology (NIST), March 2014
16. Fiat, A., Shamir, A.: How to prove yourself: practical solutions to identification and signature problems. In: Odlyzko, A.M. (ed.) CRYPTO 1986. LNCS, vol. 263, pp. 186–194. Springer, Heidelberg (1987). https://doi.org/10.1007/3-540-47721-7_12
17. Florêncio, D., Herley, C., Van Oorschot, P.C.: An administrator's guide to internet password research. In: Proceedings of the 28th USENIX Conference on Large Installation System Administration, LISA 2014, Berkeley, CA, USA, pp. 35–52. USENIX Association (2014). http://dl.acm.org/citation.cfm?id=2717491.2717494
18. Gennaro, R., Jarecki, S., Krawczyk, H., Rabin, T.: Robust threshold DSS signatures. Inf. Comput. **164**(1), 54–84 (2001). https://doi.org/10.1006/inco.2000.2881. http://www.sciencedirect.com/science/article/pii/S0890540100928815

19. Grassi, P.A., Garcia, M.E., Feton, J.L.: Digital identity guidelines. Technical report, 800-63-3, National Institute of Standards and Technology (NIST), June 2017

20. Grassi, P.A., et al.: Digital identity guidelines - authentication and lifecycle management. Technical report, 800-63b, National Institute of Standards and Technology (NIST), June 2017

21. Hao, F.: Schnorr Non-interactive Zero-Knowledge Proof. RFC 8235, September 2017. https://doi.org/10.17487/RFC8235, https://rfc-editor.org/rfc/rfc8235.txt

22. Haupert, V., Müller, T.: (In)security of app-based TAN methods in online banking. University of Erlangen-Nuremberg, Germany (2016). https://www1.cs.fau.de/filepool/projects/apptan/apptan-eng.pdf

23. Hayikader, S., Hanis binti Abd Hadi, F.N., Ibrahim, J.: Issues and security measures of mobile banking apps. Int. J. Sci. Res. Publ. **6**, 36–41 (2016)

24. ISO/IEC: ISO/IEC 29115. Information technology - Security techniques - Entity authentication assurance framework. International Standard, International Organization for Standardization (2013)

25. ISO/IEC: ISO/IEC COMMITTEE DRAFT 29003. Information technology - Security techniques - Identity proofing. Technical report, International Organization for Standardization (2016)

26. Jones, M.: JSON Web Key (JWK). RFC 7517, May 2015. https://doi.org/10.17487/RFC7517. https://rfc-editor.org/rfc/rfc7517.txt

27. Jøsang, A., Zomai, M.A., Suriadi, S.: Usability and privacy in identity management architectures. In: Proceedings of the Fifth Australasian Symposium on ACSW Frontiers, ACSW 2007, Darlinghurst, Australia, vol. 68, pp. 143–152. Australian Computer Society Inc. (2007). http://dl.acm.org/citation.cfm?id=1274531.1274548

28. Kerry, C.F., Romine, C.: FIPS PUB 186-4 Federal Information Processing Standards Publication Digital Signature Standard (DSS) (2013)

29. Kim, J.J., Hong, S.P.: A method of risk assessment for multi-factor authentication. JIPS **7**, 187–198 (2011)

30. Lenz, T., Alber, L.: Towards cross-domain eID by using agile mobile authentication. In: 2017 IEEE Trustcom/BigDataSE/ICESS, pp. 570–577, August 2017. https://doi.org/10.1109/Trustcom/BigDataSE/ICESS.2017.286

31. Lenz, T., Krnjic, V.: Agile smart-device based multi-factor authentication for modern identity management systems. In: WEBIST (2018)

32. Lenz, T., Zwattendorfer, B.: A modular and flexible identity management architecture for national eID solutions. In: 11th International Conference on Web Information Systems and Technologies, pp. 321–331 (2015)

33. Lindell, Y.: Fast secure two-party ECDSA signing. In: Katz, J., Shacham, H. (eds.) CRYPTO 2017. LNCS, vol. 10402, pp. 613–644. Springer, Cham (2017). https://doi.org/10.1007/978-3-319-63715-0_21

34. MacKenzie, P., Reiter, M.K.: Two-party generation of DSA signatures. Int. J. Inf. Secur. **2**(3), 218–239 (2004). https://doi.org/10.1007/s10207-004-0041-0. https://doi.org/10.1007/s10207-004-0

35. Mohammed, M.M., Elsadig, M.: A multi-layer of multi factors authentication model for online banking services. In: 2013 International Conference on Computing, Electrical and Electronic Engineering (ICCEEE), pp. 220–224, August 2013. https://doi.org/10.1109/ICCEEE.2013.6633936

36. Sarikhani, R.: Language and American social identity, January 2008. http://ezinearticles.com/?Language-and-American-Social-Identity&id=956774

37. Schnorr, C.P.: Efficient identification and signatures for smart cards. In: Brassard, G. (ed.) CRYPTO 1989. LNCS, vol. 435, pp. 239–252. Springer, New York (1990). https://doi.org/10.1007/0-387-34805-0_22
38. Taneski, V., Heričko, M., Brumen, B.: Password security - no change in 35 years? In: 2014 37th International Convention on Information and Communication Technology, Electronics and Microelectronics (MIPRO), pp. 1360–1365, May 2014. https://doi.org/10.1109/MIPRO.2014.6859779
39. Turner, S.: The application/pkcs10 media type. RFC 5967 (2010). https://rfc-editor.org/rfc/rfc5967.txt
40. Zwattendorfer, B.: Towards a privacy-preserving federated identity as a service-model (2014)

An Open Source Approach for Modernizing Message-Processing and Transactional COBOL Applications by Integration in Java EE Application Servers

Philipp Brune[1,2(✉)]

[1] Neu-Ulm University of Applied Science, Wileystraße 1, 89231 Neu-Ulm, Germany
`Philipp.Brune@hs-neu-ulm.de`
[2] QWICS Enterprise Systems, Taunustor 1, 60310 Frankfurt, Germany
`Philipp.Brune@qwics.de`
`https://qwics.de,`
`https://qwics.org`

Abstract. Modernization of monolithic "legacy" mainframe COBOL applications to enable them for modern service- and cloud-centric environments is one of the ongoing challenges in the context of digital transformation for many organizations. This challenge has been addressed for many years by different approaches. However, the possibility of using a pure Open Source Software (OSS)-based approach to run existing transactional COBOL code as part of Java EE-based web applications has just recently been demonstrated by the author. Therefore, in this paper, an overview of the previously proposed Quick Web-Based Interactive COBOL Service (QWICS) is given and its new extension to run message-processing COBOL applications via JMS is described. QWICS runs on Un*x-like operating systems such as Linux, and therefore on most platforms, but in particular on the mainframe itself. This enables a mainframe-to-mainframe re-hosting, preserving the unique features of the mainframe platform like superior availability and security.

Keywords: Web services · Message processing · Transaction processing COBOL · Java EE · Open Source Software · Mainframe computing

1 Introduction

In the recent and ongoing discussions about digital transformation and its impact for companies, in particular in the banking and financial service industries, it has been recently pointed out by various authors that the mainframe is by no means an outdated technology and probably will remain an important part of the entrprise IT landscape for a long time [16, 28, 42].

© Springer Nature Switzerland AG 2019
M. J. Escalona et al. (Eds.): WEBIST 2018, LNBIP 372, pp. 244–261, 2019.
https://doi.org/10.1007/978-3-030-35330-8_12

However, the traditional monolithic "legacy" COBOL enterprise applications are too inflexible and not open enough to fulfill the requirements of the digital age [1,38]. And despite its age, COBOL still plays a major role in enterprise application development on the mainframe [1,20,40] (with "mainframe" in this paper denoting IBM's S/390 platform and its descendants) and will continue to do so for a long time due to various reasons [1,9,18,30,36].

Therefore, the challenge of modernizing the existing COBOL applications is to convert them into service-oriented backends with well-defined APIs and using open technologies [17,19] while preserving their inherent value, making them accessible for cloud-based "Systems of Engagement" like mobile apps and web frontends [12] or distributed big data processing applications [27,39].

Migrating to Open Source Software (OSS) has recently been suggested as one approach for the banking industry to reach this goal [11]. Therefore, the recently proposed Quick Web-Based Interactive COBOL Service (QWICS) [6] discussed in this paper follows this direction. It is built on top of well-established, enterprise-ready OSS components such as e.g. the PostgreSQL relational database[1] [15].

Most of these legacy mainframe COBOL programs are online transaction-processing (OLTP) applications, which require a so-called transaction processing monitor (TPM) middleware to run in, like e.g. IBM's CICS[2] [25] or Fujitsu's openUTM[3]. Therefore, any modernization approach needs to take into account the inherent dependency of the transactional COBOL code on these TPM environments [6].

Most previous approaches [6] thus focus either on adding modern features such as RESTful APIs or Java EE support to the mainframe TPM middleware itselve, thus making use of the unique features of modern mainframes [9,30,40], or on providing a complete (mostly proprietary) replacement or emulation for the traditional mainframe TPM on other, non-mainframe platforms[4] [37,41].

In contrast, QWICS adopts another perspective on modernizing transactional COBOL applications, as it provides an open framework to run COBOL code in the context of any modern Java Enterprise Edition (EE) application server[5], using the latter to provide the TPM functionality [6]. QWICS is built using established OSS components and runs on Un*x and Linux derivates, in particular on the mainframe itself. Therefore, it combines the unique features of the modern mainframe with the platform independence and openess of Linux and OSS [6].

To further extend the capabilities of QWICS, in this paper its extension to support transactional message-processing COBOL programs is described. This is an important feature, as asynchronous, message-oriented data processing is

---

[1] https://www.postgresql.org.

[2] https://www.ibm.com/software/products/de/cics-tservers.

[3] http://www.fujitsu.com/de/products/software/middleware/openseas-oracle/openutm/.

[4] See e.g. https://www.lzlabs.com/.

[5] In this paper, for convenience still the term Java EE is used, despite it has been officially re-labeled recently to Jakarta EE (see https://jakarta.ee/about/).

an important concept for many enterprise applications [4]. Consistent with the original idea of QWICS, this is achieved by using the Java Message Service (JMS)[6] functionality of the Java EE application server.

The rest of this paper is organized as follows: In Sect. 2 the related work is analyzed in detail, while the software architecture of QWICS proposed in [6] is summarized in Sect. 3. Section 4 describes its new extension to support message-oriented transaction processing in COBOL using JMS. The experimental evaluation of QWICS and its results are illustrated in Sect. 5. We conclude with a summary of our findings.

2 Related Work

As described in [6], over the years the challenge of modernizing transactional "legacy" COBOL applications by modularization and encapsulation [31] has been addressed by numerous approaches, which my be classified into three major categories:

- *Modernization on the mainframe itself* [32]*:* Making use of new technologies such as web services and Java EE supported by the current versions of the "classical" mainframe TPM products to wrap COBOL transaction programs by web service facades or web user interfaces [19,22,35] and integrate them into service-oriented architectures [7,10,26,29]. This is well supported by various software tools from the mainframe vendors [3] as well as by third parties, and allows to make use of the unique features of modern mainframes such as extremely high availability and outstanding transaction throughput [9,40].
- *Migration to non-mainframe platforms (including cloud services)* [17,21]*:* Usually driven by the expectation to reduce the perceived high operating costs of the mainframe platform and the related vendor lock-in [17,21], this typically requires to use either the original mainframe TPM middleware [25] on these non-mainframe platforms (which is the case for the major mainframe TPM products) or an emulation mimicking the functionality of the TPM [2,37]. In particular, the latter has been addressed over the years by various hobbyist approaches[7] as well as professional commercial offerings (See footnote 4). However, these approaches have different drawbacks, since they frequently do not achieve the same transactional throughput as the original mainframes, rely on on proprietary emulation techniques (thereby creating a new vendor lock-in) or may suffer from patent-related and licensing issues [2,23,37,41].
- *Conversion of the program code to other languages and platforms:* This involves either the (automatic) conversion of the COBOL code to other, more modern programming languages and/or the extraction of the business rules and logic from the existing code (e.g. by using special analysis tools) and their subsequent re-implementation (either manually or by code generators)

---

[6] https://javaee.github.io/jms-spec/.

[7] http://www.kicksfortso.com.

using other languages and platforms [5, 8, 13, 21, 24, 34–36, 43]. Being closely related to model-driven development, this approach has gained wide interest in the scientific community on legacy systems modernization, but has been rarely used in practice since it may be too expensive or riskful for companies in many cases [36].

Despite numerous attempts for re-writing [14] or re-hosting mainframe "legacy" applications on other platforms, mainframe-based organizations after various failed migration projects [1, 9, 40] realized that the mainframe platform offers unique features like the support for high availability, vertical scalability and security [40], which could not always be recovered on other platforms [28, 42]. Therefore, to enable the digital transformation [38], in the last years the focus shifted again to the first approach, namely the modernization on the mainframe itself [42].

Since Java has overtaken the role of COBOL in enterprise application development to a large extend, Java Enterprise Edition (EE)[8] application servers for the Enterprise Java Bean (EJB) components provide functionalities similar to those classical TPM middleware does for COBOL [3, 21]. These includes support for distributed transactions and the 2-phase-commit (2PC) protocol through the Java Transaction API (JTA)[9] as well as transactional message processing via Message-driven Beans (MDB) and JMS.

Due to this analogy between Java EE application servers and classical TPM middleware, the previously proposed QWICS framework [6] demonstrated an approach to execute transactional COBOL programs integrated in a Java EE application server as part of a JTA transaction, such that the required TPM functions (such as transaction handling, resource access, access to message queues, user interfaces, etc.) are realized by the Java EE application server out of the box.

QWICS has been implemented as pure OSS, built using mature, enterprise-ready OSS components, since openess and OSS have been identified recently as cornerstones for enterprise application modernization in the age of digital transformation [11, 15]. Since QWICS adds only a thin "glue component layer" to the established OSS components to manage the native COBOL execution for the Java EE application server [6], it is fully portable among various Un*x- and Linux derivatives, with a strong focus on "re-hosting" COBOL applications to Linux on the mainframe itself using OSS[10] [6].

While the feasibility of this approach has been demonstrated already in [6], QWICS so far lacked the support for transactional message-processing. Since this is an important feature [4], in this paper together with a summary of its previously described architecture and functionality the question is addressed, how an extension of QWICS to support message processing in COBOL via JMS could be designed and implemented.

---

[8] http://www.oracle.com/technetwork/java/javaee/overview/index.html.

[9] http://www.oracle.com/technetwork/java/javaee/jta/index.html.

[10] https://www.openmainframeproject.org/.

3   Design of the Software Architecture

Figure 1 shows an overview of the software architecture of QWICS, which has been presented in [6] and will be summarized in this section. Its full source code is available as OSS on GitHub[11].

As described in [6], QWICS is based on well-established, mature and enterprise-ready OSS components selected following a "best of breed" strategy: *GnuCOBOL*[12] for compiling the COBOL sources on the respective target platform, the *PostgreSQL relational database system* (See footnote 1) replacing the original mainframe DBMS and the *JBoss WildFly application server*[13] as the Java EE runtime. Here, in particular PostgreSQL has a wide recognition by practitioners as a reliable, scalable enterprise-quality OSS database management system [15].

To execute the transactional COBOL programs in the context of the Java EE container, as the core concept the integration by a special Java Database Connectivity(JDBC)[14]-compliant driver is used. This QWICS JDBC driver provides Non-XA and XA datasources to handle distributed transactions. It acts as a TCP client for the *COBOL Transaction Server*, which actually loads and executes the COBOL binary programs, the so-called load modules. Thus, the execution of these COBOL programs is invoked and controlled from the Java code (e.g. from an EJB) by special callable statements and result sets implemented by the QWICS JDBC driver. Thus, in QWICS always a Java EE application (e.g. consisting of EJB, servlets, JPA, Web Services, ...) is needed to call the COBOL programs via the JDBC driver [6].

The *COBOL Transaction Server* itself is a separate program implemented in C, which dynamically loads and executes the COBOL load modules created by the GnuCOBOL compiler. It also serves as a client for the PostgreSQL database to execute SQL statements embedded in the COBOL programs as well as those directly send from the Java side via the JDBC driver, being able to mix both in one transaction. The transaction server uses a slightly modified version of GnuCOBOL's `libcob` library, which has an intercept added to handle special `DISPLAY` statements of the form `DISPLAY "TPMI:...` and call a function in the transaction server for these. The necessary modification is shown in Fig. 2. This mechanism allows to handle the original `EXEC ... END-EXEC` macros in the code [25], which therefore have to be converted to these special `DISPLAY` statements in a subsequent preprocessing step [6].

To keep track of the state of all running transactions, a TPM needs to handle all input/output (I/O) operations performed by the programs it executes. Therefore, transactional COBOL programs running inside a TPM may not use the normal COBOL I/O statements. Instead, all necessary I/O operations (like e.g. executing SQL statements, sending or receiving data from the screen, etc.)

---

[11] https://github.com/pbrune1973/qwics.

[12] https://sourceforge.net/projects/open-cobol.

[13] http://wildfly.org.

[14] http://www.oracle.com/technetwork/java/javase/jdbc/index.html.

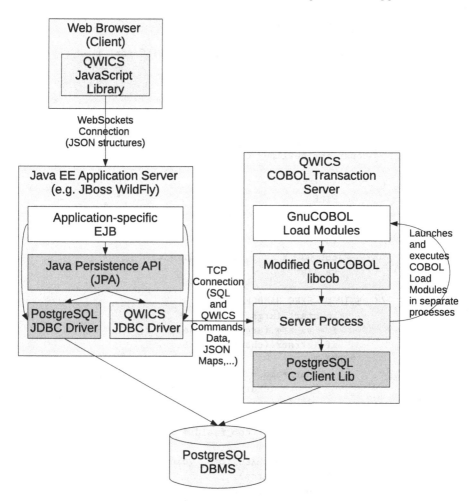

Fig. 1. Overview of the software architecture of QWICS. The arrows denote usage/invocation relationships. Yellow boxes describe the QWICS-specific components and white boxes the application-specific COBOL or Java code. The integration between the Java and the COBOL code is achieved using a specific JDBC driver calling the COBOL server via its own protocol over a TCP connection. Reprinted from [6]. (Color figure online)

are usually coded in COBOL (or that of any other supported language) by using TPM- and SQL-specific `EXEC ... END-EXEC` macros. These macros are then translated into TPM API calls in an additional preprocessing step before actually compiling the COBOL code [25]. In addition, the terminal UI screen definitions (so-called maps) referenced by these macros also need to be translated to stored COBOL code fragments (called copybooks) containing the necessary variable declarations. These copybooks are then inserted in the COBOL code during preprocessing as well [6].

```
int (*performEXEC)(char*, void*) = NULL;

void display_cobfield(cob_field *f, FILE *fp) {
    display_common(f,fp);
}


void
cob_display (const int to_stderr,
   const int newline, const int varcnt,
   ...)
{
        FILE         *fp;
        cob_field    *f;
        int          i;
        int          nlattr;
        cob_u32_t    disp_redirect;
        va_list      args;

// BEGIN OF EXEC HANDLER
        va_start (args, varcnt);
        f = va_arg (args, cob_field * );
        if (strstr((char*)f->data,
    "TPMI:")) {
            char *cmd
                = (char*)(f->data+5);
            if (varcnt > 1) {
                f = va_arg (args,
                    cob_field * );
            }
            (*performEXEC)(cmd,(void*)f);
            va_end (args);
            return;
        }
        va_end (args);
// END OF EXEC HANDLER
```

Fig. 2. Necessary modification to `termio.c` of GnuCOBOL's `libcob` runtime library. Only the lines shown between `// BEGIN...` and `// END ...` need to be added, no further modifications are necessary. This code adds an interception to DISPLAY statements of the form DISPLAY" TPMI:..., which are used to execute the EXEC-macros in the original COBOL source. Reprinted from [6].

This preprocessing needs to be mimicked by QWICS to allow to re-use the unmodified COBOL source codes. In Fig. 3, the overall process implemented in QWICS by two preprocessors written in C, `cobprep` for COBOL and `mapprep` for the map definitions, is illustrated. After the preprocessing, the resulting COBOL code is compiled to an executable load module using the GnuCOBOL compiler [6].

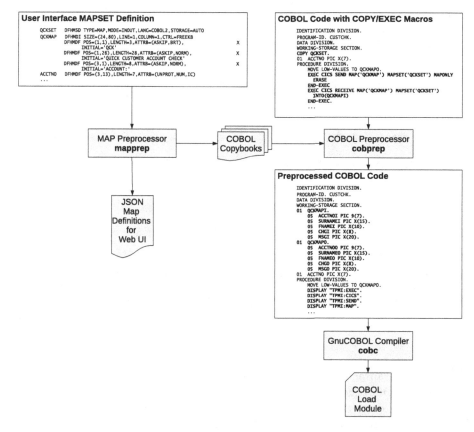

Fig. 3. Process of preprocessing the original COBOL source files and map definitions for use by QWICS. Reprinted from [6].

Last but not least a *JavaScript Library* has been implemented for QWICS, which supports the (optional) implementation of web user interfaces by converting the original TPM's map defintions [25] to JavaScript Object Notation (JSON) structures beforehand using the preprocessor [6].

4 Extension to Transactional Message-Processing

Asynchronous, transactional message-processing is an important concept of large-scale enterprise applications [4]. In traditional mainframe applications this functionality is typically provided by a message-oriented middleware invoked from COBOL programs running in a TPM. A similar concept exists for Java EE application servers through the Java Message Service (JMS).

Following the general approach of QWICS, transactional message-processing was therefore implemented by using JMS from the COBOL code by extending the QWICS JDBC driver. To do so, the COBOL program calls for getting and

```
// BEGIN OF CALL HANDLER
void* (*resolveCALL)(char*) = NULL;
// END OF CALL HANDLER

void *
cob_resolve_cobol (const char *name, const int fold_case, const int errind)
{
        void    *p;
        char    *entry;
        char    *dirent;

// BEGIN OF CALL HANDLER
        p = resolveCALL(name);
        if (p != NULL) {
            return p;
        }
// END OF CALL HANDLER
```

Fig. 4. Necessary modification to `call.c` of GnuCOBOL's `libcob` runtime library. Only the lines shown between `// BEGIN...` and `// END ...` need to be added, no further modifications are necessary. This code adds an interception to COBOL `CALL` statements, which executes the function denoted by the pointer `resolveCALL(..)` if it is set.

putting messages from and into queues or topics [4] need to be intercepted by the QWICS transaction server. Therefore, again a patch has been added to the GnuCOBOL `libcob` library to intercept and redirect the respective `CALL` statements to corresponding C functions provided by the transaction server. Figure 4 shows the respective modification to the `libcob` library.

The transaction server communicates with the QWICS JDBC driver to send and receive messages via JMS. Figure 5 shows a conceptual overview of the interplay between the components involved in this process. Since JDBC datasource management, JTA and JMS are independent subsystems of Java EE, a JDBC driver should not depend on any JMS API or call it directly. Therefore, the integration of COBOL with JMS requires a custom Java EE application using message-driven beans (MDB).

While the JDBC driver only offers interfaces representing abstract wrappers for queues or topics (`QueueWrapper`) and a factory for creating them (`QueueManager`), the Java EE application implements these interfaces to actually access the JMS functionality. It registers a `QueueManager` implementation with the JDBC driver, so the latter could create instances of these classes. The UML class diagram in Fig. 6 illustrates the relevant Java classes of the JDBC driver and the example Java EE application and there relations.

For every JMS queue or topic for which messages should be processed within a transaction by a COBOL program, a corresponding MDB needs to be implemented, for which the example `QwicsMDB` may serve as a blueprint. When such a MDB receives a message, its method `onMessage(Message message)` is invoked by the EJB container, wrapped into a distributed JTA transaction. This method

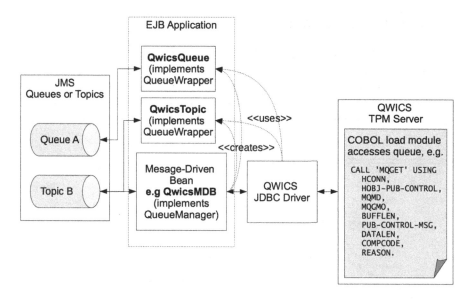

Fig. 5. Conceptual overview of the integration between COBOL and JMS via the QWICS framework. The actual access to JMS is implemented within an EJB application and not inside the QWICS JDBC driver to keep the different Java EE subsystems independent from each other. A message-driven bean listens at a queue or topic and upon reception of a message triggers the corresponding COBOL program using the JDBC driver. The COBOL program accesses the JMS queues via the JDBC driver and the EJB application.

now uses the QWICS JDBC driver via a XA datasource to trigger the respective COBOL program.

Figure 7 shows an excerpt from the source code of the example QwicsMDB to illustrate this. The COBOL program invoked here is a demo program called QPUBCBL. By the statement maps.updateObject(''QMGR'', this);, the MDB registers itself as the QueueManager implementation with the JDBC driver.

The invoked COBOL load module now may access the JMS queues itself by executing CALL statements to the (emulated) routines "MQOPEN", "MQCLOSE", "MQGET" and "MQPUT". Intercepted by the transaction server as described above, these calls are forwarded to the JDBC driver, which again uses the implementation classes QwicsTopic or QwicsQueue provided by the Java EE application to access the respective JMS artifacts.

With this mechanism, analogous to the previously described QWICS functionality, COBOL programs will be triggered by JMS messages are able to send and receive messages via JMS.

5   Experimental Evaluation

To evaluate the functionality and usefulness of QWICS, in a first step an existing transactional COBOL application was ported to the QWICS evironment [6]. To avoid a bias, a representative COBOL application written for training purposes using the IBM CICS TPM a consulting company was used for this [33], since its developers are not related or known to the author [6].

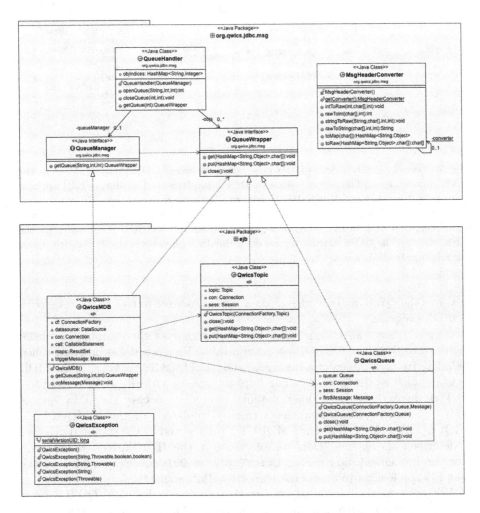

Fig. 6. UML class diagram describing the Java-side implementation of an example Message-Driven Bean (`QwicsMDB`) using the newly added message-queueing functionality of the QWICS JDBC driver. The MDB class listens for and reacts to received messages from a JMS queue or topic and provides the driver with appropriate `QueueWrapper` implementation classes (labeled `QwicsQueue` and `QwicsTopic` here) for accessing the respective JMS objects.

```
@MessageDriven ( ... ,
        messageListenerInterface = MessageListener.class)
public class QwicsMDB
        implements MessageListener, QueueManager {
        ...
        @Resource(mappedName="java:jboss/datasources/QwicsDS")
        DataSource datasource;

        private Connection con;
        private CallableStatement call;
        private ResultSet maps;
        private Message triggerMessage = null;
        ...
        public void onMessage(Message message) {
           try {
                triggerMessage = message;
                con = datasource.getConnection();
                call = con.prepareCall("PROGRAM QPUBCBL");
                maps = call.executeQuery();
                maps.updateString("QNAME","MyQueue");
                maps.updateString("ENVDATA","MyStatQueue");
                maps.updateObject("QMGR", this);
                maps.next();
                try {
                        String ac = maps.getString("ABCODE");
                        throw new QwicsException("ABEND "+ac);
                } catch (Exception e) {
                }
           } catch (Exception e) {
                throw new QwicsException(e);
           }
        }
}
```

Fig. 7. Excerpt of the example Java EE message-driven bean (MDB) listening for messages on a JMS queue or topic. Upon reception of a respective message, the method **onMessage(Message message)** is invoked by the container, wrapped into a distributed XA transaction. The message is only removed from the queue of this transaction is committed successfully. The method invokes a sample message-processing COBOL program via the QWICS JDBC driver.

The original sources were passed through the preprocessors as described above, compiled using GnuCOBOL and then run in the QWICS environment. The screenshot shown in Fig. 8 illustrates how this COBOL application running in QWICS may appear to user in a web browser window. This original evaluation was repeated two times, first on an Apple MacBook Air laptop running MacOS X 10.11.6 (thus, a BSD Un*x- derivative), and second on a IBM zBC12 mainframe computer running Linux on Z. Both tests worked smoothly, delivered identical results regarding the functionality and thus demonstrate the feasibilty of the approach in principle [6].

Subsequent to the original publication of these evaluation results [6], in a second step a public community website (https://qwics.org) including a free demonstration and testing environment for QWICS has been set up, to further evaluate the QWICS framework and move it towards production readiness.

This website provides further information on QWICS, links to the source code repository and after a free online registration offers everyone the possibilty to run a personal QWICS environment in a Virtual Machine (VM) based on a Docker container[15]. Besides the actual QWICS framework, this environment offers the user a web-based administration console for the PostgreSQL database (using the OSS phpPgAdmin[16]) and a web-based source code editor to write COBOL code and edit UI screens online (using the Codiad IDE[17]). Figure 9 shows screenshots of the dashboard and the online code editor of this environment. As can also be seen from the screenshot, the QWICS online environment currently still runs on an Intel x86-based server running Ubuntu Linux. It is planned also to provide a demo running on the mainframe under Linux on Z in the future.

The QWICS server VM offered on https://qwics.org to the public already contains a simple but ready-to-run transactional COBOL example written by the author for demonstration purposes, in the form of a small guestbook web app. This online version of QWICS not only allows to demonstrate and explore the framework, but also may serve as an easy to use and free opportunity to learn and practice transactional COBOL programming online.

The availability of this QWICS online trial has been promoted via a press release and internationally via social media so far. Until now, a small number of interested persons from different countries have registered, but it is yet too early to obtain results from the analysis of user feedback.

It has been pointed out before that QWICS is different from other mainframe modernization approaches with respect to its focus on using OSS to integrate existing COBOL code into Java EE applications to use modern web technologies with COBOL [6]. Therefore, it requires a partial adaption and recompilation of the existing sources instead of achieving full binary[18] or source-level compatibilty [2,37] on other (commodity), non-mainframe platforms [6]. Instead, it enables customers to modernize transactional COBOL applications on the mainframe itself using Linux.

The next research steps will focus on evaluating the potentials of QWICS in real-world case studies, on the one hand by an extended Proof-of-Concept using a real "legacy" COBOL application in a company, on the other hand by further

---

[15] https://www.docker.com/.

[16] http://phppgadmin.sourceforge.net/doku.php.

[17] http://codiad.com/.

[18] https://www.lzlabs.com/

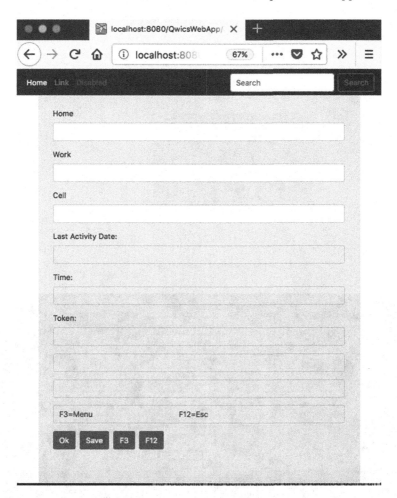

Fig. 8. Screenshot of a map screen converted to JSON and displayed in web page by the JavaScript library. Reprinted from [6].

exploring the use of the QWICS online platform for COBOL programming education. The first will also need include an extended analysis of the performance and scalability of the approach compared to the original mainframe TPM. As described in [6], there definitely will be a performance tradeoff due to the design of the used OSS components, but it remains an open issue how big it will be in practice.

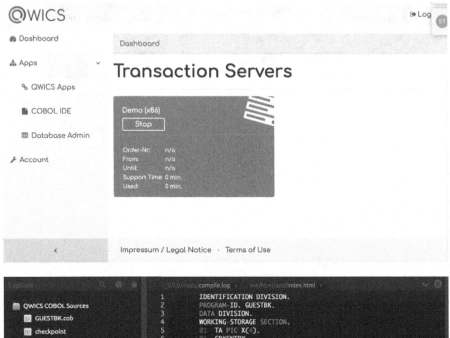

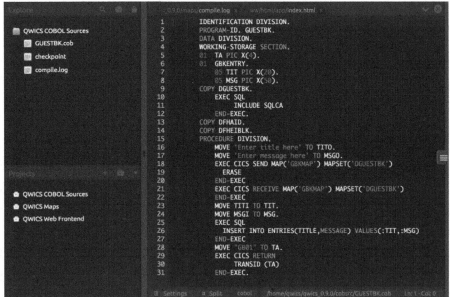

Fig. 9. Screenshots from the free QWICS online demonstration and testing environment: Admin Dashboard showing a running QWICS VM instance (above) and the online source code editor showing a COBOL example (below).

6 Conclusion

In conclusion, in this paper the previously proposed Quick Web-Based Interactive COBOL Service (QWICS) [6] was presented and its extension to support asynchronous, transactional, message-oriented communication in COBOL via the Java Message Service (JMS) API was introduced. The latter is in particular important for building large-scale enterprise applications.

Therefore, QWICS now allows to run the most relevant types of transactional COBOL applications (synchronous and asynchronous) within the context of a Java EE application server using a pure OSS stack. Therefore, it allows to mix COBOL and Java code for extending and converting "legacy" applications into web services. Its pure OSS stack runs on most Un*x and Linux platforms, allowing in particular to modernize "legacy" applications on the mainframe itself using Linux.

The feasibility of the approach has already been evaluated by porting a semi-realistic third-party COBOL application to QWICS [6], as well as by making it available for public use via an online demonstration and testing environment at https://qwics.org. Also, meanwhile the community feedback received via the GitHub source code repository of QWICS (See footnote 12) has been taken into account as far as possible.

However, since QWICS is still a proof-of-concept implementation and thus not feature-complete, or its production readiness further extensions and adaptations may be necessary, which should be detected and addressed during migration of a real-world application. Therefore, further research is needed to explore the approach in a real industry case study.

References

1. Abbany, Z.: Fail by design: banking's legacy of dark code. https://m.dw.com/en/fail-by-design-bankings-legacy-of-dark-code/a-43645522 (2018). Accessed 05 Jan 2019
2. Apte, A., et al.: Method and apparatus for migration of application source code, US Patent App. 15/397,473 (2017)
3. Bainbridge, A., Colgrave, J., Colyer, A., Normington, G.: CICS and Enterprise JavaBeans. IBM Syst. J. **40**(1), 46–67 (2001)
4. Banavar, G., Chandra, T., Strom, R., Sturman, D.: A case for message oriented middleware. In: Jayanti, P. (ed.) DISC 1999. LNCS, vol. 1693, pp. 1–17. Springer, Heidelberg (1999). https://doi.org/10.1007/3-540-48169-9_1
5. Bodhuin, T., Guardabascio, E., Tortorella, M.: Migrating COBOL systems to the WEB by using the MVC design pattern. In: Proceedings of the Ninth Working Conference on Reverse Engineering, 2002, pp. 329–338. IEEE (2002)
6. Brune, P.: A hybrid approach to re-host and mix transactional cobol and java code in java ee web applications using open source software. In: Proceedings of the 14th International Conference on Web Information Systems and Technologies - Volume 1: WEBIST, pp. 239–246. INSTICC, SciTePress (2018)
7. Calladine, J.: Giving legs to the legacy–web services integration within the enterprise. BT Technol. J. **22**(1), 87–98 (2004)
8. El Beggar, O., Bousetta, B., Gadi, T.: Getting objects methods and interactions by extracting business rules from legacy systems. J. Syst. Integr. **5**(3), 32 (2014)
9. Farmer, E.: The reality of rehosting: understanding the value of your mainframe (2013)

10. Ferguson, D.F., Stockton, M.L.: Service-oriented architecture: programming model and product architecture. IBM Syst. J. **44**(4), 753–780 (2005)

11. FinTech Futures: How open will your bank become?. https://www.bankingtech.com/2018/11/how-open-will-your-bank-become/ (2018). Accessed 05 Jan 2019

12. Hashem, I.A.T., Yaqoob, I., Anuar, N.B., Mokhtar, S., Gani, A., Khan, S.U.: The rise of "big data" on cloud computing: review and open research issues. Inf. Syst. **47**, 98–115 (2015)

13. Huang, H., Tsai, W.T., Bhattacharya, S., Chen, X., Wang, Y., Sun, J.: Business rule extraction techniques for COBOL programs. J. Softw.: Evol. Process **10**(1), 3–35 (1998)

14. Kanter, H.A., Muscarello, T.J.: Reuse versus rewrite: an empirical study of alternative software development methods for web-enabling mission-critical COBOL/CICS legacy applications. Fujitsu Software, CICS Legacy Applications (2005)

15. Karremans, J.: Postgres in the enterprise: real world reasons for adoption. https://www.enterprisedb.com/blog/postgres-enterprise-real-world-reasons-adoption (2018). Accessed 05 Jan 2019

16. Khadka, R., Batlajery, B.V., Saeidi, A.M., Jansen, S., Hage, J.: How do professionals perceive legacy systems and software modernization? In: Proceedings of the 36th International Conference on Software Engineering. pp. 36–47. ACM (2014)

17. Khadka, R., et al.: Does software modernization deliver what it aimed for? a post modernization analysis of five software modernization case studies. In: 2015 IEEE International Conference on Software Maintenance and Evolution (ICSME), pp. 477–486. IEEE (2015)

18. Kiefer, C.: COBOL as a modern language. https://digitalcommons.northgeorgia.edu/honors_theses/17/ (2017). Accessed 27 July 2018

19. Knoche, H., Hasselbring, W.: Using microservices for legacy software modernization. IEEE Softw. **35**(3), 44–49 (2018)

20. Lämmel, R., De Schutter, K.: What does aspect-oriented programming mean to COBOL? In: Proceedings of the 4th International Conference on Aspect-Oriented Software Development, pp. 99–110. ACM (2005)

21. Lancia, M., Puccinelli, R., Lombardi, F.: Feasibility and benefits of migrating towards JEE: a real life case. In: Proceedings of the 5th International Symposium on Principles and Practice Of Programming in Java, pp. 13–20. ACM (2007)

22. Lee, M.S., Shin, S.G., Yang, Y.J.: The design and implementation of Enterprise JavaBean (EJB) wrapper for legacy system. In: 2001 IEEE International Conference on Systems, Man, and Cybernetics, vol. 3, pp. 1988–1992. IEEE (2001)

23. Lymer, S.F., Starkey, M., Stephenson, J.W.: System for automated interface generation for computer programs operating in different environments, US Patent 6,230,117, 8 May 2001

24. Mainetti, L., Paiano, R., Pandurino, A.: MIGROS: a model-driven transformation approach of the user experience of legacy applications. In: Brambilla, M., Tokuda, T., Tolksdorf, R. (eds.) ICWE 2012. LNCS, vol. 7387, pp. 490–493. Springer, Heidelberg (2012). https://doi.org/10.1007/978-3-642-31753-8_51

25. Malaika, S., Park, H.: A tale of a transaction monitor. IEEE Data Eng. Bull. **17**(1), 3–9 (1994)

26. Mateos, C., Zunino, A., Misra, S., Anabalon, D., Flores, A.: Migration from COBOL to SOA: measuring the impact on web services interfaces complexity. In: Damaševičius, R., Mikašytė, V. (eds.) ICIST 2017. CCIS, vol. 756, pp. 266–279. Springer, Cham (2017). https://doi.org/10.1007/978-3-319-67642-5_22

27. Moore, G.: Systems of engagement and the future of enterprise IT: a sea change in enterprise IT. AIIM Whitepaper (2011)
28. Nelson, J.: Why banks didn't 'rip and replace' their mainframes. https://www.networkworld.com/article/3305745/hardware/why-banks-didnt-rip-and-replace-their-mainframes.html (2018). Accessed 05 Jan 2019
29. Rodriguez, J.M., Crasso, M., Mateos, C., Zunino, A., Campo, M.: Bottom-up and top-down cobol system migration to web services. IEEE Internet Comput. **17**(2), 44–51 (2013)
30. Sagers, G., Ball, K., Hosack, B., Twitchell, D., Wallace, D.: The mainframe is dead. Long live the mainframe!. AIS Trans. Enterp. Syst. **4**, 4–10 (2013)
31. Sellink, A., Sneed, H., Verhoef, C.: Restructuring of COBOL/CICS legacy systems. In: Proceedings of the Third European Conference on Software Maintenance and Reengineering, 1999, pp. 72–82. IEEE (1999)
32. Sellink, A., Sneed, H., Verhoef, C.: Restructuring of COBOL/CICS legacy systems. Sci. Comput. Program. **45**(2–3), 193–243 (2002)
33. SimoTime Technologies and Services: The CICS connection, sample programs for CICS. http://www.simotime.com/indexcic.htm. Accessed 21 Feb 2018
34. Sneed, H.M.: Migration of procedurally oriented COBOL programs in an object-oriented architecture. In: Proceedings of the Conference on Software Maintenance, 1992, pp. 105–116. IEEE (1992)
35. Sneed, H.M.: Wrapping legacy COBOL programs behind an XML-interface. In: Proceedings of the Eighth Working Conference on Reverse Engineering, 2001, pp. 189–197. IEEE (2001)
36. Suganuma, T., Yasue, T., Onodera, T., Nakatani, T.: Performance pitfalls in large-scale java applications translated from COBOL. In: Companion to the 23rd ACM SIGPLAN Conference on Object-Oriented Programming Systems Languages and Applications, pp. 685–696. ACM (2008)
37. Talati, K., Lackie, C.W.: Virtual software machine for enabling CICS application software to run on UNIX based computer systems, uS Patent 6,006,277, 21 December 1999
38. The Financial Brand: The four pillars of digital transformation in banking. https://thefinancialbrand.com/71733/four-pillars-of-digital-transformation-banking-strategy/ (2018). Accessed 05 Jan 2019
39. Tommy, R., Ravi, U., Mohan, D., Luke, J., Krishna, A.S., Subramaniam, G.: Internet of Things (IoT) expanding the horizons of mainframes. In: 2015 5th International Conference on IT Convergence and Security (ICITCS), pp. 1–4. IEEE (2015)
40. Vinaja, R.: 50th aniversary of the mainframe computer: a reflective analysis. J. Comput. Sci. Coll. **30**(2), 116–124 (2014)
41. White, J.W.: Portable and dynamic distributed transaction management method, US Patent 6,115,710, 5 September 2000
42. Wilkes, A.: The mainframe evolution: banking still needs workhorse tech. https://www.finextra.com/blogposting/16067/the-mainframe-evolution-banking-still-needs-workhorse-tech (2018). Accessed 05 Jan 2019
43. Zhou, N., Zhang, L.J., Chee, Y.M., Chen, L.: Legacy asset analysis and integration in model-driven SOA solution. In: 2010 IEEE International Conference on Services Computing (SCC), pp. 554–561. IEEE (2010)

Author Index

Printed in the United States
By Bookmasters